# THE NEVILLS
## OF MIDDLEHAM

### ENGLAND'S MOST POWERFUL FAMILY IN THE WARS OF THE ROSES

## K.L. CLARK

*for my mother*

First published 2016

The History Press
The Mill, Brimscombe Port
Stroud, Gloucestershire, GL5 2QG
www.thehistorypress.co.uk

British Library Cataloguing in Publication Data.
A catalogue record for this book is available from the British Library.

ISBN 978 0 7509 6365 7

Typesetting and origination by The History Press
Printed and bound in Great Britain by TJ International Ltd

# CONTENTS

# ACKNOWLEDGEMENTS

I should like to thank, first, my late mother who was so looking forward to holding this book in her hands. Her belief and pride in her children was understated but firm. Her last gift from me was the (not quite finished) manuscript, which she immediately set about reading … and immediately found a typo.

My husband, Martin Heskins, as always read every chapter as it was written and gave valuable feedback and invaluable encouragement and support. My children were variously and severally subjected to hours of discussion, and I thank them for their love and forbearance.

To Susan Higginbotham and Geanine Teramani-Cruz, my eternal thanks for their love and support. Words are an inadequate means of expressing just how important they have been to me over the last few years, and continue to be.

My thanks also to Amy Licence for throwing my name into the ring, Sharon Bennett Connolly for her help with translation, Tim Byard-Jones for clearing up some of my confusion regarding medieval warfare and Geoffrey Carter for help with some of the less well-documented aspects of fifteenth-century battles. I am indebted to a small core of readers of my almost-final draft for their feedback, enthusiasm and encouragement. My thanks also to Linda Clark and David Grummit for providing hard-to-get information.

My special thanks to Rhoda Friedrichs for generously sharing much of her research and writing about the lives of Maud Stanhope, Thomas Nevill and Ralph, lord Cromwell.

# NEVILL FAMILY TREE

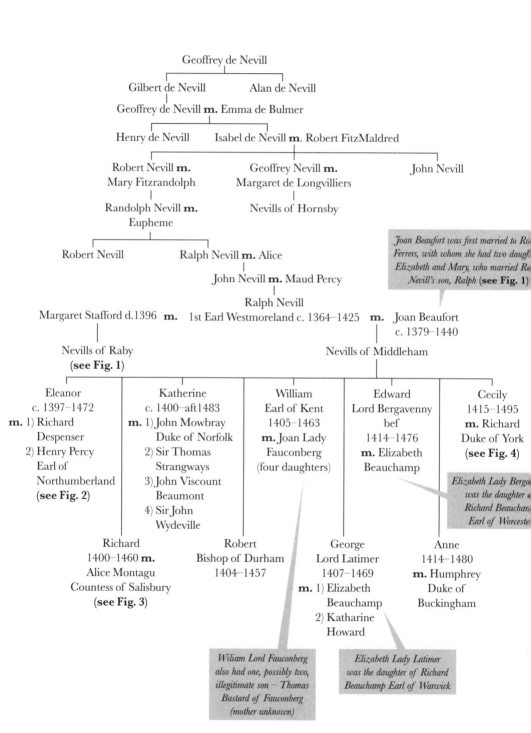

Geoffrey de Nevill

Gilbert de Nevill      Alan de Nevill

Geoffrey de Nevill **m.** Emma de Bulmer

Henry de Nevill     Isabel de Nevill **m.** Robert FitzMaldred

Robert Nevill **m.**     Geoffrey Nevill **m.**     John Nevill
Mary Fitzrandolph     Margaret de Longvilliers

Randolph Nevill **m.**     Nevills of Hornsby
Eupheme

*Joan Beaufort was first married to Ro[...]
Ferrers, with whom she had two daugl[...]
Elizabeth and Mary, who married R[...]
Nevill's son, Ralph (**see Fig. 1**)*

Robert Nevill     Ralph Nevill **m.** Alice

John Nevill **m.** Maud Percy

Ralph Nevill

Margaret Stafford d.1396 **m.**   1st Earl Westmoreland c. 1364–1425   **m.**  Joan Beaufort
                                             c. 1379–1440

Nevills of Raby                Nevills of Middleham
(**see Fig. 1**)

| Eleanor | Katherine | William | Edward | Cecily |
|---|---|---|---|---|
| c. 1397–1472 | c. 1400–aft 1483 | Earl of Kent | Lord Bergavenny | 1415–1495 |
| **m.** 1) Richard | **m.** 1) John Mowbray | 1405–1463 | bef | **m.** Richard |
| Despenser | Duke of Norfolk | **m.** Joan Lady | 1414–1476 | Duke of York |
| 2) Henry Percy | 2) Sir Thomas | Fauconberg | **m.** Elizabeth | (**see Fig. 4**) |
| Earl of | Strangways | (four daughters) | Beauchamp | |
| Northumberland | 3) John Viscount | | | |
| (**see Fig. 2**) | Beaumont | | | |
| | 4) Sir John | | | |
| | Wydeville | | | |

*Elizabeth Lady Berga[...]
was the daughter [...]
Richard Beaucha[...]
Earl of Worceste[...]*

Richard         Robert         George         Anne
1400–1460 **m.**   Bishop of Durham   Lord Latimer   1414–1480
Alice Montagu     1404–1457      1407–1469   **m.** Humphrey
Countess of Salisbury           **m.** 1) Elizabeth   Duke of
(**see Fig. 3**)                  Beauchamp    Buckingham
                                  2) Katharine
                                  Howard

*Wiliam Lord Fauconberg
also had one, possibly two,
illegitimate son – Thomas
Bastard of Fauconberg
(mother unknown)*

*Elizabeth Lady Latimer
was the daughter of Richard
Beauchamp Earl of Warwick*

# Fig. 1: The Nevills of Raby

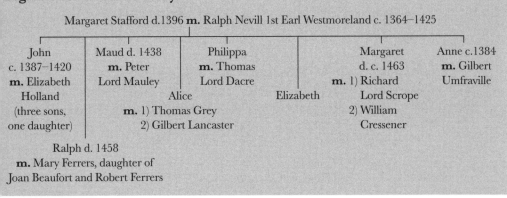

Margaret Stafford d.1396 **m.** Ralph Nevill 1st Earl Westmoreland c. 1364–1425

| John c. 1387–1420 **m.** Elizabeth Holland (three sons, one daughter) | Maud d. 1438 **m.** Peter Lord Mauley | Philippa **m.** Thomas Lord Dacre | Margaret d. c. 1463 **m.** 1) Richard Lord Scrope 2) William Cressener | Anne c.1384 **m.** Gilbert Umfraville |

Alice **m.** 1) Thomas Grey 2) Gilbert Lancaster

Elizabeth

Ralph d. 1458 **m.** Mary Ferrers, daughter of Joan Beaufort and Robert Ferrers

# Fig. 2

Eleanor Nevill Countess of Northumberland c. 1397–1472 **m.** Henry Percy Earl of Northumberland 1493–1455

| Henry Percy Earl of Northumberland 1421–1461 **m.** Elizabeth Poynings (four daughters, one son) | Thomas Lord Egremont 1422–1460 Illegitimate son and daughter (mother unknown) | Ralph 1425–1464 | Richard c. 1426–1461 | Henry Bishop of Carlisle 1428–1462 | Others |

# Fig. 3: The Nevills of Middleham

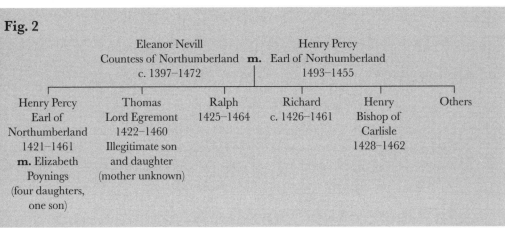

Richard Nevill Earl of Salisbury 1400–1460 **m.** Alice Montagu Countess of Salisbury 1407–1462

| Joan c. 1423–1462 **m.** William Fitzalan Earl of Arundel (see Fig. 5) | Richard 1428–1471 **m.** Anne Beauchamp Countess of Warwick (see Fig. 6) | George Bishop of Exeter & Archbishop of York c. 1432–1476 | Alice Lady Fitzhugh d. aft 1503 (see Fig. 8) | Margaret c. 1444–1506 **m.** John de Vere Earl of Oxford |

Cecily c. 1424–1450 **m.** 1) Henry Beauchamp Duke of Warwick (one daughter, Anne d. 1448) 2) John Tiptoft Earl of Worcester

John Lord Montagu & Earl of Northumberland c. 1430–1471 **m.** Isobel Ingoldisthorpe (see Fig. 7)

Thomas c. 1429–1430 **m.** Maud Stanhope c. 1425–1497

Alianor c. 1438–1471 **m.** Thomas Lord Stanley Earl of Derby (see Fig. 9)

Katherine c.1442–1503 **m.** 1) William Bonville Lord Harrington 2) William Lord Hastings (see Fig. 10)

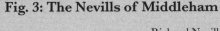
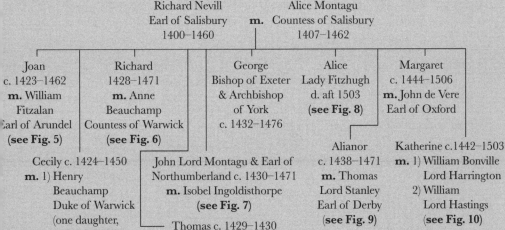

**Fig. 4**

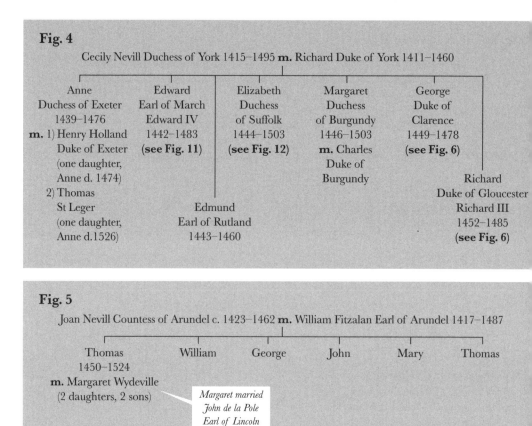

Cecily Nevill Duchess of York 1415–1495 **m.** Richard Duke of York 1411–1460

| Anne Duchess of Exeter 1439–1476 **m.** 1) Henry Holland Duke of Exeter (one daughter, Anne d. 1474) 2) Thomas St Leger (one daughter, Anne d.1526) | Edward Earl of March Edward IV 1442–1483 **(see Fig. 11)** | Elizabeth Duchess of Suffolk 1444–1503 **(see Fig. 12)** | Margaret Duchess of Burgundy 1446–1503 **m.** Charles Duke of Burgundy | George Duke of Clarence 1449–1478 **(see Fig. 6)** |

Edmund Earl of Rutland 1443–1460

Richard Duke of Gloucester Richard III 1452–1485 **(see Fig. 6)**

**Fig. 5**

Joan Nevill Countess of Arundel c. 1423–1462 **m.** William Fitzalan Earl of Arundel 1417–1487

| Thomas 1450–1524 **m.** Margaret Wydeville (2 daughters, 2 sons) | William | George | John | Mary | Thomas |

*Margaret married John de la Pole Earl of Lincoln*

**Fig. 6**

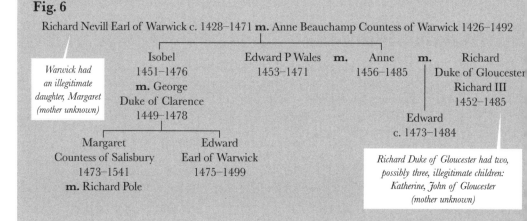

Richard Nevill Earl of Warwick c. 1428–1471 **m.** Anne Beauchamp Countess of Warwick 1426–1492

*Warwick had an illegitimate daughter, Margaret (mother unknown)*

| Isobel 1451–1476 **m.** George Duke of Clarence 1449–1478 | Edward P Wales 1453–1471 **m.** | Anne 1456–1485 **m.** | Richard Duke of Gloucester Richard III 1452–1485 |

Margaret Countess of Salisbury 1473–1541 **m.** Richard Pole

Edward Earl of Warwick 1475–1499

Edward c. 1473–1484

*Richard Duke of Gloucester had two, possibly three, illegitimate children: Katherine, John of Gloucester (mother unknown)*

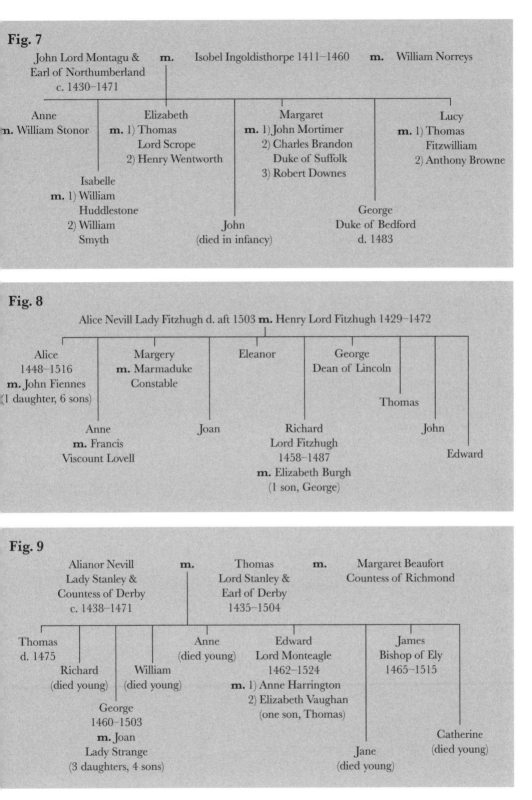

**Fig. 7**

John Lord Montagu & **m.** Isobel Ingoldisthorpe 1411–1460 **m.** William Norreys
Earl of Northumberland
c. 1430–1471

Anne
**m.** William Stonor

Elizabeth
**m.** 1) Thomas
Lord Scrope
2) Henry Wentworth

Margaret
**m.** 1) John Mortimer
2) Charles Brandon
Duke of Suffolk
3) Robert Downes

Lucy
**m.** 1) Thomas
Fitzwilliam
2) Anthony Browne

Isabelle
**m.** 1) William
Huddlestone
2) William
Smyth

John
(died in infancy)

George
Duke of Bedford
d. 1483

**Fig. 8**

Alice Nevill Lady Fitzhugh d. aft 1503 **m.** Henry Lord Fitzhugh 1429–1472

Alice
1448–1516
**m.** John Fiennes
(1 daughter, 6 sons)

Margery
**m.** Marmaduke
Constable

Eleanor

George
Dean of Lincoln

Thomas

Anne
**m.** Francis
Viscount Lovell

Joan

Richard
Lord Fitzhugh
1458–1487
**m.** Elizabeth Burgh
(1 son, George)

John

Edward

**Fig. 9**

Alianor Nevill
Lady Stanley &
Countess of Derby
c. 1438–1471

**m.**

Thomas
Lord Stanley &
Earl of Derby
1435–1504

**m.**

Margaret Beaufort
Countess of Richmond

Thomas
d. 1475

Richard
(died young)

William
(died young)

Anne
(died young)

Edward
Lord Monteagle
1462–1524
**m.** 1) Anne Harrington
2) Elizabeth Vaughan
(one son, Thomas)

James
Bishop of Ely
1465–1515

George
1460–1503
**m.** Joan
Lady Strange
(3 daughters, 4 sons)

Jane
(died young)

Catherine
(died young)

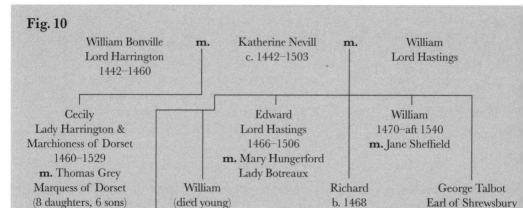

**Fig. 10**

William Bonville
Lord Harrington
1442–1460

**m.**

Katherine Nevill
c. 1442–1503

**m.**

William
Lord Hastings

Cecily
Lady Harrington &
Marchioness of Dorset
1460–1529
**m.** Thomas Grey
Marquess of Dorset
(8 daughters, 6 sons)

William
(died young)

Edward
Lord Hastings
1466–1506
**m.** Mary Hungerford
Lady Botreaux

William
1470–aft 1540
**m.** Jane Sheffield

Richard
1464–1465

Richard
b. 1468

George Talbot
Earl of Shrewsbury
(11 children)

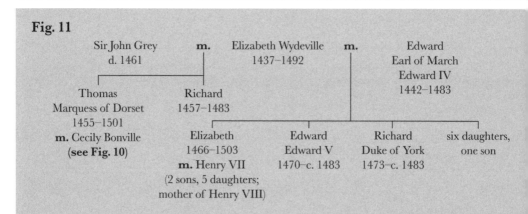

**Fig. 11**

Sir John Grey
d. 1461

**m.**

Elizabeth Wydeville
1437–1492

**m.**

Edward
Earl of March
Edward IV
1442–1483

Thomas
Marquess of Dorset
1455–1501
**m.** Cecily Bonville
(**see Fig. 10**)

Richard
1457–1483

Elizabeth
1466–1503
**m.** Henry VII
(2 sons, 5 daughters;
mother of Henry VIII)

Edward
Edward V
1470–c. 1483

Richard
Duke of York
1473–c. 1483

six daughters,
one son

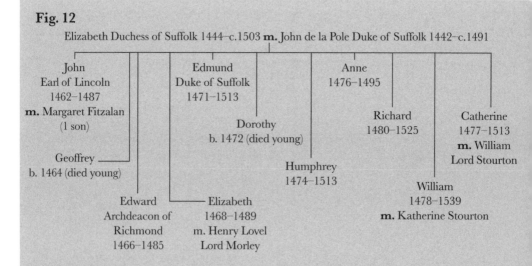

**Fig. 12**

Elizabeth Duchess of Suffolk 1444–c.1503 **m.** John de la Pole Duke of Suffolk 1442–c.1491

John
Earl of Lincoln
1462–1487
**m.** Margaret Fitzalan
(1 son)

Edmund
Duke of Suffolk
1471–1513

Anne
1476–1495

Geoffrey
b. 1464 (died young)

Dorothy
b. 1472 (died young)

Richard
1480–1525

Catherine
1477–1513
**m.** William
Lord Stourton

Humphrey
1474–1513

Edward
Archdeacon of
Richmond
1466–1485

Elizabeth
1468–1489
m. Henry Lovel
Lord Morley

William
1478–1539
**m.** Katherine Stourton

# INTRODUCTION

The Nevills rose from humble beginnings through royal service and favourable marriages to become one of the wealthiest and most powerful families in fifteenth-century England. They were larger than life, even in their time.

Dominant in the north of England, the earl of Salisbury and his sons were determined to stamp their mark on the nation as a whole. The separate strands that led to the Nevills – John of Gaunt, the Beauchamp earls of Warwick, the Montagus of Salisbury and the Nevills of Raby – wove in and out of English politics over generations. They supported kings, opposed kings, fought by the side of kings and against them.

The earl of Salisbury's sons married resilient women who shared their triumphs and setbacks, who brought up children in sometimes difficult situations and faced widowhood and separation with stoicism and determination. The earl of Salisbury's daughters married men as active in war and politics as their brothers. Together, they took their place in English society and English politics, rising and falling as the wheel of fortune turned.

It was not easy wrangling such a large and active family, nor keeping track of all the small events that provided turning points in their fortunes. A feud that set cousin against cousin and forged the sides in a thirty-year civil war. The death of a child, devastating to her mother and foster mother, paved the way for Richard Nevill to become earl of Warwick. The secret marriage of a king sent a hairline crack through a partnership and friendship that had helped that king to his throne. In earlier generations, the legitimisation of the children of a duke and governess, the execution of an earl and the deposition of a king set the wheels in motion.

Through it all, like a colossus, strode Richard Nevill earl of Warwick. Determined to hold on to power forged in the white heat of civil war and rebellion, he turned against the king he had helped to his throne, dying in a hopeless attempt to change the world. He was 'the flower of manhood', 'a second Caesar', 'a famous knight and excellent', 'the most courageous and manliest knight living', 'as astute a man as ever was Ulysses'. In later centuries, he became known as 'the Kingmaker', though this is an easy label that obscures much of his character and ambition. Dismissed more recently as 'an overmighty subject' and 'the last of the barons', Warwick's reputation ebbs and flows. Hated in Burgundy, portrayed as little more than raw ambition and temperament in popular fiction, alternately admired and derided over the centuries, he was all of these things and more. He was a complex human being who knew the value of his own worth. A father and a husband as well as a soldier, administrator and diplomat, our admiration for him must always be tempered by a recognition of his faults and failings. Though he dominates this work, as he dominated his family and his times, there was more to the Nevills than Warwick alone.

Thomas Nevill died before his potential could be realised. Warlike and determined to hold on to what was his, he defied the executors of his wife's uncle and championed her cause when her dower was stolen. John was a ferocious and successful military commander who loved his wife and tried to cut his own path through life. In the end, the call of family could not be ignored and he died in the cause of a king he had done so much to depose. George, a talented and able administrator, twice Chancellor of England and Archbishop of York, followed his brothers into politics and suffered greatly after their fall.

Joan, beautiful and serene, earned the undying love of her husband. Cecily lost her only child and died herself not long after. Alice stood by her husband through all he did and, in widowhood, threw her support behind her cousin the duke of Gloucester. Alianor suffered the heartbreak of losing as many as ten children. Katherine was widowed first at 18 then again at 51, both husbands dying by violence. Margaret knew both the depths of poverty and despair and the heights of a close connection to a king.

These women had role models like few others. Their mother, Alice countess of Salisbury, attainted and forced to flee England for the safety of Ireland, did all she could to support her husband and her sons. Their father, grandson of John of Gaunt and the son of a Lancastrian princess tried, and failed, to walk the fine line between loyalty and rebellion. They were determined their children would reach as high as they could, through service, preferment and marriage.

Over the centuries, the Nevills climbed inexorably up the social ladder, from Lincolnshire gentlefolk to northern barons, then earls and duchesses and, finally, to the dizzying heights of the crown itself. Warwick did not live to see his daughter crowned Queen of England or his grandson invested as Prince of Wales. Nor did he live to see them both die before their time, the hopes and ambitions of the Nevills brought to an abrupt end.

N.B. Middle English quotes have been given modern spellings throughout for the sake of consistency and ease of reading. Syntax has not been changed, nor have archaic words or words that have since changed in meaning.

# PART 1

# THE NEVILLS AND THE LANCASTRIAN KINGS

# 1

# THE BEGINNINGS
# OF GREATNESS

In February 1396, a wedding was celebrated in Lincoln Cathedral that changed the course of English history and helped set the scene for thirty years of sporadic civil war. The wedding was quiet, private, possibly even secret. Certainly there is no evidence the groom sought blessing and permission from his nephew, Richard II. For the bride, now in her forties, the wedding was something of a vindication. After more than twenty years of constancy to her married lover, her reputation in ruins, she was finally to be his wife. More than that, she was to be his duchess.[1]

The groom was John of Gaunt, duke of Lancaster, fourth son of Edward III, and his bride was his long-time mistress and mother of four of his children, Katherine Swynford. Neither bride nor groom was in the first flush of youth, he being somewhere in his fifties. Their relationship, which scandalised England's court, had begun decades earlier while both were married to others. With the death of his second wife Constance of Castile two years earlier, duke John was finally free to formalise his relationship with Katherine, but rather than this being simply the romantic culmination to a long attachment, the couple married, quite literally, for the sake of their children.[2]

Despite its magnificent setting, the wedding was no glittering royal occasion. There are no records of who was in attendance, what the bride wore, who officiated or where they might have feasted afterwards. Quite apart from the personal feelings of the couple, there was some urgency about the wedding. John of Gaunt was suffering from increasing ill health and both he and Katherine were keen to see their children legitimated and their futures secure. Marriage was an essential step towards achieving this.[3]

For decades, since the death of his first wife, Blanche of Lancaster, Katherine had been an almost constant presence in John's life. When their relationship began, she was the governess of his children and continued to maintain a close and loving relationship with them throughout her life. Her reputation had suffered greatly, though duke John's public acknowledgement of her and their children, his gifts and his ongoing need of her must have gone some way towards ameliorating her feelings. As it was, as her now-husband's health rapidly failed, she had only four years of married life to look forward to.[4]

In September 1396, a papal bull was issued legitimating John and Katherine's children. In February 1397, Parliament approved a royal patent to the same effect. Later this was to be amended with a proviso that they had no place in the succession. All four were given the surname Beaufort, though it is not at all clear where this comes from. Though there have been suggestions it relates to Chateau de Beaufort in Anjou, it is also possible the name was chosen in honour of Roger Beaufort, brother of Pope Gregory XI, who was an 'honourable captive' of John of Gaunt's during the 1370s.[5]

John and Katherine's children were born over a roughly six-year period in the 1370s, in the early years of John's marriage to Constance of Castile. All four were to rise to some prominence in English society. The oldest, John, was granted the title earl of Somerset and founded a dynasty that was to play a crucial role in the upcoming political and military conflicts. He died in 1410 and his title passed to his son. Henry Beaufort was installed as Bishop of Lincoln in 1399 and elevated to the see of Winchester in 1404. In 1417, the newly elected Pope Martin V named Henry a cardinal as a reward for his support. Thomas Beaufort was granted the title duke of Exeter for life; he died in 1447.[6]

Shortly after her parents' marriage and the issuing of the papal bull, John and Katherine's youngest child, 18-year-old Joan, married the widowed Ralph Nevill. This was another marriage that was to have far-reaching consequences for the future of England.[7]

The connections between the Nevills and John of Gaunt were not insignificant. Ralph Nevill's father was a retainer of duke John's for much of his life. The Nevills had wealth and prominence in the north of England and this was a good match for Joan. For Ralph, it brought a connection to the royal family and the possibility of patronage to come.[8]

Ralph Nevill was born around 1364, probably at Raby Castle in the Durham Dales. His father was John Nevill, 3rd lord Raby and his mother Maud Percy, daughter of the earl of Northumberland. The Nevills, originally Lincolnshire gentlefolk, had amassed a small fortune in land, as well as growing power in the north of England through astute marriages and sometimes inconsistent service to the crown. The earliest Nevill of note was Alan de Neville, appointed Henry II's chief justice of the forest in 1166, who did himself no favours with his harsh implementation of the forest laws.[9]

Now this Alan, as long as he lived, enriched the king, though he ceased not from vexing both the clergy and the laity. Thus to please an earthly monarch, he was not afraid to offend the King of Heaven. But how much gratitude he obtained from the king whom he was thus careful to ingratiate, the sequel proved. When he was brought near his end, the brethren of a certain monastery, desiring, as it seems, a portion of his substance for their house, went to the king, beseeching him to allow them to take his body and bury it with them. The king evinced his regard for him in these terms: 'I,' quoth he, 'will have his wealth but you may have his carcass and the demons of hell his soul!' Behold the wretched recompense; see the miserable disposal of him and his substance! This may well be a lesson to officials of every degree of power – to mark how this man, who studied to please the king by his wicked deeds, got neither thanks nor respect thereby, while he incurred the displeasure of the King of Heaven.[10]

Over the centuries, Alan de Neville's successors variously served their royal masters and joined in rebellions against them. A series of advantageous marriages brought them further and further north, Raby Castle coming to the family through the FitzMaldreds. The name 'Nevill' had come to mean something, however, and when Isabel Nevill married Robert FitzMaldred around 1190, her son took his mother's name, passing it on to his three sons. By the time of Ralph's birth, the Nevills were well entrenched in the north of England, owning extensive property in Durham and Yorkshire, including Middleham Castle, and had a prominent role in upholding marcher law along the border with Scotland.[11]

Along with his eight siblings, Ralph Nevill grew up in some comfort. Raby Castle was by far the finest property the family owned. With a population rivalling that of some small towns, and with an estate of some 2 acres, Raby was the most significant building in its landscape. It was surrounded by a park of more than 900 acres, in which the family hunted and from which firewood was collected. The nearest town, situated hard on the estate's southern edge, is Staindrop, which became a market town in 1378 when Ralph's father was granted a charter. Many of Ralph's ancestors, both FitzMaldred and Nevill, are buried in Staindrop church. Raby Castle was the most visible sign of how far the Nevills had come since Lincolnshire landowner Alan de Neville first came to public notice.[12]

Ralph's day began with matins in the chapel in the company of his parents and siblings. The rest of the household heard mass in the great hall, except for those whose duties required them to keep working, such as cooks, sewers, botlers and those responsible for making beds and setting up the great chamber and hall for the morning meal. The family dined in relative privacy in the great chamber, with younger children in the nursery. *Privacy* did not mean then what it means now. This was no informal family meal, and the ceremonies involved in serving and eating were not just performed in the presence of the family, they also took place behind closed doors.[13]

> Also half an hour before the lord go to meat or supper the marshall shall take the Rod in his hand and command the panter and ewer to cover and make ready for the lord and the household; and as soon as it is made ready the marshall shall command the sewer to await when the cooks be ready; and then shall the sewer go to the ewry and take a towel upon his shoulder and the marshall and he to go together and show before the lord so that he may know thereby when his meat is ready.[14]

This went on for every meal of every day and required such precision and training that books, known as courtesy books or household ordinances, were written to 'teach every man that is willing to learn to serve a lord or master in every thing in his pleasure'. There were ceremonies for rising, attending mass, eating in private and eating in public. There were ceremonies for receiving guests, for leaving home and returning, and even for going to bed at night. All this was designed to make visible and clear the status of the master of the household. Mistakes and omissions might call attention to his newly ennobled state, and the more newly made men joined the ranks of the aristocracy, the more elaborate the rituals needed to be for those families of long-standing pedigree. Upward mobility was not uncommon and could be achieved through a number of means. The Nevills represented both those who rose through the ranks through service to their king and those who did so through marriage. Ralph Nevill knew how this worked and, later in life, would do all he could to improve the lives of his children. By the time his grandson Richard, 16th earl of Warwick came to prominence, it was as if the family had been in the ranks of the aristocracy for countless generations.[15]

In his childhood, Ralph and his younger brothers took formal lessons with a tutor, joined by his father's wards and young pages sent to live at Raby so that they might acquire something of an education before moving into more formal service. As the oldest son of a warrior, Ralph's training began early, his father's knights and men-at-arms a constant presence throughout his childhood. The life of a soldier in the late middle ages, even the son of a baron, was neither easy nor comfortable. Ralph needed to learn not only to fight, but to command, to ensure his army was supplied, well-trained and in good health and good spirits.[16]

Ralph's father, John, 3rd lord Raby, was a military man. He was Admiral of the North and in 1370 gathered ships to transport troops for an expedition to France; in 1372, he led a small army to Brittany; and in 1378, as King's Lieutenant, he was crucial to the defence of English territory in Gascony.[17]

Like many Nevills before him, John also served as warden of the marches towards Scotland. A good part of Ralph's training would have been designed to ready him to take over from his father in this capacity. The role of the warden was initially judicial, overseeing marcher law. In England, this set of laws was designed to deal with Scots who committed crime south of the border and, in Scotland, to deal with Englishmen who committed crime north of it. Over time, the role became more military and diplomatic, the legal aspects dealt with by ordinary courts. In the thirteenth century, one Robert Nevill travelled to Scotland several times and was instructed to 'visit the king's daughter, the queen of Scotland, as often as possible, to give her comfort and assistance, and to supply her with funds'. Another, later, Robert was taken prisoner at Bannockburn and was shortly afterwards killed in Berwick in retribution for a murder he and his brothers were accused of committing. Over several centuries, Nevills were included in, and sometimes led, embassies to Scotland. It was important for the king, far away in London, to know he had people he could trust policing his northern border.[18]

The administrative centre of the west march was Carlisle Castle and Ralph, along with his father and his father's trusted retainers, travelled frequently between Carlisle and Raby, a distance of some 60 miles. As one of the major responsibilities of the warden was to keep the garrison supplied and armed, Ralph learned to assess need, order what was required, oversee deliveries north and keep accounts of expenditure. Apart from his formal schooling, all this he would have learned from watching his father both at home and in Carlisle.[19]

In 1380, when he was just 16, Ralph took part in his first military campaign, to Brittany, under the command of Thomas Woodstock, earl of Buckingham. By this time, his father had been impeached, in part for an earlier military failure in Brittany and in part for a discrepancy between the size of the retinue he took to Brittany and the terms of his engagement. He was accused of profiteering, though the charges were later withdrawn. Restored to favour, though minus his former court appointments, John Nevill concentrated for the next few years on making improvements to Raby Castle, including crenellations, a new gate and a new tower. He continued to serve in France until 1381, but from that time on concentrated his energies and attention in the north of England, particularly in the marches, a responsibility he shared with the Percy earls of Northumberland. Dividing the marches towards Scotland between the two most powerful northern families served three purposes: it helped protect the integrity of the border; it prevented either family from developing overwhelming military might; and, in theory at least, it kept those families, and their considerable armies, occupied.[20]

Young Ralph Nevill had a good deal to live up to, for not only did his father serve in France and the marches but had fought, alongside his own father, at the battle of Neville's Cross in 1346 against an invading Scots army. Apart from his single foray into Brittany, however, Ralph's own military career was confined almost entirely to the north. Just 24 when his father died in 1388, he had already served as warden of the west march for two years, a role he was to hold until 1414. In 1403, after the battle of Shrewsbury, he was granted wardenship of the east march as well, which he also relinquished in 1414.[21]

Ralph Nevill and his first wife, Margaret Stafford, had either eight or nine children – two sons and six or seven daughters. Their second son, also Ralph, married his stepsister Mary Ferrers. He died, childless, in 1458. Ralph and Margaret's oldest son John died in 1420, making *his* son Ralph his grandfather's principal heir.[22]

Ralph senior's second marriage, to Joan Beaufort, and their subsequent fourteen children, put great pressure on the Nevill inheritance, leading to open and ongoing hostility between the two branches of the family. This feud, as with others, was to have dire consequences for the Nevills of Middleham in time to come.[23]

Joan was just 18, and a young widow with two daughters, when she married the 33-year-old Ralph Nevill. Ralph had been a widower for a little over six months and Joan had been a widow for about a year. The three events at the end of 1396 and the beginning of 1397 – the marriage of John of Gaunt and his long-time mistress Katherine Swynford; the legitimating of their children by papal bull and parliamentary decree; and the marriage of Joan Beaufort and Ralph Nevill – each came so fast on the heels of the last that it is difficult not to speculate the third event depended on the second as much as the second depended on the first.

Married at 13 to Sir Robert Ferrers, the mother of two daughters by the time she was 16 and widowed at 17, Joan had already seen much of life when she married for the second time. The sixteen years between her and Ralph did not prevent a strong bond of affection, perhaps love, certainly shared purpose, developing between them. Joan's father did not hide his children away and it is likely that she and Ralph had been acquainted for some time.

The Nevills had long been in the service of John of Gaunt and the offer of marriage to his daughter may have been a reward for this service. Certainly, Joan was young and her connection to the royal family stood to bring great benefit to her new husband. Less than a year after the wedding, Ralph was further elevated by Richard II, created earl of Westmorland in September 1397. Thus, in the space of twelve months, Joan Beaufort went from being the widowed illegitimate daughter of a prince and a governess, to the legitimated daughter of a duke and duchess, and the wife of an earl.[24]

Joan and her Beaufort brothers, John, earl of Somerset, Henry, Cardinal Beaufort and Thomas, duke of Exeter, had always been acknowledged by their father and brought up, at least partially, in his household. Joan benefited from the same education as her legitimate half-sisters, and the two sides of duke John's family remained close, if not always in complete harmony, for the rest of their lives.[25]

Joan was well read and had quite a library, which she cared for so much that she petitioned for the return of two books she had lent to her nephew Henry V, which were still in his keeping at the time of his death. Her literary connections were not insignificant, her mother's sister Philippa Roet was married to Geoffrey Chaucer. Philippa provided her husband a connection to John of Gaunt's circle and, through that, to wider court and aristocratic circles.[26]

The court of Richard II was criticised, in its time, for being 'feminised' and 'soft', with 'more knights of Venus than of Bellona, more vigorous in the bedroom than on the field of battle, armed with words rather than the lance'. This was demonstrated by a fluidity of movement between the king's household and the queen's. Richard II and Anne of Bohemia enjoyed a particularly close and affectionate marriage and her female attendants had a higher profile at court than was usual, so much so that it was frequently remarked upon. One result of this was the rise in the number of women admitted to a sorority of one of the most prestigious orders in England, the Order of the Garter. Women had attended Garter ceremonies before, such as Edward III's queen, Philippa of Hainault, and his daughter Isabella. Richard II admitted a number of women to the Ladies of the Garter, including Joan Beaufort and her half-sisters Philippa, Elizabeth and Catherine, and sisters-in-law Mary Bohun and Margaret Holland. These women were literate and, to some extent at least, worldly, and they may have influenced Chaucer to widen his readership beyond a 'Westminster-London audience of gentlepersons and clerks'. When Joan married Ralph Nevill, she took her love of books north with her and proved to be a strong influence on her daughters and daughters-in-law.[27]

There is a well-documented tradition of book ownership, readership and patronage among Joan's female descendants. The stepmother of her son Richard's wife was Alice Chaucer, granddaughter of the poet. Joan herself owned several books, as did her daughters Anne, duchess of Buckingham, and Cecily, duchess of York. Reading and discussing books was an abiding tradition in the household of the duchess of York and there are a number of bequests of books in her will. Joan's grandson Thomas and his wife Maud owned a copy of *The Canterbury Tales* and her granddaughter Cecily was married the year before her death to John Tiptoft, earl of Worcester, a widely travelled collector of books. Joan's father's first wife, Blanche of Lancaster, was herself a significant literary patron. Though she died before

Joan's birth and had no direct influence on her, John of Gaunt's household would seem to have been decidedly bookish.[28]

Joan's recorded texts are largely devotional and she was a woman of some piety. A curious incident, recorded in Margery Kempe's *Book*, tells of a visit to Joan Beaufort, some time around Easter 1413. Kempe, a well-known religious figure, particularly in Norfolk, has been criticised by modern writers for being a mediocre mystic or lauded for being a proto-feminist. It is likely she was neither, simply a conventionally pious woman of some social standing who saw her own religiosity as something greater than it was. Her *Book*, as one writer argues, can be seen as auto-hagiography, an attempt to set down the happenings of her life, both spiritual and temporal, to ease her future canonisation. At a time when opposition to Lollardy was official state policy, Kempe, was from time to time, swept up in this and examined by members of the clergy. On one such occasion, Kempe was accused by an archbishop of counselling Joan's daughter Elizabeth, lady Greystoke to 'forsake her husband, that is a baron's wife and daughter to my lady of Westmorland, and now has said enough to be burned for'. Kempe admitted to seeing the countess of Westmorland 'this two years and more', saying she was sent for.[29]

'… if it pleases you, I will go again to her for record that I moved no such matter.' 'No,' said they that stood about, 'let her be put in prison and we shall send a letter to the worshipful lady, and, if it be truth that she says, let her go quite without danger.'[30]

Kempe goes on to relate a story she told the countess of Westmorland, about a 'lady that was damned for she would not love her enemies and of a bailiff who was saved for he loved his enemies and forgave that they had trespassed against him, and yet he was held an evil man'. On hearing the tale, the archbishop gave Kempe his blessing and let her go. There is no contemporary evidence that Elizabeth Greystoke was planning to leave her husband and Margery's willingness to seek Joan Beaufort's testimony to prove her innocence was sufficient to clear her of wrongdoing.[31]

If Joan did send for Margery Kempe and listen to her parables, it need not suggest she was drawn to a specifically female or feminine mysticism, or that her own piety was somehow unconventional. It does suggest, however, that she was more than a little familiar with Kempe's activities and religious reputation. While others might associate Kempe, albeit briefly, with Lollardy, there is nothing to suggest Joan had any sympathies in that direction.

In 1414, Joan and Ralph had been married for seventeen years, and only their youngest child, Cecily, was yet to be born. They were enjoying a period of calm; the Nevill dominance in the north of England had stood unchallenged for almost ten years. The illegitimate daughter of a prince was now a countess, the mother of a swarm of children and a religious and literary patron – a woman of wealth, culture and status. Her husband was about to give up his role as warden of the marches towards Scotland and, essentially, retire. Reaching this point had not been easy, the years between the usurpation of Henry Bolingbroke and the final (and, seemingly, irrevocable) fall of the Percies in 1405 had been particularly tumultuous. During those years, one king was deposed and the new king faced armed rebellion in both Wales and England. Within a year of Ralph's retirement, a battle that was to go down in legend was fought at Agincourt in France.[32]

# 2

# RICHARD II, BOLINGBROKE AND HOTSPUR

n 25 October 1415, a battle was fought on French soil that was to reverberate down the centuries as one of England's finest hours. Just two years on the throne, and determined to regain lost English territory, 29-year-old Henry V had almost immediately accelerated the war against France that had been going on in fits and starts since 1337. His victory at Agincourt, which is often attributed to the superiority of English longbow men and their weapons, cemented his place in the roll call of warrior kings.[1]

Cut off from the English town of Calais, Henry V sought a way to cross the River Somme, shadowed all the while by the French army. Forced to take position at Agincourt, Henry ordered stakes be driven into the ground as protection for his archers. An impulsive French cavalry charge against the longbow men failed miserably and many men died. With their foot soldiers too densely packed and hemmed in, they were no match for the more mobile English.

> In the opinion of the French, it was what injured them the most which assured the English of victory, especially the continuous hail of arrow shot which rained down on our men. As the English archers were lightly armed and their ranks not too crowded, they had freedom of movement and could deal mortal blows with ease. Many of them had adopted a weapon until then unknown – great lead-covered mallets from which one blow to the head could kill a man or knock him senseless to the ground.[2]

Along with the defeat of the Spanish Armada and the Battle of Trafalgar, Agincourt has a particular magic about it: a victory against the odds, a charismatic commander and proof of the glory of England. Shakespeare gave his most memorable eve-of-battle speech to Henry V and turned this young warrior king into a hero for the ages.[3]

The day after Agincourt, Henry V's brother John, duke of Bedford won a naval battle that gave the English the port of Harfleur. After another three years of almost continual campaigning, the English occupied a good part of Normandy and were pushing towards Anjou. With the fall of Rouen in 1418 after a six-month siege, Henry V was in control of Upper Normandy and, by the following summer, the whole of the duchy was in his hands. The Treaty of Troyes, and Henry V's marriage to Catherine de Valois, daughter of the French king Charles VI, saw Henry named as heir to the French throne. In the seven years since his father's death, Henry V won vast territories in France by conquest and, by marriage, the throne of France for himself and his successors. The Lancastrian dynasty looked to have secured itself a glittering future.[4]

However, the dynasty proved to be short-lived: just three kings from John of Gaunt's legitimate line ruled England from 1399 to 1461, the last of them dying ten years after that in decidedly suspicious circumstances. The Lancastrian line began and ended in rebellion and the deposition and death of a king. The first of those kings was Richard II.

Like many kings before and since, Richard II's loyalty to unpopular friends, favourites and counsellors got him into trouble. Two in particular, Michael de la Pole and Robert de Vere, were promoted in rank and given considerable gifts of land and official posts. This was resented by other nobles, who felt themselves excluded from royal patronage, their income and influence declining. On top of this, Richard II was seen as personally extravagant at a time when the people of England were suffering economically, and the seemingly endless war with France was not going well. There were also tensions between the young king and his uncle John of Gaunt, which eased only when duke John left England in 1386 in hopes of pursuing his claim (through his second wife, Constance of Castile) to the Castilian throne. John of Gaunt, despite his difficult relationship with Richard II, provided a measure of political stability. His departure left something of a vacuum into which stepped another of the king's uncles, Thomas of Woodstock, duke of Gloucester, and Richard Fitzalan, earl of Arundel. Both men were determined to put an end to the influence of de la Pole and de Vere.[5]

The first moves against the king's favourite ministers came during the 1386 Parliament, when the Commons demanded the dismissal of Michael de la Pole as chancellor. Refusing to attend Parliament, and rejecting the demand, Richard was visited by Gloucester and Arundel at his palace in Eltham. After a heated exchange, the king was forced to concede and de la Pole was removed.[6]

Another of Richard II's closest, and most unpopular, advisors was Alexander Nevill, Archbishop of York and Ralph Nevill's uncle. Alexander

was, by all accounts, a less than competent clergyman who had been promoted beyond his abilities. He spent much of his time in legal disputes and
tangles and, in the ten years after his elevation to archbishop, spent very
little time away from his home at Cawood Castle. In 1385, he was thrust
into the limelight and the hothouse of English politics, leaving the north
and joining Richard II's intimate circle at court. Alexander was not well
loved and his corruption was well known. The king, however, would hear
not a word against him: 'he makes to his king as if he were a saint but all
the world knows it well, the fairer he speaks the falser he is'. He enriched
himself through extorting payment for the proving of wills: 'there was never
such a tyrant in holy church, nor among the commons of this country, for
he oppresses more the country than the king and all the lords of England'.[7]

In 1388, when it looked as if things might come to armed conflict,
Alexander attempted to leave England but was captured. Stripped of his
rank as Archbishop of York, he was demoted to the see of St Andrews in
Scotland. Alexander chose instead to flee the country and lived the rest
of his life in obscurity and poverty, eking out a living as a schoolmaster
in Flanders.[8]

All three of these men – Michael de la Pole, earl of Suffolk, Robert de
Vere, Marquis of Dublin and Alexander Nevill, Archbishop of York – were
subjected to a civil indictment for treason (or 'appeal') lodged directly with
the king by Gloucester, Arundel and Thomas Beauchamp, earl of Warwick.
Known as the Lords Appellant, this group included others who took less
prominent and public roles, among them John of Gaunt's oldest son, Henry
Bolingbroke, later Henry IV. Richard II delayed his response to the appeal
to give de Vere time to gather troops in Cheshire to support him should the
war of words erupt into armed conflict.[9]

The Lords Appellant immediately rode out of London to prevent de Vere
reaching the city. Shadowing his army, they led him into a trap at Radcot
Bridge on the Thames. Caught by Bolingbroke on one side of the river and
with the rest of the Lords Appellant closing in behind him, de Vere escaped
by removing his armour and swimming a borrowed horse across the river.
When the discarded armour and de Vere's own warhorse were found, it
was assumed he had drowned. He had, however, made good his escape.[10]

Now in the hands of the Lords Appellant, Richard II had no choice but
to agree to summon Parliament so that his favourite counsellors could be
tried for treason. All three – de Vere, de la Pole and Nevill – had fled the
country by this time. They were tried and found guilty *in absentia*. Richard II
himself was firmly under the control of the Lords Appellant, who may even
have confined him in the Tower of London while they quarrelled about
who should replace him on the throne. The young king had not yet seen his
twenty-first birthday.[11]

By the end of 1388, Richard had regained his authority and his differences with the Lords Appellant seem to have been forgotten. Stability was restored when John of Gaunt returned from Castile the following year and, for the next decade, Richard's reign was more or less peaceful, witnessing a flowering of culture and literature which, as we have seen, was well established in John of Gaunt's household. The only thorn in Richard II's side was the ongoing opposition and blunt criticism of the earl of Arundel.[12]

Arundel berated both the king and John of Gaunt in Parliament. Duke John accused Arundel of failing to take action against a potentially dangerous rising in Cheshire in 1393. Arundel accused Richard of being too dependent on his uncle and John of Gaunt of being so overbearing in Parliament that no one else dared speak up. Without support from the other lords, however, Arundel was on his own. He was forced to apologise publicly to duke John and, in April 1394, secured a general pardon from Richard II.[13]

Tragedy struck Richard II's life in June of that year with the death of his queen, Anne of Bohemia. Richard was distraught with grief and ordered the queen's palace of Sheen destroyed. At her funeral in August, the earl of Arundel so upset the king with his lack of respect – he arrived late and immediately asked for permission to leave – that Richard struck him over the head with a baton. Arundel was sent to the Tower for a week.[14]

In July 1397, Richard moved against the Lords Appellant without warning. Gloucester, Arundel and Warwick were all arrested. All three were charged with plotting against the king and usurping royal authority, and all three were found guilty of treason, despite a spirited defence. Gloucester, who had been imprisoned in Calais after his arrest, was murdered before the trial began. Warwick was initially condemned to death but his sentence was reduced to exile on the Isle of Man. Arundel was sentenced to death. Others of the Lords Appellant, such as Henry Bolingbroke, were exiled for life.[15]

Though Ralph Nevill took little active part in court life, he remained loyal to Richard II at this time and played a small role in Arundel's trial.

> The court being seated, Richard earl of Arundel was immediately put on trial, clad in a robe with a scarlet hood. Then John, duke of Lancaster and steward of England, who had been appointed to undertake this task, formally told lord Nevill, 'Remove his belt and his hood', which was done.[16]

It was for this ongoing support that Nevill was awarded his earldom. He will be referred to by his title Westmorland from this point on.[17]

When the exiled Henry Bolingbroke returned to England in 1399 after the death of his father John of Gaunt, Westmorland's loyalty to his king was tested. The last two years of Richard II's reign have been described as 'tyranny'. He ruled without any meaningful opposition and had even managed to sideline the powerful and stabilising figure of his uncle in the months before duke John's death. While Bolingbroke may have been concerned for the well-being of England and hoped for better government than the king could provide, his actions were also prompted by Richard II's attempts to rob him of his inheritance. Bolingbroke landed at Ravenspur in Yorkshire on 4 July 1399, announcing he returned to England only to reclaim that inheritance. As he travelled south and east with his small band of men, he was joined by many others, including Henry Percy, earl of Northumberland, his son Hotspur, Ralph Nevill, earl of Westmorland and lord Willoughby.[18]

The king was in Ireland, his uncle Edmund, duke of York left in charge of the kingdom in his absence. Immediately on hearing of Bolingbroke's arrival, York set about mustering troops in St Albans. Though he was joined by many loyal lords, all were reluctant to move against Bolingbroke. 'Even the duke of York stated publicly that the duke of Lancaster had been wrongfully disinherited, and that he had no intention of attacking someone who came in a just cause and to ask for the restoration of his rightful inheritance'. The rapid growth of Bolingbroke's army alarmed York, however, and urgent letters were sent to the king warning him to return to England if he did not want to lose his crown.[19]

Richard II did, eventually, return from Ireland and immediately disbanded his army. According to one source – Jean Creton, a Frenchman who was with Richard II in Ireland and Wales during this time – within four days, 40,000 men gathered near Conwy Castle in support of their king, who was reported to be there. John Montagu, earl of Salisbury addressed them in stirring tones.

> Let us go from here and march straight toward them if we are determined to assault them, then God will help us for, according to our law, it is the duty of every man to support a just cause unto death, indeed in a situation such as this God expressly commands us to do so.[20]

When it became clear the king had not yet arrived at Conwy, the Welsh grew disheartened and dispersed. Some went immediately in search of Bolingbroke and others went home, 'leaving the earl alone in the middle of the field with only his own men, who amounted, I think, to less than a hundred. He was greatly saddened by this and declared "Let us make our retreat for our enterprise goes very badly…"'[21]

Salisbury was a man known for his many accomplishments. He was both a lover of poetry and a poet himself. Though suspected of Lollard sympathies, he was never charged with any offence or subjected to examination. Philosopher and poet Christine de Pisan, who met him in Paris, was so impressed by him she sent her son to be brought up in his household along-side Salisbury's own son Thomas. After Richard II's surrender, one source has Salisbury 'sent to the north in the custody of the earl of Westmorland', but there is little evidence of this. A more amicable connection was later established when Montagu's granddaughter Alice married Westmorland's son Richard.[22]

Bolingbroke sent the earl of Northumberland to Conwy Castle to per-suade the king to give himself up. Hiding the bulk of his army behind some rocks, Northumberland made his way to the castle with around twenty men, in the hopes of assuring the king of his peaceful intentions. Telling Northumberland he would travel the next day to Flint Castle to meet with Bolingbroke, Richard neither trusted him nor intended to keep his word. According to Creton, Richard planned to march against Bolingbroke as soon as he had gathered enough men. Northumberland heard mass with the king and swore neither he nor Bolingbroke intended any deceit: 'then the earl without further hesitation took the oath upon the body of our lord. Alas, his blood must have run cold at it, for he knew well to the contrary.'[23]

Northumberland left Conwy and returned to where he had hidden his army. Richard and his followers walked straight into the trap. After spend-ing the night at Flint Castle, Northumberland sent word of the success of his mission to Bolingbroke. The king was escorted to Chester, where Bolingbroke and Westmorland were waiting and, from there, to London. Richard II was immediately lodged in the Tower.[24]

Along with Northumberland, Westmorland was present in the Tower on 28 September 1399, representing England's earls in discussions with Richard about resigning his crown. They took with them a document that set out the charges against the king and a statement of resignation for him to sign. Richard promised he would consider the question overnight. Adam Usk reports that Richard was in a pitiful state, recording the fates of England's deposed kings and 'musing on his ancient and wonted glory and on the fickle fortune of the world'. The next day, when the same men returned to the Tower, Richard told them, 'he would not do it under any circumstances and he was greatly incensed, and he declared that he would like to have it explained to him how it was that he could resign the crown, and to whom'.[25]

Richard finally agreed to resign to his cousin Henry Bolingbroke but, he insisted, there would be conditions attached. Bolingbroke's delegation went home, leaving the beleaguered king to spend another night in misery and lamentation. Westmorland was again with the party that rode to the Tower a third day in a row. Again the king stated he would abdicate 'upon certain conditions that he would state'. He was told there would be no conditions and, understanding he had no choice, Richard read aloud from the prepared document and resigned his throne. Westmorland was among several witnesses whose names were entered in the record. It must have been both humiliating and demoralising for Richard II to read, agree to and sign a document that condemned his kingship in such blunt terms.[26]

> I confess, acknowledge, recognise, and from my own certain knowledge truly admit that I have been and am entirely inadequate and unequal to the task of ruling and governing the aforesaid kingdom and dominions and all that pertains to them, and that, on account of my notorious insufficiencies, I deserve to be deposed from them.[27]

When Parliament met, Henry Bolingbroke took his late father's seat in Westminster Hall. The Archbishop of York, Richard Scrope, announced the resignation of Richard II, which was enthusiastically accepted by the assembled lords. Westmorland had one more important part to play in the drama. He represented the lords of England on a procuracy formally surrendering homage and allegiance to the former king. The Bishop of St Asaph then read out the procuracy and declared the crown vacant.[28]

It was not vacant for long. Bolingbroke immediately set out his claim and each man present was asked if they would accept him as their king, the Treasurer asking the lords spiritual and Northumberland asking the lords temporal. Not surprisingly, each body gave their consent and agreement. Bolingbroke was then led to the throne by the two archbishops. He knelt before it in prayer and, 'to the great joy of all the people, who cried out loudly both inside the hall and outside, they sat him down on the aforesaid throne as king'.[29]

Some time before Christmas, Richard II was taken from the Tower to Pontefract Castle. Bolingbroke was crowned as Henry IV the following month. A failed attempt in January 1400 to restore Richard to his throne sealed his fate. He probably died on 14 February but the cause of his death is not known for certain. Starvation, either by refusing to eat or others withholding food, seems to be the most likely cause. He was buried in Kings Langley but, later in the reign of Henry V, was removed to Westminster Abbey and laid to rest alongside the tomb of his queen, Anne of Bohemia.[30]

The earl of Salisbury was involved in these failed plots to restore Richard II, which included a plan to put Henry IV and his sons to death. This was to take place at Windsor during Christmas but Henry was forewarned and left for London. When Salisbury and his fellow conspirator, the earl of Kent, turned up with 400 men, they found the king not only gone but aware of their plans. At this point, they left Windsor and rode to Sunning Manor, where the queen, Henry's second wife Joan of Navarre, was spending Christmas with a daughter of the King of France.[31]

The earl of Kent did his best to persuade the queen to join them, telling her that her husband had taken refuge in the Tower of London, that Richard had escaped and stood at the head of an army some 100,000 strong. Unable to convince her of the truth of this, Kent and Salisbury fled, fetching up in Cirencester. 'But the inhabitants of the town, becoming suspicious of their display of arms, and believing, quite rightly, that they were not telling the truth, during the night secretly blocked all the entrances and exits from the lodgings where they were staying.' Kent and Salisbury attempted to escape but found themselves under siege. After some hours of desperate fighting, both earls gave themselves up and were taken to a nearby abbey. One of their followers set fire to some houses, hoping to create a diversion allowing Kent and Salisbury to escape. The people of Cirencester responded by marching to the abbey and demanding the two earls be handed over to them for summary justice. [32]

> Eventually, therefore, when the sun was almost setting, they were duly handed over, and the earls of Kent and Salisbury were beheaded at the hands of the people, by which act the Lord took his revenge upon them with such punishment as bad faith and lack of belief merited. For they were both unfaithful to their king, who had spared them and shown them so much mercy. And if what is commonly said is true, then the earl of Salisbury, who all his life had been a follower of the errors of the Lollards, a despiser of holy images, and a spurner of the sacraments, ended his miserable life without the sacrament of confession. [33]

Arguably, it was this rash act of rebellion that led directly to the decision that Richard was too dangerous to be allowed to live. The earl of Salisbury was posthumously attainted in Parliament in 1401, which was to have repercussions for the family of his granddaughter Alice. [34]

What made Westmorland change his allegiance in just two short years? Despite his involvement in the trial of the earl of Arundel, and his enduring – though often distant – support of Richard II throughout his reign, Westmorland threw in his lot with Bolingbroke not only quickly but with vigour and enthusiasm. He was not the first Nevill, nor would he be the last, to change his mind about supporting the reigning king.

One Hugh Nevill, Alan de Neville's son, initially supported King John during the First Barons' War of 1215–17. He was beside his king at Runnymede and is listed in the preamble to Magna Carta. Hugh's loyalty was rewarded with grants of land confiscated from more rebellious barons. He also held Marlborough Castle for King John throughout the course of the First Barons' War, when it was used as an alternative royal treasury. In 1216, the political situation worsened and Prince Louis of France invaded

England to lead the rebels. Hugh Nevill surrendered the castle and was later punished by King John, who seized his lands. After John's death, Hugh made his peace with his son Henry III and, like his father, was appointed chief justice of the forest.[35]

During the Second Barons' War (1264–7), two Nevill cousins stood on opposing sides. Robert Nevill, a direct ancestor of Westmorland, remained staunch in his support of Henry III, while his cousin Hugh supported the barons and Simon de Montfort. When de Montfort demanded Robert attend a council meeting in London, and that his person be seized if he continued to refuse, two high-profile supporters of de Montfort – the earl of Gloucester and Prince Edward (later Edward I) – distanced themselves from him. This led to the battle of Evesham in August 1265, and de Montfort's death. Immediately after Henry III was restored to power, Robert resumed many of his previous offices. In May the following year, he came face to face with his rebellious cousin Hugh, who was holding out in Kenilworth Castle with de Montfort's son.[36]

Westmorland's life-long connection with John of Gaunt and the house of Lancaster proved stronger and more important than his loyalty to Richard II. He was married to Bolingbroke's half-sister, and when Richard II took control of the Lancastrian inheritance on the death of John of Gaunt it affected her too, though to a lesser extent. Westmorland's decision to support Bolingbroke was based not only on what might have been best for England – the deposition of Richard II – but what was best for himself and his family. Enlightened self-interest is often a driving force for change, no more so than in the case of the earl of Westmorland and Henry IV.[37]

Henry IV, like kings before him, saw the value of the Nevills and the Percies in the north of England. Once again, the business of protecting the border with Scotland was left in their hands. Westmorland seems to have been content with his lot. He was brother-in-law to the King of England, which he could not have foreseen when he married the young daughter of John of Gaunt.

Within a few short years of his coronation, Henry IV had other problems to deal with. Rebellion in Wales took up much of his time and attention. Closer to home, the earl of Northumberland and his son were making known their discontent with the king they had helped to his throne.

Henry Percy, earl of Northumberland had a son and, like every earl of Northumberland before and after him, he named him 'Henry'. The younger Henry earned himself a nickname that has endured: owing to his habit of riding his horse fast and furious, his Scots enemies called him 'Hotspur'. He was known for his impulsiveness and won battles he might just as easily have lost, and lost those a commander with a cooler head might have won. Hotspur was active and enjoyed some measure of success in Wales against the rebellion of Owain Glyndŵr and soon came to feel aggrieved at the lack of financial support from Henry IV. After Hotspur's return to the north of England, Glyndŵr's actions went unchecked for some time and, in 1401, Henry IV himself led an expedition to Wales that ended in failure. Northumberland attempted to broker peace between Henry and the rebellious Welsh prince and there was a strong sense of mutual respect between Glyndŵr and Northumberland's son. Despite his successes in Wales, Hotspur, too, championed a peaceful settlement.[38]

In 1402, Hotspur faced a Scots army at Homildon Hill, where he was reinforced in part by men sent by the earl of Westmorland. Hotspur won a decisive victory and took a number of prisoners, including the earl of Douglas. Henry IV ordered all prisoners brought to Westminster, depriving the Percies of considerable ransom. The king considered himself to be in greater need of funds than his northern lords. While Northumberland was willing to obey the king's instructions, Hotspur was not, and did not accompany his father to London nor send Douglas with him. Northumberland reminded the king of moneys owed to the Percies, but was given no satisfaction. Relations between Henry IV and the Percies, particularly Hotspur, never recovered, and as Westmorland's power grew in the north, the good working relationship he had enjoyed with the Percies began to break down. Not known for his calm approach to life, Hotspur grew more and more defiant.[39]

Despite the difficulties, Henry IV granted the Percies the earl of Douglas's estates in southern Scotland, so long as they could take possession, a condition he may have hoped would keep them busy for some time. By this point, shored up by a sense that they had put the king on his throne and Hotspur's reputation in battle, Percy ambitions grew until they wanted nothing less than to control the whole of the north of England and the Borders. Hotspur's attempts to take custody of the Douglas lands were unsuccessful and another refusal by Henry IV to provide much-needed financial aid pushed Hotspur and his father into open rebellion.[40]

In the summer of 1403, Hotspur gathered his forces, including the earl of Douglas, with whom he seems to have developed some kind of friendship, and marched south. Henry IV was in Nottingham when news reached him that Hotspur's standard had been raised in Chester. Despite Richard II's death being common knowledge, Hotspur attempted to gather men to his cause by claiming the deposed king would soon be with them in person.[41]

Henry IV was in Lichfield in Staffordshire when he sent an urgent message to his council in London to join him. Meanwhile, Hotspur's failure to produce Richard II caused some disappointment. He attempted to counter this by issuing a proclamation expressing his regret for his family's involvement in the deposition of Richard II and his replacement by Henry IV.[42]

Hotspur marched towards Shrewsbury, hoping to take possession of both the king's 16-year-old son and heir and the city's substantial military resources. Shrewsbury held firm to Henry IV. Inside the town, Prince Henry, outnumbered and no doubt hoping his father would soon arrive, stayed firm in the face of danger.[43]

From Shrewsbury, Hotspur issued a manifesto accusing the king of oath-breaking, asserting that he and his father would never have supported him on his return to England had they known his true intentions.

> … you swore an oath to us at Doncaster upon the holy gospels, which you personally held and kissed, concerning the kingdom and the status of the king, excepting only your own inheritance and that of your wife in England; and that our lord king Richard would remain king for the term of his life …[44]

This was a cynical exercise in finding justification for their own rebellion. Northumberland could not in all conscience claim he had been unaware of Bolingbroke's plans to seize the throne, whether they were made before the two men met in Doncaster or some time later. Northumberland himself had sworn a similar oath in the presence of Richard II, yet he had asked each of the lords in Parliament if they would accept Bolingbroke as their king.

Henry IV was in the town by 20 July and the Battle of Shrewsbury was fought the following day. Hotspur came close to victory, his forces reaching the royal standard and slaying Sir William Blount, Henry IV's standard-bearer. With the outcome in doubt, the king himself took to the field and his son sent his forces in to attack Hotspur's flank. At this point, Hotspur was killed in circumstances that are far from clear.[45]

On 23 July, Henry IV commissioned Westmorland to find Northumberland and bring him in. Northumberland, protesting that he had no part in his son's rebellion and treason, attempted to take shelter in Newcastle but was refused entry. Instead, he sent his army home and took refuge in Warkworth Castle. With the prospect of Westmorland's army against him, and his son dead, Northumberland had no choice but to throw himself on Henry IV's mercy. When he came face to face with the king in York, he rejected all responsibility for his son's actions. In order to control the situation, or at least avoid making things any worse, Parliament found Northumberland guilty of lesser charges than treason and he was immediately pardoned.[46]

Despite this, Northumberland was again plotting in 1405, this time with Glyndŵr and Edmund Mortimer, earl of March. Mortimer's daughter Elizabeth was Hotspur's widow, and he considered himself Richard II's heir and rightful successor. The Archbishop of York, Richard Scrope, who had just five years earlier proclaimed Richard II's resignation in Parliament, was deeply involved in the plot, as was the earl marshal, Thomas Mowbray.[47]

Early in May, Northumberland attempted to capture Westmorland in Durham but Westmorland was forewarned. At this point, Northumberland would seem to have considered their enterprise doomed and abandoned his fellow conspirators. This did not save him, however, and he soon fled to Scotland. He was later attainted *in absentia* by the following Parliament.[48]

Westmorland was instrumental in the capture and arrest of Scrope and Mowbray at Skipton in Yorkshire on 27 May 1405. His own forces outnumbered, he greeted them in a sympathetic and friendly manner before persuading Scrope to disband his army. As soon as the men left Skipton, Westmorland arrested both Scrope and Mowbray. Henry IV arrived on 3 June and five days later both men were beheaded.[49]

With the Percies in ruin, defeated or in exile, Westmorland was the undisputed power in the north of England. He was rewarded with forfeited Percy lands and castles in Cumberland. After the death of Henry IV's son and successor Henry V, he sat on the council of regency for the infant Henry VI, but Westmorland kept himself very much to the north of England for the remainder of his life.[50]

Henry IV's reign lasted just thirteen years. He was succeeded by his son who, at the age of 16, had played such a decisive role at the battle of Shrewsbury. In the year Henry V won his most famous victory at Agincourt, Joan Beaufort gave birth to her youngest surviving child, Cecily. In the roll call of marriages negotiated by Westmorland and, after his death, by his widow, Cecily was to make the greatest match of all. In her long life, she was to know triumph and tragedy, none of which could have been foretold as she enjoyed a privileged childhood at Raby Castle.

# 3

# Joan Beaufort's Daughters and the Young Duke of York

In August 1415, while waiting for his treason trial to begin, a young and impoverished nobleman wrote two heartfelt letters to his king, begging for compassion and mercy. 'I know well I have highly offended your Highness; beseeching you at the reverence of God that you like to take me into the hands of your merciful and piteous grace'. He was Richard, earl of Cambridge, barely 30 years old and the father of two young children. Cambridge and his fellow conspirators had been betrayed by one of their number, the figurehead they hoped would raise rebellion in Wales and topple Henry V. None of them had, in fact, committed treason as it was defined at the time. Plotting rebellion, even supporting rebellion, was not included in the Statutes of Treason. Imagining the death of the king and his heirs was. In order to make the charges stick, the beginning of the rebellion had to be assumed, as well as its successful conduct and the eventual fulfilment of its aims. This must, it was reasoned, involve the death of the king and his brothers.[1]

The earl of Cambridge was the fourth son of Edmund of Langley and Isabel of Castile and a grandson of Edward III. His older brother Edmund was duke of York and one of England's wealthiest men. Cambridge had nothing. Through his first wife, Anne Mortimer, he had hopes of future prosperity after the deaths of her brothers, neither of whom was permitted to marry. Her death in 1412, however, shortly after the birth of their son, ended those hopes. Cambridge had something of an income through his second wife, Maud Clifford, who had a life interest in the property of her first husband John Nevill, lord Latimer. Cambridge and his family lived at Conisborough Castle, not the finest of the York estates, and was little esteemed by more senior members of the royal family.[2]

Left out of his father's will entirely, Cambridge's cause was taken up by his mother. She left her entire estate to Richard II and begged him to make provision for her youngest son. After the fall of Richard II, Cambridge found himself pushed wholly into the background by Henry IV. He did his bit for king and country, fighting against Glyndŵr in Wales, defending Herefordshire with a handful of poorly paid men and supporting the defence of Abergavenny Castle, but was little rewarded. In 1406, he accompanied Henry IV's daughter Philippa to her wedding in Denmark, where he made the acquaintance of Henry, lord Scrope of Masham, who was later to marry Cambridge's stepmother.[3]

In 1408, Cambridge secretly married Anne Mortimer, sister of Edmund Mortimer, earl of March, and was fined for failing to seek permission or a dispensation. After applying for and receiving papal dispensation, the couple were forgiven and allowed to legally remarry. They had two children, Isabel and Richard.[4]

Cambridge's main grievance was his lack of funds. He owned no land in his own right. He had expectations of succeeding his brother Edmund as duke of York, which would have made him a wealthy man, but York was not much older than he was. York's marriage to a woman considerably older than him meant children were unlikely, but it could still be a long time before Cambridge achieved financial stability, if he achieved it at all.[5]

Things did not improve after the death of Henry IV and the succession of his son. In fact, Henry V made things worse in 1414 by granting Richard the earldom of Cambridge without any means of making an income from it. The company of two other men in similar financial peril, his brother-in-law Mortimer and Sir Thomas Grey of Heton, encouraged Cambridge to imagine rebellion and a more sympathetic king than Henry V. The plot was ridiculous and doomed to fail. Cambridge and Grey were to help Mortimer get to Wales, where he was to foment rebellion. Cambridge claimed to have the support of the Scots, though it is highly unlikely they took him or his plotting seriously. Just like that of the earls of Salisbury and Kent a decade and a half earlier, the rebellion was to be fought in the name of Richard II, though few believed him to still be alive. Putting Mortimer on the throne was the aim all along but it was presented as a back-up plan, in the event Richard II proved unavailable.[6]

Scrope's part in the plot is more difficult to determine. The claim in his confession that he was only in communication with the plotters in order to see what they were up to and, eventually, stop them failed to convince anyone. Of the four, his actions seem least to resemble treason. Mortimer, who saw himself and was seen by others as Richard II's heir, had finally been granted permission to marry but the fine that was levied, 10,000 marks, was exorbitant and one he could not hope to pay in his lifetime. Sir Thomas

Grey was married to Westmorland's daughter Alice and himself had serious financial worries. Ambitious for his family and himself, he did everything he could to raise their status and not just through prudent marriages. In 1412, his son married Cambridge's daughter Isabel. This allowed him to buy the lordship of Wark-in-Tyndale for around half its market value but still at a cost he could not afford. He threatened to default on the first payment. Like Mortimer and Cambridge, Grey hoped a change of king would bring with it a change in fortune.[7]

The conspirators' hopeless plot was uncovered just before Henry V and his nobles were to sail to France. Mortimer, suddenly overcome by the futility of the plan, confessed all to the king, in return for a pardon. Cambridge, Grey and Scrope were called to a regular council meeting at Portchester Castle and arrested. They were locked up in Southampton Castle, where they confessed to varying degrees of complicity and Cambridge wrote his heart-wrenching letters begging for mercy.[8]

Cambridge, Scrope and Grey were all beheaded for their part in the plot. Had Henry V not been about to embark on his expedition to France, they may have been dealt with more leniently. He could not, however, afford to have three loose cannons, even locked up in a castle, alive on the other side of the Channel while he and a large part of England's nobility were fighting in France. At the time of Cambridge's execution, his son was just 4 years old. Within a few months of his father's death, young Richard would receive what Cambridge had been too impatient to wait for – the estates and title of his uncle, Edmund, duke of York, who was killed at Agincourt.

Young Richard's inheritance was not affected by his late father's attainder and, still aged 4, he succeeded his uncle as duke of York. He spent the next eight years in the household of Sir Robert Waterton who, in 1423, sold his wardship to the earl of Westmorland for 3,000 marks. There can be little doubt Westmorland bought York's wardship, which came with the rights to his marriage, in order to provide a husband for one of his daughters.[9]

Westmorland had provided good, though unspectacular, marriages for his children from his first marriage, including a match between his second son Ralph and Joan Beaufort's daughter Mary Ferrers. With his daughters provided for and his oldest sons either dead or childless, Westmorland seems to have given little thought to his three senior grandsons. Ralph, the eldest, was to inherit his grandfather's title and Raby Castle. However, Westmorland spent considerable time and energy in his later years securing the bulk of his lands for Richard, his oldest son with Joan Beaufort. This led to great tensions within the family that would have dire consequences much later.[10]

Westmorland and, after his death, his countess took particular care with their children's marriages.

Between 1412 and 1436 there occurred what must certainly be the most amazing series of child marriages in English history – eleven marriages involving thirteen children under sixteen years of age, a young man at the most seventeen, two girls of eighteen or less and five men between twenty and twenty-three.[11]

By 1436, eight of Joan Beaufort's surviving children had married and married well. The exceptions were Robert, who was destined for the Church, and Joan, who became a nun. By the time of her own death four years later, the countess of Westmorland was the mother of an earl, three barons, a countess, three duchesses, a bishop and a nun.

Medieval aristocratic marriage was rarely about romance, though marital love was an ideal to be aspired to. Though often depicted in chivalric terms, courtship was a matter for hardnosed fathers or guardians to negotiate, hammering out conditions and financial settlements. Many factors had a bearing on the choices families made for their children – wealth, title, ancestry, prominence and influence all had a part to play. Older sons needed connections to other noble families, brothers-in-law to help build strong affinities as they grew to military manhood. Younger sons needed incomes and, where possible, titles. Heiresses needed husbands strong enough to protect their wealth and worthy enough to carry their titles. Everyone needed healthy, fertile partners so bloodlines on both sides could continue. Older widowed fathers of daughters sought out young wives who might bear them sons. Men whose titles would descend through a daughter sought out vigorous young men who would pass those titles to their own sons. Bloodlines were of paramount importance. The longer a title remained within a single family, passed down in an unbroken line, the more status it conferred. A father's bloodline was almost always more important, though a mother's line was never forgotten.[12]

This was not a hard and fast, non-negotiable rule. Westmorland's grandson, the earl of Warwick, set as much store by his wife's bloodline and almost as much by his mother's as he did his father's. His rather complicated coat of arms gives prominence to both, though the Nevill saltire was the largest single element. Warwick's brother John chose to take his mother's name Montagu as his title in 1461. There was clear precedent for the acknowledgement of a mother's lineage over a father's several generations back when the son of Robert FitzMaldred took his mother's Nevill surname.

Matters other than money and title were also of concern when it came to choosing marriage partners. Social standing, knowing how to behave, good manners, skills in hawking and hunting, and more genteel arts, such as the writing of verse, were all considered important. Marriage to a rich merchant's son or daughter may be of financial benefit to a family but without an understanding of social graces acquired in childhood, there was a risk of attracting scorn or ridicule.[13]

Despite this businesslike pragmatism, the myths of chivalric romance in courtship and marriage endured, particularly in the form of noble genealogies, such as the Rous Roll and the Salisbury Roll. A woman's authority over her man peaked in courtship. After he had proved himself worthy of her and the marriage was celebrated, she yielded her power to his.[14]

In truth, many fifteenth-century marriages had more in common with business partnerships than idealised chivalric romances. Margaret Paston oversaw much of her husband's legal practice and shared family business from Norfolk while he was in London. In 1450, the duke of Suffolk urged his son to heed his mother's advice and counsel above all others. Until her death in 1422, Elizabeth Berkeley, countess of Warwick had to contend with threats to her inheritance largely on her own.[15]

Despite everything, marital love was what many couples aspired to. When decisions were made, or wedding ceremonies took place when couples were children, this allowed time for friendship and affection to develop. While the cliché of noble couples meeting for the first time at the church door may not be entirely true, older couples who knew little of each other faced a steep learning curve.

While future prospects in matches were usually of paramount importance, this was sometimes overridden by the more immediate concerns of parents. Fathers of daughters might seek strong and well-connected sons-in-law to add to their sonless affinities. Others in need of funds might sell their children's marriages with little thought for their future happiness. Judging from the end results, Ralph Nevill and Joan Beaufort had a knack for finding a happy balance, as did Ralph's son Richard in the next generation. While we have only circumstantial evidence of happy and fulfilling Nevill marriages, there is even less evidence of any great misery. Happy marriages do not seem to have been noticed, much less remarked upon. On the other hand, spectacularly unhappy and unsuccessful marriages were. One particularly happy marriage that was noted at the time was that of Cecily Nevill and Richard, duke of York.

In May 1415, Joan's youngest surviving child, Cecily, was born at Raby Castle. By this time, Richard, her oldest brother in the full blood, was already close to manhood. Their worlds were almost completely separate and the two siblings would not have had much to do with each other in the ordinary course of events. Certainly, by the time Cecily was 6 or 7, Richard was married and living in his own household in southern England. In childhood, Cecily spent most of her time in the company of her next oldest sister, Anne, her nursemaids and governess. Richard would have spent his time with his younger brothers, his father and his father's wards and retainers.

Cecily's time with her mother was spent in quiet industry, learning the fine arts of sewing and embroidery but also household management, account keeping and child-rearing. It was from their mother that Cecily and her sister Anne got their love of books. Reading aloud and discussing what was read accompanied many of the more mundane activities. Men rarely intruded into this closed world of women. Meal times and hunts, Christmas festivities and celebrations, such as weddings and baptisms, were times when men and women came together. Whether Cecily paid much attention to the young boy who came into her home and her life when she was just 8 is difficult to say. Two years later, the young duke of York became a very large part of her future. Even then, it is unlikely they spent any considerable time in each other's company.

It was Joan's job as a mother to keep her daughters chaste until they married. She, like her daughter-in-law Alice after her, took this one step further. Perhaps it was her own experience of pregnancy and motherhood around the age of 15 that influenced her, but Joan took care not to expose her daughters and daughters-in-law to the potential dangers of childbirth before they were 17 or 18. As some of her daughters married very young, this sometimes meant keeping married couples apart for years. During a long period of betrothal, as was the case with Cecily and York, or the years after an early marriage, wise parents would have striven to encourage affection, but not intimacy, between couples. In 1424, Cecily was betrothed to the duke of York. Her father died the following year and it is not clear where York spent the next few years of his life. As the earl of Northumberland was involved in the management and settlement of two of York's estates, it is possible he was sent to live with him for a time before the wedding itself was celebrated in 1429.[16]

Northumberland, Hotspur's son, was married to Westmorland's daughter Eleanor. This was Eleanor's second marriage, her first husband having died just two years after their wedding, when she was 11 and he no more than 13. Northumberland was some ten years older than his bride and eager to be restored to his family's title and estates.[17]

Just 9 years old when his father died at the battle of Shrewsbury, Northumberland had spent the last ten years of his life in the custody of the Scots duke of Albany, who had also sheltered Hotspur's father until his death in 1408. When Henry IV died in 1413, his son embarked on a long and complicated process to return Northumberland to England and at least part of his inheritance. This involved an exchange of prisoners and was almost scuppered by the Southampton Plot. The terms of the agreement were finally settled in July 1415 and Northumberland began his journey south. In February the following year, Eleanor and her parents travelled to Berwick, where the couple married. Their oldest son, Henry, was born in 1421 when Eleanor was 19. She and Northumberland were to have a further eight children together.[18]

This marriage was just one of many Nevill–Percy matches made over the years. The two families were both natural allies and natural rivals. It is possible that a marriage between Northumberland and a daughter of Joan Beaufort, who was the young king's aunt, was crucial to his rehabilitation. In the middle of campaigning in France, Henry V needed more than ever to trust those who protected England's northern border. As experienced and accomplished as Westmorland was, this was not a responsibility he could continue to shoulder on his own. His son Richard was appointed warden of the west march in 1420 and it would have been assumed he and his brother-in-law Northumberland would work together, as Nevills and Percies had done in the past. However, ties of marriage did nothing to prevent Richard Nevill and Henry Percy developing a strong mutual antipathy that was, later, inherited by their sons.[19]

Joan's second youngest daughter, Anne, was married some time before 1424 to Humphrey Stafford, later duke of Buckingham. He was some twelve years older than his bride and of modest means. Stafford spent the first few years of his marriage fighting in France, where he was given the posts of Governor of Paris, Constable of France and Lieutenant-General of Normandy. Along with Joan Beaufort's brother, Henry, Bishop of Winchester, Stafford advocated peace with France. On the death of his mother in 1438, his financial position was transformed and he became one of the greatest of English landowners. Though he came to be known as a moderate and something of a conciliator, his relationship with his wife's family was not always amicable. During their thirty-year marriage, he and Anne had ten children.[20]

Unlike her sisters, Ralph Nevill and Joan Beaufort's oldest daughter Katherine had a chequered and – in the end – scandalous marital history. She was first married at 12 or 13 to John Mowbray, who was eight years her senior. Mowbray was the younger brother of the earl marshall, Thomas Mowbray, who had just eight years earlier been arrested by Westmorland and executed by Henry IV. Westmorland had bought John Mowbray's wardship in 1411 with a view to marriage with one of his daughters and in the hope that the young man's loyalty to Henry IV could be assured. The hereditary role of earl marshal – lost when Thomas was executed and held ever since by Westmorland – was restored to John on his marriage. In this capacity, in 1415, he investigated the Southampton Plot and was one of the judges who sentenced the rebels, including his brother-in-law Sir Thomas Grey, to death. Though he fought in France, Mowbray was sick with dysentery and missed the battle of Agincourt. He and Katherine had only one child, John, who was born in 1415. In 1425, John Mowbray was restored to the dukedom of Norfolk. He died in 1432, leaving the bulk of his estate to Katherine and naming her chief executor of his will.[21]

Katherine's second marriage is a little more obscure and may not have actually taken place before the births of two daughters. The first mention of this marriage comes in 1442 when she and her husband, Thomas Strangeways, were fined for failing to secure a licence. Thomas died within a year and Katherine quickly married for a third time. John, Viscount Beaumont was some nine years younger than his bride and a much more fitting husband for the daughter of an earl. They were married for seventeen years but had no children together. By the 1450s, Beaumont was not on the friendliest terms with Katherine's family. Whether this had an effect on the marriage is not known. When Beaumont died in 1460, Katherine was about 60 years old.[22]

It was Katherine's fourth marriage that caused the greatest scandal. Some time in 1464 or 1465, Katherine married the much younger John Wydeville, brother of Edward IV's queen, who was somewhere in his twenties. Despite the great disparity in their ages, Katherine outlived him too.[23]

Cecily Nevill was 14 and Richard of York 18 when they married in 1429. Joan had been a widow for four years and her husband's grandson Ralph was now earl of Westmorland and master of Raby Castle. Joan and her younger children were living at Middleham at this time, which, along with Sheriff Hutton, was part of her dower lands. Later, she leased Middleham to her son Richard and it became the principal home of his family until his death. Some time between 1429 and 1439, when their first child was born, Cecily left her mother's care and set up her first household with her husband at Fotheringhay.[24]

Cecily and York spent many of the early years of their marriage in France, where York served as Henry VI's lieutenant. He was ably assisted by John, lord Talbot, reputedly one of the greatest of English soldiers, and his brother-in-law Richard, now earl of Salisbury in right of his wife. Though he was an able administrator and may have seen himself as more than just a military governor, York failed to distinguish himself in battle.[25]

Their first child, Anne, was born at Fotheringhay in 1439 and their next four children – Henry, Edward, Edmund and Elizabeth – were all born in Rouen in Normandy. Henry died in infancy, as did several other children over the years, leaving Edward as the principal heir to York's English estates. It was York's intention to provide lands in France for Edmund, lending a personal dimension to his determination to hold on to English territory in France.[26]

After the death of Henry V in 1422, the success of the English army in France slowed and, eventually, went into reverse. Despite the infant Henry VI being crowned King of France, the French were not about to accept defeat and rule by a foreign dynasty. In codicils to his will, written when he knew he was dying, Henry V had left provisions for the care of his young son. His brother Humphrey, duke of Gloucester was to be Protector of England until Henry VI came of age. Thomas Beaufort, duke of Exeter and lord Henry Fitzhugh were to be in charge of the young king's person. Though he left no sign in writing, witnesses to Henry V's final hours testified it was his wish that his other brother, John, duke of Bedford, be in charge of the future conduct of the war in France.[27]

England was stretched financially and maintaining territory in France was costly. Resistance within English-occupied France and renewed activity by French armies strained resources and affected morale. When the duke of Bedford died in 1435, a sense of cohesion was lost and the English commanders in Gascony and Normandy, the dukes of Somerset and York, had to compete for resources.[28]

It was in France that York first developed a strong sense of his own destiny and a distrust, which later turned to bitter enmity, for John Beaufort, duke of Somerset. The two dukes were in fierce competition and Somerset's actions in France ultimately ended in disaster, both political and military.[29]

That Somerset was Cecily Nevill's cousin did not soften her husband's opinion of him. Returned from France in disgrace, he was exiled from court and died at Corfe Castle, a sick and broken man. Though there is no clear evidence to support the claim, his death may have been suicide.[30]

Beaufort was succeeded, both in his title and in France, by his nephew Edmund. Though there was nothing to suggest any difficulties at this point, York would later engage in a bitter dispute with the new duke.[31]

In what must have been a welcome respite from war, in 1445, York and Cecily enjoyed high-profile roles in the reception of Henry VI's bride Margaret of Anjou in Rouen. The bridal party was in Rouen for a fortnight before York accompanied them to the port of Honfleur for Margaret's voyage across the Channel.[32]

York's term as Governor of Normandy expired in late 1445 and he left France for England, fully expecting to have his commission extended, but this failed to come to pass.[33]

His next appointment was to Ireland, where he was to serve as Governor. Cecily gave birth to another son, George, in Dublin in 1449. By this time, York's disaffection with Henry VI's councillors, particularly Somerset, had grown. This was to culminate in 1452 in a stand-off at Dartford, with York and a handful of supporters on one side, demanding that Somerset be tried for treason, and Henry VI and York's brother-in-law, the earl of Salisbury, on the other.

# 4

# JOAN BEAUFORT'S SONS AND THE FAMILY FEUD

We have now late heard and well understand to our great displeasure of certain misgovernances and debates late moved and stirred betwixt our cousin the earl of Westmorland, sir John Nevill and sir Thomas Nevill on the one part, and our cousins the countess of Westmorland, the earl of Salisbury and the lord Latimer on the other part. Of which several, either against other, by manner of war and insurrection have late assembled great routs and companies upon the field and do furthermore other great and horrible offences in slaughter and destruction of our people.[1]

Joan Beaufort and her sons were expected to appear before the king 'wheresoever we may be in this our realm' on St Hillary's Day, 13 January 1438. The middle of winter was not the best time to be on the road in the fifteenth century, especially for a woman close to 60, and neither party made the journey.[2]

The earl of Westmorland summoned to London was Ralph Nevill's grandson. Sir John and Sir Thomas were his younger brothers. The countess of Westmorland was still Joan Beaufort; the earl of Salisbury and lord Latimer were her oldest son Richard and third son George. The nature of the 'war and insurrection', the 'routs and companies' and the 'slaughter and destruction' was not recorded by any of the known chroniclers. That anyone actually died by violence is unlikely. Acts of vandalism, intimidation and threats, and the taking of property by force are not. With small private armies at their disposal, young Westmorland and his uncles had the resources to both attack and defend. Through her sons, Joan had the means to defend her property against threat. She herself was more than capable of mobilising the inhabitants of a castle or manor and directing their actions.

The dispute, whatever form it took, was over the Nevill inheritance. Ralph Nevill made a new will before he died, leaving little to the children of his first wife. Since his second marriage, he had been funnelling properties, particularly those he held jointly with Joan, to their children. His second son, Ralph, husband of Joan's daughter Mary Ferrers, his own stepsister, had no children. His oldest son, John, died when his sons, the young earl of Westmorland and his brothers, were young. Young Westmorland did not have Salisbury's powerful connections, though he was not entirely without support. It was not, however, nearly enough to stand up to the combined might of his stepgrandmother and her sons.[3]

What prompted Ralph Nevill to favour the children he had with Joan is not entirely clear. He may have been concerned for their futures and sought to leave them well provided for. He may have been conscious of their direct descent from Edward III. He may simply have been fonder of them. Whatever his reasons, he went well beyond simply seeking a way to make sure their lives, particularly the life of the eldest, were comfortable. Ralph had managed to redirect almost everything he owned away from his grandson and to his son Richard. The second earl of Westmorland was not about to accept his disinheritance without a fight.[4]

Though no details of the level of violence, or the seriousness of its threat, have come down to us, it had to have been serious for the king to get involved. Trouble in a remote part of the kingdom close to the border with a traditionally hostile neighbour needed to be dealt with quickly and decisively. Henry VI, barely out of the schoolroom, took the only action he knew – he sent for the warring parties with a view to brokering peace between them.

A second letter was sent in February, requiring Joan and her stepgrandson to be in London on 'xv Pasq', which refers to the fifteenth day of Lent or 20 March 1438. A second entry in the Proceedings of Privy Council later in February mentions 'a covenant to be made betwixt them'.[5]

In February 1438, 16-year-old Henry VI had only just taken the reigns of personal kingship into his own hands. His education and preparation for the role had been overseen by Richard Beauchamp, earl of Warwick, but now Warwick had taken up the governorship of Normandy and Henry was acting in his own name. As every king before him, he needed his nobles to be at peace with each other, particularly in the north of England.

If Joan obeyed the summons, it would have taken her up to two weeks to get to London from Middleham in a litter or light carriage. Her stepgrandson, not restricted to a slower pace, could have got there in half the time.[6]

Along the way, Joan and her considerable armed escort would have stayed the night in family properties, or as guests of friends or her late husband's retainers, or, if necessary, strangers. Religious houses also offered hospitality. Travellers were not turned away when they needed a meal or a bed for the night. Someone of Joan Beaufort's standing and status would have been greeted by many with a mixture of respect and apprehension. Would there be enough food for her retinue? Did she offer supplies from her own store? Would she find her bed comfortable? Would she look down her royal nose or would she treat her hosts with respect and friendship? For her part, Joan was likely glad just to be out of her jolting litter and off the muddy roads.[7]

Once in London, she would have taken up residence in the Erber, the great Nevill house on the banks of the river. The Erber was just one of many properties that found its way into Nevill hands through marriage. Leased in 1373 by William Latimer, lord of Danby, whose daughter married Ralph Nevill's father after the death of Maud Percy, it was later granted to Ralph and Joan permanently by Henry IV.[8]

The Erber did not begin its existence as a nobleman's manor but the house of a merchant. Fronted by streets on three sides with the river at its back, it was a sprawling rectangle built around a series of courtyards. The property had numerous outbuildings for stabling horses, storing hay and timber and a sizeable garden. It included several shops and an inn that brought an annual rent of some £12. The Erber was a comfortable, if unpretentious London base for members of the Nevill family for several generations. After the attainder of the duke of Clarence in 1478, the Erber reverted to the crown. Henry VII granted it to the earl of Oxford, who was married to a daughter of the earl of Salisbury. On his death, the property was restored to Clarence's daughter Margaret, countess of Salisbury, who held it until her arrest and execution in 1541. The Erber was one of many properties destroyed in the great fire of 1666.[9]

The Erber was on the north bank of the Thames between Westminster and the Tower of London. Travelling by barge, flanked by her sons, with the Nevill saltire and the Beaufort arms on proud display, the countess of Westmorland would have made a magnificent spectacle as she made her slow way upriver to meet with the king.

Richard, earl of Salisbury was now 38 years old and the father of seven children. George, lord Latimer was 31 and newly married. Young Westmorland had twice before been bound over to keep the peace while his half-brother Salisbury was serving in France, so the threat of violence was not trivial. If Westmorland felt aggrieved at his grandfather's machinations, it is entirely understandable. The conventions of primogeniture should have seen him a wealthy man, not an earl with little property. His yearly income, he claimed, had been reduced to less than a quarter of what it should have been. Salisbury, ably assisted by his mother and younger brothers, was going to hold on to what he had, however he had come by it. In 1430, Westmorland entered into recognizances with Joan Beaufort not to pursue his claim by use of force.[10]

Joan was no helpless widow at the mercy of powerful men. In an attempt to have his grandfather's later will overturned, Westmorland tried to retrieve an earlier one from its place of safekeeping at Durham Priory. Joan beat him to it and both wills were safely in her possession.[11]

Westmorland was not without potentially powerful allies. His second wife was Margaret Cobham, sister of Eleanor, duchess of Gloucester, whose husband Humphrey was Protector of England during the minority of Henry VI. Even this failed to turn things in Westmorland's favour, however, the fall of the duchess of Gloucester in 1441 wiping out any advantage a Cobham connection might have brought. After Joan Beaufort's death in 1440, a settlement was reached between Westmorland and Salisbury, Westmorland securing the lordship and castle of Raby and the little he had inherited, and Salisbury getting the rest.[12]

Joan Beaufort's efforts were not confined to fierce protection of Salisbury and his interests. Her fourth son Robert entered the Church at 9 years old when he joined the community of the collegiate church in Auckland. By the time he was 15, Robert held a number of prebends in the see of York as well as revenue from the parish of Spofforth. Robert's uncle Henry, Bishop of Winchester, chancellor and, in 1417, cardinal, did much to support him. Robert spent some time in Henry Beaufort's household and, in 1417, travelled with him to Europe, though he did not accompany his uncle on his subsequent pilgrimage to Jerusalem.[13]

Robert was elevated to the see of Durham in 1437, again with his uncle's support. This was at the height of the dispute between Joan Beaufort and the 2nd earl of Westmorland. It was more likely designed to put the considerable resources of the palatinate of Durham in friendly hands rather than a reflection of Robert Nevill's worth. Generally, Robert left much of his work to others, living away from his see and taking little part in administrative or clerical duties. Apart from one 'disastrous exception', the focus of Robert's life was pleasing his older brothers.[14]

This 'disastrous exception' was Robert's part in a long dispute between Church, state and the Beauchamp family over the lordship of Barnard Castle. Seized in 1293 by Edward I and granted by Edward II to Guy Beauchamp, earl of Warwick in 1307, the castle was the subject of centuries of legal wrangling and changing hands. When Richard Beauchamp, earl of Warwick died in 1439, Bishop Nevill took possession, only to be ejected by his brother Salisbury, whose son was married to Beauchamp's daughter. Thereafter, Robert Nevill concentrated his efforts on supporting his brothers and their children. He died in 1457.[15]

In 1443, George Nevill married Elizabeth Beauchamp, daughter of Richard Beauchamp, earl of Warwick and his first wife Elizabeth Berkeley, and together they had four children. For many years he was Salisbury's trusted lieutenant in the west march and led an army against the Scots in 1435. During the 1440s he suffered some kind of mental breakdown from which he never fully recovered and Salisbury became his legal guardian.[16]

Edward Nevill, Joan Beaufort's youngest surviving son, was knighted in Leicester in 1426. He held his title, lord Bergavenny, in right of his wife Elizabeth Beauchamp, daughter of Richard Beauchamp, earl of Worcester. The complications of noble marriage and remarriage – and the scarcity of given names – leads to a somewhat confusing situation. After the death of her father, the earl of Warwick became Elizabeth's stepfather. Both were called Richard Beauchamp. Warwick already had a daughter named Elizabeth who had married Edward Nevill's brother George. The lordship of Abergavenny, from which Elizabeth's title came, was soon in dispute between Edward and his nephew Richard. At one point, Edward took possession of Abergavenny Castle by force and was removed by the duke of York on the orders of Henry VI.[17]

Young Richard Nevill was in dispute with both his aunts Elizabeth Beauchamp – over the lordship of Abergavenny on the one hand and the Warwick inheritance on the other. This did not, however, force Edward Nevill into open hostility towards his nephew. Though he maintained a far lower profile than his brothers Salisbury and Fauconberg, Edward did support the duke of York's first protectorate in 1454 and fought at the battle of Northampton in 1460. Edward married twice, first to Elizabeth Beauchamp, with whom he had four children, and second to Katherine Howard, with whom he had three daughters.[18]

By far the most influential, powerful and politically active of Joan Beaufort's sons were Richard, earl of Salisbury and William, lord Fauconberg. William was Joan's second son and the one most closely associated with his brother Salisbury and, later, his nephew Richard. Before April 1422, he married Joan, only daughter of John, lord Fauconberg, who had died when Joan was still an infant. From 1436 to 1439, alongside Talbot and Scales, Fauconberg had been in charge of the defences of Normandy, after which he returned to England in hopes of gaining more support from king and Parliament. In 1440, he was elevated to the Order of the Garter.[19]

William's wife Joan is described in much of the literature as 'an idiot from birth' though there is no contemporary mention of this before 1463. Whatever questions there may have been as to her mental competency, Joan and William had four daughters together. The existence of a long-standing mistress in William's life, with whom he had at least two sons, could suggest his marriage was neither emotionally nor sexually fulfilling, but it is by no means a closed case. In 1463, a commission was sent to examine Joan but there is no record of its findings. Whatever the case, the marriage between 15-year-old Joan and 17-year-old William endured for some forty years.[20]

Fauconberg returned to France in 1448 but was soon wounded and captured. He remained a prisoner for some three years. Shortly after his release, the political situation in England worsened with the sudden illness of Henry VI and Fauconberg soon joined his brother and nephew in support of the duke of York. He was to continue in York's service, and later his son Edward IV, until his death in 1462.[21]

By 1421, Joan's oldest son, Richard, was married to 15-year-old Alice Montagu, sole heir to the Salisbury title and fortune. The posthumous attainder of her grandfather John in 1400 was repealed in 1409 and Alice's father, Thomas, was restored to the family estates and title. Thomas Montagu spent many years in France as a soldier and diplomat and, in 1419, he was appointed Henry V's Lieutenant of Normandy. He was a trusted battlefield commander and military governor. He returned briefly to England in 1427 and spent most of his time planning his next expedition to France. Alice's mother, Eleanor Holland, had died some time before 1421. Within three years, Thomas married Alice Chaucer, granddaughter of the poet. Alice Chaucer was very close in age to her stepdaughter Alice Montagu. The two women maintained a close relationship throughout their lives.[22]

Alice Chaucer was said to have been quite beautiful, so much so that she caught the eye of Philip, duke of Burgundy during a feast he was hosting in Paris. Philip had something of an eye for the ladies and paid her rather too much attention for her husband's liking. This hardened Montagu's heart against the duke and in 1427, against the interests of Burgundy, he laid siege to Orléans. The following year, he was seriously wounded in the face by a splinter from a French cannon. He died a few days later.[23]

> But sorrow it is to tell, and doleful to write, while one day the said good earl, sir Thomas Montagu, rested him at a bay window and beheld the compass of the city and talked with his familiars, a gun was levelled out of the city from a place unknown, which broke the timber and stone of the window with such violence that the pieces thereof all to quashed the face of the noble earl in such wise that he died within three days following ...[24]

Montagu's daughter Alice inherited her father's estates and the earldom of Salisbury. Richard Nevill was unofficially recognised as earl of Salisbury in her right soon after his father-in-law's death, though this was not confirmed by Parliament until 1429 or by Henry VI until 1443.[25]

Salisbury and his countess settled into life among the extensive Montagu and Nevill estates spread across England. Between 1428 and 1444, Alice gave birth to ten children in rapid succession. Life was not peaceful, however, what with Salisbury's obligations in the marches towards Scotland, membership of the king's council, his concerns about the escalating inherit-ance dispute and service in France.

Joan Beaufort died in 1440 and Salisbury moved his family north to Middleham Castle, which he had held under lease from his mother since the death of his father.[26]

In 1443, Salisbury once again took up the accustomed Nevill role of warden of the west march, appointing a series of lieutenants who were paid from his salary of around £1,000 a year.

The 1440s also brought a new distraction. Disputes with his brother-in-law the earl of Northumberland threatened to turn into open conflict. The historical cooperation between the wardens of the west and east marches, crucial to the protection of the border with Scotland, began to break down. A breach of protocol on Northumberland's part and a bitter precedence dispute might, in time, have been mended. But as the earls' sons grew to manhood, they took up the quarrel their fathers had largely conducted with words, added a good measure of violence and turned it into one of the most destructive blood feuds in English history.

# PART 2

# THE NEVILLS AND THE DUKE OF YORK

# 5

# The Road to Dartford

he year 1450 was one of great turmoil, particularly in south-eastern England. The duke of Suffolk was murdered as he crossed the Channel to start a five-year exile. The commons of Kent and Sussex rose and threatened the peace and safety of London. The duke of Somerset returned from France with a beaten and demoralised army. And the duke of York returned from Ireland without royal permission, determined to find redress for the shoddy treatment he had received from the king.

With the government in disarray, and aware of his growing popularity, York was determined to step into the breach left by the absence of Suffolk. He feared, as did the populace, that if he did not move quickly, Henry VI would draw Somerset further into his personal circle, perhaps even name him as his heir presumptive. York had already been replaced by Somerset once. He was not about to let it happen again.

From Dublin, York could do nothing but watch. We do not know who he might have been corresponding with, probably a number of people, but he was certainly receiving news and little of it was good. He would have known the commons of Kent had invoked his name, and he certainly knew that some suspected he was behind the rising. He would have known of the surrender of Rouen and the loss of Normandy. This must have been a bitter blow to a man who had spent many years and a good deal of energy consolidating England's hold on the duchy. He would also have known of the fall of Suffolk, who had never been his friend.

Suffolk had for many years been Henry VI's chief councillor. He guided the young king and placed himself squarely between Henry and the rest of the world. For this, he was much criticised at the time and continues to be criticised now. Though there is no doubt he benefited personally from his close association with the king and the royal household, he also worked hard in the interests of England, particularly in the pursuit of peace with France.[1]

It was in France that Suffolk first came to prominence. After the deaths of his father at the siege of Harfleur and his older brother at Agincourt, Suffolk began thirteen years of military service under both Henry V and his son, Henry VI. He worked closely with Henry VI's uncle Bedford as both a soldier and a diplomat. It was his dealings with the French, particularly his later friendship with Charles, duke of Orléans, that allowed his enemies to stir up public resentment against him.[2]

In France, Suffolk was most closely associated with Thomas Montagu, earl of Salisbury. They were at the siege of Orléans together, where Salisbury was killed and Suffolk captured by Joan of Arc herself. He was soon released, on condition he use his influence to secure the release of high-profile French prisoners in England.[3]

It was during this time of imprisonment that Suffolk penned several love poems addressed to an anonymous woman. She was most likely Alice Chaucer, widow of his old friend Salisbury. Suffolk undoubtedly knew her and must have known of the offence caused by Philip of Burgundy at the Paris wedding feast. If Suffolk had lost his heart to her before her husband's death, he was far more discreet than Philip the Good. He certainly seems to have kept the memory of her alive during his captivity. He and Alice married shortly after his release.[4]

Sworn in as king's councillor in November 1430, Suffolk soon established himself as the chief conduit between Henry and his council. Though his personal sphere of influence was in East Anglia, he preferred to spend his time at his wife's home at Ewelme in Oxfordshire. Here, the couple built themselves a house and established a hospital for impoverished soldiers. It was probably at Ewelme, some ten years after their wedding, that their only son John was born.[5]

For a time during his long imprisonment in England, Charles, duke of Orléans was in Suffolk's custody. He is said to have influenced Suffolk to pursue peace with France but there is no direct evidence for this. What does seem to have developed between the two men is a genuine friendship. They shared a love of poetry and it has been suggested that four English poems that found their way into a collection put together by Orléans were written by Suffolk. Orléans was released in 1440 and the two men met several times over the next few years.[6]

Suffolk's value as a diplomat was quickly recognised and he led a major embassy to France in 1444 to negotiate a short truce and a marriage contract. Henry VI was now in his twenties and in need of a wife and queen. Margaret of Anjou was the bride chosen and, the following year, Suffolk led the party sent to Rouen to welcome her and escort her across the Channel.[7]

Suffolk's fall began in 1447 with the arrest of Humphrey, duke of Gloucester on charges of treason. Gloucester died a few days later and rumours soon circulated that he had been poisoned. More modern speculation suggests he died of a stroke brought on by the stress of his arrest and imprisonment. Whatever the cause of Gloucester's death, Suffolk was held responsible in the popular imagination and he soon became isolated from the other lords. The loss of Normandy and the government's poor financial position were blamed on Suffolk. He was accused of working secretly for the French and even of plotting to kill Henry VI and put his own son on the throne.[8]

A marriage had been contracted between young John de la Pole and Margaret Beaufort, the only legitimate child of Somerset's older brother and predecessor, John. Though the Beauforts had been disbarred from the succession by Henry IV, it would not have taken much effort to reinstate them. What would have been difficult was pressing Margaret's claim over that of the current duke, her uncle Edmund. The charge was both highly speculative and ludicrous. Suffolk's vociferous denial was enough to satisfy Henry VI.[9]

Suffolk demanded that formal charges be laid against him so he could respond. The commons duly obliged and he was able to dismiss the more obviously spurious accusations. He waived his right to a trial in return for his case being heard directly by the king. In a room packed with all the available lords, Henry VI exonerated Suffolk but sentenced him to five years' exile, in all probability to get him out of the way of any immediate threat to his life. Suffolk had six weeks to organise his affairs in England before leaving the country on 1 May 1450.[10]

When John de la Pole was 7 years old he received what proved to be his father's last letter, written on the eve of Suffolk's journey into exile.

> [N]ext [to God], above all earthly thing, to be true liege man in heart, in will, in thought, in deed unto the king our most high and dread sovereign lord, to whom both you and I be so much bound to; charging you, as father can and may, rather to die than to be the contrary, or to know any thing that were against the welfare or prosperity of his most royal person, but that as far as your body and life may stretch, you live and die to defend it, and to let his highness have knowledge thereof in all the haste you can.[11]

The letter contains further advice along the same lines – trust in God, serve the king – and is rendered all the more poignant because we know something Suffolk did not. He would never see his son again.

The *Nicholas of the Tower* was a privateer that prowled the Channel looking for easy pickings. Though several attempts were made to locate it, it proved elusive until it disappeared from the record entirely in 1455. In May 1450, the ship intercepted Suffolk's small fleet just off Calais. The crew demanded that Suffolk leave his own ship and be taken aboard the *Nicholas of the Tower* to answer charges. After a mock trial, he was taken onto a smaller boat, held down over the gunwale and his head hacked off with more than a dozen strokes of a rusty sword. His body was tossed onto the beach at Dover, his head set on a pole. His servants, despoiled of all they carried but unharmed, were let ashore with their master's body.[12]

There have been many theories and speculations about conspiracies concerning Suffolk's murder. Some said he was killed on orders of the duke of Somerset; others that he was smuggling treasure out of England, or that the *Nicholas of the Tower* was owned by the duke of Exeter and that the latter gave the order for Suffolk to be hunted down and killed. None of them are sustainable. In 1453, supporters of the duke of York were accused of conspiracy to murder. In the summer of 1451, two men were arrested and indicted with Suffolk's murder and both pleaded not guilty. No record of their trial or sentence remains.[13]

Alice Chaucer was widowed for the third and last time at the age of 46. Suffolk seems to have been deeply fond of his wife and twice commended their son to her care and keeping. In his will, written in 1448, he wrote: 'And last of all, with the blessing of God and of me as heartily as I can give it, my dear and true son, I bequeath between him and his mother love and all good accord and give him to her wholly'.[14]

In his final letter to his son, he wrote:

> Thirdly, in the same wise, I charge you, my dear son, always, as you're bound by the commandment of God to do, to love, to worship your lady and mother, and also that you obey always her commandments and to believe her councils and advice in all your works, the which dread not, but shall be best and truest to you. And if any other body would stir you to the contrary, to flee the counsel in any wise, for you shall find it nought and evil.[15]

Whatever the truth behind the tales of conspiracy, Alice Chaucer lost a husband who valued her most highly and John de la Pole lost a father who undoubtedly loved him.

It may seem strange to some that Alice Chaucer turned to her husband's enemies after his death, but in truth she had little choice. Her connection to the Nevills was still strong and if she and her son were to survive and prosper they needed powerful support. She soon broke her son's betrothal to Margaret Beaufort and contracted a marriage for him with the duke of York's daughter Elizabeth. This would suggest that, though she was perhaps aware of the ill feeling between her late husband and York, she did not share the suspicions of those who held him directly responsible for Suffolk's death.[16]

Justified or not, Suffolk, alongside the equally hated Somerset, was widely hated and held responsible for the loss of Normandy. Many pinned their hopes on one man – the duke of York, at the time in Ireland serving as Governor. In the course of the next few years, his enemies were to use his popularity against him, holding him responsible not only for the death of Suffolk but for the great upheaval that followed – Jack Cade's rebellion.[17]

> And this year came Jake Cade of Kent, and made himself a captain with a great multitude of people unto Blackheath, and there abode seven days continually until that the king with his lords that lay that time at Saint John's in Smithfield and in divers places came riding through London towards Greenwich, and then Jake Cade fled and removed from there towards Tunbridge, Maidstone and Sevenoaks.[18]

England's woes in 1450 were not only political or military. The economy was in a mess and the commons of England were suffering. Population loss meant unproductive farmland and shortages of food. Coin was in short supply and prices fell. The wages of day labourers were cut and part-paid in meals. The wool industry was on the brink of collapse. When population began to decline faster than production it led to a reversal in the situation and gluts of food and wool. As wages were also low and producers were getting far lower prices for their own output than could sustain them, few people had money to spend. Economic woes on the continent meant England's surplus could not be exported. Times were hard. Add to this perceptions of misgovernment and corruption by Henry VI's chief ministers – real and imagined – and the humiliating situation facing the armies in France, and the rumblings of discontent soon turned into calls for action.[19]

> And in the month of June this [year], the commons of Kent assembled in great multitude, and chose themselves a captain, and named him Mortimer, and cousin to the duke of York, but of most he was named Jack Cade. He kept the people wondrously together, and made such ordinances among them, that he brought a great number of people of them to Blackheath, where he devised a bill of petitions to the king and his council, and showed therein what injuries and oppressions the poor commons suffered by such as were about the king, a few persons in number, and all under colour to come to his side. The king's council seeing this bill, disallowed it, and counselled the king, which by the second day of June had gathered to him a strong host of people, to go against his rebels, and to give to them battle.[20]

Leaving Humphrey and William Stafford, lord Say and 'other certain gentlemen' to give chase, Henry VI retired to Greenwich, believing the danger would soon pass. The Staffords gave fight at Sevenoaks and were both killed. Lord Say was arrested and sent to the Tower. When Henry received this news, he went immediately to London. Cade returned to Blackheath with his people and parlayed with the duke of Buckingham and the Archbishop of Canterbury. However, 'they could not cause him to lay down his people, and to submit himself into the king's grace'. Again, Henry left London, taking his queen to Killingworth and leaving the city essentially undefended with lord Scales once again in command of the Tower.[21]

Cade moved his people to Southwark, just south of the river. The mayor called a common council to discuss what should be done and found opinion divided – there were those who said the rebels should be let into the city and others who strongly opposed the idea. Cade sent assurances that there would be no trouble and he and his followers entered the city that afternoon,[22]

> and made in sundry places proclamations in the king's name, that no man, on pain of death, should rob or take anything by force without paying therefor. By reason whereof he won many hearts of the commons of the city; but all was done to beguile the people, as after shall evidently appear.[23]

Lord Say, who had been sent to the Tower after his capture in Sevenoaks, was removed and beheaded, as were two other men, one named Cromer who had spoken up on Say's behalf: 'and so [Cade] entered again the city with the heads of the lord Say and of Cromer; and as they passed through the streets joined the poles together and caused either dead mouth to kiss the other divers and many times.'[24]

An alderman's house was ransacked and robbed. The following day, Cade robbed the property where he had dined 'like an uncourteous guest'. By this time, he had 'lost the people's favour and hearts' and the mayor had had enough. He joined with lord Scales and the city militia to drive the Kentishmen from London, engaging them as they attempted to cross the bridge from Southwark. The battle continued all through the night until eleven the next morning, and many on both sides were killed or drowned.

> … after the Kentishmen were put to the worse, a truce was agreed for certain hours, during the which truce, the archbishop of Canterbury, then chancellor of England, sent a general pardon to the captain himself, and another for his people, by reason whereof he and his company departed the same night out of Southwark, and so returned every man to his home.[25]

Almost immediately, a price of 1,000 marks was put on Cade's head and he was killed in Sussex, possibly while in hiding.

[Cade] was brought to Southwark the ____ of the month of [September] and there left in the king's bench for that night. And upon the morrow the dead corpse was drawn through the high streets of the city to Newgate, and there headed and quartered, whose head was then sent to London bridge, and his four quarters were sent to four sundry towns in Kent.[26]

Henry VI sent commissions of enquiry into Kent and Sussex and several men were tried and executed.[27]

Into this chaotic and dangerous situation came the duke of York, returned from Ireland without the permission or foreknowledge of his king. Several attempts were made to stop him landing in Wales, under direct orders from Henry VI, who feared York had come to take his crown. An ill-considered rising in Sussex in the duke's name, but most likely without his encouragement or even knowledge, did nothing to ease the king's concerns.[28]

The immediate cause of York's hurried return to England was the recall from Normandy of the duke of Somerset. Despite returning in defeat, with a dispirited and depleted army, Somerset quickly resumed his seat in the king's council. The past year had been traumatic for the king, with lawlessness and the rebels' occupation of London and, on a more personal note, the exile and murder of his friend and trusted councillor, Suffolk. That York's name featured in the *Articles of the Commons of Kent*, written up under the guidance of Jack Cade, did not help to ease his fears. First, in relation to rumours of treason plotted by York or, at least, on his behalf,[29]

they say that the commons of England would first destroy the king's friends and afterwards himself and then bring the duke of York to be king, so that by their false means and lies they make him to hate and destroy his friends, and if there were no more reason in the world to know, he may know they be not his friends by their covetousness.[30]

The *Articles* urged the king, after the removal and punishment of 'the false progeny and affinity of the duke of Suffolk', 'to take about his noble person his true blood of his royal realm, that is to say, the high and mighty prince the duke of York, exiled from our sovereign lord's person by the noising of the false traitor the duke of Suffolk and his affinity'. York was not the only lord named. Henry was also urged 'to take about his person the mighty prince the duke of Exeter, the duke of Buckingham and the duke of Norfolk, and his true earls and barons of his land, and he shall be the richest Christian king'.[31]

York had loaned considerable money to the king over several years, some £26,000. He was also owed nearly £39,000 from his tenure as Governor of Normandy. Attempts to repay had been sporadic and unsuccessful.

This failure to pay York's salary followed him to Ireland and he had to mortgage some of his property to stay afloat. He also felt some resentment for what he saw as the more favourable treatment of the dukes of Somerset, John Beaufort and his successor Edmund. This included some advance payments for their soldiers' wages in France, paid at a time when York was being urged to be patient. This resentment was further fuelled by Somerset replacing York as Governor of Normandy and his poor conduct of the war with France. When Somerset surrendered Rouen in 1449, York was angry – this was where he had lived with his duchess, this was where four of his children were born.[32]

As York rode towards London, he had four things on his mind: Somerset's return from France; fears that his name was being linked to insurrection and treason; his personal financial grievances with the crown; and his resolve to be the one to fill the gap left by the murdered Suffolk. He certainly seemed to have been linked with this last in the popular imagination – York was back and soon all would be right with the world.[33]

Along the way, York collected a considerable number of followers and entered London in a show of force. He went straight to Westminster to present his case to the king and was graciously received, his protestations of loyalty accepted without question, on the surface at least.[34]

York presented two bills to the king, putting forward his own case and that against the men who had brought England to its current sorry situation.

> Please it your highness, that since my departure out of this your realm, by your commandment, I have been informed that divers language, has been said of me to your most excellent estate which should sound to my dishonour and reproach, and charge of my person, howbeit I have been and ever will be your true liegeman and servant, and if there be any man that will or dare say the contrary, or challenge me otherwise, I beseech your rightwiseness to call him before your high presence and I will declare me for my discharge as a true knight ought to do.[35]

York was only asking for what Suffolk had received when the commons set out their accusations against him – the chance to hear and answer the charges. Henry attempted to reassure him: 'Cousin, we have seen the bills late taken to us and have understood the good humble obeisance that in yourself you show to us as well in word as in deed.' But he would not give York the satisfaction he sought, even going so far as to gently remind him about his 'sudden coming [to England] without certain warnings'.[36]

York was not about to give up and, in his second bill, offered himself to sit in judgement on 'all such that are indicted or openly so named' of committing treason. This did not much please Henry, either, and he stated in his second response that he would set up a council 'giving them more ample authority and power than ever we did before … in the which we have approved you to be one'. But Henry would not 'take a conclusion or a conduct by advice of one person by himself'.[37]

In October, Henry VI dashed any hopes York had of replacing Suffolk in government and the king's confidence. Henry intended to establish a council and, contrary to his promise, York was not going to be part of it. Both Henry and York were the subject of rumour and innuendo, neither of them truly thinking the best of the other and both quick to believe the worst. York soon left London again, making a progress around his various estates, meeting with the duke of Norfolk to discuss the upcoming parliamentary elections and conducting personal business. Norfolk was a potentially powerful ally of some wealth and resources, including a sizeable number of household knights and several castles. He felt at least as strongly as York about bringing Somerset to justice for his conduct of the war.[38]

There was considerable popular support for York in London, which did nothing to ease Henry VI's mind and he gathered his men around him in anticipation of the upcoming Parliament. When York returned to the city in late November, he had some 3,000 men with him, his sword carried before him like a king and the duke of Norfolk and the earl of Devon following in his trail. York made sure his army was well supplied and self-sustaining, not wanting to add to the worries of the citizens of London.[39]

On 30 November, rioting broke out after demands to bring Somerset and his allies to justice were not met. An attempt on Somerset's life was foiled, Devon smuggling him out of Blackfriars to the safety of the Tower. This would seem to have been on the duke of York's orders – he may have had serious issues with Somerset, but sitting back and allowing him to be lynched by a mob was not the way to deal with them. The mob had to satisfy itself with ransacking Blackfriars.[40]

York rode through the city with a sizeable army behind him, in an attempt to restore peace: 'And he made to be cried in several places that what manner of man that robbed or rifled any person should have as hasty justice as the man had.' York backed this up with action, executing a looter to stand as an example to others. He had essentially declared martial law in the city, on his own initiative. This overstepping of authority did not please Henry VI and, to counter it, on 3 December, the king made his own presence felt in the streets of London, riding through the city 'with the duke of York and the highest in substance all the lords in this land with their retinues of defensible men'. Peace was eventually restored, but all who attended Parliament made sure they were well defended, the earl of Warwick arriving with 'a mighty people arrayed for war'.[41]

Parliament continued peacefully and effectively until the last weeks of January 1451. Despite Cade's death and the collapse of his rebellion, the people of Kent had not remained silent. A man who had spent a year with York in Ireland, Stephen Christmas, stirred up trouble by claiming that the king intended to raise forces in Lancashire and Cheshire to lay Kent to waste. On 28 January, Henry VI rode to Kent with the dukes of Exeter and Somerset, the earl of Shrewsbury, a number of barons and a force of some 3,000 men, to deal with the trouble once and for all: 'and there they held sessions for four days and there were damned many of the captain's [Cade] men for their rising and for their talking against the king, having more favour with the duke of York than unto the king'.[42]

All through this, York sought to be formally recognised as Henry's heir presumptive, with all that went with it. This Henry was reluctant to do, not least because of the prominence it would give York, a prominence many saw as potentially dangerous, given York's popular support and presumed ambitions.[43]

Though York was a strong candidate for heir presumptive, he was not the only one, and it was perhaps this that drove him to press his claim. He may have had concerns that Edmund Beaufort's preferential treatment was a prelude to Henry naming *him* heir, despite the Beauforts' disbarment from the succession.[44]

In September 1451, trouble broke out in Somerset between members of the Bonville family and supporters of the earl of Devon. York intervened and managed to stop the situation getting out of control. In an attempt to establish lasting peace between the feuding families, Henry VI summoned all involved to meet with him. Neither York nor Devon obeyed. This did not please the king and York retreated to his castle at Ludlow. Despite his efforts, his concerns about England, his own personal issues with the king and the matter of the succession, York had achieved nothing but to push himself even further from Henry VI's government.[45]

# 6

# THE EDGE OF REBELLION

There are two versions of the events of the early months of 1452 that saw the duke of York come perilously close to armed rebellion and equally close to charges of treason. In one, understanding the impossible situation he was in, York submitted meekly to Henry VI in the king's tent on Blackheath. In the other, he was tricked into disbanding his army with false promises and delivered himself up for rebuke and humiliation. In both versions, he was taken to London, virtually a prisoner, and required to swear an extraordinary oath in St Paul's.

His attempts two years earlier to bring down his enemies, particularly the duke of Somerset, had failed. He had used the channels available to him, both king and Parliament, and Somerset still stood firmly by Henry VI's side. In York's eyes, no one bore more responsibility for the loss of Normandy than Somerset. For a man who had spent so many years governing the duchy, who lived there with his wife and growing family, it was a bitter blow to see it in French hands once again. York was single-minded in his pursuit of Somerset and, in February and March 1452, this led him to take action that might well have been interpreted as treason.

In January, York sent yet another letter to Henry VI protesting his loyalty. He invited the earl of Shrewsbury and the Bishop of Hereford to come to his castle at Ludlow to witness his oath and report it personally to the king. He would, he said, repeat the oath in front of anyone Henry might name.[1]

> For as much as I, Richard duke of York, am informed that the king my sovereign lord is my heavy lord, greatly displeased with me and has me in mistrust by sinister information of my enemies, adversaries and evil willers.[2]

It is not clear whether this was a disclaimer for what would follow or if events and connections now lost to us changed York's mind and focus. There were concerns about the security of Calais, and Parliament was called specifically to discuss those concerns. Henry VI planned to cross the Channel to visit the town and garrison himself. Somerset was Captain of Calais and York trusted him no more to hold on to this foothold on the edge of France than he had held on to the rest of Normandy. In a letter to the citizens of Shrewsbury asking them to join him in journeying to London, York lamented that Henry had ignored the advice offered him in 1450: 'the which terms of advice, though they were thought full necessary, were laid apart, and to be of no effect, through the envy, malice and untruth of the duke of Somerset; who ... labours continually about the king's highness for my undoing.'[3]

York meant to go to London to sort things out once and for all.

> I, seeing that the said duke ever prevails and rules about the king's person, that by this means the land is likely to be destroyed, am fully determined to proceed in all haste against him ... in such a way that it shall prove to promote ease, peace, tranquility and the safeguard of this land.[4]

York needed men behind him, a show of force that would intimidate but not threaten. When they came to him, he was sure they would 'behave in such a manner ... that they do no offence, robbery or oppression upon the people, in injury of justice'. Men were also gathering at Fotheringhay, Ludlow and other places within York's sphere of influence. Demonstrations were organised by York's supporters in various of his towns as he travelled south. He hoped to score a public relations victory by these 'spontaneous risings' in his name and, perhaps, to intimidate the king himself.[5]

Meanwhile, Henry VI had left London with a sizeable retinue, including the earl of Salisbury, and was moving to intercept York and his force. On 22 February, York was in Northampton. Here, Henry sent the Bishop of Winchester, lord Stourton and York's own brother-in-law Viscount Bourchier to see just what it was York was up to.[6]

There is no question that Henry was worried about York and his intentions – any medieval king would have been. And there is little question that, for every word York spoke against Somerset, Somerset had an equally uncomplimentary word about York. Henry must have recognised the two dukes would never be able to work together and he had made his choice, for good or ill. He would not turn Somerset over to York; he would not call on Somerset to answer the charges laid against him; and he would not set Somerset aside so York could take his place.

The king sent letters to the mayor, aldermen and commons of London, requiring them to 'keep the city and suffer not the duke of York to come therein; wherefor was made great watch in the city, the which was told the duke of York, wherefor he left the London way and went over Kingston bridge'. York then moved to Dartford, hoping the men of Kent who had marched behind Jack Cade would join him. This they failed to do and York was backed into a corner, unable to enter London and, cut off by the royal army, unable to return to his estates. Henry VI had raised his forces so quickly, including many with close family connections to York, that York had no time to strengthen his own army. His brothers-in-law the duke of Buckingham and the earl of Salisbury were with the king, as was Salisbury's son the earl of Warwick. Henry, viscount Bourchier, married to York's sister Isabel, also stood with Henry VI. York had only the earl of Devon and lord Cobham. Even Norfolk had abandoned him. York had no choice but to make a stand and hope it would not end in death and disaster.[7]

York's articles against Somerset laid out his case that Somerset was not only responsible for the loss of Normandy but was plotting to hand Calais to the duke of Burgundy. Burgundy's son was to be married to one of Somerset's daughters in return for the English outpost. If this was not enough to convince, York held Somerset responsible for England's domestic woes as well. Soldiers returning from France were not only displaced but unpaid and this had led directly to lawlessness in England. York branded Somerset corrupt. On taking over as governor, he said, Somerset had removed from their positions 'all the true and faithful officers', restoring them only on receipt of 'great gifts and rewards'. York further accused him of imprisoning other officials without cause 'and by that means did great extortions and raised unlawfully great sums under colour of amends and compositions'. Somerset gave up Rouen, York claimed, on condition he be allowed to leave with his family and property unharmed. York finished with the claim that he made the charges against Somerset with only the good of his king and country in mind. He hoped that 'judgement … be had and executed' in the matter.[8]

York left out much of the context to Somerset's actions in France and the accusations of plotting to turn Calais over to Burgundy were a triumph of imagination over substance. The articles, like the show of force on Blackheath, were ill-conceived and did York's position immeasurably more harm than good.[9]

All the chroniclers agree on what happened next – the king sent York's kinsmen, the earls of Salisbury and Warwick, the Bishop of Ely Thomas Bourchier and the Bishop of Winchester to talk with York 'till a peace was made between them; the [duke] was sworn'.[10]

And at the last the duke of York came with eleven horsemen to the king about noon, and obeyed him to his liegance; and with [him] the earl of Devon and the lord Cobham, the which held with the duke of York and were in host with him. And the king took them to grace and all.[11]

All chroniclers have York backing down entirely, with no negotiation and no conditions. His brothers-in-law and nephew had nothing to offer him except pardon and his life. York knelt before the king in his tent and received his grace. His great gamble was over and he had nothing to show for it.

There is another version of events, however, which shows not only Henry VI but Salisbury, Warwick, Bourchier and the Bishop of Winchester in a very poor light. This version has promises made to York that Somerset would be arrested and presents this as the condition on which he was willing to submit to the king.

> And there [at Blackheath] the lords both spiritual and temporal took the matter in hand and entreated them of rest and peace, the which the said duke at the last agreed to on this condition, that his petitions for the well-being of the king and the realm might be had and his enemies to the Tower to await the law … Soon the duke sent home his men again and himself meekly obeyed the king at Blackheath, and his adversaries stood present contrary the agreement.[12]

> … and there was agreed that the duke of Somerset should be had unto ward to answer such articles as the duke of York should lay unto his charge. Upon which promise the duke of York broke up his field. And when he came to the king's tent, the duke of Somerset was still awaiting upon the king and chief about him …[13]

Both versions have the duke returning to London between two bishops, as though a prisoner, and swearing an oath at St Paul's before being allowed to freely go on his way.

While the second version of the story puts York in a positive light – on the brink of achieving his aims, he had them snatched away by the duplicity of the king and his lords – its truth is questionable. First, while there was no great connection yet forged between York and his Nevill in-laws, they had no more positive feelings towards Somerset than he did, particularly Warwick. It is difficult to imagine them colluding with Somerset to this extent. Second, it seems greatly out of character for Henry VI to come up with, or even support, such a blatant lie. Lastly, the intermediaries were hardly likely to be given the power to negotiate such terms on their own. If York demanded Somerset's arrest as a condition for his supplication, it was never going to be granted.

At St Paul's, York swore on the Bible, the Cross and the Sacraments: 'When so ever I shall feel myself wronged or aggrieved I shall sue myself humbly for remedy to your highness and after the course of your laws…' It was a devastating back down, the oath itself designed to be humiliating and remind York of his place, which was not to be at the king's side.[14]

As a sop to York, Henry VI set up a panel of nobles, heavily weighted in favour of Somerset, to give judgement on York's claims. This judgement was never reached. Several of York's supporters, including his chamberlain, William Oldhall, were accused of meeting at York's principal London residence, Baynard's Castle, to plot rebellion in the Welsh Marches and in Kent. They were even accused of plotting the king's death and intending to set York in his place. As Oldhall was in St Martin's sanctuary at the time, these charges are untenable. This did not stop Oldhall being outlawed in April 1453 and his property confiscated.[15]

Although a general pardon was offered to those who had stood with York at Blackheath, it was not automatically applied. Each man had to sue for his pardon and then present it to a court of law should he be indicted on any relevant charge. Nearly 400 pardons were issued after Blackheath, by no means the total number of York's men. York himself was confined to his estates and it was at Fotheringhay that his youngest surviving child, Richard, was born in October 1452.[16]

Sporadic unrest continued for some time but Henry's show of force and unity at Blackheath went a long way towards stabilising the situation. Margaret of Anjou's pregnancy, confirmed by Easter 1453, helped settle things. The question of the succession was to be answered at last.[17]

Somerset resumed his role as Henry's chief councillor. In August 1453, he was forced into a difficult decision. The king showed signs of a mysterious mental illness. This was, at first, concealed by Somerset who attempted to carry on the business of government alone. When Prince Edward was born on 13 October, Somerset had to take action and called a great council to discuss the king's illness and what was to be done. He initially planned to exclude the duke of York but others realised he was needed and sent for him. York's summons was worded in such a way as to give him hope that his charges against Somerset were to be revived and properly addressed at last.[18]

# 7

# THE NEVILLS OF MIDDLEHAM AND THE PERCIES OF ALNWICK

In November 1448, fire raged through the outskirts of Carlisle. An army of Scots had blazed their way through Cumberland and now threatened the most important city in the west march. The people of Carlisle lived on the frontline of a perpetually brewing war with Scotland. Despite treaties and truces, and the benefits of living close to a border, the threat of strife was never far away. Now it had erupted in earnest and the city itself was in danger of being burned to the ground. The wardens of the marches had failed in their duties to protect the border.[1]

Raiding parties of Scots had been encroaching on English territory all summer. In October, lord Poynings, Northumberland's oldest son, led an army north of the border and engaged the Scots on the River Sark. His defeat was comprehensive: many lives were lost and Poynings himself captured. Salisbury's attempt at retribution a month later also ended in disaster. Neither guardian of Henry VI's northernmost lands had covered himself in glory.[2]

The Percies were still struggling to re-establish themselves after the restoration of Northumberland to their lands and titles. The Nevills, on the other hand, had slid comfortably into the gap left by Hotspur's fall. The marriage between Northumberland and Salisbury's sister Eleanor should have cemented the relationship between the two families, but subsequent events were to prove how fragile that connection was.

A dispute over precedence between the two earls had been conducted largely on paper over several years and was resolved in Salisbury's favour in 1443. In the complex world of fifteenth-century nobility, precedence was a serious matter, resting on when a title was created and bestowed and establishing an unbroken line of descent. Northumberland's case rested on the 1400 attainder of John Montagu. Salisbury's response referred to the 1405 attainder of Northumberland's grandfather, thus asserting his title's precedence. When John Montagu's son Thomas was restored to the title, it was as his father's son; the attainder was reversed by act of Parliament. On the other hand, Northumberland's title, despite him being the grandson of the previous holder, was deemed a new creation. This made Richard Nevill the fifth earl of Salisbury, whereas Henry Percy was only the first earl of Northumberland.[3]

A series of documents passed between Northumberland, Salisbury and the king's council in London. Only one of these survives. In his *Answers of Richard Earl of Salisbury to the Replications of Henry Pretending to be Earl of Northumberland*, Salisbury sets out his responses to an earlier document in such a way that we can glean the gist of what that document contained. For his part, Northumberland had responded to an even earlier document, presumably written by Salisbury.[4]

Each earl was trying to prove two things: first, that he had every right to hold his title; and, second, that the other did not. Both made reference to the attainders in previous generations, both attempted to minimise the effect of those attainders on themselves while maximising the effect on the other. Salisbury claimed Northumberland had not followed correct procedure when he entered into some of his restored properties. Northumberland claimed Salisbury could not possibly be an earl because Thomas Montagu's heir was a woman. To this, Salisbury responded with unassailable logic:

> And where the said Henry in the same replication says that the honour, name and dignity of an earl may not descend to a woman because a woman may not bear the name of earl etc, and so may not the said Richard be earl in the right and title of Alice his wife, thereto says the same Richard earl of Salisbury that all manner of things and inheritance that her father, whose heir she is, had … come to the said Alice as daughter and heir unto him, and though she may not bear the name of earl yet she must have as her inheritance of fee in the name of countess of Salisbury and that name bear.[5]

Salisbury went on to say that at the time of his death in 1428, Thomas Montagu had a male heir – his grandson Richard. Whoever held the title in the meantime, one day, after the death of his mother, young Richard Nevill would be earl of Salisbury, the line of blood and descent unbroken. Whatever had triggered this dispute, it was resolved in Salisbury's favour.[6]

This issue of precedence was not the only problem for the Percies in the 1440s. Northumberland was also involved in a dispute with John

Kemp, then Archbishop of York. Twice this dispute descended into violence with some loss of life. Northumberland was ordered to London
and imprisoned for a time in the Tower, the blame for the violence laid
squarely at his feet.[7]

Perhaps Northumberland had inherited something of his father Hotspur's
intemperate nature. He certainly seems to have passed it on to his younger
sons, Thomas lord Egremont, Richard and Ralph. All three were to play
major roles in the escalation of the feud in the 1450s.

All of the Percy brothers but one were older than their Nevill cousins.
The oldest, Henry, lord Poynings, was born in 1421 and the youngest,
William, Bishop of Carlisle, in 1428. Northumberland's second son Thomas
was created lord Egremont in 1449. Though he never married, he had two
acknowledged children: John, who carried on the tradition of Percy rebellion in the 1490s, and Mary.[8]

By 1448, all ten of the Salisburys' children had been born, and four were
married. There has been some speculation there was at least one set of twins
in the family and, given the number born in the short period between 1428
and 1434, there may well have been two. While it is entirely possible for
the countess to have given birth to six children in six years, circumstantial
evidence that Richard and Cecily might have been born on the same day,
and difficulty in finding Alice's place in the order of birth, could indicate a
pattern of multiple births.

Generally, in the fifteenth century, children got their names from one of
three sources. They were named after their parents, their godparents or the
saint on whose day they were born. The Salisburys' second oldest daughter
Cecily may have been named after her aunt, the duchess of York, who may
have been her principal godmother. Given that her brother Richard was
born on 22 November, St Cecelia's Day, and given their joint wedding in
1436, they may have been twins.[9]

The birthdates of children were often not recorded, particularly if there
was little likelihood that proof of age would be required in the future. Proof
of age was frequently established by linking the child's birth to specific
family events of known date, such as weddings or recorded deaths, or
national events, such as coronations or battles.

Alice, who married Henry, lord Fitzhugh, gave birth to their first child in
1448. If Alice was then 17 or 18, this puts her birth around 1429 or 1430,
the presumed birth years of her brothers Thomas and John. Unless one of
them was Alice's twin, the only available spot for her in the birth order is
between George and Alianor, or sometime after 1433. This would make her
no more than 15 at the time of her oldest daughter's birth, which would be
an anomaly worth exploring further. None of this is clear evidence of twins
in the family but it is an interesting possibility.

Whether or not they were twins, in 1436, when Richard was 6, he and Cecily were married to Anne and Henry Beauchamp, children of Richard Beauchamp, earl of Warwick and his second wife Isabel Despenser. Anne was around 9 at the time and her brother 11.

Richard Beauchamp's first marriage to Elizabeth Berkeley had produced three daughters. Margaret married John Talbot, earl of Shrewsbury, Eleanor's second husband was Edmund Beaufort, duke of Somerset and Elizabeth married Salisbury's brother George, lord Latimer. Beauchamp's second wife, Isabel Despenser, was a wealthy widow in her own right. Salisbury had achieved quite a coup in marrying his daughter to the heir to the earldom of Warwick. Henry stood to inherit a substantial fortune from his parents, extensive properties across England, as well as the Warwick earldom. Apart from a connection to Henry Beauchamp and a most suitable bride, Richard Nevill was not expected to gain a great deal.

The Salisburys' youngest son George was a man of the cloth. From around 1448, he studied at Balliol College Oxford, attaining his BA in 1450 and his MA two years later. He was granted both degrees without fulfilling all the requirements, which is often interpreted as a result of aristocratic privilege. While there was probably an element of this, George was not simply fast-tracked through the system to qualifications he neither earned nor deserved. Most of the crucial requirements were met. George was relieved of some of his teaching duties at least in part because he sponsored a number of students, whose fees he paid. Providing the university with students, who would later be masters, more than made up for any lack of teaching on George's part.[10]

George Nevill had a suite of rooms at Balliol where he lived much of the time. Compared with the halls of residence, where ordinary students had to squeeze in together, these rooms were luxurious and spacious. George also sponsored building works at Balliol, which was undergoing something of an expansion in the 1450s.[11]

> The west side, which contains part of the lodgings belonging to the Malter, Buttery and Refectory, was built with monies of William Grey, bishop of Ely, George Nevill, archbishop of York, and others, as their arms in the stone walls and the windows of the said building show.[12]

George later applied for his doctorate of theology, and again received it faster than usual and without fulfilling all the requirements. Though his supplication was accepted, there is no record he was ever formally granted the qualification.[13]

MA graduates of wealth and standing were expected to host a feast for a large percentage of the university population. In October 1452, George was given permission to exceed the usual limit on expenditure and provided a two-day feast for around 900 people. Six hundred were feasted on the first day and 300 on the second, including the scholars and members of George's family. This was no mean feast – pheasant, swan, crane, peacock, quail, custard and baked quinces, among much else, featured on the menu.[14]

George's generosity was not restricted to those who were invited to the feast days. There were 'provisions made for the poor and other ordinary sort of people of the University, which were of considerable value'. George Nevill was undoubtedly one of life's great feasters though his generosity and largesse would suggest he was no mere glutton. He liked to celebrate his achievements with those around him, and he liked to celebrate them with food.

On 9 June 1453, George was officially sworn in as Chancellor of Oxford University. His appointment was part of a change in policy from electing scholars to men of influence and wealth. In 1451, William Percy, Bishop of Carlisle was elected Chancellor of Cambridge and George himself replaced the Bishop of Winchester, William Waynflete. George was no absentee chancellor who got others to do the work, though he did appoint deputies from time to time. Far from the usual image of the privileged son of an earl filling an essentially empty and honorary position, George took his role seriously. He was involved in the administration of the university, sat on select committees and oversaw disciplinary and other judicial hearings. He used his family's influence on at least one occasion, while his father was briefly chancellor of England. He drew attention to the presence of French scholars at the university at a time when there were no reciprocal arrangements for English scholars in France. When he resigned after his customary two-year term, he was immediately re-elected. He held the position and remained living in Oxford until he was appointed Bishop of Exeter in 1457.[15]

As yet unmarried were Salisbury's second and third sons, Thomas and John, and his three youngest daughters, Alianor, Katherine and Margaret. In 1453, a wife was found for Thomas who promised to bring him great wealth in the future and, possibly, a title. Twenty-eight-year-old Maud Stanhope was the niece of Ralph, lord Cromwell and, along with her sister Jane, co-heir to a not inconsiderable fortune. Recent widowhood had put her in need of protection, and the hastily arranged marriage was to provide that. Her husband Thomas was some five years younger than her, but the promise of future wealth, and the possibility of one day bearing the Cromwell title in his wife's right, were fine incentives.[16]

Maud, who had once worked in the household of the disgraced duchess of Gloucester, was considered something of a beauty, with a fiery temper and a quick wit. Married in her early twenties to her uncle's associate

Robert, lord Willoughby, her recent widowhood should have given her the financial security to choose to remarry, or not, in her own time. But events forced her to seek shelter and the protection of her uncle in Tattershall Castle. Turned out of her dower property by her stepdaughter Joan Welles, Maud was in need of a champion. In May 1453, just a little less than a year after lord Willoughby's death, the marriage was contracted with Thomas Nevill. Three months later, the couple were married at Tattershall and almost immediately went north to Middleham. Lady Willoughby was no innocent, overprotected maiden, but her introduction to Yorkshire, and her new family, could not have been more dramatic. Just outside York, the wedding party was attacked by Northumberland's younger sons and a band of hundreds of their followers.[17]

That the Nevills and Percies were first cousins did nothing to quell the enthusiasm and violence with which they picked up their fathers' differences. A particular dislike sprang up between Thomas Percy and Thomas Nevill, though its precise origins are a mystery. In the 1440s, both young men were sent to the marches by their fathers, wardens of the east and west march respectively, and it was there that their mutual dislike seems to have been forged. Shortly after Salisbury appointed his son steward of the manor of Bolton-in-Allerdale, Egremont led a raid on the property, inflicting over £23 in damage. 'Quarrelsome, violent and contemptuous of all authority, [Thomas Percy] possessed all the worst characteristics of a Percy for which his grandfather Hotspur is still a byword.'[18]

History has not been kind to Egremont though, from the little we know, this may not be entirely unjust. He certainly did his bit against the Scots, safeguarding his family estates in Cumberland and leading his men into battle. He was, however, also responsible for more than his fair share of lawlessness and violence. Anyone who held a grudge against the Nevills was welcomed into Egremont's circle. With the city of York in economic decline following the collapse of the wool trade and stiff competition from other English cloth-making centres, Egremont had found a fertile recruiting ground.[19]

In June 1453, he was summoned by the king for service in France. Egremont disobeyed the summons, which turned out to be a less serious breach than it might have been. With the fall of Castillon, England's hold on Gascony was forever ended and the planned expedition did not set sail.[20]

Thomas Nevill's involvement in the feud had lessened by this time, his place being taken, with great enthusiasm, by his younger brother John. By July 1453, Henry VI had had enough and planned to go north to deal with the situation himself. Unfortunately, his sudden illness prevented him. With the king incapacitated, Henry's councillors did their best, sending a stream of letters to both Egremont and John Nevill, as well as their fathers. These letters demanded a cessation of their activities and, in the case of

Egremont, his attendance before council to answer questions. The letters grew more and more exasperated, and more overtly threatening, as time went on. All of them were ignored. A letter to John Nevill dated 26 July stated: 'it is come to our knowledge how by occasion of certain discords and debates between you and the lord Egremont divers things and novelries contrary to our peace have of late days been committed betwixt you to great trouble and vexation of our country and subjects.'[21]

And to Salisbury, with a copy to Northumberland, on 27 July the council wrote:

> We therefor write to you at this time exhorting and in the straitest wise also charging that you by all the ways and means possible to you do your effectual labour and diligence that the said assemblies and gatherings of people be put down and utterly ceased.[22]

Another letter to both Egremont and John written about the same time commands them – again – to cease their 'riotous assemblies and gatherings of people'. Similar letters were sent to high-profile supporters on both sides, with an added threat: 'upon pain of forfeiture of all your lands and goods'. On 8 August, letters were sent to the earl of Westmorland and the Bishop of Durham praising them for their neutrality and asking for their continued help in dealing with the situation. This was something of an error of judgement. Westmorland's neutrality can be put down to having no wish to support his uncle Salisbury's family any more than he wished to support the Percies. As for the Bishop of Durham, he would do what his brothers required of him, whatever the king's council might say about it. On the same date, the newly appointed Archbishop of York, William Bothe, was written to, urging him to help keep the peace and not 'depart from that country until the time the said trouble and unlawful assemblies be fully appeased'.[23]

Two further letters are worth noting for their change in tone. No longer simply commanding obedience and an end to the violence, they contain overt threats to the recipients. The first is a long letter to Salisbury and Northumberland, reminding them of their privileged position and the responsibility this carried 'to the worship of God and to the advice and supportation of us in keeping of our laws'. They should 'in no wise take upon you the rule thereof at your own hand'. They were reminded that 'in our parliament … you and other lords were warned that if any of you felt him aggrieved against another should put his grievance in writing'. And, in tones of stern desperation, they were warned that if anyone should die as a result of the unlawfulness the earls had failed to prevent, they would be held responsible: 'we shall in no wise spare you in this case but rather more grievously punish you than we would do the least person of our land the which nevertheless as our lord knows we would be right loath to do.'[24]

On 8 October one last letter was sent to John Nevill and Egremont. The latter was told that he had been raised 'to the worship and estate of Baron' not in recognition of past service to the crown but in hopes of future service. His title was not yet earned and could easily be taken from him.

> [Y]ou have not in any wise obeyed nor accomplished our said commandment but as it appears in contempt thereof have multiplied and daily do gatherings of people of our subjects ready to go to the field ... you in restful and peaceable wise depart such people as you have assembled and cease such novelries as you have begun ... upon pain and forfeiture of all that you may forfeit unto us.[25]

John Nevill, more anxious his cousin be hauled before the king than he was to answer his own summons, made a plan to ambush Egremont as he travelled to the Percy estate of Topcliffe. John attempted to rouse the tenants of Topcliffe against their lord's son, going so far as to threaten to hang them if they refused. Either Egremont escaped or stayed a safe distance away; on that occasion, there was no satisfaction for John Nevill and he returned home without his cousin.[26]

In July, a commission was established to investigate the general lawlessness in Yorkshire and, more specifically, the trouble between the Nevills and the Percies. Though some of the commissioners, such as Viscount Beaumont, could be seen to be impartial, others very much were not. Ralph Nevill (not the earl of Westmorland) was a retainer of Salisbury's, as was John, lord Scrope of Bolton. Henry Fitzhugh was Salisbury's son-in-law and several others either were or would soon be working for him. There was no equivalent presence of Percy partisans, leading to accusations that the commission was deliberately stacked in favour of the Nevills. A second commission, less Nevill-friendly, was set up, headed by Sir William Lucy, who took some action, ordering several prominent members of both factions to cease and desist. It did little good.[27]

On 23 August, on Heworth Moor, just south of York, the feud descended into something close to open warfare. The Percies gathered their men and lay in wait for the Nevill wedding party to pass. It is not entirely clear what happened next. Despite the rather dramatic words of the annalist at Whitby Abbey – 'there arose ... a great disturbance betwixt him [Northumberland] and Richard, the earl of Salisbury his wife's brother, insomuch as many men of both parties were beaten, slain and hurt' – later hearings in York did not mention deaths or even much in the way of injury. The Nevills were able to continue their journey to the safety of Salisbury's castle at Sheriff Hutton.

On his arrival, Salisbury immediately wrote to his oldest son, Richard, earl of Warwick. Warwick intercepted the letter on his way from Wales to Warwick Castle, sent his countess on without him and turned his feet north, for the first time in more than five years.[28]

Whatever concerns Salisbury might have had for his and his sons' safety, and that of the 500 men who rode behind them, were likely eclipsed by the very real danger faced by his wife, daughters and new daughter-in-law. While they had not been exposed to any real danger in the past, the Nevill women would have been well aware of the depth of feeling between their menfolk and the Percies. Maud, whose own family was not immune from such troubles, was thrust headlong into someone else's feud. Just a few days married, and fewer in Yorkshire, her life was in real danger, and would be until they reached the walls of Middleham.[29]

Warwick was not the only person of power and importance to be summoned to Middleham. The Archbishop of York William Bothe, Salisbury's brother the Bishop of Durham and the mayor of York all arrived at the castle in quick succession. Something had to be done about the Percy threat, and it had to be done quickly.[30]

The attack at Heworth caused alarm in York and further futile attempts were made to mediate between the parties. After the failed assault, Richard Percy set off on a 'tour of pillage'. At Gargrave church on 9 September, he and his followers attacked one Lawrence Caterall, bailiff of Staincliff, dragging him from his hiding place in the vestibule. The vicar was saying mass and begged them to leave after they jumped onto the altar. Once they had what they came for, they took Caterall to Cockermouth, where he was imprisoned until his term as bailiff had expired. The story behind his abduction and imprisonment remains intriguingly obscure. Another vicar, William Hebdon, had his house raided on 23 September.[31]

The concerns of Thomas and John Nevill might have been confined to Yorkshire, but both Salisbury and Warwick had bigger matters to contend with. News of Henry VI's strange illness was trickling out of Westminster. His queen Margaret of Anjou was soon to give birth to their first, and only, child. In Parliament, the commons demanded something be done – they urged the lords to establish a council to govern England in the absence of her king. Henry's chief councillor, Somerset, did not have sufficient support to lead such a council, certainly not the support of the Nevills. Salisbury's brother-in-law York looked to be the most likely candidate. If he was to prevail, then the elder Nevills needed to be in London. Leaving Yorkshire in such a time of trouble, with two hot-headed sons unlikely to sit at home peacefully awaiting their father's return, was not an option. Salisbury had to act. The situation grew even more urgent when on 24 September John, sent to Sheriff Hutton on his father's business, rode the 26 miles to the Percy manor of Catton and exacted his own revenge for the attack at Heworth. Threats were made, windows broken and tiles dislodged from the roof.[32]

On 20 October 1453, Thomas Nevill left his new bride at Middleham Castle and set out with his father and brothers, and the Archbishop of York to help conduct negotiations, to Sandhutton village, close by the Percy manor of Topcliffe. They demanded that Northumberland turn his troublesome sons over to their uncle's custody, to be delivered to London and the council. Wherever Egremont and his brothers Richard and Ralph were, it was not at Topcliffe, and the earl of Northumberland was unlikely to have meekly handed them over if they were. A tenuous peace was brokered, and the Nevills returned home in good order. Salisbury and Warwick immediately left for London.[33]

Unlawfully removed from her dower property at Eresby in Lincolnshire, a begrudged guest at her uncle Cromwell's house at Tattershall and survivor of the fall of the duchess of Gloucester, Maud Stanhope now found herself married to a man whose family was enmired in a feud.

In Thomas Nevill, Maud's uncle had found a young man of proven mettle from a family of wealth, status and power, a family he could turn to for help with the conflicts that beset his own life. Maud was the currency in this transaction – the promise of future wealth for Thomas Nevill in exchange for his support and the support of his family while Cromwell lived. That she agreed to the match so soon after the death of her first husband suggests she understood the benefits to herself. If Thomas had half his brother Richard's determination and energy, Maud's dower property would soon be back in her hands.

# 8

# The Beauchamp
# Earls of Warwick

On the eve of Henry IV's coronation on 13 October 1399, 17-year-old Richard Beauchamp went to his bedchamber to await the start of a long and solemn ceremony. He was put to bed by his squires and covered with rich bedclothes provided by the king. Across London, more than forty other young men, including three of the new king's sons, were doing the same.[1]

> And upon that, the king shall command his chamberlain to go to the esquire's chamber that is to be made knight and to take with him the most worthy and wittiest knights that be then present to the intent that they shall the same esquire truly counsel, inform and teach wisely of the order of knighthood.[2]

Outside his door, minstrels sang and young squires danced. Hot water was brought and a bath was filled, a barber sharpened his tools. Beauchamp was taken from his bed to be shaved and his hair cut, the minstrels silent now, the dancing squires still. He was undressed and lifted into the bath. The door opened and the king's chamberlain entered and spoke to the knights, asking who would be the first to speak to the young man. One by one, the knights knelt down by the bath and spoke soft words of wisdom and advice, telling Beauchamp what was expected of him, his obligations to his brother knights and their obligations to him. Each of them scooped water in their cupped hands and let it fall over his shoulders. When the last word was spoken, he was taken from the bath and laid in his bed to dry.[3]

He was then dressed in warm clothes, wrapped in 'a cape of russet black with long sleeves, the hood sewn into the cape in the manner of a hermit', another gift from the king. He was taken to the chapel, minstrels leading the way, squires dancing and singing again. At the doors of the chapel, his escort was thanked, gifts were bestowed and he was handed a cup of spiced wine. Then he was led inside, and the doors shut.[4]

> In this wise, shall the esquire all night till it be day abide ever in his prayers … And when the dawning comes, he shall have a priest and be confessed, if it will please him, of his sins and trespass, which thing done, he shall have matins and mass and take communion, if he will.[5]

Beauchamp's prayers were private. Perhaps he prayed for guidance in his life to come; perhaps he gave thanks for the restoration of his scattered family; or prayed his young wife would bear healthy children. Perhaps he prayed he would bring no shame and only honour to the new brotherhood he was about to enter. The Order of the Bath was but the first step on a young knight's journey to honour and worship. Many went no further.

Whatever was on the young man's mind and in his heart, surely he prayed for a long and peaceful reign for the king who was soon to be crowned. Like others in England, like the great lords of the north, Westmorland and Northumberland, so many of Beauchamp's hopes were pinned on the young man who had landed at Ravenspur just months earlier with a handful of men. Beauchamp had sent Bolingbroke secret messages of support and welcomed him to Warwick Castle while the man who had usurped the Beauchamp properties and title was in Ireland with the king.[6]

A taper passed between Beauchamp and one of the knights, back and forth during the mass, in Beauchamp's hands when the priest said this and in the knight's when he said that. Beauchamp's hood was removed and when the priest fell silent he offered the taper and a penny to the lord. His long vigil over, his knees stiff and sore, he was led back to his chamber and put to bed to rest. While he slept, a coverlet of cloth of gold was laid over him – the king's third gift. A message from the king roused the young man from sleep. He was dressed in a red gown and black silk hose, a white leather girdle, armour his mother had spent a good deal of time and money purchasing or having mended and made ready. A red mantle trimmed with white silk was laid across his shoulders, white gloves put on his hands. Outside, a horse waited to take him to Westminster Hall, two young squires carrying his sword and spurs. All along the journey minstrels led the way 'making their minstrelling'. The wise knights who had been with him all night escorted him into the hall, by his side the squires with the sword and spurs.[7]

Inside the hall, young men were seated at the second table. Closer to the dais was a table crowded with senior members of their order, waiting to welcome their new comrades. Prince Henry, aged just 13, and his two younger brothers were the first to be presented to the king, then came the sons of England's dukes. Richard Beauchamp was the first of the earls' sons. He stood before his king in his new red mantle and lifted his feet as first the right then the left spur was buckled to his heels. The king, 'of the meekness of his high might', buckled Beauchamp's sword about his waist, clasped him in his arms and struck the side of his neck. 'Be you a good knight,' he said.[8]

It took a long time, for there were more than forty esquires to be spurred and belted, but the king showed no sign of impatience or fatigue. Tomorrow, he would be crowned and this ceremony was his gift to England, his pledge to her future. Richard Beauchamp's loyalty to Henry IV and his successors would never be questioned – he would live and die in their service.

Though this was the focal point of the ceremony, the day was not yet over. There were more prayers to pray and masses to be heard. Room was found for each of the new knights among their colleagues and a feast was served. The young knights did not eat, nor did they speak. Their bellies must have rumbled for they had spent the night in fast and prayer with only sips of wine to sustain them. They would eat back in their chambers, where one final gift from the king awaited them.

> [A] robe of blue with straight sleeves and … upon the left shoulder a white lace of silk hanging, and that he shall keep in this wise above his clothing forth from that day henceforth until the time he get some manner of worship by deserving by witness of worthy knights and squires of arms and heralds duly afterward reported.[9]

Richard Beauchamp had taken the first step in a lifelong journey. His investiture as a Knight of the Bath was no trivial matter and he was to take his obligations seriously throughout his life. For him, knighthood was no empty honour. He did what he could to help his brother knights, raising ransoms for those captured in battle and paying for masses and prayers for those who died.[10]

Generations of Beauchamp earls stood behind him and, almost to the Conquest itself, the title had been passed in an unbroken line from father to son and from brother to sister.

The first post-Conquest earl of Warwick was Henry de Beaumont, granted the title by William II in 1088. There were 'eorls' in Warwick before then and, in the brief reign of Richard III and his queen Anne Nevill, John Rous wove for them a fantastical genealogy. Mixed with more verifiable information from records and chronicles, it began with King Guthelyne, who ruled the entire island of Britain and divided it between his sons – the eldest, Locryne, getting 'the chief part from the Trent to the south sea'. The great city of this realm was Warwick.[11]

Rous told the story of the origins of the Warwick badge of ragged staff and bear:

lord [Gwayr] or one of his successors of the Britons on a time met with a giant that ran on him with a tree shred and the bark off, but that lord had grace with him and was a fearsome man and overcame the giant and in token thereof then forward bore on his arms a ragged staff of silver on a field of sable, and so his heirs bear continually after him.[12]

As for the bear, Rous claims it stems from a later lord of Warwick, Arthal, 'The first syllable of [whose] name, that is to say Arth or Narth, is as much to say in Welsh as a bear.'[13]

Mixing in a good helping of Virgil, Rous traces the descent of the Briton and Saxon eorls of Warwick to Aeneas, 'a king's son and a queen's' whose siblings 'by enchantment were foreshaped into swans with collars and chains of gold and of the chains a cup with them'. Rous claimed the silver cup was kept in the treasury of Warwick Castle and not only had he seen it, he had drunk from it.[14]

One of the most celebrated pre-Norman eorls was Guy, who fell in love with his master's daughter, Felice the Fair, who 'by true inheritance was countess of Warwick'. She was wooed by Sir Guy and 'caused him for her sake to put himself in many dangers and perils'. Guy is a model of medieval love, courtship and marriage. He represents an ideal – the young man in servitude to his beloved, who must do her bidding to win her heart and hand. She, like all women of her class and time, has ultimate authority over her suitor. Only when he has proven himself and she consents to be married does her power give way to his. Guy fulfils all the requirements of a husband and a knight. Once his lady's heart has been won and she places herself under his authority, once his son is born, thus securing both his bloodline and hers, then his mind can turn to more spiritual concerns. '[C]onsidering what he had done for a woman's sake, [he] thought to beset the other part of his life for God's sake', and dressed himself in the robes of a pilgrim. He fought many great battles and, towards the end of his life, came home to his wife and 'by her leave had his abiding at Gibcliff' [Guy's Cliff]. An angel foretold his death and his wife's, just a fortnight later, and they were buried together at Guy's Cliff, where miracles were later said to take place.[15]

Guy's son, Raynbroun, was kidnapped from his home as a child and 'sold to a heathen king where he proved to be a noble knight'. After many adventures, he was rescued and returned home, where he was 'full cheerfully received by king Athelstan and received his lands with the king's daughter to his wife'.[16]

With the Norman Conquest, Rous's history of the earls of Warwick becomes more grounded in historical reality. In the early months of 1088, among the most trusted men of the newly crowned William II were his uncle, Bishop Odo, and Henry de Beaumont. By Easter, Odo was in open rebellion, awaiting the arrival in England of William's older brother, Robert Curthose, duke of Normandy. There had long been tensions between Robert and his late father, William I. It was the Conqueror's intention to divide his realms of England and Normandy between his oldest sons, Robert and William, but Robert was impatient to take possession and control of his inheritance.[17]

When William I died in 1087, he was succeeded by his second son, William Rufus, and Robert was confirmed as duke of Normandy. Almost immediately, Robert set in motion plans to take England from his younger brother. Despite many defections to Robert's cause, Henry de Beaumont stayed loyal to his king and was principal accuser at the rebellious Bishop Odo's eventual trial.[18]

Around July 1088, Henry de Beaumont was granted the earldom of Warwick as a reward for his loyalty and service. By that time, faced with the failure and capture of his agents in England, Robert abandoned his plans to invade, for the time being.[19]

Beaumont was likely with William Rufus when the king died, hunting in the New Forest. He was certainly one of the lords who chose his successor, Henry I, who had been his ward, and supported him during his later troubles, when Curthose revived his plans.[20]

Earls and countesses of Warwick followed Beaumont in an unbroken line, though with marriage the family name changed, first to Maudit then to Beauchamp. For the most part, they were loyal to the crown, though one was involved in the execution of Edward II's favourite and refused to fight at Bannockburn. In 1348, another became a founding member of the Order of the Garter and his son Thomas, 12th earl, carried the third sword at Richard II's coronation.[21]

Thomas Beauchamp was with King Richard II in the Tower during the Peasants' Revolt but soon turned against him, joining the Lords Appellant and fighting against Robert de Vere at the battle of Radcot Bridge in 1387. Along with his fellow Lords Appellant, Thomas Beauchamp held the reins of government for the best part of two years before Richard II resumed his authority and power. In May 1397, Beauchamp was arrested on charges of treason connected with the Gloucester/Arundel rebellion. He pleaded guilty and was attainted, his estates forfeited. Through the queen's intercession, he escaped execution and was exiled to the Isle of Man.[22]

In January 1382, Thomas's only son, Richard, was born into the rarefied atmosphere of England's high nobility, having as his godfathers Richard II and Richard Scrope, later Archbishop of York. He spent some of his youth at court, where he received part of his education. Richard II's court was famed for its chivalry, refinement and love of learning and young Beauchamp was to carry the legacy of this throughout his life.

In October 1397, he was married to Elizabeth Berkeley. Beauchamp's mother, Margaret Ferrers, suffered greatly during Thomas's years of exile and was forced to seek shelter in a convent in 1398. Her son was powerless to help her and it must have caused him both anger and grief when Kent had Richard II's badges carved into the very stones of Warwick Castle.[23]

When news came of Bolingbroke's landing at Ravenspur, the 17-year-old Beauchamp took advantage of Kent's absence and made contact in secret, presumably pledging his support in return for restoration of the family's estates and titles. On his way south and west, Bolingbroke stopped at Warwick and ordered the badges to be removed. The family was soon reunited, with the release of Thomas Beauchamp and the countess's return home. Both father and son were rewarded at the coronation of Henry IV, Richard knighted and Thomas taking a prominent place in the procession to Westminster Abbey. Henry's trust was to be well rewarded, for Richard Beauchamp gave lifelong support to the Lancastrian kings.[24]

After the death of his father in 1401, Richard Beauchamp became earl of Warwick. He was soon given his first chance to prove himself when Henry IV led an expedition to Wales in an attempt to end the rebellion of Owain Glyndŵr. Beauchamp was left in charge of the defences of Paincastle, near to some long-neglected family estates.[25]

Throughout his youth, Beauchamp was famed for his skills in the tournament, first coming to public notice in 1403 during the coronation celebrations for Henry IV's second wife and queen, Joan of Navarre: 'earl Richard kept jousts for the queen's part against all comers, where he so notably and so knightly behaved himself, as redounded to his noble fame and perpetual worship.' In 1404, he and Elizabeth welcomed the birth of their first child, Margaret, who was later to marry John Talbot, earl of Shrewsbury.[26]

The following year, Beauchamp fought alongside Henry IV and Prince Henry at Shrewsbury, where Hotspur was defeated and killed. After the victory, he was admitted to the Order of the Garter. It was around this time that a close and lifelong friendship developed between Beauchamp and the young prince. Over the next few years, between them they retook much of the land captured by Glyndŵr. The campaigns against the rebels in Wales were hardly conventional warfare and both young men carried the lessons they learned into future battles and campaigns, most notably in France.[27]

Life for the young nobleman was not all the glory of battle and the spectacle of the tournament. In 1405, Richard Scrope, Archbishop of York and Beauchamp's godfather, rebelled with Thomas Mowbray. Following their capture by Ralph Nevill, Beauchamp was one of the judges appointed to try them in a hastily convened court. Sentencing his godfather to death cannot have been easy, and the execution of a man of the cloth was shocking and all but unprecedented. Soon after the birth of his second child, Eleanor, in 1407, Beauchamp set out on a long pilgrimage which may, in part, have been prompted by the role he played in Scrope's death. He travelled through France and Italy to Rome, then to Jerusalem before setting out on the long journey home. Along the way, he dined with kings and dukes, jousted with great champions and joined crusading knights in 'other feats of war'. In Jerusalem, Beauchamp made an offering at the Holy Sepulchre, gave gifts to the worthy, receiving many in return, and dining with the Patriarch. In the 1400s, a pilgrimage to Rome and the Holy Land was neither trivial nor cheap. Beauchamp had to ensure not only that he had fine gifts for those he would meet, particularly English cloth, but also sufficient money for himself and his entourage to travel in comfort and style. This had required the mortgage of some ten properties and money deposited with his London bankers that could be forwarded to him as required.[28]

On his way to Rome, Beauchamp had accepted a challenge from Pandolfo Malalesta. On his return, he stopped at Verona to honour his promise, 'he and his challenger … should first joust, then go together with axes, after with arming swords and last with sharp daggers'. Beauchamp so comprehensively got the better of his opponent that 'if lord [Galeas of Mantua] had not the sooner cried peace, sir Pandolf, sore wounded on the left shoulder, had been utterly slain in the field'.[29]

Beauchamp returned to England via Eastern Europe, where he briefly accompanied the Teutonic Knights in their constant crusade against 'heathens', as his father and grandfather had done before him. Finally back in England, Beauchamp had little time to rest. Henry IV was ill and his son Prince Henry established a council to oversee the governing of England and the royal finances. Beauchamp was immediately appointed and, in October 1410, he was formally retained for life by the prince. After a brief but successful campaign in France, the two young men returned home to find Henry IV recovered and their services no longer required. Though he was publicly thanked, the prince's council was disbanded as the king once again took up the reins of government.[30]

After years of ill health, Henry IV died in 1413. The following year, Beauchamp was appointed Captain of Calais, a prestigious and sought-after post that came with unique pressures and difficulties. The garrison's wages were permanently in arrears and the first task of any newly appointed captain was to try and wrest at least promises of payment from the exchequer, if not the money itself. Calais was essentially a company town, shared between the garrison, England's only standing army, and the wool staple. It was a small enclave on the coast of France just 15 miles long and around 10 miles wide. To the east, between Calais and Flanders, was low-lying country, farmed in times of peace and flooded to provide a defensive barrier in times of war or siege. The town of Calais was the administrative centre of the enclave, with the imposing bulk of the castle on its west side. This was not just a garrison town, however, a significant population of civilians, mainly involved in the wool trade, had their permanent homes here. The largest building was the Staple Inn, where the captain and lieutenant conducted administrative business and where the treasury was housed. The town was ringed by fortresses. The most important of these was Guines, which remained crucial to the defence of England's last foothold on French soil for decades to come, particularly after most of the other castles were reduced to rubble during a Burgundian raid in 1436.[31]

By the early 1400s, the Company of the Staple of Calais held something of a monopoly on the export of English wool. Though wool could be traded domestically, both to foreign brokers and cloth manufacturers, without attracting the sizeable duty paid by the staplers, no English exporter could operate legally outside the staple.[32]

The staple was an important source of income to the crown, both in terms of the duty paid and loans raised on surety of that duty. The merchants of the staple were frequently called upon to lend sufficient money to pay the garrison's wages when they again fell into arrears. They were also called upon to help finance the repair of the town's defences. Though there were sometimes tensions between the garrison and the merchants, there was a level of mutual dependence between the two. Incoming captains of Calais frequently had to prove their worth to both soldiers and civilians before they were allowed to take possession of the enclave. This regularly involved the outlay of considerable sums of money and, even more regularly, securing loans from the staple to be paid back through tax exemptions.

As with many before and after, Richard Beauchamp frequently left the day-to-day running of Calais to his lieutenant and treasurer. In November 1414, almost as soon as he had established himself in the post, he left for the Council of Constance. This meeting, convened by the Holy Roman Emperor Sigismund, was important to the future of the papacy and attended by representatives from across Christian Europe. Beauchamp was the highest-ranking English lay lord in attendance and received much praise for his contribution to the talks. He also found time to compete in the several tournaments held, catching the eye of one particularly high-born woman. 'And then the Empress took the earl's livery, a bear, from a knight's shoulder and for great love and favour she set it on her shoulder. Then earl Richard made one of pearls and precious stones and offered her that, and she gladly and lovingly received it. Emperor Sigismund was so impressed with Beauchamp that he declared that 'if all courtesy were lost it might be found again in him'.[33]

In August 1415, Beauchamp was at Harfleur with Henry V but had to take command of a vessel carrying many men suffering from dysentery and some prisoners to Calais while Henry continued overland. Beauchamp thus missed the battle of Agincourt. He and Henry V were as close as brothers and to be anywhere but at his king's side during his greatest triumph must have been a bitter disappointment.[34]

Beauchamp remained in Calais for the next year, entertaining Emperor Sigismund, who stayed in Calais for a month on his way to visit Henry V in England. He was in London in August 1416 and enjoyed a brief reunion with his wife. Their last child, Elizabeth, was born the following year. At that time Henry V was already planning a second military expedition to France, secretly treating with both Sigismund and the duke of Burgundy while keeping up the pretence of pursuing talks with France. Along with Beauchamp, a sizeable army and shiploads of supplies, he set sail for France at the end of July 1416. The most important city in lower Normandy, Caen, was besieged and surrendered in September. Truces were signed with Brittany, Maine and Anjou and by the spring of 1418, Henry had control of most of western Normandy. Beauchamp laid siege to Domfront and Henry V began the siege of Rouen. Beauchamp successfully negotiated with the leaders of a nearby town who were blocking English river traffic and soon sufficient supplies got through to allow Henry to complete the blockade of Rouen. The city surrendered in December.[35]

The duke of Burgundy, John the Fearless, had taken Paris and appointed himself protector of the mentally ill king Charles VI. He was, to all intents and purposes, ruler of France. The Queen of France, Isabella of Bavaria, was closely allied to Burgundy and, though she was forced to give up her role as regent, she supported his takeover and worked alongside him. Her then 15-year-old son, the dauphin Charles, refused to cooperate with the new regime and fled Paris.[36]

The way was now clear for Henry V and by the spring of 1419, England controlled the whole of Normandy. Richard Beauchamp organised a meeting between Henry, Charles VI and Queen Isabella to discuss a marriage between Henry and Charles's daughter, Catherine de Valois. The meeting, held on 30 May 1419, was a complex mix of diplomacy, logistics and spectacle. Three large areas were marked out on the ground, divided by trenches, for Henry, for the French king and his family and for those who were to lead the negotiations. At the centre were three large, richly decorated tents 'draped with cloth of gold and rich hangings, embroidered with lilies and leopards', where the two kings would meet first with their advisors then with each other.[37]

As it turned out, Charles VI was too ill to play his part, leaving his queen to represent the interests of France and their daughter. This elaborately choreographed meeting ended in failure when the French withdrew. On 10 September, the dauphin arranged to meet with the duke on the

Montereau bridge, where his followers hacked the duke to death. In response, the people of Paris wreaked a bloody revenge on the dauphin's supporters and Queen Isabella was left with no choice but to return to the negotiating table in hopes of forging an alliance with England against her son.[38]

Philip the Bold succeeded his father as duke of Burgundy and Henry V sent Beauchamp to treat with him. On Christmas Day, an alliance was forged and duke Philip agreed to negotiate the marriage on Henry's behalf. This was accomplished in May 1420 with the Treaty of Troyes, which gave Henry everything he could have wanted – the throne of France after Charles VI's death, marriage to his daughter and powers of regency during the French king's intermittent bouts of madness. The dauphin was now isolated and his strongholds besieged.[39]

Beauchamp managed to return home, again briefly, in 1421. His countess Elizabeth Berkeley was fighting her own battle with her cousin James over control of her inheritance. She was readying Berkeley Castle for an attack and her husband was able to give her some much-needed support. But he was soon to return to France, leaving her to carry on as best she could on her own. Before very long, she moved with her daughters to Salwarpe Manor, one of her favourite houses, where she died in 1423.[40]

Henry V had secured Paris by 1422 but he died that August, leaving a young widow and a son who was less than a year old. Beauchamp was with his friend and king when he died and returned to England with his body. Charles VI died just two months later, leaving Henry V's son and successor king of both England and France, if the latter could be secured for him.[41]

Now 41, widowed and with no son to follow him, Beauchamp's thoughts turned to remarriage. He chose the widow of his cousin, the 23-year-old Isabel Despenser, a wealthy woman in her own right. They married in November 1423 at Hanley Castle in Worcestershire.[42]

Beauchamp's relationships with his wives are not easy to tease out. His military commitments in Calais and France, combined with her need to stay in England to defend her inheritance, meant he and his first wife Elizabeth spent little time together. Isabel, on the other hand, was to accompany him to France on at least two occasions. As widow and widower, both had more choice when it came to a second marriage than either had with their first. Beauchamp wrote a ballad in honour of his new wife, which may have been an expression of heartfelt longing or a more formulaic exercise in chivalry. Isabel's attractions to Beauchamp are clear. She was young, rich and of royal blood. Her first marriage had produced a daughter, Elizabeth, who was 8 at the time of her mother's marriage to Beauchamp, so there was hope for a much-needed and longed-for son. From Isabel's perspective, Beauchamp was one of the most powerful and respected men in Christendom, victorious in war and famed in chivalry. Isabel's first husband had served in France with Beauchamp and the couple would have known each other well. Their first child, Henry, was born in 1425. Anne was to follow just eighteen months later.[43]

Beauchamp had been remarkably successful throughout his military career in France, despite missing the famous victory at Agincourt. When he next returned to France, he faced ignominy and defeat at Montargis, where the townspeople withstood a determined siege long enough to be relieved by the Bastard of Orléans. Sir John de la Pole failed to keep watch and his men were massacred by the French, leaving around 1,500 dead. Beauchamp tried to rally those who remained but was forced to flee, leaving his guns behind.[44]

In 1427, Beauchamp was relieved of his post as Captain of Calais, the duke of Bedford appointing himself in his place. His dismissal caused Beauchamp a good deal of grief and he blamed three men: the treasurer of Calais, the warden of the mint and Bedford's chamberlain. Though all three denied any responsibility, Beauchamp's anger was obvious. '[O]ur lord of Warwick shows himself always heavy lord to [Richard] Wydeville, Lewis John and Richard Bokeland, charging them that they were causes thereof.'[45]

Beauchamp was owed a considerable amount of money by the crown for his service in Calais, more than £46,000. In an effort to show his goodwill and mend fences, Bedford asked Bokeland, Treasurer of Calais, to make good that debt. Bokeland, who understood the financial realities of Calais, knew this was impossible.[46]

> that I should govern me as tenderly as I can in preferring the payments due to my said lord of Warwick, God knows my will were to please my lord of Warwick in that or in any other thing to me possible; but it is hard for me to prefer those payments without insupportable ill will on other parties. Considering that all the assignments of Calais will not suffice yearly to pay my lord and his soldiers and the remnant of the captains of the marches …[47]

It would seem that Bedford's chamberlain, Richard Wydeville, tried to distance himself from all of this. Bokeland wrote to him: 'as I am informed, that you be busy to excuse yourself to his lordship and charged the default wholly upon Lewis John and me.' Wydeville also claimed Bokeland had written a letter 'against his lordship'. This caused Bokeland a good deal of distress and he demanded to see the letter, stating that he never 'wrote to you anything that should cause my said lord of Warwick to be thus displeased towards my person'.[48]

Deeply unhappy with this state of affairs, Beauchamp returned to England, possibly with a view to retiring from public life and settling down with his young wife and family. Though he was owed considerable money by the crown, he had done well out of the war with France, amassing large ransoms of prominent prisoners and plunder from captured towns and cities. He embarked on a building programme, including a new stable and other additions at Warwick Castle, and acquired several manors.[49]

Beauchamp was far too valuable to be allowed to settle down to a quiet life. In 1428, he was appointed the young king's tutor, responsible for overseeing his education and general upbringing. Until then, Henry VI had lived in a world of women, headed by his mother and lady Alice Butler, though Henry, lord Fitzhugh had ultimate responsibility for the security of his person. Now the young king was old enough to leave the nursery, Richard Beauchamp's skill in war and learnedness made him a most suitable candidate to oversee the next stage of Henry's development. Beauchamp stayed close to Henry VI for the next nine years. His son Henry became the young king's close companion, as perhaps, after 1434, did his son-in-law Richard. Perhaps Beauchamp saw a similar relationship as he had enjoyed with Henry V developing between the two boys. He left the day-to-day management of Henry's education to others, mostly trusted men of his own household, but he had general oversight and was deeply involved in all of it, including the vexed question of discipline and chastisement.[50]

In the meantime, in France the dauphin's position was growing stronger, particularly after the appearance of the charismatic and inspiring Joan of Arc. He was crowned Charles VII in July 1429 and it became imperative, if England was not to lose the crown of France altogether, that Henry VI's coronation take place. As he must be crowned in England first, arrangements were hastily made. Beauchamp took the young king to Westminster Hall and, at the age of 7, Henry was crowned King of England.[51]

Beauchamp, his wife and son with him, led the expedition to France where, it was hoped, Henry VI would be crowned king at Reims Cathedral. The city was in enemy hands, however, and the English party spent some months in Rouen. The coronation was further delayed when Joan of Arc, captured by the Burgundians, was sold to the English and put on trial for heresy. In order to discredit the dauphin, it was determined that Joan must be sentenced to death. She was tried by an ecclesiastical court and Beauchamp was not directly involved. He did, however, work behind the scenes and was possibly involved in the sleight of hand that saw Joan retried after an initial sentence of life imprisonment was handed down. Joan of Arc was burned at the stake on 30 July 1431. In December, Henry VI rode triumphantly into Paris, accompanied by Beauchamp and his uncles, the dukes of Bedford and Gloucester, where he was crowned in Notre Dame Cathedral.[52]

Henry VI and his entourage were back in London in February 1432. Beauchamp and his family finally arrived back at Warwick Castle in March, after eighteen months away from home. Beauchamp stayed in England for the next five years, the longest time he had spent at home in close to two decades. He dedicated this time to his family, his own personal affairs and his continuing responsibilities to Henry VI.[53]

Between 1434 and 1437, Beauchamp arranged marriages for four of his children with members of the extended Nevill family. First, Henry and Anne were married to the earl of Salisbury's daughter Cecily and son Richard. Then his widowed daughter Elizabeth and stepdaughter, also Elizabeth, were married to Salisbury's brothers George and Edward.

In 1434, the duke of Bedford died and England's fortunes in France began to go downhill. The young duke of York replaced Bedford as Lieutenant of Normandy and set out for France in 1436 with the largest army England had sent across the Channel in years. Far from enjoying a quiet retirement, Beauchamp, now in his middle fifties, was recalled to service in Calais, where he successfully defended the town against a siege. Though York did the best he could with limited resources, he could not prevent Paris falling to Charles VII and he was replaced by a protesting Beauchamp as Lieutenant.[54]

> My going over at this time is full far from the ease of my years and from the continual labour of my person at sieges and daily occupations in the war, seeing the length of time that I have belaboured in the service of noble kings of good memory, your grandsire and father, and about your self, as well as in your wars as about your noble person.[55]

Henry VI was insistent and Beauchamp made preparations to leave, once again taking his wife and son with him. The seas were rough and several attempts were made to cross, Beauchamp's ships driven back to shore time after time.

> … in short space rose a grievous tempest and drove the ships into divers coasts, in so much that they all feared to be perished. And the noble earl, forecasting, let bind himself and his lady and Henry, his son and heir … to the mast of the vessel to the intent that wherever they were found they might have been buried together worshipfully by the knowledge of his coat armour and other signs upon him.[56]

They eventually made it to Normandy and arrived in Rouen in November 1437. Beauchamp appointed his son-in-law Talbot field commander of the English forces and dug in in the city, almost in ruins after years of war and siege. Attempts were made to sue for peace with both Charles VII and the duke of Burgundy. The French were in a far stronger position than they had been for decades and wanted nothing more than England's complete withdrawal from France.[57]

In May 1439, already ill and exhausted, Beauchamp died, his wife and son at his bedside. It was not until October, however, that his body was returned to England: 'his corpse was honourably conveyed, as well by water as by land, from Rouen unto Warwick, and there worshiply buried in the College of Our Lady Church, founded by his noble ancestors.' He was later laid to rest in the beautiful Beauchamp Chapel at Warwick Castle. His widow Isabel, already ill herself and aware she was unlikely to recover, died some six months later. In later years, their daughter Anne commissioned the stunning Beauchamp Pageant in celebration of his life. In words and pictures, it shows a man larger than life, whose chivalry was unsurpassed and whose fame spread from England to the Holy Land.[58]

Along with the Beauchamp Pageant, the Rous Roll celebrates the lives and achievements of the earls of Warwick. Of Richard Beauchamp's children, Rous saves his most lavish praise for Anne, mother of the Queen of England and grandmother of the Prince of Wales when he compiled his Roll. Beauchamp's oldest daughter, Margaret, countess of Shrewsbury and only son Henry, duke of Warwick, are also praised. Of the first, Rous tells us that 'This lady, to the honour of God, made a decree in her house, not her own children outset, that whatever person blasphemed our Lord by unlawful swearing he should lack that day ale and wine and cooking and only have but bread and water. And, of Henry: 'he also would suffer no officer of his to oppress any man sorely and if it come to his knowledge he would punish them, and yet they would not mend thereby, they should not serve him.' Anne is most likely the one who commissioned the Roll and the praise for her is both heartfelt and touching.[59]

Dame Anne Beauchamp, a noble lady of the blood royal, daughter to earl Richard and whole sister to sir Henry Beauchamp duke of Warwick and, after the decease of his only begotten daughter Anne, by true inheritance countess of Warwick, which good lady had in her days great tribulation for her lord's sake, sir Richard Nevill, son and heir to sir Richard earl of Salisbury and, by her title, earl of Warwick, a famous knight and excellent, greatly spoken of through the most part of Christendom … and was ever a full devout lady in God's service, free of her speech to every person familiar according to her and their degree. Glad to be at and with women that travailed of child, full comfortable and plenteous then of all things that should be helping to them. And in her tribulations she was ever, to the great pleasure of God, full patient, to the great mercy of her soul, and example of all others that were vexed with any adversity. She was also gladly ever companionable and liberal and in her own person seemly and beauteous and to all that drew to her ladyship, as the deed showed, full good and gracious.[60]

Anne was the last holder of the Warwick title to be born with the Beauchamp name. Rous's loyalty and personal devotion to her extended to her children, her sons-in-law and her grandchildren. It lasted through the reigns of Henry VI, Edward IV and Richard III. They died in the same year, 1492, both in their seventies, tenacious survivors of turbulent times.

Anne's husband Richard Nevill held the title earl of Warwick in her right. Not only did he have a great deal to live up to when it came to his own father, the Earl of Salisbury, but his father-in-law had laid down a firm template for chivalric behaviour. Beauchamp had been a force of nature in his own time. The young Warwick must have felt both inspired and intimidated by the legend. Throughout his life, he was aware of the legacy and burden of the Warwick title, as well as the great benefits and privileges it brought. Though he ultimately failed, he worked hard for much of his life to fill the place beside Edward IV that Richard Beauchamp had beside Henry V.

# 9

# Death of a Grandchild and the Making of an Earl

n 3 June 1449, in a nursery at Ewelme in Oxfordshire, a 5-year-old child breathed her last. She was the ward of the duke of Suffolk. His duchess, Alice Chaucer, was most likely nearby, if not nursing the child herself. Alice had hoped to be the child's mother-in-law in time to come and her death was a blow not only to her mother but her foster family as well. Alice had ties with the child's family, having once been stepmother to her grandmother, Alice, countess of Salisbury.[1]

Anne Beauchamp was the only daughter of Henry, duke of Warwick and Cecily Nevill, daughter of the earl and countess of Salisbury. Her death not only grieved her family but set her aunts at odds. As the heir to young Anne's title would be one of four women, the line of Beauchamp earls that stretched back 200 years was about to be broken.

Anne's parents were married at Abergavenny in 1436 when they were children. Sharing their wedding were her mother's brother Richard and her father's sister Anne. When Anne and Henry's father Richard Beauchamp, earl of Warwick died in 1439, Henry inherited his lands and title. The earldom was upgraded to a dukedom in posthumous recognition of Beauchamp's service to the crown and his personal service to Henry VI. When Henry Beauchamp died seven years after his father, he was succeeded by his only child Anne, then just 2 years old.[2]

Young Anne had good people looking after her and her interests. The practice of wardship after the death of a father might seem cruel but, in practice, it helped preserve an inheritance during the child's minority. With wardship came marriage rights and, most usually, a planned marriage between the fatherless child and a member of the guardian's family.

Wardships were sometimes given as rewards for service but most often bought. Not only did the guardian gain the future revenue from the inherited estates, he was also securing the future of a son or daughter, niece or nephew. It was, therefore, in his interests to take good care not only of the child but of their inheritance as well. That is not to say mothers could not be trusted but remarriage might bring a stepfather less inclined to care for his predecessor's children than any he and his new wife might have in the future. The Suffolks no doubt took as much care of Anne as they did their own son John, if not more.

Suffolk and Salisbury, along with lord Sudeley and John Beauchamp of Powick, formed young Anne's council and worked hard to keep the Warwick, Beauchamp and Despenser fortunes intact. Salisbury was specifically acknowledged as 'her grandfather and would therefore be more friendly and favourable to Anne than any other person'.[3]

After duke Henry's death, John Beauchamp of Powick, a distant cousin of Richard Beauchamp, initially pressed a claim to the title but formally renounced it early in 1447. He seems to have done this in good faith, not wishing to cross his more powerful colleagues. Had Anne lived to reach her majority, it would have been these four men she thanked for the integrity and security of her inheritance.[4]

Salisbury shifted his focus with such speed after his granddaughter's death that, within a fortnight, his son Richard was earl of Warwick. Salisbury, Suffolk, Sudeley and Beauchamp of Powick had managed to gather and keep everything together, so it passed to Richard and his wife swiftly and smoothly.[5]

When the double marriage was celebrated between the Beauchamp and Nevill siblings, their future lives were full of promise. This was truer for Cecily and Henry than for Richard and Anne, though both bridegrooms stood to inherit an earldom when their fathers died. We do not know how the children felt about each other, nor do we know how Cecily and Henry's relationship developed as they grew to adulthood. Their first child was born when they were both 18, so they must have established their own household about that time.

For several years after their joint wedding, Richard Nevill's life was closely entwined with that of his brother-in-law. As it was customary for a young husband to live with his bride's family, Richard may have spent part of his childhood at Warwick Castle and other Beauchamp estates. Henry Beauchamp was one of Henry VI's boyhood companions and the relationship between them was close. Though there is nothing more than an oblique reference in later letters patent, it seems likely Richard was at least a peripheral member of this select group.

However close the relationship between the young brothers-in-law, Richard's destiny still lay in the north of England. Whatever physical distance may at times have separated him and his brothers, later events would suggest that nothing was quite strong enough to break the close bond forged between them.

When Richard Beauchamp died, his son and heir was just 14 years old, seven years short of his majority. Without a powerful guardian and protector of his future wealth, Henry Beauchamp was vulnerable to those who could find a way to divert some of it to themselves. Prior to her own death in the same year, his mother worked to protect as much of her son's inheritance as she could. It was also in Salisbury's interest to use what influence he could on his son-in-law's behalf. Though we do not know where Henry and Cecily lived prior to 1443, it could well have been at Middleham, though Henry would seem to have maintained his links to the young king. It was also probably to Middleham that Richard and Anne returned after Richard Beauchamp's death.[6]

Young Richard Nevill was knighted in 1443, possibly during Margaret of Anjou's coronation. It would have been around this time that he and Anne established their own household, though we do not know which of the Nevill or Beauchamp estates it might have been. It was also around this time that Richard first started acting as his father's lieutenant in the marches towards Scotland.[7]

Wherever their main place of residence, Richard spent a good deal of his time in and around Carlisle. That Anne did not accompany him on all his trips is suggested by the birth of an illegitimate daughter there, probably around 1443 or 1444. Margaret Nevill's mother is unknown to us now and, if her father and his wife were not already established in their own home, her birth may have moved things along in this regard. Margaret was acknowledged by her father and brought up alongside his legitimate children, later establishing a place for herself in the nursery.

On 11 June 1446, Henry Beauchamp died, leaving a young widow and 2-year-old daughter Anne. He was just 21 years old. Cecily either was or believed she was pregnant, but no child was subsequently born. In September of that year, the duke of Suffolk bought Anne's wardship and she went to live at Ewelme.[8]

Cecily needed to secure her dower and her daughter's inheritance, not always an easy process for a young widow. The carefully protected fortune Henry Beauchamp had inherited just three months earlier was once more vulnerable to plunder. Though they moved quickly to secure it, Suffolk, Salisbury, Sudeley and Beauchamp of Powick were not quite quick enough.

More than fifty grants were made in the five weeks after [duke Henry's] death, mainly to members of the royal household: to the king's secretary, the controller of the royal household, the marshal of the hall, to carvers, ushers of the chamber and yeomen to the crown, to a clerk of the signet, several serjeants, and to the usher and groom of the queen's chamber and to pages of her robes and her bed.[9]

This damage needed to be limited and, where possible, undone. Immediate steps were taken to do this and in July 1446 the king's council issued an order that all those who held grants at the time, or were to in the future, must have 'letters of confirmation thereof under [the duke of Warwick's] great seal during the minor age of Anne, daughter and heir to the said duke'.[10]

In April 1449, her dower secure, Cecily married John Tiptoft, who was granted the title earl of Worcester soon after. Two months later, her only child was dead. Cecily herself died in June the following year.[11]

On 23 July, letters patent were issued to Richard Nevill, confirming him as earl of Warwick.

> Whereas Henry, late duke of Warwick, brother of Anne, wife of Richard Nevill, knight, first-born son of Richard Nevill, earl of Salisbury, of which Henry she is heir, was earl of Warwick and his ancestors from time imme-morial were earls of Warwick; the king has granted to Richard the son, and Anne and her heirs, for good service about the king's person and in Scotland on the punishment of the king's enemies at his own costs, he being still in his minority, the estate and title of earl of Warwick.[12]

Not only was Richard (whom we will now call Warwick) an earl six months shy of his twenty-first birthday, he was premier earl, holder of the oldest earldom in England. For the grandson of a new-made earl, the weight of this, as well as the glory, must have been awesome. Warwick now had one of the finest castles in England as his principal place of residence, as well as estates the length of the country. It might have been overwhelming but Warwick, aware of the value of both the title and the wealth of the Beauchamps to himself and his family, set about securing as much of that wealth as he could. Despite the swift transfer of the Warwick title, the set-tling of the Beauchamp, Warwick and Despenser estates was to prove a long, complex and sometimes violent matter.[13]

The first obstacle to overcome came in the form of the new countess of Warwick's older half-sisters. The estate of their late mother, Elizabeth Berkeley, was also in dispute but Anne had no claim over that. Margaret, countess of Shrewsbury, Elizabeth lady Latimer and Eleanor, duchess of Somerset all saw themselves as joint heirs of their father, along with Anne. However, it was not earl Richard's estate that was under discussion but that of his granddaughter, the young countess Anne.[14]

Salisbury was in a better position than the husbands of Anne Beauchamp's sisters, who were all in France at the time of the child Anne's death. With access to court, and possibly king, he moved quickly, shifting the machinery that had protected his grandchild to protect his son and daughter-in-law. Warwick only needed a little breathing space. Within six months, he would reach his majority and have all he had been able to secure in his own hands.

Warwick and Salisbury had to battle on two fronts. First, the dispute with Anne's half-sisters and, second, a dispute over the Despenser inheritance with Salisbury's brother, Edward, lord Bergavenny. Edward had married Isabel Despenser's daughter Elizabeth, and it was their son George who had a claim to half her estate. Warwick set about occupying as much Despenser property as he could. Though he was entitled to his half when he came of age in 1457, George did not press his claim and was formally dispossessed by act of Parliament in 1461.[15]

Also in dispute between Warwick and his uncle was the Bergavenny title and lordship. Edward Nevill was summonsed to Parliament as lord Bergavenny in September 1450. Possession being nine-tenths of the law, Warwick held firm to several properties found to belong to his cousin George, among them Abergavenny Castle. Helping him to resist any attempt to oust him was his brother Thomas, who was appointed sheriff of Glamorgan in 1450.[16]

While some legal disputes in the fifteenth century descended into open hostility, ongoing conflict and, sometimes, generational feud, others were remarkably amicable. Salisbury may have sworn Bergavenny would get nothing, and Bergavenny may have sworn to fight for his son's rights to the bitter end, but the matter seems not to have spilled into personal animosity. The two brothers remained supportive of each other in many other aspects of their lives. Warwick's conflict with the duke of Somerset, on the other hand, did descend into enduring personal enmity. Not only were the two men connected through their wives but also their common Beaufort ancestry – Somerset was the grandson of Joan Beaufort's brother John. As with the Nevills and the Percies, shared blood seems not to have had a particularly positive effect on Warwick and Somerset's regard for each other.

At first, Warwick seemed willing to compromise and prepared to recognise at least part of the sisters' claim. He later changed his mind. An inquisition post mortem was held in several places over a period of time to sort out what property Henry Beauchamp (and his daughter) had. This process was chiefly designed to identify anything that belonged to the crown, but it also served to identify the rightful heirs of separate properties or parcels of properties. On each occasion the inquisition met, Anne Beauchamp's claim was upheld. As duke Henry's only full sister, and the child Anne's only aunt of the whole blood, Anne Beauchamp's relationship with the deceased overrode those of her older half-sisters. Despite the findings, between them, Margaret, Elizabeth and Eleanor managed to secure nine manors.[17]

It was not until 1466 that Warwick conceded that Margaret, countess of Shrewsbury might keep what she had managed to get her hands on. It was further conceded that, should Warwick have no male heirs, the Warwick title and estates would pass to her descendants. Not everything went Warwick's way. Henry Beauchamp had secured the lordship of the Channel Islands, to be his after the death of Humphrey, duke of Gloucester. As Gloucester was still alive at the time of duke Henry's death, Warwick's claim to it was not upheld. However, John Nanfan, who had once worked for Richard Beauchamp and now worked for Warwick, was appointed Governor of the Channel Islands in 1452. This would prove most fortunate for Warwick in time to come.[18]

No sooner did Somerset arrive back in England from Normandy than he set about trying to make good his duchess's claims on the Warwick inheritance. Whatever the findings of the various enquiries, Warwick was firmly in possession, and control, of the disputed properties and would not be shifted. A large part of his time in 1451 and 1452 was spent consolidating his hold on land in Wales and the Midlands.[19]

In June 1451, licences were granted to all four sisters and their husbands

> to enter all possessions and hereditaments whatsoever, which Cecily, late duchess of Warwick, held in dower of the endowment of Henry, late duke of Warwick, sometime her husband, in England and the marches of Wales, which ought to descend to the said daughters [of Richard, late earl of Warwick] … licence also to Richard Nevill, now earl of Warwick, to enter into all possessions which the said late duke, or as kinswoman and heir of Anne, daughter and heir of the said duke, after the death of Cecily.[20]

There were other calls on his time, however. In 1450, Warwick accompanied the king for the first time as earl, to Blackheath to protect the security of the realm against the rebels from Kent. Prior to his departure, he wrote to lord Ferrers of Charteley, asking him to raise men to ride under Warwick's banner.[21]

> [T]he king has desired and charged me to be with him at St Albans on Saturday next coming accompanied with such a fellowship as that I may and be content in case the commons of Kent well be rebel and be not to obey the laws, that then I with my fellowship to be assisting and advancing upon his person that by the grace of our good lord we shall be of the power to withstand their malice and evil will, wherefore I pray you with all my heart with such persons as you now array and secure you will send to me at Warwick, to be [here] on Wednesday at night next coming in semblable wise.[22]

Unfortunately, Ferrers died the day after this letter was sent so his men probably did not get to ride with Warwick to London.[23]

On 5 September 1451, when Warwick was 22 and his countess 25, their first child, Isobel, was born at Warwick Castle, the family's principal place of residence.[24]

In 1452, Warwick was again at Blackheath with an army at his back and his father by his side, this time to negotiate with his uncle of York. At this time in his life, Warwick remained staunchly loyal to the king he had known since childhood, for whose grandfather's sake his own grandfather had helped overthrow Richard II. It would take an escalation of his brothers' feud with the Percies, and his own with Somerset, a crisis of government in England and the strange illness of the king to threaten that loyalty.

# 10

# A Crisis of Government

n the early hours of 17 October 1452, an army of 3,000 Englishmen under the command of one of England's great warrior heroes slipped into the city of Bordeaux through a broken gate. They had landed in the Gironde estuary while Charles VII of France was expecting an English force in Normandy. Friendly faces waited for them in Bordeaux, merchants and traders who feared their commercial links with England would be cut under French rule, leading citizens who had sworn their oath of allegiance to Charles and since thought better of it. John Talbot retook Bordeaux without breaking into a sweat.[1]

Gascony had been an important English territory for centuries. Brought to England in 1153 when Eleanor of Aquitaine married Henry II, it had never sat quite safely in English hands. Successive kings had fought to hold on to it by force of arms or diplomacy. In October 1453, after a devastating defeat and the loss of Talbot, it changed hands for the last time.[2]

Talbot's warm welcome in Bordeaux did not last long. His men behaved badly, looting homes and churches and sending the spoils back to England. The presence of 5,000 soldiers, behaving more like an army of occupation than liberators, put a strain on the citizens' goodwill. When Talbot raised taxes for the defence of the city, that goodwill was stretched to breaking point. With many outside the city holding firm to France and Charles VII, Talbot's hold slipped.[3]

Charles VII had treated the people of Bordeaux well when the city was in his hands, paying his soldiers on time and rewarding them for good service. Talbot's soldiers had last been paid in July 1452. Two English commanders had to pay their men from their own funds and from hasty loans.[4]

On 17 July 1453, Talbot attacked a strongly defended French army near Castillon, about 20 miles east of Bordeaux. Cannon fire ripped through his army, killing both Talbot and his son. Despite the loss of their governor and commander, the English at Bordeaux held out for a further three months. In August, realising there was to be no further threat to Normandy, Charles VII blockaded the Gironde and laid siege to Bordeaux. Facing starvation, the city surrendered to the French in October. When the news reached England, the psychological blow was massive, both for the people and the king.[5]

It had been business as usual in July and August. Henry VI was at Sheen, where his council was trying to find a way to establish peace between Somerset and the absent Warwick. Their dispute was about the towns and castles associated with the lordship of Glamorgan and Morgannock. Somerset had been granted the keeping of these properties and Warwick resisted him with force at Cowbridge and Cardiff. Right was on Warwick's side, these were part of Anne Beauchamp's Despenser inheritance and her half-sisters and their husbands had no claim on that. Nevertheless, letters were sent to Warwick and his countess ordering them to disband their armies and surrender the towns and castles. News from the north of England, and an urgent letter from his father summoning him home, diverted Warwick's path towards Yorkshire.[6]

Henry VI had taken it upon himself to resolve the various disputes and feuds between his lords and was travelling west through Wiltshire when he stopped at the royal hunting lodge at Clarendon. Something happened there that either no one quite understood or had the chance to fully record. One chronicler writes that 'the king, being at Clarendon indisposed, suddenly was taken and smitten with a frenzy and his wit and reason withdrawn'. It seems Henry took fright at something, suffered a sudden shock, perhaps similar to the one that presaged his grandfather's first bout of mental illness. This was almost immediately followed by news of the death of Talbot and the loss of Gascony. Whether the psychotic episode alone was enough, or the dreadful news from France exacerbated it, Henry VI fell into a state of catatonia. The king was 'deprived of his senses and memory, unable to speak or use his limbs, incapable of even moving from the place where he sat'. Even the news of the birth of his son on 13 October failed to rouse him.[7]

At first, Henry's illness was kept secret. Somerset presided over the council for two months as if nothing were amiss. As hope for a speedy recovery faded, a great council was convened. The duke of York was initially excluded but the more neutral lords, including Buckingham, prevailed and a belated summons was sent. If they hoped for some kind of reconciliation between York and Somerset, they would soon be disappointed.[8]

When great council met in London in November 1453, there were only a few absentees. The duke of Exeter did not attend, possibly in protest at York's presence and likely precedence. Westmorland was too ill to leave home. Henry VI's half-brother Edmund Tudor, earl of Richmond was busy in the king's service in Wales. Others were too ill or old to travel, or were concerned with the security of their estates. Northumberland and his two oldest sons, lords Poynings and Egremont, were reluctant to leave Yorkshire while Thomas and John Nevill were at home, unchecked by the authority of their absent father. Also absent was William Fitzalan, earl of Arundel, married to Salisbury's oldest daughter, Joan. He was neither a conscientious nor enthusiastic member of council and preferred to spend his time at home with his family.[9]

On 12 November, York arrived in London with a relatively small following, accompanied by Norfolk. John Mowbray, duke of Norfolk was the son of Salisbury's sister Katherine, but this was not the reason he attached himself to York and his supporters. Norfolk shared York's dislike and distrust of Somerset. He had prepared a set of articles denouncing him for his conduct of the war in France and calling for him to be indicted for treason. He accused him of 'falsehoods and lying', of bribery and treason. To those who suggested Somerset might be tried on lesser charges of trespass, he responded with strong feeling and uncompromising zeal.[10]

> Whereas every man that is true to the said crown might greatly marvel that any man would say that the loss of two so noble duchies as Normandy and Guyenne, that be well worth a great realm, coming by succession of fathers and mothers to the said crown, is but trespass, whereas it has been seen in many realms and lordships that, for the loss of towns and castles without siege, the captains that have lost them have been dead and beheaded and their goods lost.[11]

Norfolk's words worked. Somerset was arrested and sent to the Tower to await trial. Having got what he wanted, Norfolk then retired into the background. The way was now clear for York to set up a council and a government, unhindered by personal feud and potential challenge to his authority.[12]

York was operating on a very thin margin of support, however. So long as he remained within the limits of whatever powers he might be granted, he could count on those lords, like Buckingham and Worcester, whose main concern was for continuity of government during the king's absence. He could afford to lose those who were partisans of Somerset, or even the queen, so long as those who did support him did so wholeheartedly.

On 30 November, great council met with a view to setting up a smaller council to govern England in the king's absence. The lords there present swore 'on a book' to keep the peace with each other and to uphold the laws of England. The task ahead of them would be impossible without some level of cooperation and a good measure of peace.[13]

A smaller group met on 5 December. York was appointed Henry VI's lieutenant and prepared a petition to be put before Parliament to be named protector and defender of England. Little else was decided and it was left to the chancellor, Cardinal Archbishop Kemp, to keep the wheels of government turning.[14]

> [A] great many matters were daily moved among them of great weight and charge concerning the wellbeing of our said sovereign lord the king, his lands and subjects, [for] the king's infirmity, of the which these were as sorry as they could be, suffered him not to attend to the politic rule and governance of this his land and to the observance and keeping of his laws as the necessity asks and requires.[15]

Nothing more was done and many of the lords went home to their estates for Christmas, returning to London in January for the next sitting of Parliament the following month. As these lords arrived, the citizens grew nervous about their retinues.

> The earl of Salisbury will be at London on Monday [25 January] or Tuesday next coming with seven score knights and squires besides other men. The earls of Warwick, Richmond and Pembroke come with the duke of York, as it is said, each of them with a goodly fellowship. And nonetheless the earl of Warwick will have 1,000 men awaiting on him besides the fellowship that comes with him.[16]

Without the calming presence of the king, the various bands of armed men guarding the assembled lords might grow restless.[17]

With Somerset out of the way, at least one source of potential trouble had been avoided. However, Somerset did not let his imprisonment render him entirely impotent and idle. He was reported to be making 'him ready to be as strong as he can make him'. 'The duke of Somerset's harbinger has taken up all the lodgings that may be got near the Tower, in Thames Street, Mart Lane, Saint Katherine's, Tower Hill and thereabout.' He was confident his affinity and well-established network of spies would remain loyal and vigilant, whatever the outcome.[18]

> The duke of Somerset has spies going in every lord's house in this land: some gone as friars, some as shipmen taken on the sea and some in otherwise, which report to him all that they can see or hear touching the said duke [of York].[19]

In January, the queen brought Prince Edward to Windsor to meet his father, where

> [t]he duke of Buk took him in his arms and presented him to the king in goodly wise, beseeching the king to bless him; and the king gave no manner

of answer. Nevertheless, the duke stayed with the prince by the king and when he could no manner of answer have, the queen came in and took the prince in her arms and presented him in like form as the duke had done, desiring that he should bless [him]; but all their labour was in vain, for they departed thence without any answer or countenance saving only that once he looked on the prince and cast down his eyes again without any more.[20]

Queen Margaret, herself from a long line of strong women who were used to standing in for absent, ailing or deceased husbands, had prepared a set of five articles offering herself as regent until her husband recovered.[21]

John Stodeley reported in his newsletter of 19 January that the queen desired 'to be given the whole rule of this land' and authority to 'make the chancellor, the treasurer, the privy seal and all other officers of this land, with sheriffs and all other officers that a king should make'. She desired also '[t]hat she may give all bishoprics of this land and all other benefices belonging to the king's gift' and 'that she may have sufficient livelihood assigned her for the king, the prince and herself'. As for the fifth item, Stodely wrote that he 'cannot know what it is'.[22]

This kind of thing might suit the counts of Anjou, but it would not do for the lords of England. We have no other evidence of Margaret's articles than John Stodeley's newsletter. How, and if, they were presented, how they were received and what response Margaret got is not recorded. That, in itself, can be taken as a fair indication of the lack of credit England's lords were prepared to give to the political abilities of their queen.

The true nature, and full extent, of Henry's illness was not understood by the assembled lords until yet another crisis forced them to confront it. On 22 March 1454, Chancellor Kemp died. While the government of England could be carried out without a king, and the Church could manage for a time with only one archbishop, the death of the chancellor was disastrous. No official business could be done and the wheels of government ground to a halt. A chancellor must be appointed and the king's advice must be sought. To that end, the lords decided 'that certain lords, that is to say, the bishops of Winchester, Ely and Chester, the earls of Warwick, Oxford and Shrewsbury, viscounts Beaumont and Bourchier, the prior of St John, lords Fauconberg, Dudley and Stourton, should ride to Windsor to the king's high presence'. They found the king insensible, unable to talk and dependent on attendants for his every need. They spent the best part of a day attempting to get him to answer two questions: Who should replace Kemp as Archbishop of Canterbury? Who should replace him as chancellor? They got a response to neither. In Parliament the following day, Bishop Waynflete delivered the sad news, revealing, for the first time in public, the full extent of King Henry's illness.[23]

Urgent action was needed, both in the matter of appointing a chancellor and a protector. Who was to be the new Archbishop of Canterbury was a far easier decision. York's brother-in-law, Thomas Bourchier, Bishop of Ely, was elevated to archbishop. An attempt to fill his empty see with Salisbury's youngest son, George, was unsuccessful. York was named protector and defender of England until such time as either the king should recover or his infant son Edward come of age.[24]

York's response to the appointment was partly formulaic – what one says when offered a prestigious post – and gave no hint he might not have been praying too strenuously for Henry's quick restoration 'to healthful disposition'. He could not, he said, do it alone. He required the support of the other lords and he was not, he feared, 'sufficient of myself of wisdom, cunning nor ability, to take upon me that worthy name of protector and defender of this land'.[25]

He did not, he insisted, take up the role through

any presumption of myself … but only of the due and humble obedience that I ought to do unto the king, our most dread and sovereign lord, and to you the peerage of this land, in whom by the occasion and the infirmity of our said sovereign lord rests the exercise of his authority, whose noble commandments I am as ready to perform and obey as any of his liege men alive.[26]

Terms and conditions were hammered out, taking as a template those that had applied to the duke of Gloucester's protectorate during Henry VI's minority, and the business of Parliament continued.

On 4 April, council met again and the duke of York's first act was to appoint Salisbury as chancellor, and the great seals of England were duly delivered to the Erber. Far from signalling an irrevocable switch to York's camp, Salisbury's appointment needs to be seen in context rather than in light of what came later. York required the approval of the council, not just his own supporters. He also needed those more closely connected to the king and his household or to the queen, as well as the sizeable group of neutral lords exemplified by Buckingham. Salisbury's loyalty to Henry VI had never been in question. His thirty years of council attendance, his military background, both in France and in the marches, and his legal experience stood him in good stead. Most importantly, he was not seen as a partisan of York, despite their connection through marriage. After all, Buckingham and Beaumont both shared similar ties and they conferred no particular closeness; in Northumberland's case, it conferred no closeness at all.[27]

York was not about to take the responsibility of governing England fully onto his shoulders and Salisbury's. Each lord was asked in turn by the new chancellor 'whether it was his will to take upon him the same name and charge of councillor'. 'So many pleaded that they were handicapped by illness that the naïve might be pardoned for concluding that a serious epidemic was raging among the lay peers of the realm.[28]

The duke of Norfolk, who only a few months earlier had burned with a fiery zeal to condemn Somerset, claimed

> he was that person that would, with all his heart, do all that was in him that might be to the king's pleasure and the will of his lords and subjects, and would not spare to do the service he could, and to give attendance and assistance as he should and ought do, without that infirmity with which he is many times vexed.[29]

The duke of Buckingham 'could not take upon him to attend daily and continually, specially for such sickness as he is at divers times visited with and that he may not at such times endure to ride'. If that meant the other lords felt he should be discharged as councillor, he was willing to live with that, he said. The lords, however, particularly York and Salisbury, were not about to discharge him. Buckingham remained on the council.[30]

The Archbishop of York 'would give such assistance as he could and reasonably so'. The Bishop of Winchester claimed that 'his conscience would not suffer him continually to attend but as he might reasonably, he would'. The Bishop of Worcester committed himself to be 'ruled as the lords would have him'. The Bishop of Norwich claimed that responsibilities in his diocese would not allow him to attend regularly. The Bishop of Lincoln asked that 'in certain times of the year he might be spared especially in Lent and Advent'. The Bishop of Chester would do as the other bishops had said they would.[31]

As for the other lords temporal, Warwick rather disingenuously protested that he was 'young of age and younger of discretion and wisdom so that he was unable to [attend] that occupation. Notwithstanding, he would, with right goodwill, do that which was in his power.' The earl of Oxford would do whatever he could 'as far as his sickness would suffer him with which, as he said, he was many times full vexed with'. The earl of Shrewsbury was 'ready to do his part as other men did'.[32]

The earl of Worcester and Treasurer of England John Tiptoft, who had once been married to Salisbury's daughter Cecily, cut through a lot of the lords' anxieties.

> It was thought to him necessary and full expedient to all the lords that should take upon them the said charge to have knowledge of the execution of their power and find means how such charges as rest upon the king should now

be borne. Also, in which ways the lords of the council should be contented of their duty and, as for himself, he would be ready to do such service to the king as he could.[33]

Viscount Bourchier, married to York's sister, and probably counted on to be of immediate and unhesitating support, wavered a little but finally declared himself ready to serve. The Prior of St John's was anxious to know what serving on the council would involve and declared the commons should make it clear just what was required of them. Lord Cromwell also had concerns, 'alleging the great age he is of, his infirmity and feebleness, desired as he might be excused'. When the assembled lords urged him to 'use his great laud and merit, he granted to take it upon him and do his part as far as his said age, sickness and feebleness would suffer him'. Twice before assaulted and fearing for the safety of his person, he asked that the safety of council members travelling between home and meetings be assured.[34]

Lord Scales vacillated as well as anyone, claiming 'uncunning and inexperience', but finally agreed he would do his best, so long as he was not to be expected to attend every meeting nor be held to account for any remuneration he might receive.[35]

Viscount Beaumont, married to Salisbury's sister Katherine and a member of the queen's household, needed some persuasion. He particularly asked that it be

> remembered that he was with the queen, for the which he would not depart in taking upon him this charge; he said also it was contained in the articles of the council that every man should have full freedom to say what he thought in matters as of councils, without any displeasure, indignation or wroth of any other person for his saying the which he would, should be kept observed; he also said he had far to come to council and therefor would take upon him not to come at all times but at such times as he goodly might, and said his poverty and little discretion constrains him to desire his excuse; notwithstanding, since the lords willed him, he would perform their will and to do [his] part with the others.[36]

Margaret of Anjou, mother of the Prince of Wales and wife of an ailing king, having tried and failed to put forward her own claim for the regency, was to be fully – and openly – represented in York's council. Lord Stanley, whose son Thomas was later that year to marry Salisbury's daughter Alianor, had no illusions about his value to council: 'he knew well he was named to the charge only to do such errands as the lords would lay upon him.' John Say, council's official messenger, 'said the same'. Lastly, the Dean of St Severin's told them that 'he was poor, the which made a man to be reputed no great wisdom, yet he would do such service as he could with right good will'.[37]

A small but representative council was established and could now get on with the business of government. For York and Salisbury, it must have felt like drawing blood from a stone. York himself took the captaincy of Calais left vacant by the arrest and imprisonment of Somerset. This was not the easiest of positions to take on. Calais might be a possession of the English crown but the merchants of the wool staple and the permanent garrison were not always easy to deal with. Somerset had had little success and York struggled to achieve an understanding with either the staple or the garrison.[38]

Events in the north of England, however, swiftly overtook other considerations. The duke of Exeter, as reported by John Stodeley in his newsletter: 'has been at Tuxford beside Doncaster, in the north country, and there the lord Egremont met him and the two be sworn together'.[39]

Now they were stirring trouble in Lancashire and Yorkshire. With only Thomas and John Nevill to counter them, urgent action needed to be taken. Accompanied by Cromwell, who had his own quarrel with Exeter to resolve, the duke of York rode out of London to confront the rebels and bring them to heel.

# 11

# A TIME FOR WOMEN

In the last week of November 1453 there came a day when the noblemen of England set aside their discussions of great matters of state and made their way with their wives and daughters to Westminster Palace. All were dressed in their finery, robes of office and estate, elaborate hats and beautiful gowns. Women had travelled from as far as Yorkshire on wintry roads; furs and jewels, gowns of silk and cloth of gold kept safely locked in stout coffers, well guarded by armed escorts. In London, houses that had been the domains of men, where they gathered to discuss the coming day's events, to gather allies and identify their enemies, rang with the voices of women. Great barges made their slow and solemn way along the Thames to Westminster. Crowds gathered to watch them pass.

On a curtained bed in the middle of the great chamber, Queen Margaret, dressed in scarlet and sable, waited to be ceremoniously brought back into the world after the birth of her son some six weeks earlier. Two duchesses drew back the curtain, and their husbands extended their hands, lifted the queen from her bed and set her feet upon the floor. A lit candelabra was put into her hand and a long day of celebration and ceremony began.[1]

Queen Margaret had last been seen in public on 10 September when, again with much ceremony, a barge took her down the river to Westminster to await the birth of her child. The mayor and aldermen, dressed in crimson robes, witnessed her journey. London and all of England waited anxiously for happy news.[2]

This came at last on 13 October, more than eight years after Margaret married her king and shortly after he fell into his strange illness. Bells rang and the good news was carried to the city and beyond. England, and Margaret, had waited a long time for this. Her joy at safely giving birth to a healthy boy must have been tinged with sorrow, fear and deep concern for the well-being of her husband. When Henry had received the news of Margaret's pregnancy earlier in the year, he greeted it with great joy, rewarding the courtier who brought it with a lifetime annuity of £40.[3]

The birth of a child was a time for women. Had Henry been in good health and of sound mind, he would likely have received word of his queen's confinement and the subsequent birth while at Windsor. It would have brought him great happiness, not just for himself but for his kingdom. It is often said, rather dismissively, that a medieval queen's only job was to produce an heir. While a king had other responsibilities, none was more crucial than the one he shared with his queen. A king with living legitimate brothers might have a little breathing space, but royal brothers did not always make the most promising heirs presumptive. The pressures on a king were only less intense than those on his queen because they were masked by other responsibilities.

Finding a suitable queen was only the start. The king also had to make sure he visited her bedchamber as often as he could. Henry VI's reputation as a pious and prudish man may have made this more difficult for him than for other kings but – at long last – he and Margaret had fulfilled their most pressing duty. He should have been awaiting the news but was not. Possibly the saddest outcome of his illness was his inability to share his kingdom's celebrations and bask in the glow of a job well done.

In a letter to the queen, Cecily, duchess of York gave extravagant expression of her own joy and that of England at the news of Margaret's pregnancy: 'that blessed lady to whom abounds plenteously mercy and grace, by whose mediation it please our lord to fulfil your right honourable body of the most precious, most joyful and most comfortable treasure that might come to this land and the people thereof'.[4]

Now this treasure was born, feted and fussed over, baptised with great ceremony and wrapped up tight in swaddling, away from the long and arduous ceremonies his mother must endure and enjoy.

From the point of view of the Church, and probably of contemporary men, a churching was a time of cleansing. For women, it was a time for celebrating the survival of both mother and child or, if the outcome was grim, of quiet sorrow and silent solidarity. For Margaret, it was a triumph. The succession of England was, for the time being at least, secure. There was time enough to worry about childhood illness and the almost surely fatal results of infection. For today, she need only think about getting through the mass, the feasting and the dancing.

Margaret had come to England in 1445, a 16-year-old bride, dowerless and ill. The daughter of René, count of Anjou and Isabella of Lorraine, she had been largely brought up by her grandmother, Yolande of Aragon. With her son away from home a good deal, Yolande frequently served as regent. Count René's court was cultured and literate and Margaret grew up well educated and independent of mind.[5]

In 1442, count René turned his attention to arranging marriages for his children. Two years later, Suffolk arrived from England with an embassy to negotiate a match between Margaret and Henry VI. The betrothal took place on 24 May, with Suffolk standing proxy for the king. In November, the marriage treaty was finalised. Suffolk may have committed England to the surrender of Maine on Henry VI's behalf, but the details are not entirely clear. In spring 1445, Margaret travelled to Rouen with the duke and duchess of Suffolk. There was a great celebration to welcome her but Margaret was too ill to appreciate it fully. She enjoyed both the hospitality and friendship of the duke of York, then Henry VI's Lieutenant of Normandy, and stayed in Rouen for some time, arriving in England on 9 April, still quite unwell. Margaret and Henry were married on 22 April at Lichfield Abbey. Six days later, she enjoyed a state entry into London, and was crowned queen two days after that.[6]

The surrender of Maine, captured by Bedford in 1425 and occupied by the English ever since, was closely connected to the fall of both Suffolk and the king's uncle, Humphrey, duke of Gloucester. It was also, in later years, the cause of some hostility towards the queen herself.[7]

Margaret knew well the vulnerability of women, even those married to men of power and status. The death the previous year of the imprisoned duchess of Gloucester, found guilty of witchcraft and sorcery, her husband powerless to help her, was an object lesson in the limits of a noblewoman's power and independence. Desperate to provide her husband with a legitimate heir, Eleanor Cobham had stepped outside the bounds placed on her by church and state by consulting astrologers and purchasing love potions from the Witch of Eye. Ruin, imprisonment and the deaths of her co-conspirators had been swift. That those who accused the duchess of Gloucester were at least as interested in bringing about her husband's fall as her own was little consolation. At the time of her downfall, the duchess had been married to England's heir presumptive. Speculation and hopes for a glittering future led her into folly.[8]

Gloucester struggled to regain his place as Henry VI's trusted councillor, opposed at every turn by men of power and ambition. The death of Suffolk provided an opportunity for his rehabilitation but the spectre of his duchess was never far away. It did not take much to convince Henry that his uncle was plotting to take his throne. Gloucester was arrested in 1447 and died before he could face his accusers and answer the charges against him. As he was likely to have counselled Henry quite firmly against keeping his word to René of Anjou and surrendering Maine, this may have been the reason for his downfall.[9]

Henry VI was determined to keep his promise and both he and Margaret sent letters to Charles VII of France assuring him that Maine's transfer would come to pass. Henry wanted his French uncle's support and goodwill. Margaret has been accused, at the time and since, of putting undue pressure on Henry to surrender Maine. Certainly, it was in the interests of her family but Henry was at least as determined to see it done as she was. It was not universally opposed in king's council though, in later years, it was used as an example of his weakness and Margaret's willingness to step outside the bounds of queenship and the 'natural' role of women.[10]

One person who did oppose the surrender – or would have, had he a voice in council and were Henry prepared to listen to him – was the duke of York. While this does not seem to have led to ill feeling between him and Margaret at the time, it would take on great significance as time went on.

York and his duchess had welcomed Margaret most warmly in Rouen as she made her way to England and her wedding. Years later, duchess Cecily certainly felt she had a strong enough relationship with the queen to write to her, asking her to intercede with the king on behalf of her lord and husband, 'whose infinite sorrow, unrest of heart and of worldly comfort, caused of that that he hears him to be estranged from the grace and benevolent favour of that most Christian, most gracious and most merciful prince, the king our sovereign lord'. This was the same letter in which Cecily expressed her joy, and England's, at news of Margaret's pregnancy. This joy may well have been unfeigned, reflecting relief that the matter of the succession was now settled and one potential cause of danger removed from her husband's life. York's eagerness in 1450 and 1451 to be named Henry's heir presumptive could have been seen by Margaret as a comment on her failure to produce an heir and an assumption of barrenness.[11]

The young Prince Edward was baptised the day after his birth, 'at Westminster and his godfathers were the cardinal archbishop of Canterbury, chancellor Kemp, and the duke of Somerset and his god-mother, duchess of Buckingham. Of his birth the people spoke strangely.' The chronicler does not expand on the 'strange' talk and some have taken the reference to mean the general citizenry had doubts, even then, about the prince's paternity. This is unlikely, as rumours of Margaret's adultery are closely associated with later efforts to set aside the succession in favour of York and his sons. In 1453 there was no incentive to call Margaret's reputation into question. Far more likely is that this talk related to concerns for the infant's future. Here was the son of a king rendered impotent and silent by an illness no one understood.[12]

The ship of state was rudderless. It might be thought that Somerset would simply step into the breach until the king recovered. His arrest and imprisonment in the Tower, perhaps just days before Queen Margaret's churching, put paid to that possibility. As one of prince Edward's godfathers and a good friend to the queen, his absence on this special day must have caused her grief. But there was a far more frightening question than who was to govern England. *Until the king recovered…* What if the king never recovered?

Henry's grandfather, the similarly afflicted Charles VI of France, had lived for twenty-nine long years after his first bouts of psychosis. During that time his kingdom had been wracked with strife. It was only after the accession of his son Charles VII that things settled down. England had experienced strife and war enough with a healthy king at the helm. Could her people wait until the young prince was of an age to rule in his own name before lasting stability could be established?

The king's two closest kinsmen, the dukes of York and Exeter, could each be counted on to step in, but they could not work together. The queen thought to offer herself as regent, which might have been fine in Anjou or France, but England was not ready to hand such power and responsibility to a woman, and a French woman at that. Not even the most prominent members of her household, such as Viscount Beaumont, were prepared to support her bid. York was the sensible choice and the sensible choice was made. Margaret had other things to concern her, an ailing husband and an infant son. So long as her interests, and the prince's, were well represented, and so long as her household continued to be supported, there was nothing she could do but hope Henry would soon recover.

Her churching, a most splendid and solemn occasion, was a signal that life must go on. Whatever ailed the king, he had a son who would one day succeed him. The queen spared little expense, ordering a gown of 20 yards of russet cloth of gold trimmed with more than 500 sable backs. Margaret was not about to hide. The king might be shut away but his son's birth would be celebrated in the full light of day. Margaret would set herself as a symbol of dynastic continuity and regality.[13]

Choirs sang and maidens danced as Margaret walked from Westminster Palace to the cathedral. Behind her, ranked in order of precedence, came the nobility of England, dukes and duchesses, earls and countesses, lords and ladies. With a lighted candelabra in her hand, and the duchess of York behind her carrying Prince Edward's chrisom gown, Margaret walked to the great doors of the cathedral where the Cardinal Archbishop of Canterbury awaited her. Here she was blessed and sprinkled with holy water before being led inside.[14]

A celebration of the mass followed, with Margaret offering up the candelabra she carried and the duchess of York the gown. Gathered inside the cathedral were the great and good of England, hostilities and enmities postponed for the occasion. Many had a direct connection to the Nevills, through blood or marriage. The countess of Salisbury, her oldest daughter Joan and daughters-in-law Anne and Maud; four of Salisbury's sisters and the wives of two of his brothers; the countess of Warwick's half-sisters; the married daughters of the duchess of York and countess of Shrewsbury; and Alice Chaucer, once the countess of Salisbury's stepmother, whose son was to marry the daughter of the duchess of York. Of those who were not in attendance, Alice, lady Fitzhugh was either preparing for or recovering from the birth of a child and lady Fauconberg may not have been well enough to travel.[15]

Some of these women would have been delighted at the chance to spend time together; others may have exchanged tense but polite greetings and moved on. Men who refused to attend king's council headed by York, such as Northumberland and York's son-in-law Exeter, dared not excuse themselves from the queen's churching without good cause. This occasion, though none in attendance could have known, would mark the last time for many years to come that so many of England's nobles were gathered together in one place on an occasion of peace. So many of the men would lose their lives during the conflicts to come; so many of the women would be widowed.

When the mass concluded, Margaret stepped out of the cathedral and back into the world. The procession reformed and snaked its way back to Westminster Hall, where a feast awaited. The men departed and the women knelt in silence as the queen ate, moving only to attend to those tasks assigned to them – bringing her a cup of wine and taking it away when it was empty, carving meat, holding a towel for her to dry her hands. When the queen's feast was done, the men returned and there was dancing. Without her husband to take her hand, Margaret would have danced with dukes, their wives looking on, exhausted and hungry after their long day.[16]

The following day, life would return to normal, as far as it could under the circumstances. The men would go to the council chamber, or gather their families for the journey home. Many of the women made their way to their estates, though some stayed in London to spend Christmas with their husbands. Two women were without their husbands: Queen Margaret and the duchess of Somerset. The first could do little but hope her lord and king would recover from his illness; the second could do little but hope hers would survive the duke of York's protectorate.

# 12

# A Reckoning
# in the North

enry Holland, the young duke of Exeter and York's son-in-law, was not pleased with the way his life was turning out. A prince of the blood royal, he considered himself a better candidate for Protector of England than York. Already hereditary admiral and keeper of the seas, this descendant of Edward III, essentially landless and with little income, had a strong sense of his own status and worth. While his status was not in dispute, others' assessment of his worth did not necessarily match his own.[1]

Exeter's grandmother was a sister of Henry IV and he carried his royal connection with understandable pride. Shortly before his death, Exeter's father John, as chronically short of funds as his son would be throughout his life, negotiated a marriage between 15-year-old Henry and Anne, oldest daughter of the duke of York. A substantial dowry of 4,500 marks was promised, but John Holland died before the payments were finalised. Ordinarily, Exeter might have expected the balance of the dowry to come to him, but his father had died so deep in debt that most of it was used to settle his accounts. Exeter got nothing from the marriage but a 6-year-old bride he resented and continued to resent for as long as their marriage lasted. On his father's death, Exeter was placed in the wardship of his father-in-law and accompanied the family to Ireland, which did nothing to endear him to either York or Anne.[2]

On paper, this was in many ways a good match. In dynastic terms, both were of royal blood, and a young man of Exeter's energy and vigour should have made an excellent ally for York. However, Exeter's resentment at his less than satisfactory financial position could not be eased by marriage to a duke's daughter. If his interests had been paramount, rather than York's, a bride might have been sought among the ranks of wealthy heiresses. Exeter's greatest problem was his lack of land from which he might derive an income. Though he inherited five manors in Northamptonshire from a distant relative in 1451, his income came mainly from shipping and trade. Most of the estates he might have expected to inherit from his father were lost when Gascony and Normandy fell to the French.[3]

Already in dispute with Cromwell over the manor of Ampthill, Exeter now risked everything and launched open rebellion against York's protectorate. Disaffected and ambitious, possibly beyond his abilities, he joined forces with Egremont, coming to an agreement in the house of lady Willoughby's mother at Tuxford in Nottinghamshire. Whether lady Stanhope was actively involved in the plotting, or her house was just a convenient place to meet, is not at all clear. Certainly, it would be peculiar if she was involved, as she was Cromwell's sister. Still, as is already abundantly clear, blood kinship was no guarantee of support and alliance. The involvement of her mother, or at least this meeting taking place at her mother's house, may have caused some friction between lady Willoughby and her new husband's family. While wives were presumed to support their husbands in every way, including politically, Maud's personal views are not known to us.

The first documented action of the rebellion occurred on 6 May, when a group of Percy associates broke into Salisbury's house in York and attacked one of his tenants. Council sent letters to various people in the north of England urging them to resist the rebels and ordering those who had given them aid and assistance to cease. That same month, York left London to deal with matters himself.[4]

> For as much as we be informed that the lord Egremont, accompanied by other of like disposition as he is … has now late made and daily makes great assemblies of our liege people in the country about you and other places there and, over that, of his own presumption without any authority or power from us, makes divers and strange proclamations to stir our true subjects into rebellion and breaking of our laws and peace.[5]

Lord Clifford, not known for his friendship with the Nevills or York, was urged to give the Protector all the 'assistance, help and aid' as was in his power. Council's faith in Clifford to stand firm against his erstwhile friends and allies was not misplaced. Though it was a short-term alliance, Clifford did what was asked of him. Similar letters were sent to the mayors and citizens of York and Hull.[6]

Along the way, York also wrote to his son-in-law Exeter with 'fatherly and cousinly affection'.

> I, having consideration in the nighness wherein we be knit together in nature and alliance, which of reason must drive and steer and so drives and steers me

to will and to desire of the good zeal and tender affection that God knows I have borne and bear to you and your honour, worship and prosperity, advertised, moved and exhorted you to lay apart and forbear the insolent rule and misgovernance which has been by you used, and to drive from your fellowship such persons approved of riots and unrestful conversation as of their conditions and importunes, motions and provocations have been and be, as it is deemed, causers and occasioners of your insolence.[7]

Whether York expected Exeter to abandon his plans on receipt of the letter is open to question, as is York's intent in writing and sending it. A clue might lie in the last few lines.

I will open and show unto the king and his council, and make to be open and showed to all this land to the intent that, whatsoever happen hereafterward through the continuance of the said misrule, it shall be verily known what diligence I have done and in what manner to reconcile it to such worshipful, substantial and lawful governance that you owe to us as a prince of this land, and to put your humble obedience to our said sovereign lord and his laws.[8]

York was painfully aware of the difficulties he faced. Suffolk, Gloucester and Somerset had shown how quickly and easily a man could fall from power to imprisonment or even death. His protestations of loyalty to his king no doubt had a ring of sincerity to them, but he had a healthy sense of his own self-worth and his rightful place in the world. Right now, on his way to York to deal with feud and rebellion, he was in his element, though aware that he must tread carefully to avoid any suspicions that he wished to usurp the authority of others. At this point in York's career, he had no designs on the throne itself.

With him on this journey was lord Cromwell, who had his own reasons for wanting Exeter brought to book. With his niece married to Thomas Nevill, he could look forward to the support of a strong and influential family. The Nevills had hitched their star to York's wagon and Cromwell hitched his to the Nevills. Cromwell was an experienced soldier, having served in France under the command of Henry IV's brother Thomas, duke of Clarence. He was at Harfleur with Bedford and at Agincourt with Henry V. In 1420, he participated in the talks that led to the Treaty of Troyes and, the following year, was appointed Captain of Harfleur. After Henry V's death, he had served on the council that governed England on behalf of the infant King Henry VI and attended his coronation in Paris. In 1433, Cromwell was appointed Treasurer. England's finances were in a mess, expenditure far exceeding income. Cromwell's attempts to remedy the situation were ultimately unsuccessful, but he remained in the post for the next ten years.[9]

Cromwell became one of England's richest barons through the luck of inheritance and good personal financial management. Though he urged England's nobles to forgive their debts to the crown in order to get finances back on track, he was not so forgiving of debts owed him. The dowry for his niece Maud's first marriage to Robert, lord Willoughby took the form of the cancellation of a debt and, in the year after her second marriage to Thomas Nevill, he sent her an account for moneys expended on her behalf while a guest at Tattershall Castle.[10]

With his experience as a soldier, diplomat, politician and businessman, Cromwell should have spent his later years in comfort and ease. However, a significant event in 1449, and ongoing trouble with Exeter, shook his confidence and equilibrium to the point where he largely withdrew from public life. The nephew of his estate agent, William Tailboys, was a man with a bad reputation who had accusations of extortion and murder against his name. Cromwell, along with lord Willloughby and Willoughby's son-in-law lord Welles, attempted to bring him to justice but no case was ever brought. Tailboys, it would seem, was under the protection of Suffolk, then the most powerful lord in England. Tailboys ambushed Cromwell as he was leaving the council chamber at Westminster and assaulted him with a small band of like-minded men, perhaps hoping this would end his troubles with the law. He was unsuccessful in his attempt to kill his neighbour and enemy, and was arrested. Cromwell escaped unhurt but shaken. He suspected Suffolk was behind Tailboys's actions and managed to have accusations to this effect inserted into the articles of impeachment brought by the commons against Suffolk.[11]

Imprisonment did not end Tailboys's vendetta against Cromwell and he made two further attempts: another failed ambush and a plot to blow up the house next to Cromwell's London lodgings so he could be quietly murdered while everyone's attention was on putting out the fire. The man who confessed to this, Tailboys's chaplain, very sensibly failed to put the plan into action, despite being given a bag of gunpowder.[12]

Even then, Tailboys was not quite finished. He made accusations of treason against Cromwell that saw him suspended from council and investigated. Nothing came of this but Cromwell's influence was over. He remained chamberlain of the exchequer and was reinstated to council but no longer enjoyed the prominence and authority he once had.[13]

When York became Protector of England in May 1454 and brought the Nevills with him into a new sphere of influence, Cromwell was ready to join them. It was clear from his concerns in council that he still feared for his personal safety, be it at the hands of Tailboys and his associates or Exeter. He accompanied the Protector to York, there to sit in judgement over the rebels as they were rounded up. The principals, Exeter and Egremont, took flight from the city just before the Protector's party arrived on 13 May.[14]

The rebellion was no trivial matter. The city of York was in turmoil, trouble spilling into the surrounding countryside. Nevill properties, tenants and associates were quite deliberately targeted. Egremont was at Spofforth, gathering his men. On or about 21 May, Exeter joined him, raising his standard and handing out livery in the name of the duke of Lancaster.[15]

Sir Thomas Stanley and lord Bonville were sent into Lancashire to subdue those who would rise in Exeter's name. Stanley, a loyal servant of council, was doing no more than his expected duty. Bonville, who was embroiled in his own feud with the earl of Devon, had turned to York for support just as Devon was turning away.[16]

Establishing himself in York Castle, England's new Protector heard the grievances of the citizens, including mayor Nelson and recorder Roucliffe, who had been set upon by Egremont's men and severely beaten after seeking shelter in York Minster. On 23 May, there was a half-baked plot to lure York out of the city and assassinate him. Just what this was supposed to achieve, beyond York's death, is not immediately clear. Such an act would surely have resulted in a swift and possibly fatal response, even from those who had stood aloof from a York-led council.[17]

Despite his high profile, Exeter was not the driving force behind the rebellion and contributed few men. Those who were with him, including his illegitimate brothers Robert and William, were drawn from a close circle of associates. It is difficult to understand just why Exeter involved himself in what was, essentially, a local Yorkshire feud. He had no great following among the nobility. If he had succeeded in his plan to assassinate his father-in-law, it is highly unlikely he would have been welcomed as a member of king's council, let alone invited to lead it. As it was, there was little chance the rebellion would succeed. Even with Egremont's size-able and largely conscienceless following, they were no match for York's more organised forces. Egremont had no property that might be forfeit should he be called to account for his actions, unlike his father and older brother, who took no part in the rebellion. Even staunch Percy allies, such as Clifford, were working against them, and the rebellion quickly fell apart. By 15 June, when the first accusations against the rioters were heard in York Castle, it had collapsed altogether and Exeter was on his way to London. Abandoned by their ally, Egremont and his younger brothers were left to their fate.[18]

Among those who sat in judgement were the earl of Warwick, who had travelled from London, his brother-in-law Henry Fitzhugh, *his* brother-in-law Ralph, lord Greystoke and lord Clifford. Many of the accused were pardoned though some were arraigned to appear later before king's bench. Most were treated leniently, as the aim of the Protector's mission in York was to establish peace in the county rather than exact retribution or administer punishment. While the hearings were going on, York returned to London to deal with his recalcitrant son-in-law.[19]

Exeter took an enormous risk returning to London. He may have hoped to find support and shelter, even to set his case before council and defend his actions. If he expected to keep his presence in the capital a secret, he failed miserably. As John Paston noted in a letter home: 'It is said the duke of Exeter is here covertly. God send him good counsel hereafter.' Once in the city, Exeter and his half-brother Robert took sanctuary at Westminster, from which he was forcibly removed by York. He was then sent north to Pontefract Castle and the custody of the earl of Salisbury. That left the Percies to be found and dealt with and York, almost immediately, returned to the north.[20]

In September and October, Egremont was at Spofforth with his brothers Henry lord Poynings and Richard. The manor was fortified 'for the safe-keeping and defence of the township and lordship at the time of the quarrel between the lord and the earl of Salisbury'. As the living expenses at Spofforth were considerable, some £50, it would seem there was a considerable number of Egremont's men there at this time. Meanwhile, Salisbury visited his estates, taking with him some chancery clerks and the great seal, ensuring the business of government was not interrupted. York joined him at Middleham Castle some time in August.[21]

The opportunity to take Egremont and his brothers came in November. They were at Pocklington, some 17 miles east of York. They had with them the bailiff of Pocklington and around 200 of his men. At Stamford Bridge, a Nevill property on the road to York, they were intercepted by two of Salisbury's sons, who had with them a fair sized force and a band of poorly armed tenants. 'This year on All Hallows Eve, the lord Egremont was taken by sir Thomas Nevill and sir John Nevill, knights, by great battle in the north country where were many men slain.' Despite this rather dramatic reporting, only one man is known to have been killed. Egremont was taken first to Middleham then to York, where he was 'condemned in a great sum of money to the said earl of Salisbury and therefore committed to prison in Newgate in London'.[22]

Egremont was in fact ordered to pay a total of £16,800 in restitution to members of the Nevill family for his attack at Heworth the previous year. His imprisonment in Newgate was the result of his inability to pay this exorbitant sum. Even then, this was insufficient to subdue him: 'when he had been a certain space, he broke the prison, three prisoners with him, and escaped and went his way.'[23]

Thomas and John Nevill had, at long last, triumphed over their cousin and bitter enemy. They had been tracking the Percies for months, ever since their uncle York had arrived from London. Years of abuse and violence, not always one-sided, had come to an end. With the younger Percies neutralised, and their father and older brother keeping a low profile, the Nevills were kings of the north.

The following month, Alianor Nevill married Thomas Stanley, son of the Sir Thomas Stanley commissioned by York to ensure peace in Lancashire during the short-lived rebellion. Alianor was the Salisburys' fourth daughter and probably around 16 at the time of her marriage. Little is known about her beyond that she had something of a forceful personality, which is a trait she shared with her mother and most, if not all, of her sisters. Alianor died some time before 1472, thirty years before her husband. Depending on the source, they had anything between nine and thirteen children, though only three sons survived to adulthood. She must have made a good impression on her husband for he requested to be buried alongside her, despite his second marriage to Margaret Beaufort.[24]

York's protectorate was short-lived but eventful. He had neutralised the powerful enemy he shared with his nephew Warwick. With the support of the Nevills, Cromwell, Stanley and, more surprisingly, Clifford, he had dealt with the half-baked rebellion led by Exeter and Egremont. This had also served to bring an end, for the time being at least, the Nevill–Percy feud. In lord Bonville, York found himself both a new ally and a new client. Bonville lent his support to York in subduing Exeter and the Percies in return for York's future help to quell the Courtenay–Bonville feud in the West Country. If this was York's next planned move, events were soon to overtake him.

Early in 1455, Henry VI recovered his senses as suddenly as he had lost them more than a year before. He greeted his infant son Edward with great delight and set about taking up once more the reins of kingship. York was thanked for his service as Protector and courteously dismissed. Salisbury found himself in an impossible position, ordered to release Exeter from imprisonment in Pontefract Castle. This, in all conscience, he could not do, and he was compelled to resign the chancellorship. The fall of the York–Nevill alliance was swift and there were real fears it would prove fatal, particularly when one of Henry VI's first acts was to order the release and rehabilitation of the duke of Somerset.[25]

# 13

# 'LOYAL LIEGEMEN'

hen Henry VI recovered his senses in the New Year of 1455, he found the world changed. He had a son, Prince Edward. Two of his closest kinsmen, one a trusted friend and councillor, were imprisoned. Chancellor Kemp was dead, replaced by the earl of Salisbury, and the duke of York sat at the head of king's council, protector and defender of England.

> And on the Monday afternoon, the queen came to him and brought my lord prince with her. And when he asked what the prince's name was, and the queen told him Edward; and then he held up his hands and thanked God thereof. And he said he never knew till that time, nor knew what was said to him, nor knew not where he had been while he had been sick until now. And he asked who was godfathers, and the queen told him, and he was well pleased.[1]

As always, and as he would until forced to understand this approach would get him nowhere, Henry wished for peace among his lords. 'And he said he is in charity with the world and so he would all the lords were.'[2]

That they were not, and had not been during his illness, was abundantly clear. Queen Margaret, or his twelfth night visitors, Bishop Waynflete of Winchester and the Prior of St Johns, must have told him what had taken place over the last year. All were delighted and relieved to see him returned to his senses. The two clergymen were reported to have 'wept for joy' when they left his chamber.[3]

When his council next met, the king's immediate concern was securing the freedom of Somerset and Exeter. Somerset was released on bail on 4 February, though it is possible his physical release was arranged some days earlier in anticipation of council's decision: 'the 26th day of January the duke of Somerset was strangely conveyed out of the Tower by the duke of Buckingham, earl Wiltshire and lord Roos.'[4]

Somerset's chief accuser, Norfolk, did not attend the council meeting and York, who had failed to prosecute Somerset for over a year, could do nothing to prevent his release. Bail was set to expire on 3 November, by which time Somerset would be required to answer the charges against him. In the event, even this was overturned by the king who overthrew all charges against Somerset at a meeting of great council on 4 March, reinstating him as his most trusted councillor.[5]

York could not have expected his protectorate to be permanent but he had as little warning of its end as he had of its beginning. With the king fully recovered, he had no option but to resign. Though the precise date is not recorded, some time after the release of Somerset, he 'gave up the king's sword and no longer would occupy protector'. With regard to their personal enmity, Somerset and York were bound over to the sum of 20,000 marks each 'to abide the decision of Thomas archbishop of Canterbury, William bishop of Ely, Humphrey duke of Buckingham and five others, as to the differences against them'.[6]

On 3 February, King Henry ordered Exeter released. Initially, Salisbury, as chancellor and constable of Pontefract Castle, simply ignored the order. Unable to continue disregarding Henry's wishes, and unable, in all conscience, to comply with them, Salisbury was removed from his post.[7]

Memorandum that on Friday 9 March, 33 Henry VI, between the eleventh and twelfth hour at Greenwich in a small chapel above the gate, in the presence of the king, Thomas archbishop of Canterbury, William bishop of Carlisle, Humphrey duke of Buckingham, Henry earl of Northumberland, James earl of Wiltshire, John viscount Beaumont, Henry viscount Bourchier, Thomas Clifford [and several others named, including the keeper of the chancery rolls and a chancery clerk] and other notable persons, Richard earl of Salisbury, the chancellor, laid upon a stool before the king one great seal of silver in a black leathern bag and two others, one of gold and one of silver severally in two bags of white leather, all previously in the said chancellor's keeping under his seal.[8]

Half an hour later, the seals were examined and delivered to the Archbishop of Canterbury. Salisbury's short tenure as chancellor was over. Under threat of an exorbitant fine if he refused, the Archbishop of Canterbury ordered Exeter's release.[9]

Exeter was not rehabilitated or taken immediately into the king's confidence, but Somerset slipped seamlessly into his former role. After a year in the Tower without the opportunity to answer the charges laid against him, bond or no bond, Somerset could not be expected to be positively disposed towards York or his Nevill allies. With York out of power as swiftly, and as decisively, as he had gained it a year earlier, Somerset's newly re-established authority, and easy access to the king, made him a dangerous enemy. York left London for Sandal Castle; Salisbury and Warwick for their own estates, evidently without taking their leave or seeking the king's permission to do so.[10]

Great council was summoned to Leicester for 21 May. Henry had not given up hope his quarrelling lords could be reconciled. He failed to understand that the difficulties between York and Somerset, and between Warwick and Somerset, went a little deeper than merely 'personal'. Later Yorkist propaganda claimed this meeting was called to accuse York and the Nevills of treason, and that Somerset was the driving force behind it. Whatever the purpose, York and his allies immediately set about gathering their armies, rapidly and in secret.[11]

Salisbury and Warwick were in a difficult position. For years, nothing had been done to quell the troublesome young Percies beyond the sending of letters, bearing varying levels of threat, and the establishment of commissions of enquiry. Within months of York taking power, the threat from that quarter was all but eliminated. Neither Northumberland nor his heir Poynings showed any inclination to carry on the feud now Egremont and Richard Percy were in prison. There was still ill feeling between Salisbury and Northumberland. It must have been galling for Salisbury to have his resignation as chancellor witnessed by two members of the Percy family, but there was no immediate threat of a renewal of hostilities. In that regard, the alliance with York had done its job. The failure to permanently remove Somerset from the king's side had failed, which may have caused Warwick to fear further attempts by Somerset to get his hands on part of the Beauchamp inheritance. Had either of the Nevill earls been hoping to distance themselves from York, it was no longer possible. They were too closely linked, and any risk York might face charges of treason when the council met at Leicester must be shared by the Nevills. They had no choice but to continue the alliance; simply withdrawing from political life was not, at this point, an option.[12]

Salisbury looked to the men who served him in the marches, some of them for decades. Some would continue to serve him in the difficult times to come. Principal among these were Sir Robert Ogle, Sir James Pickering and the Conyers, father and son. Though there is no clear record of either Thomas or John Nevill accompanying their father south in May 1455, it would seem strange if both remained at Middleham. A later reference to John advising York to remove one of his estate stewards on the grounds that he 'refused to assist the duke's rebellion in the journey to St Albans' and to grant the stewardship instead to John Nevill and James Pickering would suggest that John, at least, was with his father. Pickering had been a close associate of John's in his dealings with the Percies during the height of the feud.[13]

Whatever concerns York, Salisbury and Warwick may have had about what awaited them in Leicester, Henry VI departed London with an entourage of lords that was not notably well defended. If the intention was to accuse York and his allies of treason, the king lacked the necessary military might to back it up, should the need arise. While it is possible the summons to council was a thinly disguised trap, it is also possible there was, in fact, no such plan. But perceptions count for a good deal and it is clear from letters signed by all three that York, Salisbury and Warwick had genuine concerns for their liberty and safety.

Though their preparations had been kept secret for some time, by 18 May Somerset knew something was afoot. The progress south of York and his allies seemed designed to prevent the king and his party from reaching Leicester. Somerset immediately dispatched a letter to the mayor and citizens of Coventry, requiring that 'you, accompanied with such fellowship as you goodly may in their best and most defensible array, to do us service, and such as you will answer for, will do our commandment and pleasure, and none otherwise fail not to be with us wheresoever we be, in all haste possible'. The letter, duly received, was discussed and the mayor and aldermen of Coventry took immediate action.[14]

> [H]aving tenderness of our sovereign lord the king as a very true liegeman ought, they ordained that a hundred good men, defensibly with bows and arrows, jacketed and saletted, should be made ready in all haste possible to go to our sovereign lord to Saint Albans, and to abide with him and to do him service such as it should please his highness to command them to do.[15]

As Somerset's letter was received on 22 May, events overtook the hundred good men of Coventry and they never left the town.[16]

Another contemporary report seems to have missed the significance of the king's journey to Leicester, putting responsibility for the decision to leave London squarely on Somerset's shoulders.

> When the duke of Somerset and those who were of his party then in the town of London heard that the duke of York and several other lords … were coming against him with a power of 5,000 men, and when he considered what he had done against the said duke of York and how also he was in very bad odour with the people of London, he came to the conclusion that he would not await them in the town of London.[17]

Henry's decision to leave the city for Leicester had, of course, already been taken and the news that York, Salisbury and Warwick were on their way south would have surprised no one. That their line of march was set to intercept the king's was a cause for caution, if not alarm.

On 21 May, Henry was at Watford; York, Salisbury and Warwick were at Ware, some 24 miles away. St Albans lay between them and there the king planned to stop to eat before moving on to Leicester. It was at this point, possibly as a conciliatory move or an attempt to reassure York of his peaceful intentions, that Henry VI replaced Somerset as Constable, appointing the duke of Buckingham in his stead.[18]

The decision to hold the council meeting in Leicester had been taken at an earlier, smaller meeting from which York, Salisbury and Warwick were excluded. Whatever was on the agenda at this meeting, their understanding was that the discussions at Leicester were to include the 'surety of [the king's] most noble person'. This, they claimed, implied 'a mistrust to some persons'. As they were the most notable of the lords to be excluded from that meeting, the conclusion drawn was that *they* were the ones mistrusted. They wished to clear their names.

> [F]or as much as we understand that other lords of this land have been late sent for, by the king's commandment under his letters, to come to his council privately called at Westminster, whereunto we have not been among the said lords called, we conceive a jealousy had against us, whereof we purpose with God's grace to declare us and show us such as we be in our troth, duty and allegiance to our said sovereign lord, indenting in all ways to remove the said jealousy which we will eschew to have lying dormant upon us.[19]

The 'petitions, requests, demands and other things' sent to the king via Salisbury's brother Fauconberg are lost to us. According to the sources we do have – two letters sent and received on 21 and 22 May and three accounts of the ensuing battle – York and his allies wanted three things: their loyalty to be recognised by the king; to be admitted to the king's presence and accompany him to Leicester; and for those who wished them, and the king, ill to be recognised and dealt with.[20]

The king sent letters under the great seal instructing York to reduce his escort to 200 men and for Salisbury and Warwick to reduce theirs to 160 each. These instructions were ignored, though the letter was not. The size of their armies could not be reduced, they feared, as this would leave them ill defended.[21]

> We also understand what colourable and subtle means be made by our enemies, holding them colourably about the said most noble person of our said sovereign lord, of might of men and habiliments of war have the more surely accompanied us, to the intent that at our coming to his most high presence, we must be of power to keep ourselves out of the danger whereunto our said enemies have not ceased to study, labour and compass to bring us.[22]

Neither side backing down or giving much ground, both moved steadily towards St Albans. On the night of 21 May, the combined armies of York, Salisbury and Warwick marched from Ware and took up position in Key Field, just east of the town. The king's journey the next morning was more leisurely, and it was with great surprise that he found York and his Nevill allies already there, 'within range of a crossbow'.[23]

Somerset opened the negotiations, sending Exeter's pursuivant, Lesparre, with the demand they 'quit at once and withdraw, on pain of their allegiance and breach of honour'. Not only was Somerset not authorised to negotiate, sending Exeter's herald was a calculated insult, an attempt to demoralise York and a reminder of his powerlessness now that his two prisoners were both free, one, at least, fully restored in the king's confidence. Lesparre was ignored and given no message to take back to Somerset.[24]

It was only when he was approached by Buckingham Herald, accompanied by Bonville's pursuivant, Joyeux, that York responded. Mowbray Herald conducted the negotiations on behalf of York and the Nevills, though his master Norfolk was nowhere to be seen. Apart from Buckingham Herald, the go-betweens at St Albans were officers of lords who were not themselves present. This was by no means unusual, for it signalled alliances that were broader than might, at first, be seen.[25]

Negotiations went on for several hours, Buckingham and Mowbray Heralds both making several trips to and from York's camp. York laid his cards on the table with regard to Somerset: 'Wherefor, gracious lord, please it your high Majesty to deliver such as we will accuse, and they to have like as they have deserved and done.'[26]

To this, Henry VI was reported to have responded with uncharacteristic vehemence. If the message was genuine, it was likely written by Buckingham or Somerset. It is also entirely possible it was written, or at least embellished, after the fact as part of the programme to exonerate York and lay the blame for the battle at the feet of others.

> I, king Harry, charge and command that no manner person, of what degree or state or condition that ever he be, abide not, but void the field, and not be so hardy to make any resistance against me in my own realm; for I shall know what traitor dare be so bold to raise a people in my own land, where through I am in great disease and heaviness. And by the faith that I owe to St Edward and to the Crown of England, I shall destroy them every mother's son, and they be hanged and drawn and quartered, that may be taken afterwards for them to have example to all such traitors to be aware to make any such rising of people within my land.[27]

Such extraordinary words, as it was later claimed, left York with no choice. When Mowbray Herald returned for the last time, refused access to Buckingham, he met York and his army on their way to the town.[28]

York's pre-battle speech is likely as fabricated after the fact as at least some of Henry VI's uncharacteristically belligerent message. He and the Nevills had done their best to make the king understand why they had 'come here and assembled forth and gathered at this time'.[29]

Now, York claimed,

> there is none other way but that he will with all his power pursue us and, if we be taken, to give us a shameful death, losing our livelihood and goods and our heirs shamed forever. And therefore, since it will be no other wise but that we shall utterly die, better it is for us to die in the field than cowardly be put to great rebuke and shameful death.[30]

When it came, the battle was short. York and Salisbury commanded those who sought to find a way through the town's defences. Clifford commanded the royal forces at the barricades and was killed in the thick of the fight. Warwick and his men, including 600 led by Sir Robert Ogle, were positioned at the back of a row of houses looking out on to St Peters Street. They saw a way into town through the gardens, and 'they and their people broke down violently houses and pales on the east side of the town and entered into St Peters Street slaying all those that withstood them'; 'and anon as they were within the town, suddenly they blew up trumpets and set a cry with a shout and a great voice "A Warwick! A Warwick! A Warwick!" and until that time the duke of York might never have entered into the town'.[31]

But enter the town he did, where he found the royal army ill-prepared and scrambling for arms and armour, the royal standard thrown down and abandoned. Henry VI had taken a slight arrow wound in his neck and sought refuge in the house of a tanner. With great courtesy and respect, York escorted the king to the abbey, where he might rest: 'and during the battle, the duke of York and the other lords had the king into the abbey and there kept him unhurt and there the king granted to be ruled by them'.[32]

Just who threw down the royal standard is disputed. One source has 'the lord Sudeley bearing the king's banner'; another states that it was the earl of Wiltshire who 'bore the king's banner that day … and set [it] against a house end and fought manfully with his heels'. A third says, 'Sir Phillip Wentworth was in the field and bare the king's standard, and cast it down and fled … He is in Suffolk now and dare not come about the king.'[33]

In the meantime, the battle continued. At some point, possibly deliberately targeted by Salisbury or his sons, Northumberland was killed. Somerset, having taken refuge in a house, came under attack. He came out fighting but was cut down. This was a welcome outcome for York, though he was not directly responsible, nor do any of the records suggest he ordered the killing.[34]

The death of Somerset signalled the end of the battle, though there was extensive looting, particularly on the part of Salisbury's northerners, 'and the substance of the king's party were despoiled of horse and harness'. William Percy, Bishop of Carlisle was 'stripped of jewels and horses so that, deserted by his household, he had to flee on foot'.[35]

Though the abbey offered safety to the king, it did little to shield others. When a group of men broke in, seeking to murder Buckingham and Wiltshire, York sent his herald to Henry, demanding that both be handed over to his custody if he did not want to see them killed before his eyes. Only Buckingham could be found. Wiltshire had already fled with 'many others', leaving 'their harness behind them cowardly'.[36]

In the abbey, York, Salisbury and Warwick knelt before the king and 'besought him of grace and forgiveness for what they had done in his presence'. Their intention had not been to fight, they said, and they certainly offered no threat to the person of the king. Henry ordered an end to the fighting. York relayed the order to his men and 'so ceased the … battle'.[37]

The following day, Norfolk, Cromwell and Sir Thomas Stanley arrived in St Albans. There is no record of the welcome they received from York but it is likely to have been somewhat frosty. Some time that day, or even the night before, a new government was formed, with York as Constable of England and Viscount Bourchier appointed Treasurer in place of the vanished Wiltshire. The Archbishop of Canterbury continued as chancellor. The earl of Warwick, a young man of just 25 years old with little experience but boundless confidence, was appointed Captain of Calais. 'And they brought the king the second day after to the city of London in great honour. And the said duke of York riding on his right side and the earl of Salisbury on the left side and the earl of Warwick bore his sword.[38]

Two men wounded at St Albans are worth mentioning here. Sir John Wenlock, who had been the queen's chamberlain and fought in the royal army, quickly came to terms with the new power in England and was elected speaker of the commons. This marked the start of a long association with York and a longer attachment to Warwick. Somerset's young son Henry was taken into Warwick's care and custody while he recovered from his wounds. He failed entirely, and understandably, to be reconciled to the new regime.[39]

Once Warwick found a way into the town, winning the battle had been easy. Now came the difficult part. There seems little question that, had their forces been defeated, the actions of York and the Nevills would have been viewed as treasonous. Prior to the battle, they had worked to establish their loyalty. Now they must work to establish their innocence and the best way to do so was to find someone else to cast as the guilty party. Someone had to take responsibility for the battle, the deaths, the fright and injury to the king, and the victors of St Albans were determined it would not be them.[40]

This required some creative rearrangement of the facts. First and foremost, the loyalty of York and the Nevills had to be irrefutably established. The battle had achieved its aim, Somerset was permanently out of the picture. Neither York nor Warwick need worry about him again, though they would surely have preferred to have achieved that without undue bloodshed. Prior to the battle, the justification for taking up arms had been to protect themselves from undeserved threats of attainder as traitors. If only the king had read their letters and the 'petitions, requests, demands and other things' they had sent via Fauconberg. Then, surely, Henry would have seen through the mischief stirred against them by others and welcomed them as his true and loyal liegemen.[41]

The fiction that Somerset had concealed their correspondence from the king was established and enrolled in the record of the 1455 Parliament. Somerset, and two men of lesser rank and little importance, were held entirely responsible for the battle and the spilling of noble blood. York and his allies were fully and unconditionally pardoned. The king, in words that must surely have been written for him, declared them so and further declared that the matter must not be spoken of again. In doing so, he endorsed the fiction that important letters had been cruelly kept from him by his most trusted councillor.[42]

> [T]here passed a bill both by the king, lords and commons, putting Thorpe, Joseph and my lord of Somerset in all the default, by the which bill all manner of actions that should grow to any person or persons for any offences at that journey done, in any manner of wise, should be extinct and void, affirming all things done there well done and nothing done there never after this time to be spoken of, to the which bill many a man grudged full sore now it is passed.[43]

The transition of power and authority from Somerset to York and Warwick may have been quick but it was far from smooth. Warwick, York and Salisbury's men were reported to be 'go[ing] about … in harness with strong weapons and have stuffed their lords' barges full of weapons daily into Westminster'. Warwick was confirmed as Captain of Calais and almost immediately prepared to take up the role.[44]

Then there is the strange tale of 'language' between Warwick and Cromwell:

> lord Cromwell would have excused himself of all the stirring or moving of the unfortunate journey of St Albans; of the which excuse making my lord

Warwick had knowledge and in haste was with the king and swore by his oath that the lord Cromwell said not truth but that he was the beginner of all that journey at St Albans; and so between my said two lords of Warwick and Cromwell there is at this day great grudging, in so much as the earl of Shrewsbury has lodged him at the hospital of St James, beside the mews, by the lord Cromwell's desire for his safety.[45]

Just what Warwick meant is not at all clear. Perhaps he referred to Cromwell's delay in reaching St Albans. It is possible Warwick and company had been relying on Cromwell to intercede on their behalf, to carry messages and present their case better than it had been. Whatever the reason, Cromwell, already conscious of his own vulnerability to physical attack, retreated from his alliance with the Nevills with devastating results for Warwick's brother, Sir Thomas.

# 14

# LADY WILLOUGHBY'S TROUBLES

aud Stanhope was little more than 16 when her mistress Eleanor, duchess of Gloucester was arrested on charges of treason. Perhaps she joined the crowds who watched the disgraced duchess's barefoot walks of penitence to St Paul's Cathedral. Perhaps she was too preoccupied with concerns for her own future to give her fallen mistress much thought. Maud was, of course, not implicated in the duchess's treason and witchcraft; she may have known nothing of it before the story broke, but the affair brought an end to her comfortable existence in the duchess's household. She must hope a new position could be found for her or she would have to go home to her mother's house at Tuxford.[1]

Maud was as yet unmarried and with few prospects. On his death, her uncle Cromwell's vast fortune and title would go to her brother Henry. Maud and her younger sister Jane had little to recommend them beyond their youth. Maud was one of thousands of women of gentle birth who held relatively low-status positions in noble households. They were not on intimate terms with their mistresses, though they were much in their company. Maud's duties in the duchess of Gloucester's household would not have been onerous, leaving her plenty of time to participate in the intrigues of a small, claustrophobic enclosed community. Innocent love affairs, the reading and writing of poetry, genteel arts such as embroidery, took up much of Maud's time. Away from her mother and sister, she grew into her womanhood – passionate, quick of wit and temper, a sufferer of no fools.

Just 11 years old when her father died, Maud was dependent on her uncle Cromwell for everything, from her position at court to her future marriages. Her mother, also Maud, was Cromwell's sister; her father, Richard Stanhope, had been a man of some wealth, a soldier and Member of Parliament, rambunctious and sometimes lawless. Stanhope had already amassed a sizeable fortune in land before Maud was born. Originally from

Northumberland, the family had moved south when Richard's father, John, inherited manors at Rampton and Haughton in Nottinghamshire. Richard himself was to inherit yet more property around Egmanton, Tuxford and Laxton from a distant relative of his mother.[2]

Stanhope first married Elizabeth Staveley, with whom he had five children. He arranged good marriages for them and continued to expand and consolidate his land holdings. In 1412, he disposed of his Newcastle properties, using the proceeds to buy more land in Nottinghamshire.[3]

When Bolingbroke landed at Ravenspur in July 1399, Stanhope was among the lords, knights and gentry who greeted him. He had with him an armed force of unspecified size which he was able to equip and arm from his growing income. Two months later, he provided the new king, Henry IV, with a bodyguard during his first Parliament. He was knighted soon after and, over the course of his life, returned to Parliament nine times. In 1405, Stanhope fought in Henry IV's army at Shrewsbury. He acquitted himself so well both in that battle and, later, against the Welsh rebels, that he was rewarded with a little over £100.[4]

After the death of his first wife, around 1412, Stanhope married Maud Cromwell. They had four children, Henry, Maud, Jane and Katherine, who died young. Stanhope made a home with his second family at Rampton.[5]

Stanhope was not a notably peaceable man. He was involved in several property disputes that often descended into violence. On one occasion, in October 1411, he was briefly consigned to the Tower of London. Soon after his release, he sued for, and received, a general pardon. In 1414, shortly after he succeeded his father, Henry V took stern measures against the growing violence in the Midlands and Stanhope was again locked up, this time for three weeks in Kenilworth Castle. Stanhope was fiercely supportive of those who looked to him for protection and, not long after his release, found himself imprisoned in Kenilworth again, 'pending the outcome of a royal commission of oyer and terminer set up to examine a whole catalogue of his misdeeds'. Once again, he secured a general pardon on his release.[6]

Maud was born around 1425, presumably at Rampton. Nothing is known of her relationship with her older half-siblings, nor with her brother Henry, though she and her sister Jane enjoyed a relatively close relationship throughout their lives. As her mother was later closely associated with Tuxford, it might be safely assumed she and her children went to live there after Stanhope's death in 1436. The bulk of Richard Stanhope's property was inherited by his grandson from his first marriage, though his widow was well provided for.[7]

What is known of Maud's time at court is sketchy and relies heavily on picking out clues to be found in the poetry of Sir Richard Roos. Roos was closely associated with both the duke and duchess of Gloucester and Maud's lifelong association with the poet began during those few years she spent in the duchess's household in Greenwich. It is likely due to Maud collecting his work and passing it on to her heirs that we know anything of it today. As a woman of gentle rather than noble birth, Maud's position in the duchess's household was of middling importance and status. Her time there, though brief, would seem to have been happy.[8]

The property at Greenwich was given to Gloucester after the death of Thomas Beaufort, duke of Exeter. Gloucester immediately set about making improvements, fortifying the existing manor house and turning some 200 acres into a park. He later rebuilt the manor, giving it the name Pleasaunce. It was here that Maud learned about her own strength of mind and she enjoyed her first passionate but chaste love affair. It was also here that her heart was broken for the first time.[9]

In the poems of Richard Roos, Maud's name is linked with the three oldest Beauchamp sisters, with lady Strange and, most notably, with William Nevill, lord Fauconberg. The poems offer a glimpse of Maud, most often associated with the Roman god Mercury, known for his quick wit and eloquence. We can also catch a glimpse of a series of love triangles, Fauconberg's heart stolen from lady Strange by Maud then lost to the splendidly named Barbalina Herbequyne, Margaret of Anjou's German-born attendant. This last, and the reference to Maud's married name, Willoughby, in some of the poems, might also give us a clue as to Maud's continuing connection with the broken Pleasaunce circle. One member of that circle, Gloucester's treasurer, Sir Gervase Clifton, was to re-enter Maud's life in the years to come.[10]

After Gloucester's death in 1447, Pleasaunce was immediately granted to Margaret of Anjou. Maud's continuing presence at court may suggest she secured a position in another noble household, perhaps even that of the queen.[11]

Some time around 1447, Maud married for the first time. Her husband was Robert, lord Willoughby, a close friend and associate of Cromwell. Willoughby, a veteran of the French wars, was a widower somewhere in his sixties. Throughout his military career in the 1420s and 1430s, he had been most closely associated with Bedford. At the battle of Verneuil in 1424, he and Sir John Fastolf captured several prisoners, including the 15-year-old duke d'Alençon. Later, Willoughby accompanied the young Henry VI to France for his coronation. After the death of his first wife, Elizabeth Montagu, the countess of Salisbury's aunt, he sought permission to go on a pilgrimage to the Holy Land.[12]

The marriage between Maud and Willoughby benefited both parties in different ways. Maud was young and offered Willoughby the possibility of a son; Willoughby was a man of wealth and title, a far grander husband than the daughter of a knight might have expected. Not then the heiress she would become on the death of her brother, Maud had a good deal to thank her uncle for. Always canny when it came to money, Cromwell not only cancelled a debt Willoughby owed him in lieu of a dowry but negotiated a lucrative settlement for Maud. Should her husband predecease her – which, given his age, was more than likely – she would enjoy a more than comfortable widowhood.[13]

Willoughby's only child, Joan, was of an age with Maud. The two women did not develop a close relationship. Joan could hardly be expected to welcome Maud with open arms. As the only child of a wealthy landowner, she had a substantial inheritance to look forward to. If Maud and Willoughby had a son, all that would be gone. Even the birth of a daughter would put quite a dent in Joan's expectations. As it was, there were no children from this marriage.[14]

When he died in 1452, Joan Welles and her husband forcibly seized her father's properties, including those that should have gone to his widow. Maud was forced to flee. The woman who emerges from the coded poetry of Richard Roos as gifted by Mercury with wit and eloquence, with a strong will and a tongue as sharp as arrows, was no match for a band of armed men determined to turn her out of her home at Eresby.[15]

In his will, Robert Willoughby left his wife

> two standing cups covered, four bowls with a covering, two small pots and a great pot, and sixteen pieces of silver vessel in the kitchen, and a basin and a ewer of silver, a red bed of tapestry and a green bed of worsted, three featherbeds (that is to say one of the best and two minor), a tun of wine, a great salt cellar covered and another salt plain covered and a young palfrey white.[16]

Willoughby also enfeoffed several manors and tenements to various of his associates, including William, lord Fitzhugh, Viscount Beaumont and Cromwell, in order that Maud's dower might be assigned to her immediately. This was on condition she persuaded Cromwell not to sue the executors for any debts Willoughby owed him at the time of his death.[17]

None of these provisions prevented the unlawful seizure of Eresby. Fearing for her life and safety, Maud sent an urgent message to Cromwell to send someone 'to help convey her to Tattershall so that she might be there for her most comfort, surety and worship'. In widowhood, Maud should have been free to exercise her right to choose whether, and who, to marry. Instead, she found herself dependent on her uncle for everything. It cannot have been easy for her, after running her own household and her own affairs for five years, to suddenly find herself a supplicant in Cromwell's house at the age of 27. As we know nothing of her relationship with Willoughby, we cannot gauge her feelings at his death. The age difference alone would not necessarily have ruled out affection between them, nor does their failure to have children indicate a lack of physical intimacy. However, when Cromwell suggested Thomas Nevill as a husband, it would seem a fairly safe supposition that the thought of an energetic 23-year-old gave Maud a different view of marriage the second time around. The reputed, and reported, lawlessness of the Nevills may also have given her hope that here was a man who could help her recover her stolen lands.[18]

In February 1453, the Escheator of Lincolnshire was ordered to 'take of Maud, who was wife of Robert Willoughby knight, an oath etc in the presence of Joan daughter and heir of the said Robert, or of her attorneys, to assign dower to the said Maud'. This did nothing to shift Joan Welles nor allow Maud to move back to Eresby. Thinking of his own need for political protection by one of England's more notable heavy mobs, as well as relieving himself of the burden of his niece and her household, Cromwell and Salisbury set about negotiating the marriage. The death of their brother, also in 1452, changed the circumstances of the Stanhope sisters dramatically. Now they were co-heirs to a vast fortune and one of their husbands could look forward, one day, to holding the Cromwell title. On 1 May 1453, a licence was granted for Maud and Thomas Nevill to marry.[19]

The wedding took place in August at Tattershall Castle. Richard Roos, presumably commissioned by the bridegroom, wrote a poem for the occasion. The Nevills came to Tattershall with a large armed escort and the bride left the day after the wedding with her new family, escorted by her small household. For the next year, at least, she was to make her home at Middleham.[20]

Just as we know nothing of Maud's relationship with her first husband, we know nothing about her relationship with her second. We have none of the letters they must have written to each other nor do we have Thomas's will, which might have given a clue about his regard for his wife. Thomas spent much of his time away from home but it is not possible to determine whether, how often or for how long his wife accompanied him. The birthplaces of children are clues to the movements of their mothers, but Thomas and Maud remained childless. It is difficult to determine whether they were happy together or their marriage was cold and distant. There was certainly plenty of scope for conflict between them but it would be a mistake to assume such conflict led to unhappiness.[21]

Three manors in Yorkshire were given to the couple by the groom's parents: at Catterick, Danby Wiske and Aldborough, all within a 30-mile radius of Middleham. In 1459, Thomas styled himself 'of Eresby', though it is not clear exactly when they took possession and set up house there. The escalating feud with the Percies stretched the Nevills' resources. Until the danger subsided, or until Eresby was restored to her, Yorkshire would be Maud's home.[22]

While Maud was no sheltered genteel knight's daughter, her welcome to Yorkshire was both brutal and unexpected. When the Percies attacked the wedding party just outside York, the women must have felt particularly vulnerable. Maud most likely travelled in a litter though, at times, she may have ridden pillion behind her husband, or on her own slow-moving horse. She was unarmed and defenceless, relying entirely on the men to deal with the threat that faced them. There must have been great relief when they reached Sheriff Hutton and then, the following day, finally arrived at Middleham.

There was little time for a honeymoon. Within weeks, Warwick arrived, sent for by his father. Then, in October, Salisbury and his sons set off for Topcliffe, hoping to secure the younger Percies so they could be taken to London to face the king's council. Though Thomas returned home and did not accompany his father and older brother south, he and John were still preoccupied with their feud with their cousins.

Maud spent most of her time in the company of her mother-in-law and unmarried sisters-in-law Alianor, Katherine and Margaret. In between the more mundane tasks, Maud most likely enjoyed hunting or hawking in Middleham's nine deer parks. Perhaps the women made the 16-mile journey north to spend time with Alice Fitzhugh, visited Aysgarth Falls or Jervaulx Abbey. The capture of the Percy brothers in November 1454, the visit from the duke of York and Alianor's wedding to Thomas Stanley in December of that year provided moments of diversion and activity.

The death of Maud's mother, also in December, necessitated a journey south, and she had the opportunity to catch up with her sister Jane and uncle Cromwell. Maud Cromwell did not have an extensive estate to leave her daughters, but they did inherit her third share in Tuxford. This would provide them with a small but steady income, something both sisters were in need of. It was around this time that Jane married Sir Humphrey, younger son of viscount Bourchier.[23]

Just as we can glean little about Maud's relationships with her husbands, we know nothing of her political views. What correspondence she left was written in her later years and dealt almost entirely with matters of finance. During her marriage to Thomas, all such things would have been dealt with largely by him. Two such matters arose early in 1456.

In January, Ralph Cromwell died suddenly at his manor of South Wingfield. The earl of Shrewsbury was there at the time and heard 'a great noise'. He sent a child down to find out what was going on, and shortly afterwards, a servant of Cromwell, one John Leynton, came into the room and told him Cromwell was close to death:

The said earl came in to the chamber where the said lord lay, where then was the reverend father in god the bishop of Chester, master William Gulle and others, the said lord then being in point to pass from this life. So the said reverend father took a glass and held it before the mouth of the said lord and some life appeared in the same. And after that within a while he held a glass before the mouth of the said lord and there appeared no life but was passed then when God had so determined.[24]

If Cromwell's heirs thought they knew what to expect from his will, they were mistaken. After the death of his wife in 1454, he had drawn up a new will in complete secrecy. Only Gulle and two other men knew of its existence and what it contained. After it was signed and witnessed, Cromwell hid the will in a casket owned by one of his servants, locking it securely and keeping the key on his person at all times. He had taken the box with him to South Wingfield. Immediately after his death, the key was removed from the pouch that hung from his belt, the box unlocked and the will secured. Cromwell's executors were then informed of his passing.[25]

So far as Maud and Jane Stanhope – and their husbands – knew, they were, after Cromwell's debts were paid and provisions made for his soul, his chief heirs. They expected to be left a considerable share of his fortune. These had, after all, been the terms of his will when Maud and Jane married. They would surely have been revealed to both Salisbury and Viscount Bourchier during the marriage negotiations. Neither sister had been told that anything had changed.[26]

Cromwell's new will asked that his moveable goods be gathered together in one place to be sold, the proceeds to be given to the new collegiate church he had established at Tattershall. He also requested that any property that was not entailed, and could therefore be offered for sale, also be sold. All proceeds were to go to a charity or charities of the executors' choosing. This left only twenty-two entailed properties to be inherited by Maud and Jane, worth less than half of what they had been expecting. To rub salt into the wounds, Cromwell invited his heirs to buy whatever of the unentailed properties they chose, at market rates.[27]

Even worse, though, was the provision that, until the collegiate church was completed, all revenues of these properties would not go to the heirs but towards the cost of building and establishing the church. This was highly contentious, of dubious legality and morally inexcusable. In the end, it was something the executors could not in all conscience enforce.[28]

The timing of this is interesting. Neither St Albans nor Warwick's fit of anger at Westminster could possibly have had an influence on Cromwell's decision, as both occurred in 1455. Cromwell's friendship with Shrewsbury would seem to indicate a desire to distance himself from the Nevills; his lack of favouritism – Jane inherited no more than her sister – that he was also happy to distance himself from the Bourchiers and, by implication, from York.[29]

The two couples were both at Tattershall for the funeral and the reading of the will. The changes left them shocked and bewildered. Thomas Nevill and Humphrey Bourchier took immediate action, seizing what they could get their hands on and sending their men out to take possession of livestock, crops, wine and thirty-five manors they thought should be theirs. Goods taken from Tattershall were calculated to be worth more than £2,000 and total losses to Cromwell's estate came to nearly £16,000.[30]

If Thomas and Humphrey acted out of anger, outrage and a sense that they had been cheated of their expectations, Maud and Jane must have felt personally betrayed. They had married men of their uncle's choosing, twice in Maud's case. Maud claimed Cromwell had promised her certain wall hangings but the executors demanded to see written proof, which she could not provide.[31]

An attempt was made to have Cromwell's earlier will proved and the later one overturned. Cromwell's clerk of the chapel testified he had made the fair copy of the will with his own hand and that his master had sworn him to secrecy. The sale of those properties the executors managed to get control of went ahead, though the income from properties seized by Thomas and Humphrey was never recovered. Maud and Jane were each assigned eleven properties and Tattershall, the jewel in the crown, was to be held jointly between them. The battle, both legal and otherwise, continued for some time. Finally, in 1462, Maud and Jane would be forced to accept the terms of the will and relinquish all that was not legally theirs.[32]

In February 1456, licence was granted to Maud and Thomas, Humphrey and Jane to take possession of their Cromwell inheritance, much depleted as it was.[33]

In March, the king issued a grant of survivorship to Thomas and Humphrey of various offices held by Cromwell, including 'chamberlain of the receipt of the exchequer, to hold themselves or by deputies, taking the usual fees, wages, rewards and profits'. Though Maud and Thomas were not as wealthy as they had expected to be on Cromwell's death, they were certainly far better off than they had been.[34]

Cromwell's passing prompted Sir John Fastolf to recall the ransom paid by the duke d'Alençon, still owed to the late lord Willoughby, which his widow, he thought, may be entitled to claim. Alençon had raised the 10,000 marks with some difficulty and it was paid into the hands of the late duke of Bedford. Willoughby and Fastolf had each received 1,000 marks of their share, which left 4,000 each yet unpaid.[35]

Fastolf wrote to John Paston, suggesting that

the executors, and such as most have interest in the lord Willoughby's goods, may be communed with that they make pursuit of the said 4,000 marks for his part to be had … If Master Nevill, the which has wedded my lady Willoughby, have power or interest to receive the lord Willoughby's debts, then he to be laboured unto. And my lord Salisbury will be a great helper in this cause.[36]

Unfortunately, we know nothing more about this matter. If Thomas and his father did manage to secure this sum, even after taking into account anything that might be owing to Joan Welles, it would have been a most welcome addition to Maud's treasury. An earlier attempt to secure this money had been made, presumably without success. In October 1455, John Fastolf wrote to Nicholas Molyneux: 'Hears from John de Leawe, one of lord Willoughby's executors, that they will labour to my lord Beaumont to advance the process for recovery of his part of the reward for the taking of the duke of Alençon.'[37]

In April 1457, a large contingent of Nevills descended on Canterbury for John's wedding. Shortly after the celebrations were concluded, Warwick and his young family boarded a ship and crossed the Channel. Finally, after years of negotiation with both the garrison and the staple, he was to take possession of Calais. This meant that Salisbury had to bear responsibility for the security of the marches alone. He and Warwick needed a deputy they could trust and for this they turned to Thomas.

On 20 October 1457, Thomas, Salisbury and Warwick fixed their seals to an indenture appointing him for three years as 'lieutenant of the said city, castle [of Carlisle] and marches, as well in time of peace as of war, and the keeping, safeguard, governance and tuition of the same shall take upon him, for the said earls'.[38]

Thomas's peacetime salary was just over 300 marks, from which he had to:

bear and sustain of his own proper costs the whole charge of the household that shall be kept within the said castle and all other charges that should appertain to the said earls to bear or sustain for or upon the safeguard and keeping aforesaid; the wages of the constable of the said castle for the time being and the wages and rewards of the commissaries and deputies of the said marches.[39]

Salisbury was to get a third of all spoils of war as well as custody of any Scots prisoners taken so he might negotiate a ransom for their return. Should either he or Warwick visit Carlisle, he would 'pay to the said Thomas for the costs of him and all them that come with him, to meat and drink'.[40]

Thomas was unlikely to face anything more than the usual cross-border raids during his term and, certainly, would not have been expected to face anything more serious on his own. While Warwick was too far away in Calais, and too preoccupied with his own concerns, Salisbury would have at least reinforced his son should real trouble with the Scots arise. Thomas's wages were not sufficient to cover payment fo a dedicated deputy and it is likely Carlisle was his principal home for the next two years at least.[41]

One of the things Thomas did not have to concern himself with was repairs to either the city or the castle's defences, or the supply of weapons of war. A programme of repairing and strengthening Carlisle's walls and gates had been undertaken in the 1420s and, more systematically, the 1430s. A clerk of works was appointed to undertake the necessary work in Carlisle, Berwick and Roxburgh, ensuring greater efficiency and cost effectiveness than in the past, when several interested parties had competed for the same limited funds. The clerk of works also received money to pay for guns, lances, longbows and crossbows.[42]

A chronic difficulty throughout Henry VI's reign was a shortage of cash. Many who held crown-funded posts often had to accept promises of payment from revenues not yet received by the crown in lieu of wages. As the cumulative amount of such promises often exceeded the income eventually received, those who failed to get their accounts to the exchequer in time had to wait for another revenue stream before wages were paid. This often made life difficult for those in Carlisle who supplied the garrison at a time when the garrison's wages were in arrears.[43]

It was not customary for wardens to take up residence in Carlisle, though a well-paid and well-trusted lieutenant, most likely locally recruited, would have been in the city on a more or less permanent basis. If Thomas did base himself in Carlisle, there is nothing in the record to give us a clue as to Maud's whereabouts in 1457 and 1458. If she did go with him, she would have found Carlisle very different from what she was used to. She had to be close to her husband if there were to be any children but Maud's childlessness was lifelong and cannot be used with any confidence to assess either the state of their relationship or draw conclusions on how much time they spent together.

As it was, Thomas spent little more than two years in his role as lieutenant of the west march: as an urgent call went out in September 1459 for Salisbury's sons and retainers to gather at Middleham. The situation for the duke of York – and the Nevills – had deteriorated once again and immediate action was required. Warwick returned from Calais; Thomas and John both made their way to their childhood home. Despite Henry VI's ongoing attempts at peace making, concerns about their loyalty had surfaced once more. Within months, Maud would once again find herself homeless and, this time, it was going to take more than a skirmish in St Albans to silence their enemies and restore their fortunes.

# 15

# A Murder in the West Country

ust before midnight on 23 October 1455, an old man was woken by a noise outside his window. Opening the window, he saw a sea of light, blazing torches and a fire at the gate. Men and horses, too many to count, filled his garden. Frightened, he asked who had come and what business they had with him in the middle of the night.[1]

The old man was Nicholas Radford, a much-loved and respected Devonshire lawyer among whose clients was lord Bonville, bitter enemy of the earl of Devon. The young man at the head of the 100 who invaded Radford's garden was the earl's oldest son, Thomas Courtenay. He, his father and brothers had spent the last few months harrying the county in their efforts to attack and eliminate Bonville. In April, there had been an attempt to ambush him in Exeter. Both Devon and Bonville entered into good behaviour bonds, but this failed to ease their enmity.[2]

Devon, York's sole ally at Dartford in 1452, now turned to York and the Nevills for help. Bonville had once been Devon's retainer but his growing influence in the West Country earned him the earl's enmity. In 1454, he was instrumental in aiding York's successful campaign to end Exeter and Egremont's rebellion. Bonville developed a close relationship with Salisbury and a marriage was contracted between his grandson William, lord Harrington and Salisbury's second youngest daughter, Katherine. Their wedding was celebrated some time in 1455 or 1456.[3]

As it had been earlier, during the Nevill–Percy feud, Henry VI's government seemed powerless to end the troubles between the Bonvilles and the Courtenays. Now the latter were about to demonstrate just how far they were prepared to go in pursuit of their vendetta.

When Nicholas Radford opened his window to see who had disrupted his sleep, Thomas Courtenay invited him to come down and talk with him, promising him no harm. Courtenay and his men then forced their way into the house and were given food and wine by the nervous lawyer, no doubt anxious to see them on their way. While the earl's son kept Radford talking in the parlour, his men ransacked the house, taking goods worth around 1,000 marks and £80 in cash. They even tumbled his bedridden wife onto the floor so they could take the sheets she lay on.[4]

It was not until Courtenay persuaded him to come to Tiverton to talk with his father that Radford realised what had been going on. Sending a servant to fetch a horse, as he was too old and infirm to walk, he was shocked to be told they had all been stolen. In fear of his life, bitter at the loss of his property and concerned about his wife, Radford was taken from the house and led away. They had not gone far before Courtenay gave a curt order to half a dozen of his men, spurred his horse and rode away. They immediately turned on Radford and killed him.[5]

As if this were not enough, several days later, Courtenay's men returned to Radford's house and ordered his servants to carry his body to the cemetery. There, they tipped it into an open grave, and dropped onto his naked body the stones lying ready to build Radford's tomb. The resultant crushing of the unfortunate lawyer's remains would make it impossible for anyone investigating his death to determine its cause.[6]

On 3 November, the earl of Devon led an army of over 1,000 men into the city of Exeter, where they ransacked houses and looted the cathedral, intimidating the treasurer into handing over valuable property entrusted to him by Nicholas Radford. Using Exeter as a base, Devon then sent men south along the estuary to lay siege to Powderham Castle, stopping to rob the houses of Bonville's friends and supporters along the way. Led by Devon's second son, Henry, this was no half-hearted siege. 'Great cannon and serpentines were fixed in the earth at different places near the house and putting into them powder and fire, stones were shot at the mansion of sir Philip Courtenay as if they had been in an enemy's country.'[7]

Sir Philip Courtenay, a kinsman and bitter enemy of Devon, sent to Bonville for help. Bonville was at Lympstone, opposite Powderham on the other side of the Exe estuary, and attempted a crossing. He was seen, and Henry Courtenay left off the siege long enough to intercept him and his small party, killing two of Bonville's servants. Bonville retreated across the water and made a second attempt, this time by road, reaching Clyst, some 5 miles from the city, around 12 December.[8]

Bonville immediately wrote an angry letter to Devon, demanding he meet him 'tomorrow at 12 of the clock in the field and advance thy self to abide and fight in thy proper person'.[9]

Everyone knew, Bonville wrote, that Devon

often falsely, cowardly and traitorously has arrayed and laid in wait to mischief and murder me and my servants, being the king's true liegemen ... [and] in truth has made divers and many assemblies of such as should be the king's true liege people, being arrant thieves, house burners and murderers by your abetment, procuring, receiving and maintenance.[10]

In some fury, Devon promptly responded:

I say that thou in thy saying in all such premises are false and untrue and all other of thy opinion being in thy company. And that will I, in my proper person, as a true knight and the king's true liegeman, upon thy false body prove, at time and place by me and thee appointed.[11]

Devon attempted to persuade the mayor of Exeter to prevent Bonville from entering the city. To his great credit, the mayor refused, saying he did not know what ordinance he could make to keep anyone out.[12]

On 15 December, 'the said earl of Devon departed out from the city with his people into the field by Clyst and there bickered and fought with the lord Bonville and his people and put them to flight and so returned again that night into the city again with his people.' Devon's actions, the murder of Radford and Bonville's plight, were soon known in London, where Parliament was in session. Henry VI was ill again, though this time the problem would seem to have been purely physical. He had sent for a physician in June, but was well enough to attend Parliament the following month. By November, his health was failing again and York was commissioned as king's lieutenant to open the next session of Parliament in November. Whatever the king or his doctors thought of his latest illness, the commons were concerned enough to send a deputation to the lords, led by the speaker, William Burleigh.[13]

The king, Burleigh said, 'for certain causes him moving', had appointed York his lieutenant and,

if for such causes as the king hereafter might not attend to the protection and defence of his land, that it should like the king by the advice of the said lieutenant and the lords to ordain and provide such an able person as should attend to the defence and protection of the said land, and this to be done as soon as it might.[14]

The commons were particularly concerned about 'great and grievous riots down in the west country between the earl of Devonshire and the lord Bonville, by the which some men have been murdered, some robbed and children and women taken'. York was, once again, appointed Protector and Defender of England, though it took several visits by deputations from the commons to achieve. This time, he was to remain in the position until discharged by Parliament.[15]

During the Christmas recess, York set out for Exeter. Devon came to meet him and was arrested and sent to the Tower to await trial. A commission drew up an indictment of the charges against Devon and his followers and exonerated Bonville. Peace was once again brought to a troubled county by the swift actions of the duke of York.[16]

Never had York sat so high in the estimation of Henry VI. One observer wrote that he was to be named Henry's chief councillor 'as long as it like the king'. This was what York had wanted for so long. Twice he had proved himself capable of decisive action in the face of internal strife. Twice he had taken charge of the kingdom while Henry was ill. But York was never one to do anything by halves and, when Parliament resumed, a petition was presented requesting an act of resumption. This was too much for the lords and they resisted angrily, so much so that York feared for his safety, and he and Warwick attended Parliament escorted by '300 men, all jacked and in brigantines ... whereof many men marvelled'.[17]

York's position as Protector depended on the goodwill and support of his peers. With the queen and others actively opposed to his aims, not only was the act of resumption itself doomed to fail but York risked being dismissed as both Protector and Henry's lieutenant in Parliament. That Warwick alone supported him calls into question the idea of the existence of a cohesive 'Yorkist' party at this time. York, it would seem, did not as yet have Salisbury's unwavering support.[18]

The idea of an act of resumption was popular with the commons and people more generally, but none of the lords wanted it to apply to them. Margaret of Anjou, in particular, fiercely opposed it: 'The queen is a great and strong laboured woman, for she spares no pain to sue her things to an intent and conclusion to her power.'[19]

With the lords said to have gone to the king to bring him to Parliament, and a reported quarrel between York and Henry, it was little wonder that he was swiftly dismissed as Protector. He left London soon after, while Parliament was still sitting, and did not witness the string of petitions for exemption that eviscerated the bill for resumption and defeated his attempts to strengthen the finances of the crown. A strongly worded letter was sent after the duke.[20]

[W]e, on this present 25 February [1456], in our said present parliament, with the advice and assent of the lords spiritual and temporal being in the same parliament, have discharged you from the responsibility or charge and name of [protector and defender]. We order you not to intervene at all in any further responsibility or charge and name of the protector and defender of our aforesaid kingdom of England and our principal councillor of the aforesaid. For we wish you to be completely discharged of the responsibility or charge and name of the aforesaid.[21]

York rode north to Sandal Castle in West Yorkshire, where he was to deal with a new emergency – an incursion by the Scots king James II into Cumbria. York wrote letters to James who, reportedly, offered to assist him to make good his claim on the English throne. York's appearance in the north was enough to send James back across the border. Salisbury was quickly mustering a force to ride to Carlisle, ready to give battle if called upon, and the situation was quickly brought under control.[22]

This was a pattern York was unable to break. A crisis arose in government, a feud threatened to spin out of control, and he was called on to deal with it. Once done, he was dismissed and sidelined. While this may, of course, be down to the machinations of his enemies, it may also be indicative of a difficult relationship between York and the king. As much as Henry disliked conflict, as much as he wished to banish it from his council, there was something about York that made it impossible for the two to work together for long. Matters were complicated by the fact Henry knew he could not simply wave York away and have done with him. He was one of his closest kinsmen and his high rank and popularity made it difficult to banish him to the sidelines for long. Perhaps a way could be found to bring about a reconciliation, and lasting peace between the bickering lords. With a good example set at the highest reaches of the nobility, feuds and quarrels would be a thing of the past. Old men could rest safely in their beds and the counties would be at peace.

# 16

# CALAIS AND LOVE DAY

ust as the sun was rising on 24 August 1457, the town of Sandwich came under attack. A small fleet of French ships, commanded by Piers de Breze, Seneschal of Normandy, disgorged several thousand men onto land. Taken completely by surprise, the townspeople were at the mercy of the raiders. Shops were looted, houses despoiled. Prisoners were taken for ransom, though the chroniclers tell us nothing of their fate, and 'divers persons' were slain.[1]

> And in the end of this same year came the Frenchmen and other enemies, and spoiled and robbed the good port of Sandwich, and slew much people, for they came suddenly to Sandwich in the morning when men were abed, and searched every house, and all the plate, riches, gold, silver and other merchandise and goods of value they shipped it into their ships and went smoothly away with all.[2]

The townsfolk rallied, especially when the lieutenant warden of the Cinq Ports, Sir Thomas Kyriell mounted a strong counter-offensive. '[T]he people came down and drove them away, and in their fleeing to ship there were drowned more than six score of the French party.' Three warships and thirty merchantmen were taken by the French and a good deal of damage was inflicted on the town itself.[3]

England was outraged by the French raid. It was nothing short of a national disgrace. It revived fears of a full-scale French invasion and highlighted, better than anything, the weakness and inaction of the government. As Admiral and keeper of the seas, it was Exeter's job to keep the Channel ports safe and open for business. He and others were ordered to sea.

> Commission to Henry Auger, John William, Robert Brencheley and Laurence Borough, appointing them to arrest the ships and other vessels for the conduct of Gervase Clifton, knight, and certain men in his company,

appointed to go on the sea to resist the king's enemies, and mariners for the governance thereof.[4]

Neither Exeter nor Clifton achieved what they were commissioned to do and this failure put not only England's trade in jeopardy but her very sovereignty. Something had to be done or national morale, already low, would plummet to a dangerous level.[5]

In October, the earl of Warwick was commissioned to put to sea. The following month he was appointed keeper of the seas for a three-year term.[6]

> … to war against the king's enemies and to govern all of his retinue and others flocking to him and to punish delinquents and to arrest pirates and spoilers of merchants and fishermen, both English and foreign with their ships, and ships to serve at the usual rates and masters and mariners for the governance thereof and the victuals necessary in this behalf.[7]

This did not please Exeter. He was further enraged when £500 in emergency funds was granted to Warwick, 'considering the navy of France is northward and that it might be met with and for the good direction of the English navy'.[8]

John Nanfan, Governor of the Channel Islands and staunch supporter of Warwick, also received a commission

> to arrest the carpenters, smiths, gunners and other workmen necessary for the repair and munition of a ship called the *Grace Dieu* which will sail with a fleet ordained to resist the king's enemies, and mariners for the governance thereof, from the port of Bristol to the sea to serve for the money of Richard earl of Warwick and to purvey victuals, timber, iron, nails, guns and powder for the same.[9]

In the 1450s, the *Grace Dieu* was England's only royal ship. Built in 1446, she operated as a merchant ship in times of peace, under the command of her builder, John Taverner, and, later, members of the Palmer family. In times of war, the king had first call on her and, after 1457, she became the property of the crown. Between 1457 and 1460, the ship was at the core of Warwick's growing personal fleet. Repairs were to be paid for out of Warwick's funds, which were extensive but not limitless.[10]

It had taken months of negotiation with both the garrison and the company of staplers for Warwick to take command of Calais. He was appointed in May 1455, but it was not until May 1457 that he, his wife and daughters were able to cross the Channel and take up more or less permanent residence. Warwick's uncle Fauconberg and York's man, Edmund Mulso, soon to be appointed marshall of Calais, made the initial overtures and a proposed settlement was first put to council late in October 1455. In the ensuing negotiations, Richard Wydeville, lord Rivers represented the garrison. Parliament set up a committee to investigate the grievances of both the garrison and staple and, ideally, find a way forward. Warwick, Salisbury and Fauconberg were all members, as were the treasurer and victualler of Calais, Gervase Clifton and John Cheyne respectively.[11]

Warwick faced three problems in taking possession of Calais. First, the garrison's wages, which were permanently in arrears; second, the staple's outstanding loans to the crown; and, third, a residual undercurrent of loyalty to the late duke of Somerset. The garrison was particularly concerned that their new captain might be something of a new broom and sweep many from their lucrative posts. They also wanted a pardon for their appropriation and sale of wool and woolfells the previous year. The staplers demanded compensation for the loss of revenue. This was granted by Parliament, but the issue of the garrison's unpaid wages remained unresolved. Even though the garrison had made £26,000 on the sale of the seized wool, there was still a substantial shortfall.[12]

In December, Henry VI wrote a long letter to the members of the garrison. He was anxious that 'our right trusty and wellbeloved cousin the earl of Warwick might [receive] our town and castle that you be in', and that the garrison's leaders should respond to letters previously sent. Accepting that promises of a payment of 20,000 marks had been made without any specified timeline, Henry assured them that 'we wish you to know that you shall be content thereof fully within twenty days after our said cousin of Warwick, his commissioners or deputies, be entered into the charge of our said town and castle'.[13]

Though Warwick would be bringing his own men at his own expense to bolster their numbers, Henry also addressed their concerns about losing their jobs: 'And where as some perhaps imagine they shall lightly be moved and put out of wages, we know for certain our said cousin of Warwick is disposed so to demean himself towards you that by reason you shall have no cause to grudge.' Henry also undertook to issue 'letters of pardon and grace' for 'any disobedience or offence done by you or any of you against our commandments or otherwise'. This pardon was issued late in May 1456.[14]

> Pardon to the soldiers of Calais of all trespasses, offences, misprisons, contempts and forfeitures committed by them, in that, because they were not satisfied of their wages, they made restraint of the wool and woolfells brought to the staple of Calais and prevented the same from being exposed for sale and refused entry into the town to various officers and ministers sent to exercise their offices there and to execute other mandates and threatened some of them and refused to receive a writ of privy seal directed to them.[15]

While he was still excluded from Calais, Warwick himself sought a pardon in Parliament 'for anything that happens while he is excluded'.[16]

Warwick made his first official visit to Calais in December 1456 but, as noted, it was not until May the following year that he officially entered his command. For the next two years, Calais was home for Warwick and his family and his base of operations.[17]

On 24 April 1457, John Nevill was married at last. His bride was 14-year-old Isobel Ingoldisthorpe, the niece of John Tiptoft, earl of Worcester and sole heir to her late father's fortune. Her parents were Sir Edmund Ingoldisthorpe and Joan Tiptoft, Worcester's sister. Sir Edmund's wealth was centred in Norfolk and Cambridgeshire. At 27, John may have been close to despairing of a suitable wife. England's noblemen frequently had difficulties finding brides for their younger sons. Heiresses were preferred but thin on the ground.[18]

Isobel was a ward of Queen Margaret and, though legally of age to take control of her own affairs, the queen insisted the marriage be paid for pending any finding to the contrary. John and Isobel later petitioned Parliament for control of Isobel's property. John and Isobel were married at Canterbury Cathedral, their wedding celebrated by the archbishop. How many members of the family attended, besides John's parents and brother Warwick, is not recorded. Around 100 miles away at Arundel, John's oldest sister Joan was the closest and may have made the journey. If she was living with her husband Sir Thomas Stanley in Cheshire, Alianor was the furthest away and unlikely to have travelled half the length of England to attend her brother's wedding.[19]

Part of the reason the wedding was held in Canterbury was that John's brother, Warwick, was based there, busy with preparations for his voyage across the Channel. With him was his uncle Fauconberg, who was to act as his unofficial deputy, and Fauconberg's illegitimate son Thomas. Not only was Warwick overseeing the preparation of ships, the recruitment of sailors and the acquisition of supplies, he was learning how to command a vessel. He had no intention of being an absentee captain, nor a captain who could not himself sail a ship.

Before he set sail, Warwick 'had the folks of Canterbury and Sandwich before him and thanked them of their good hearts and victualing of Calais, and [prayed] them continuance'. Cultivating the goodwill of the towns and people of coastal Kent would pay dividends in the future. Not only was Calais dependent on them for supplies, Warwick could not have achieved what he did in 1460 if not for the ongoing support of Canterbury and, particularly, Sandwich.[20]

Almost immediately after his brother's wedding, Warwick, his countess and young family, 6-year-old Isobel and 11-month-old Anne, took up residence in Calais Castle. Warwick's illegitimate daughter Margaret, now about 12, may have taken up her position in her half-sisters' nursery around this time. It was not unusual to acknowledge illegitimate children, nor for them to be brought at least some way into the family. Warwick's cousin Thomas, the Bastard of Fauconberg, became an important part of his affinity. Exeter was close to both his illegitimate brothers throughout his life. Gervase Clifton's illegitimacy did not prevent him from holding positions of political and military responsibility. Whatever the countess of Warwick's feelings about her husband's daughter, Margaret was welcomed into the family and given a position of some status. She was to remain close to her half-sisters throughout their lives, eventually becoming lady-in-waiting to a queen.

The countess of Warwick, who, it was later noted, did not much enjoy living in Calais, could well have chosen to remain in England. Other women whose husbands served overseas did. That she made the move with her husband suggests the couple preferred to live together, whatever compromises might have to be made. With only two daughters, they most likely both felt under some pressure to stay together in hopes of producing a son. There may also have been more to it than that. The countess of Warwick's remaining by her husband's side throughout the difficulties that lay ahead of them is highly suggestive of a strong bond between them. On two occasions when he left Calais on difficult and potentially dangerous voyages, she is recorded as greeting his return 'with joy'. Married since childhood, and living in the same household at least since the death of the countess's parents, there had been plenty of time and opportunity for affection to develop between them.

In Calais, Warwick inherited a management team that had been in place since the late Somerset's time as Captain. Three of these men would play leading roles in the conflict to come, and not necessarily to Warwick's benefit. One was Sir Andrew Trollope. As master porter of Calais, he was responsible for the town's gates and walls. He had served with Somerset in France and joined the garrison in 1451 when Somerset was appointed Captain. A career soldier, Trollope was greatly indebted to Somerset, and Warwick was never quite able to win him over completely.[21]

Another was Richard Wydeville, lord Rivers. Infamously married to the widow of Henry VI's uncle Bedford, Rivers had served as lieutenant of Calais under both Somerset and York. Though he was a representative of the garrison during the negotiations prior to Warwick's arrival in Calais, he was one of the few officers replaced by the new Captain.[22]

The third was Sir Gervase Clifton, illegitimate son of Gervase Clifton of Clifton Hall. He was appointed to the post of treasurer by letters patent on 24 May 1451 'during good behaviour' on terms as 'any other treasurer have had'. Though he was appointed at the start of Somerset's tenure as Captain, he had not been closely associated with him prior to that. Married to a wealthy widow rather older than him, Clifton also had an active political life, serving as MP for Kent, Mayor of Canterbury and Sheriff of Kent. Along with the victualler of Calais, he was required to render his accounts to Parliament once every two years. Given the confused and depleted state of the Calais treasury, he was unable to do this on at least two occasions, and was granted pardons. He developed a good working relationship and close friendship with Trollope over the years and felt little personal loyalty to any of the captains of Calais during his time as treasurer.[23]

The raid on Sandwich demonstrated the dysfunction of the English government at this time and put even more power and resources into Warwick's hands. Faced with the general ineffectiveness of her husband, and with the interests of her son to protect, Margaret of Anjou now took a more prominent role in politics, gathering a strong household around her. York may not then have been the threat to her that he would become, but Margaret felt the effects of the growing political vacuum.[24]

For King Henry, the situation seems to have been much less complex: if only there could be peace among the lords, all would be well. That such a peace was not only elusive but unlikely to establish itself without direct intervention was demonstrated numerous times between 1456 and 1458. Feelings were running high. The sons of the St Albans dead, cheated out of redress and retribution by the parliamentary pardon, took matters into their own hands.

In November 1456, Exeter and Somerset attempted to ambush Warwick on his way to London but 'thanked be God the said earl was thereof aware and purveyed a remedy against their malice and came in safety to the city … and they dare not counter him for he was named and taken in all places as the most courageous and manliest knight living'.[25]

Warwick was not the only member of the family involved in trouble and conflict. There were reports of 'certain affrays' between Egremont and Warwick's brother John. There was also 'great visaging' between John and Somerset in London, and both young men 'mustered for to have bickered together in Cheap'. Fortunately, on this occasion, it came to nothing. John's marriage served to remove him for a time from temptation to engage in further visaging and bickering.[26]

Along with his father and uncle York, Warwick was 'near entrapped' riding to Coventry in February 1458. All three lords 'should have been destroyed if they were not seen well to'. Warnings came from Buckingham, as on previous occasions, and conflict was avoided.[27]

Buckingham's wife was the sister of Salisbury and the duchess of York but it was not simply for the sake of family connections that he intervened to rescue her kinsmen in both London and Coventry. In Coventry, Buckingham also interceded in, a great affray between the duke of Somerset's men and the watchmen of the town, and two or three men of the town were killed there, to the great disturbance of all the lords there, for the alarm bells were rung and the town arose and would have jeopardied to have distressed the duke of Somerset had the duke of Buckingham not taken a direction therein.[28]

A peacemaker and moderate Buckingham may have been, and no particular supporter of York and his aims, but he was no court favourite either. At the council meeting in Coventry in late 1456, his half-brothers Thomas and Henry Bourchier were dismissed from their posts as chancellor and treasurer respectively. As reported at the time, Buckingham took this 'right strangely'. The change in personnel in two such key posts was initiated by the queen and the dismissal of the Bourchiers brought the two, at least briefly, into opposition. This did not, however, shake Buckingham's loyalty to Henry VI, or serve to drive him into York's camp.[29]

The main cause of the trouble stemmed from the deaths of Somerset, Northumberland and Clifford at St Albans. Their sons, quite understandably, held the victors of the battle responsible for their fathers' deaths. Pre-existing ill-feeling and feud did not help the situation. The parliamentary pardon swept all responsibility away from York, Salisbury and Warwick. There had been no reckoning and the new duke of Somerset, earl of Northumberland and lord Clifford aimed to resolve the matter for themselves. Payback killings may bring short-term satisfaction to fatherless young men, but it was hardly in England's interests and was likely to lead to an escalating series of ambush and murder. Something had to be done.

It was during this time of unrest and disaffection that Henry VI took rare decisive action. He summoned his lords to a great council to be held in London in January 1458. Warwick's brother-in-law, the semi-reclusive earl of Arundel, failed to show up and was sent a letter ordering him to attend, reminding him just how important the meeting was: 'considering the great causes for the which we called our said council, in especial to set apart such variances as be between various lords of this our realm'. It was at this council that Warwick was appointed keeper of the seas and granted emergency funds, which so distressed Exeter.[30]

Such were the concerns of the mayor of London that his city be free of strife he readied 5,000 armed men to help keep the peace. He refused to allow Exeter, Somerset, Northumberland, Egremont or Clifford to bring their men into the city 'because they came against the peace'.[31]

York and Salisbury, however, were both allowed to stay within the city walls, York at Baynard's Castle and Salisbury at the Erber. Warwick's crossing from Calais was delayed by unfavourable winds but he soon arrived in the city and took up lodgings in Greyfriars. All three came with stout escorts, rather disingenuously described by one partisan chronicler as 'their householdmen in peaceable manner, thinking none harm'. The mayor and citizens of London were understandably nervous and 'the city was every day armed for to withstand the malice of the young lords if need be'.[32]

In the event, this was fortunate for Somerset and Northumberland once again made a move against Warwick in late February.

> [W]ith their men harnessed and arrayed in form of war [they] went to Westminster to the intent to have met with the earl of Warwick there but certain lords seeing it went against the earl of Warwick and met him in his barge on the Thames and so returned him again and no such thing was done, blessed be God.[33]

Warwick had no intention of allowing anything to keep him from attending council and 'said he would to Westminster on the morrow in spite of them all, wherefor the mayor made great watch to keep the peace'.[34]

On 7 March, the king and queen arrived and weeks of sometimes bitter negotiations began. There can be no doubt that Henry VI wanted peace and believed it could be achieved. York and Salisbury were equally committed but the younger lords, including Warwick and his brothers, may have been a little more cynical and less receptive to the idea.[35]

Both sides were required to submit to arbitration, an investigation of grievances with arguments and evidence presented by both sides, and a final decision that was to settle all differences. Henry VI envisaged a clean new page on which the future could be written. He was not directly involved in the process himself, moving with the queen to Berkhamsted Castle before it properly began. Here he received a visit from Exeter, Egremont, Somerset and Clifford, who seem to have hoped they could influence him to throw his support behind them. If that was their aim, they were unsuccessful. At this crucial time, Henry was not interested in playing favourites.[36]

The negotiations continued despite the tense atmosphere. In the mornings, York and his party met at Blackfriars; in the afternoons, Northumberland, Somerset and Clifford met with their supporters at Whitefriars. Besides the reluctant Arundel, Salisbury's other sons-in-law Fitzhugh, Stanley and Bonville were also in the city. Whether Thomas Nevill made the long journey down from Carlisle, with or without his wife, is not recorded. Warwick's presence in London was hard to miss, given that his 600 men were 'all apparelled in red jackets with white ragged staves'.[37]

Finally, a settlement was hammered out which could not be broken or overturned without stiff penalty. A chantry was set up to pray for those who had died at St Albans, funded by the duke of York. All current lawsuits were to be dropped. York was to compensate the duchess of Somerset for the death of her husband, and the young duke for the death of his father, to a total of 5,000 marks. Warwick was to pay 1,000 marks to Clifford and Salisbury to compensate his sister the duchess of Northumberland for the death of her husband. Egremont was pardoned for his escape from Newgate, his fines to the Nevills for his actions at Heworth forgiven and he was bound over to keep the peace for ten years. Furthermore, all parties involved were bound to abide by the settlement in amounts that would bring financial ruin if they failed to do so.[38]

The king returned to London and led a procession of his lords to St Pauls 'to pray for the peace'. Soon after, the queen came to the city and the following week,

> on Our Lady's Day Eve in Lent, that was a Friday, they were made accorded together, arm in arm as friends, and after noon the king sent writing to the mayor and commanded him to proclaim through the city how his lords were accorded and on the morn that was Our Lady's Day, the king and the queen and all the lords went in procession to St Pauls solemnly thanking God that the lords were accorded, and there was seen that day one of the greatest multitudes of people that was ever seen in St Pauls.[39]

None of the lords involved were humouring the king's wild dreams of peace. The raid on Sandwich had proved how vulnerable a disunited England was to foreign attack. Nevertheless, London celebrated, poems were written. Hindsight has done much to bring Love Day and Henry VI into ridicule, reducing the former to a pointless gesture doomed to fail. All it served to do, it is often said, was highlight the naivety of the king, the sullen intractability of the queen and her favourites. This is to ignore the enormous bonds all parties entered into, the cooperation – albeit after a sticky beginning – of all involved and the general optimism and euphoria generated by the agreement. While it can be said that peace-keeping is a pointless exercise if there is no peace to keep, the subsequent breakdown of order and descent into civil war does not, and should not, imply that no one but Henry VI either believed, or wanted to believe, Love Day would succeed.[40]

In the spring of 1458, things were looking up for England. The lords were at peace. Calais was solvent and a young man with energy and drive was both Captain of Calais and keeper of the seas. If more trouble came from France, it would be met by a united realm and stiff opposition in the Channel. Henry VI had achieved his great aim. Perhaps he would now take the reins of government into his hands and guide England wisely and firmly, advised and counselled by cooperative lords who had set their own differences aside. In spring 1458, with a healthy prince, a strong queen and a newly invigorated king, the Lancastrian dynasty was secure and assured.

# 17

# BREAKING THE KING'S PEACE

ohn Jernegan was a man with thoughts of marriage. Mistress Blanche Wychynham had caught his eye and, in June 1458, he hoped his father would be willing to approve the match. It was with such hope that he began his letter to Margaret Paston. He wrote from Calais, where he was serving under the new Captain, Richard, earl of Warwick. After the pleasantries were dealt with, assurances given that the writer was in good health, a prayer to 'Almighty Jesus to preserve you and keep you to his pleasure, and to your gracious heart's desire' and the plea to be remembered to Mistress Blanche, Jernegan turned to more dramatic news. He wrote of a great sea battle that took place just days earlier, a battle he had taken part in.[1]

It came to Warwick's attention that a fleet of twenty-four Spanish ships was at sea, sixteen of them 'great ships of forecastle'. Warwick readied a fleet of just twelve ships and, as Jernegan reported:

> on the Monday [29 May], on the morning after Trinity Sunday, we met together off Calais, at three at the clock in the morning, and there we took six of their ships, and they slew of our men about four score, and hurt two hundred of us right sore; and there were slain on their part about twelve score, and hurt five hundred of them.[2]

Jernegan was with a party that boarded and took one of the Spanish ships. He stayed aboard with just two dozen others to defend the prize. After a hard fight, the Spanish regained control of the ship, and Jernegan 'was taken, and was prisoner with them six hours, and was delivered again for their men that were taken before'. It was a hard fight and, once he was locked up in the liberated Spanish ship, there was nothing Jernegan could do but wait. Perhaps he heard the sounds of battle, the boom of the *Grace Dieu*'s cannon and the cries of men, fighting and dying.[3]

He wrote:

And as men say, there was not so great a battle upon the sea this eleven winters. And, forsooth, we were well and truly beat; and my lord has sent for more ships, and like to fight together again in haste.[4]

An exchange of prisoners saw Jernegan free to return to Calais, to write his letter to Margaret Paston and to indulge in thoughts of Mistress Blanche. Whatever it was stood in the way, perhaps his father's refusal to give his consent; Jernegan's hopes came to nothing. Sometime the following year, he married another. His bride was Isabel, daughter of Gervase Clifton.[5]

News of Warwick's exploits on the sea was greeted with great joy in England, particularly in London. Calais was more than an overseas English outpost. It was a symbol of what the nation had lost. It must be held on to, however much it drained English finances.[6]

As Captain of Calais, Warwick was popular, energetic and hardworking. On the other hand, he had little experience of military command and perhaps saw the Calais post as a way to military glory and personal profit. Calais was solvent and paid up when he took over, and the garrison's future wages seemed secure. The staple no longer need fear illegal seizure and sale of their wool. If Warwick wanted the new status quo to continue, he had to trust that Calais would remain a priority for Parliament and king.[7]

The Captain of Calais was not only a military and civilian governor, he was also a diplomat. Within months of taking possession, Warwick hosted a meeting with representatives from Burgundy. While others conducted the detailed negotiations, Warwick laid on a lavish banquet at which he entertained Anthony, Bastard of Burgundy, one of the most famous jousters of his day. Warwick's brothers, Thomas and John, were among the twenty-two members of the English delegation.[8]

Warwick realised early on the power a fleet of ships could give him. Most merchant ships were not commanded by those who owned them and ship ownership was not restricted to the very wealthy. Many vessels were owned by syndicates from coastal towns and villages, with shares passing down through families. Ships were arrested in time of war, crewed and outfitted by the admiral. While this was a cost-effective way of establishing a fleet, such ships were not always nimble enough to deal with an immediate threat. Built around the *Grace Dieu* and, later, the *Trinity*, Warwick's Calais fleet could more quickly be turned from trade to war.[9]

In May, Warwick was in London, where he may have attended jousts held in the Tower to celebrate Love Day. Unlike his late father-in-law, Warwick did not take an active part in tournaments or jousts. While he may have found it difficult to applaud the skills of Somerset and Anthony Wydeville with good grace, it would have been unwise to avoid an event attended by both king and queen.[10]

Warwick also had a family matter to attend to. Among other enquiries into piracy that year, Warwick was commissioned, along with Buckingham, to investigate his uncle Fauconberg. Fauconberg was implicated in the taking of a Spanish ship 'laden with divers goods and merchandise ... by pirates in [his] company'. On 9 May, Warwick and his brother Thomas stood bail for Fauconberg, who had been imprisoned, possibly on connected charges. He was ordered to appear before chancery later in the year. When he did, the charges were dropped.[11]

The people of London had been through much in the previous few months – the tensions of the peace negotiations, the jubilance of Love Day, the shocking news of the French raid on Sandwich. In April, riots had broken out between 'men of the court and inhabitants of [Fleet Street]. In which affray the queen's attorney was slain.' These riots were far from trivial and, on the day he left London, Warwick, 'by the king's command-ment rode through the city ... with a goodly fellowship' in a show of strength intended to awe and subdue.[12]

Back in Calais, piracy continued to be an issue. Not only had Fauconberg been investigated the previous year, Warwick was commissioned to arrest Andrew Trollope for boarding foreign ships and seizing cargoes of wool. 'Calais was alive with piracy, Warwick's officers as active as anyone else, and the king's commissions came perilously close to asking Warwick to investigate himself.'[13]

Warwick's confrontation with the Spanish fleet captured the hearts of the people of England. While other lords remained safe, caring nothing for 'the profit and honour of the king and the land', Warwick took to the sea and *did* something. That it was of questionable legality and, at the very least, unethical, that it was likely to cause conflict with Spain, that it might hurt England's trading relationships with other seafaring nations, did not seem to be much of an issue in the popular imagination.[14]

While the king, and Warwick's adversaries, did nothing,

> only he [acted], for the which manhood and his great policy and deeds doing of worship in fortifying Calais and other feats of arms [that] all commonality of this land had him in great laud and charity for the substance, and all other lands in likewise, and so repute and take him for as famous a knight as was living.[15]

In July, Warwick put to sea again, this time capturing a Genoese merchant-man and three great ships of Spain. He also attacked the Hanseatic salt fleet, bringing about a crisis in international relations. After complaints from merchants and representatives of foreign powers, Henry VI set up a commission of enquiry. It was not outside the bounds of possibility that Warwick would find himself dismissed as Captain of Calais and keeper of the seas, though the only indication we have of the imminent danger of this comes from Warwick himself. He would not, he declared, give up Calais.[16]

> It is reported that if the great parliament of the king had been held as it had been proposed, the earl of Warwick would have been disappointed of the government of Calais, and this is quite notorious, and so he understands it. And on the other hand, he has declared publicly that to abandon all his lands, and whatever he has in England, he will not give up Calais before the time appointed to him, and that is still for nine years whereof only three have expired.[17]

It was the attack on the salt fleet that proved a turning point. The government could no longer ignore Warwick's actions. In July 1458 Henry VI established a commission headed by lord Rivers to 'examine … persons having knowledge of a conflict on the sea between Richard Nevill earl of Warwick and his retinue and certain of Lubeck under the king's friendship'.[18]

In October, Warwick was summoned to a council meeting at Westminster. If he was not to be dismissed outright, he could at least expect to be admonished. His authority as keeper of the seas had been laid out explicitly. By attacking foreign ships engaged in peaceful trade in the Channel, he had hugely overstepped this authority. No doubt armed with solid arguments in his own defence, he must have approached the English coast with some trepidation. He was in need of funds and promised payments from the Treasury had failed to arrive. Taking matters into his own hands was a last resort, but necessary to keep the garrison happy and the staple on side. Furthermore, he was to claim, Parliament had appointed him Captain of Calais and only Parliament could rescind his commission. In this, he was not entirely correct, being either mistaken or choosing to misstate the facts. His appointment had been granted through an indenture with the king. Parliament had nothing to do with it. If Warwick was to be dismissed, it would be on Henry VI's word alone.[19]

Despite the urgency of the summons, Warwick took his time getting to London. He stayed a while in Colleyweston in Northamptonshire, where he had recently bought property. Whatever might have been in others' minds, his was firmly on the future of Calais. His marshal, Edmund Mulsho, had recently died and Warwick had written to his uncle asking for the services of York's man, Walter Blount. York could ill afford to lose Blount but allowed that Warwick might make use of his services for a year while he looked for a permanent replacement. From Colleyweston, Warwick travelled north to Middleham to visit his family. Three letters from the king were sent after him, one carried by John Say and two more sent under the privy seal summoning him to London where he was to answer 'for divers special causes and matters … that concern the said lord king and council'.[20]

Warwick finally made it to London on 9 November. As it turned out, he never did face an investigation of his actions in the Channel. A curious incident in Westminster Hall left Warwick shaken, in fear of his life and on his way back to the safety of Calais within days of his arrival.

> [A]s the earl of Warwick was at a council in Westminster, all the king's household men gathered themselves together for to have slain the said earl; but by help of God and his friends, he recovered his barge and escaped their evil enterprise, but the cooks came running out with spits and pestles against him.[21]

This was no unprovoked attack and Warwick was not, at first, the primary target: 'a fray happened to fall between a servant of the king's and a servant of the earl of Warwick, the which hurt the king's servant and after escaped.' Another chronicler blames the king's man, for he 'trod upon the foot of one of the earl's men'. Warwick soon found himself in the thick of it, the king's cooks 'intending to have slain him' with their utensils. If the chroniclers are to be taken at their word, this spelled the beginning of the end for Henry VI's carefully constructed but tenuous peace. 'For this the old rancour and malice, which never was cleanly cured, anon began to break out'.[22]

The original perpetrator having made his escape, 'the king's other servants seeing they might not be avenged upon the party that had thus hurt their fellow', took their anger out on Warwick as he emerged. He was lucky to escape arrest, for an attack on a member of the king's household, whether provoked or not, was as good as an attack on the king himself. Warwick got to his barge and out of the city before an arrest could be made.[23]

The incident had a profound effect on Warwick. What seems to have started with a minor scuffle between two men rapidly escalated and, in Warwick's mind at least, took on serious and sinister overtones: people were out to get him. His response speaks of a distrust too deep to be mended by Love Day, a distrust that was far from one-sided. If his account is to be believed, he came close to losing his post as Captain of Calais. He came even closer to a spell in the Tower. The brawl in Westminster was not a deliberate attempt on his life. He did what anyone in his position would have done, he came to the aid of his men. In less fraught times, his presence and authority may have gone a long way to calming things down. As it was, it did the opposite. Warwick escaped Westminster, and London, by the skin of his teeth.[24]

# 18

# THE GATHERING STORM

In August and September 1459, Middleham Castle was a hive of activity. Men and horses were pouring in from all corners of Yorkshire and beyond. Despite recent incursions by the Scots, which made a strong presence in the marches more necessary than ever, Thomas Nevill left his post as lieutenant warden and returned home. John tore himself away from his wife and young family and came north. Warwick made ready to cross the Channel from Calais. Others of Salisbury's council came from closer at hand. A cloud hung over the Nevills and, whatever the future held, they would face it in solidarity – among themselves and with the duke of York.[1]

Middleham Castle, always a busy place, swung into high gear. Supplies poured in: food, ale and wine, armour and weapons of war. The kitchens doubled and tripled their output. Rooms were opened for family members and retainers of high rank and standing. There was fresh linen on beds and space allocated for tents to be pitched and beds to be rolled out in barracks.

Salisbury had called his council together for the second time in a year. He had summoned them to Middleham the previous September, 'and there at that time it was concluded by said earl and all his whole council that he and all such other men of worship as (then met) should take full part with the full noble prince, the duke of York'.[2]

This had been a long time coming. Up until this point, Salisbury's association with York had been episodic. He played no prominent role in York's second protectorate and much of what he had done since St Albans was in support of his son Warwick rather than York directly. Now their names were inextricably linked in the minds of many, including the queen and Somerset. A slight against one was a slight against all.

A letter to the Prior of Erdesby, asking him to speak to the queen on Salisbury's behalf, may have been written at this time. The letter was written in response to one from the Prior that included oblique accusations against Salisbury, his son and York. In Salisbury's reply we get a hint of the queen's suspicions of both York and Warwick. Salisbury not only wanted to reassure the queen of his own loyalty and goodwill but that she need have no concerns about York or Warwick.

> I pray you to declare me unto her said grace and where in your said letters it is expressed that you have heard language of accusations of right high estates to be made by my lord of York, my son of Warwick and me, in matters that have not been disclosed here before, to their great rebuke etc, truly it is to my great marvel by what colour, reason or ground any such language by any person earthly might be uttered or said, for as my own part, as I will answer to our lord, I never imagined, thought or said any such matter or anything like thereunto in my days, and in like wise, I dare will say for my said lord and son as far as ever I heard or in any wise knew until this hour, as I doubt not they will at all times right largely declare themselves, and therefor therein, or in any other concerning my truth, I pray you always to answer largely for me, and if there be anything that I may do to your benefit, certify me and you shall to the performing thereof find me right heartily disposed, our lord knows.[3]

The queen's goodwill towards Salisbury was clearly still very important to him, especially as her political power was starting to grow. As the king became less able to govern, and less interested in governing, someone had to fill the vacuum. York had tried twice, with limited success. Margaret of Anjou, with her own interests and those of her son to protect, could hardly be faulted for stepping into the breach.

There is no extant response to Salisbury's letter, either from the Prior of Erdebsy or the queen. That he felt the need to call his council to Middleham to put the words of the previous year into action would suggest that if there had been a response, the earl could draw no comfort from it.

Salisbury's council consisted of a wide range of men with the skills and experience required for the smooth running of his estate. Apart from his sons and his brother Fauconberg, who was retained for life on an annual fee of £20, some of these men had been closely associated with Salisbury for decades. Some had served the family for generations. Sir John Conyers, steward of Middleham, had followed his father Christopher and was in turn to be followed by his own son. So close was the relationship between the two families that another of John Conyer's sons (also John) married Fauconberg's daughter Alice.[4]

The larger baronial estates, such as Salisbury's, were so complex they required administrative machinery that mirrored that of the kingdom itself. Barons employed, either permanently or on a more ad hoc basis, career lawyers and bureaucrats to oversee the running of a network of manors and lordships that might be scattered throughout the country. In the 1450s, professionalism had not fully replaced the last remnants of feudalism. A large core of Salisbury's northern council was made up of men from the surrounding area and from Yorkshire more generally, with one or two from farther afield.[5]

Local connections remained important, particularly during this time of growing tension. Some of the men associated with Salisbury had been with him since they were young men, serving with him in France and in the marches. While this association, and friendship, was decades-long, Salisbury retained few for life. Fees to life retainers could be a crippling burden on estates. One way to get around this was to retain men on a temporary, as needs basis. This was technically against the law but that did not bring the practice to an end. The late earl of Northumberland had expended about a third of his income on fees to retainers. Salisbury spent considerably less, choosing instead to flout the law and take advantage of the flexibility and economy that fixed-term indentures provided.[6]

An indenture drawn up in 1431 between Salisbury and Henry Threlkeld sets out the requirements of each party: Threlkeld was retained for six months to serve with Salisbury in France for two shillings a day; Threlkeld was to bring with him eight men of arms, who would receive twelve pence a day, and twenty-two archers, who would be paid sixpence; Threlkeld was also to provide arms and armour for his men, to consist of '40 arrows well feathered and notched, two bows, twelve strings, a sword and buckler, a knife or a pollaxe'. Salisbury was to get a third of all 'winnings of war during the said voyage, be they prisoner money, gold or silver or jewels or any other winning of war that ought to be thirded'. For his part, Threlkeld was expected to duly obey 'all the commandments and ordinances of the said earl, his lieutenant or deputy, and generally to do truly in all points, as soldiers ought to, unto his captain'. When his term expired, if he had pleased his good lord, Threlkeld's tenure would be extended for another six months.[7]

Besides Conyers, prominent among Salisbury's retainers in 1459 were William Parr, Robert Ogle and Thomas Harrington. Ogle, who hailed from Northumberland and might have been expected to look to the Percies for good lordship, had already proven his worth at the battle of St Albans in 1455. Harrington and Parr were both to develop even closer ties to the Nevills, with sons and grandsons married to the daughters of Alice Nevill and Henry Fitzhugh. Harrington and Conyers had supported Salisbury in the marches towards Scotland in the 1440s and 1450s. Harrington might not have been bound to Salisbury through a lifetime fee but he came when he was summoned, supported his chosen lord in times of peace and followed him in times of war.[8]

One important member of Salisbury's affinity was missing – his son-in-law Henry Fitzhugh, whose home at Ravensworth was just 16 miles north of Middleham. Fitzhugh's grandfather, also Henry, served the Lancastrian kings till his death in 1425. Like Ralph Nevill and Richard Beauchamp, he threw in his lot with Henry Bolingbroke from the moment he landed his small force at Ravenspur and continued to support him throughout his life. When Henry V came to the throne, Fitzhugh served as his chamberlain and, from 1416 to 1421, as treasurer of England. He fought at Agincourt and was involved in the negotiations that led to the Treaty of Troyes in 1420. When Henry V entered Paris later that year, Fitzhugh was by his side. Along with Beauchamp, he was with Henry V when he died and accompanied his body home to England. At the time of his death, Fitzhugh was a prominent member of Henry VI's council, having been instrumental in its establishment three years earlier.[9]

As Salisbury's son-in-law, and living such a short distance from Middleham, young Henry Fitzhugh was a member of Salisbury's council. His loyalty and support for his wife's family might have been expected to continue for many years to come. His own family's close connections to the Lancastrian dynasty, however, would not allow him to stand with anyone perceived to be working against the king. We have no record of correspondence between Salisbury and Fitzhugh at this time, nor do we know how the situation might have affected their relationship, or Fitzhugh's with his wife. Despite his involvement in the indictment of Percy followers in 1454, Fitzhugh had never been closely associated with the duke of York. He did not take the field at the battle of St Albans, which may be indicative of both his unwillingness to oppose his king and his reticence to fight against his in-laws and close neighbours. It would take some years for this uncertain state of affairs to resolve itself.

Though not officially a member of his council, another person Salisbury could rely on absolutely for support was his wife of nearly forty years. For most of their marriage, Alice Montagu's role was unambiguous. She was in charge of her household; she raised their children and kept herself busy with genteel pursuits suitable for women. It was when he was away that her role shifted. Though Salisbury could trust his council to look after his interests and the interests of his family while he was away from home, his wife had to be prepared to deal with any difficulties that arose. That might include overseeing the defence of home, family and property. Now, with her menfolk under threat, she took an active role in their preparations to defend themselves before the king.[10]

Unfortunately, though we know it dated to the beginning of August 1459, we do not know the details of Alice's involvement. Her actions were connected with those of William Oldhall and Thomas Vaughan in London a month earlier. She might have been raising troops for her husband, or ordering weapons or supplies necessary for a large army. Alice's movements around this time are also unclear. When she next appears in the record, she is in Ireland. How she got there is a mystery. There are two possibilities: she may have been with her husband and sons when they left Middleham, or she may have travelled later, essentially on her own and with little protection. Either way, she had to leave behind her last unmarried daughter, Margaret, then aged 14 or 15. Again, we are left to speculate, but with Margaret's sister Alice nearby at Ravensworth, she may have been entrusted to her care.[11]

Just what was it that caused Salisbury to gather his retainers, armed and ready for war? It was not his intention to confront Henry VI in the field, nor was there an imminent threat to his life and property. Only weeks earlier, Henry VI had still been hopeful the brokered peace of Love Day would hold. Whatever suspicions his lords entertained of York and the Nevills, Henry declared York to be 'our right trusty and wellbeloved cousin', 'our approved and true liegeman and no traitor, our true subject and no rebel, our right faithful friend and no enemy'. Anything said against him was 'only by cruel and malicious exhortation of his mortal enemies'.[12]

In June, despite King Henry's hopes and his previous support of York, charges were laid against York at a council meeting in Coventry, and possibly against Warwick as well. Chancellor Waynflete laid out the charges; Buckingham led the prosecution and pronounced the guilty verdict. A sentence was handed down, possibly death. Whatever the accusations, Henry VI overruled his lords, as he had done in previous years with Exeter and the late duke of Somerset. Without a clear understanding of the background, the charges would seem to have come out of nowhere. The attempt on Warwick's life in November 1458 had inspired no sudden flaring of violence or rebellion. Salisbury returned peacefully to Middleham and Warwick crossed to Calais, where he once again took a leading role in talks with both France and Burgundy. Henry and his queen retreated to the Midlands and the government reverted to a state of flux.[13]

The royal family's retreat to the Midlands was partly precipitated by the renewal of previous conflict in London. 'This year [there] was a great fray between the city of London and the men of [the] court, which were driven with archers of the city from the Standard in Fleet Street to their inns the 13th day of April, and some were slain and some were taken.' At the end of 1458, the king's concerns for his safety and the safety of his family had prompted him to order 500 pikes and 500 leaden clubs for the protection of the royal household. Great serpentines were also purchased, sufficient, the king was told, to lay siege to the castles of rebellious lords.[14]

On 29 April 1459, Margaret Paston wrote to her husband, informing him 'that on Thursday last was there brought into this town many privy seals'. One, she told him, was endorsed to him and another was for their son, signed, as few others were, 'with the king's own hand'.

The intent of the writing was that they should be with the king at Leicester the tenth day of May, with as many persons defensibly arrayed as they might according to their degree, and that they should bring with them for their expenses for two months.[15]

The questions of why Henry was raising troops at this time, and whose castles he felt he might need to flatten with his great serpentines, cannot be answered with any great confidence. Records of the movements or actions of York and the Nevills that might have alarmed the king have not survived. Something must have prompted the charges laid at the Coventry council in June, but that *something* remains a mystery.

What is clear from contemporary chronicles, and not just those particularly friendly to York, is that the queen was behind the charges. As the king retreated further from political life, Margaret of Anjou had little choice but to take up the slack. She had previously been instrumental in the removal of York's brothers-in-law, viscount Bourchier and the Archbishop of Canterbury, as treasurer and chancellor. Now key government posts were held by those who had no particular affinity with either York or the Nevills. Even putting aside potential factional conflicts, it made sense for a court that kept itself away from the capital to choose to deal only with those who could be absolutely trusted. There were logistical difficulties to contend with. When the king was away from the capital, business had to be dealt with through a network of messengers connecting the court, the council and the officers in London who did the actual work. As the factions became more polarised, those who had previously been seen as neutral, such as Buckingham, aligned themselves more firmly with the king. With previous associates Worcester and Norfolk conveniently choosing to leave England on pilgrimage, York and his small band of allies grew more and more isolated.[16]

Whatever efforts were made, and whatever measures were put in place to keep things running smoothly, both king and government were criticised. Henry's difficulties with money were brought up once again. 'In this same time, the realm of England was out of all good governance, as it had been many days before, for the king was simple and led by covetous council, and owed more than he was worth.'[17]

Whatever money came his way through taxes and customs 'was spent in vain, for he had no household nor maintained no wars'. His subjects' hearts hardened against Henry and 'their blessings were turned into cursings'. The queen 'ruled the realm as she pleased, gathering riches innumerable'. The officers of the realm, particularly treasurer Wiltshire, 'for to enrich themselves, peeled the poor people and disinherited rightful heirs and did many wrongs'. The queen was plotting, 'making privy means to some of the lords of England for to stir the king that he should resign the crown to her son'. While this is all likely to be something of an overstatement, designed to explain and justify the later actions of York and his allies, it holds a kernel of truth. England was disaffected; her government was in trouble.[18]

When council was called to meet in Coventry in June, some prominent names were missing. When Henry overturned the sentence pronounced on York and Warwick, the lords, led by Buckingham, fell to their knees and begged him to show York no more mercy.[19]

> [S]eeing the great jeopardy for your most noble person, and also the lords so often charged, and inquieting so often the great part of your realm, that it should not like you to show the said duke of York, nor no one other hereafter, your grace, if they attempted again to do the contrary to your royal estate, or inquieting of your realm and the lords thereof, but to be punished after their desserts, and have as they deserved, as well of the security of you, sovereign lord, as the general security of all your lords and people.[20]

Whether the queen played the leading and decisive role credited to her in contemporary chronicles is difficult to judge. As they were written after the events they described, this may have been a projection of her later role back to an earlier time, an example of the skilful manipulation of reality to which the Yorkists, and particularly Warwick, resorted time and again. Margaret did hand out her son's livery to the men of Cheshire, as reported, which was a clear sign of her growing power and authority. The claims that she particularly aimed her spite and enmity at Salisbury, however, cannot easily be verified. Her later role, and her sex, made her rich fodder for propagandists. Given his nature, it would be difficult to pin motives of malice and spite on the king. The queen and the 'covetous lords' she favoured were a far easier target. It was in these heavily York-biased reports that questions were first raised about the paternity of her son, questions the king had never thought to ask. Prince Edward was not Henry's son, the rumours claimed, 'but a bastard got in adultery'. The queen may have been 'defamed and slandered', but a cynic might conclude that the defamation and slander were not so much reported as concocted at the time of writing.[21]

Whatever the charges, and whoever the driving force behind them or, indeed, their truth, this was too much for York, Salisbury and Warwick. They needed, once again, to clear their names, to ride to meet the king and recite to him their loyalty and allegiance. Though it is likely there was a little more on their minds than simply falling to their knees and begging the king's pardon, perhaps it was again only hindsight that allowed such drastic recasting of motives and events.[22]

The duke of York, the earls of Warwick and Salisbury, saw that the governance of the realm stood most by the queen and her council, and how the great princes of the land were not called to council but set apart; and not only so but that it was said through the realm that the said lords shall be destroyed utterly.[23]

Warwick spent the night of 20 September in London before riding towards Worcester, where the three lords had planned to meet. Salisbury left Middleham at around the same time, heading south with his sons Thomas and John, his most trusted retainers and around 5,000 men. Though there is no mention of whether his countess made the journey with him, given later events, it is entirely possible she did. If he left her behind, their parting cannot have been easy. Uncertainty lay ahead for them both. If Salisbury was found guilty of treason, he faced execution by beheading. If the countess's actions came to light, her death would be more horrific still. Women executed for treason were committed to the flames.[24]

If all went according to plan, Salisbury would meet York and Warwick in Worcester, then ride to Kenilworth to meet with the king. Later, it was declared that their purpose was peaceful. As at St Albans in 1455, all they wanted to do was present themselves humbly before Henry and protest their loyalty and innocence. This was not how it was seen by their enemies. From their perspective, the intentions of York and his allies were neither peaceful nor loyal. The king was told the rebels 'falsely and traitorously conspired and sought the time and means of accomplishment of their insatiable will and desire of destruction of you, sovereign lord, the queen our sovereign lady and of your succession'.[25]

According to later reports, they had intended to take the king and his family by surprise but the king, forewarned, took decisive action. This caused Salisbury to 'divert from his first enterprise and purpose and to take another way to assemble with the said duke of York and earl of Warwick that their coming together might make a mightier field'.[26]

As it was, Salisbury's party alone gave battle to the king's forces as he travelled through Staffordshire. With Queen Margaret at Eccleshall and lords Audley and Dudley approaching Market Drayton, under order to take him into their custody, Salisbury could not hope to avoid a fight, 'and keeping his journey, met with the said lord Audley at a place called Blore Heath, where both companies ran together and there was strong bickering'.[27]

Salisbury's son-in-law Sir Thomas Stanley was nearby. Ordered by both the king and queen to come to their aid, Stanley did neither. Nor did he make any move to support his father-in-law. His brother William did, bringing much-needed reinforcements. It was later reported that William had with him some of Sir Thomas's servants, including a cook who was injured in the battle and left behind in Market Drayton to recover.[28]

Lord Audley commanded a large cavalry and around 10,000 men at arms. Salisbury's force was a little more than half that number. Informed by scouts where the enemy waited, Salisbury drew his wagons into a defensive formation on the edge of a wooded area. He set his troops parallel to a stream, whose steep banks formed part of his defences. At one in the afternoon, Audley's cavalry advanced. Salisbury ordered his centre to withdraw, giving the impression he was retreating before the battle could even begin. Seeing this, Audley urged his cavalry forward in what he must have hoped would be a quick pursuit and an effortless victory. Negotiating the banks of the shallow stream was not easy and, when they reached the other side, Salisbury's archers, who had turned back, were waiting for them. Around 300 of Audley's men were killed before he ordered them to retreat. Audley himself led the second cavalry charge. Again it was met by a swarm of arrows. Audley was killed and his cavalry left the field. Forced to take command, lord Dudley abandoned any thoughts of winning the battle by cavalry alone. Setting some of them to wait nearby, he ordered the remainder to dismount and fight on foot.[29]

The two armies met and fought bitterly well into the afternoon. Slowly, inch by inch, Salisbury's forces got the upper hand, forcing Dudley's men back. When the remnant of Audley's cavalry saw how things were going, they rode away. Around 500 of Dudley's men also deserted, some rumoured to have changed sides mid-battle. Finally, the line broke, soldiers stumbling away, abandoning their heavy weapons and running for their lives. Nearly 2,000 of Dudley's men lay dead on the field. Around 500 of Salisbury's forces lost their lives. Lord Dudley himself was taken alive.[30]

Salisbury moved his army to Market Drayton, where he received a letter from his son-in-law Stanley, 'thanking God of the good speed of the said earl, rejoicing him greatly of the same and trusting God that he should be with the same earl in other place, to stand him in as good stead as he should have done if he had been with them there'.[31]

In the early hours of the following morning, Sir Thomas Harrington and Thomas and John Nevill were captured near Taporley, some 30 miles to the north-west. Just what they were doing there is a matter of some dispute. One source reports that they had been 'sore wounded' in the battle and sought shelter. A second source suggests they strayed too far in the rout and found themselves in unfamiliar territory, uncertain of the way back.[32]

But in the morning, between the field and Chester, sir John Donne … that was at home in his father's place had word that his father was slain; anon he raised his tenants and took beside a little town named [Taporley] sir Thomas Nevill, sir John Nevill and sir Thomas Harrington, and brought them to the castle of Chester.[33]

It is possible they were trying to get to a safe haven in Lancashire with Harrington as escort when they were captured, or they may have followed the rout with more than usual enthusiasm and got themselves lost. If this is the case, Harrington's presence is puzzling, as he was reported not only to have read Stanley's letter to Salisbury but 'shewed it openly, saying, sirs, be merry, for yet we have more friends'. This would suggest Harrington was in Market Drayton with the earl and not following the rout. A third possibility is that Harrington was sent out to find Salisbury's missing sons. That Salisbury lingered in Market Drayton a little longer than was safe suggests he was either waiting for Thomas and John to return or to receive word they were in a place of safety.[34]

A curious after note to the battle is the story of the Austin friar found alone in the field with a great cannon which he had set off at intervals during the night. It might have been a ruse by Salisbury to make anyone within earshot believe his forces were still in the area and to cover his tracks. Or it might have been just as the friar is reported to have claimed.

> But the earl of Salisbury had been taken save only a Friar Austin shot guns all that night in a park that was at the back side of the field … And in the morning, they found neither man nor child in the field but the friar, and he said that for fear he had abode in that park all night.[35]

The earl of Salisbury had no choice but to keep moving if he was to avoid the nearby armies of Buckingham and Somerset. He had to reach the relative safety of Ludlow Castle and at least he knew his missing sons were alive. How long any of them would remain so was for God to decide.

# 19

# LUDFORD

hen Warwick entered London on 20 September 1459, he had with him a large part of the Calais garrison. The city welcomed him as it always had, throwing open its gates and greeting England's hero. He spent just one night in the capital before moving north, towards Warwickshire, where he hoped to recruit more men to his banner. He needed to join his father and uncle as quickly, and with as much strength, as he could.[1]

With the king and his court in the Midlands, this was no easy task. Somerset was nearby and Warwick could not linger if he was to avoid battle. With Somerset preventing him from reaching the safety of Warwick Castle, Warwick led his army north of the town, narrowly avoiding a clash near Coleshill. With little rest and no time to recruit, Warwick pressed on westward towards Worcester.[2]

Along the way, he would have received news of the battle of Blore Heath and the death of Audley. This must have engendered mixed feelings: joy at his father's victory, concern for the well-being of his captive brothers and a sense of unease that things were not going according to plan.

The plan was not complicated, however. Over the last year, York and the Nevills had been seen increasingly to be acting in concert and against the safety of the king. They had come to be seen as a cohesive unit in the minds of the public and the court, a party bent on opposition. That there was already suspicion about their true intentions was clear. York, it was feared, meant to depose Henry, perhaps even kill him, and set himself up as king in his place. If only they could speak with him. Face to face, they could assure him of their loyalty and peaceful intentions. They might convince him to dispense with the services of Somerset, Wiltshire and other lords who were only out for themselves. Henry was a reasonable and compassionate man. How could he fail to see the truth of their words when they knelt before him, pledging – once again – the whole of their allegiance?

Warwick was a man who knew he was right, even when he was otherwise. He also knew the power of words. What made sense to him would surely make sense to others, if only he could get them to listen. If it came to another fight, his father had already demonstrated what he could do on his own. When he and York and Salisbury came together, no one would be able to stand against them. Warwick had behind him the only professional fighting force in England. His commitment to this force, to Calais and to England had gone a long way to winning their personal loyalty. If he had to rely on anyone, Warwick could not do better than to put his life and his livelihood in the hands of the soldiers of the Calais garrison.

When Warwick reached Worcester, he found his father at the head of a battered and depleted army. The loss of Thomas and John was not to be underestimated. The failure of Thomas Stanley to join them was to be regretted. York had managed to attract no allies of any strength. Only two barons, lord Clinton and lord Grey of Powys, were with them. Far from the overwhelming show of power they had been counting on, they were not strong enough to risk another battle, particularly not against the consolidated forces of the king.[3]

At Worcester, with Henry VI just 32 miles away at Leominster, they wrote a letter putting forward their case, as they had done nearly five years earlier at St Albans. Composed by Warwick, it spoke of the government's failure to look after the common good, the 'good politic laws' and the 'rest and peace of the realm'. These were at the forefront of York's mind, he wrote, as well as his own and his father's. The courts, trade, recourse to justice – all these had been 'piteously overturned and as who says it is forgotten'. The king was 'outrageously spoiled and robbed of his livelihood and possessions'. The commons of England had their goods and chattels taken by 'ministers of the king's household without payment'. Then there was the lawlessness in England, 'great abominable murders, robberies, perjuries and extortions … great violence [that] is not punished but favoured and cherished'. The king's laws and commandments, his presence in council and the words of his lords and judges were disregarded.[4]

On a more personal and perhaps immediate level, greedy and covetous people had turned their 'uttermost malice' against York and his Nevill allies. All this, Warwick warned, would bring England to ruin.

They would go to the king, he wrote:

> and as true subjects and liegemen, lovers of the said common weal and lovers of the honour of his estate, show thereunto the inconveniences above rehearsed and thereupon beseech his good grace as lowly as we can that he will vouchsafe to redeem his land and subjects from the jeopardy of the said mischiefs.[5]

Henry needed to listen to 'the advice of the great lords of his blood' and punish 'the said causers of the said mischiefs'. '[W]e will employ our persons and labours about the king's most noble person and thereto be assistant if it be his pleasure.' They would do none of this for personal gain or profit, nor to dredge up old grudges or seek revenge. They wanted to be of assistance to the king, to help set the realm to rights and sweep the corruption from Henry's government. No invitation came from the king to join him.[6]

He did send the Bishop of Salisbury with an offer of pardon 'for all trespasses whatsoever if they would give over their enterprise and become true and obedient subjects', but this was refused.

> [T]hey answered by the mouth of the earl of Warwick in three points: first that as concerning the pardon, they durst not trust it. Secondly, that notwith-standing such pardons, those that were about the king were unruly and cared not to break the king's commandment. Thirdly, although every lord, being called to parliament, ought freely to come and safely to depart, yet the earl of Warwick, at a certain counsel held at Westminster, was in danger of death, if the lord above had not the better provided for his escape, for the which cause he believes the king's pardon may be likened to a buckler of glass or a staff of reed, of the which there is no truth; we dare not commit ourselves to the defence of any such pardon.[7]

Accepting a pardon would be tantamount to recognising their guilt. However their actions were viewed by others – at best a flouting of royal authority, at worst an attempt to seize power – this was not how they saw themselves, nor was it a view they wished to have confirmed. Accepting the king's offer of pardon was out of the question.[8]

From Leominster on 9 October, the king summoned Parliament but no letters came for York, Warwick or Salisbury. Their omission, alongside the unusual timing for a parliamentary sitting, could only mean that Henry planned to move against them. The situation was now both dire and urgent. If they wanted to avoid charges of treason and attainder, they had to convince the king of their peaceful intentions. That same day, Warwick was replaced by Somerset as Captain of Calais.[9]

The following day, in Worcester Cathedral, they solemnly swore themselves together, for the protection of themselves and each other, for the 'prosperity and augmentation' of the king's high estate, and for the common weal of England. They swore on the holy sacraments, the 'blessed body of our lord Jhesu'. Once again, they swore the truth of their words both in writing and 'by mouth' to Garter King of Arms.[10]

Much of this letter is a repetition of things that had been said many times before over several years. They attempted to minimise the implications of the armies they had with them. They had avoided bloodshed, they claimed, as far as they could. Audley, it had to be inferred, had been the aggressor and would still be alive if he had not forced Salisbury to battle. Warwick had, after all, managed to avoid conflict with Somerset as he attempted to reach Warwick Castle.[11]

They would not, they said, attempt to approach the king without invitation, but they had been 'proclaimed and defamed in our names unrightfully, unlawfully … and untruly'. Their property had been 'robbed and spoiled'.[12] Henry was listening to the wrong people. If he wanted to do what was right, he should

> not apply your said highness nor the great rightwiseness and equity … to the importunate impatience and violence of such persons as intend of extreme malice to proceed under shadow of your high might and presence to our destruction, for such inordinate covetous, whereof God is not pleased, as they have to our lands, offices and goods.[13]

Such people had no regard for the spilling of Christian blood, nor did they care for or respect the noble blood upon which the security and sovereignty of England relied. If Henry had any concerns about the men who rode behind them, he should know they were not there because York and the Nevills feared for their own lives but they would not leave themselves undefended and open to provocation. The letter was put into the hands of Garter King of Arms to take to Henry.[14]

From Worcester, they moved south to Tewkesbury. King Henry and his army moved swiftly towards Worcester, too close for comfort, and York and his allies changed direction and retreated once again to Ludlow.[15]

Now they were both geographically and politically isolated. Bottled up, they could expect no more supporters to join them, if any wished to. While Henry VI had the fealty of the English people and the vast majority of her lords, and York's intentions were generally viewed as motivated by self-interest and self-promotion, no one was prepared to risk attainder and death by throwing in their lot with him. York and the Nevills had become inextricably linked in the popular mind since York's first Protectorate in 1454 and the battle of St Albans in 1455. Despite geographical separation and largely separate agendas over the intervening years – Warwick in Calais and Salisbury in the marches – the fall of York was always going to mean the fall of the Nevills. While by no means reluctant allies, self-preservation mattered at least as much as any publicly stated policy of reform. Despite Love Day, Somerset was proving an intractable enemy. Joined as he was from time to time by Exeter and Northumberland's brothers, his determination to see an end to the Nevills was unlikely to diminish. He would certainly relish what was to come when Parliament met: their political and symbolic death by attainder. Now they had a more immediate threat to deal with. The king raised his banner and made ready for war.[16]

The Yorkists dug in just outside the town of Ludlow, along the River Teme. 'The duke of York let make a great deep ditch and fortified it with guns, carts and stakes, but his party was overweak, for the king had more than 3,000 harnessed men, beside naked men that were compelled for to come with the king.' With the royal army approaching, banners displayed, they had to move fast. Their armies, exhausted from a forced march from Worcester to Tewkesbury, then back to Ludlow, were low on morale. All along, they had been assured they would not be asked to take up arms against the king, and now York turned his guns on Henry, firing into the darkness. The reality confronting them now was frightening as, led by their lords, they edged closer to treason. They were outnumbered more than two to one and a growing unease swept through their ranks, particularly those of the Calais garrison.[17]

As the only professional standing army England had, the veterans of the garrison were of great value to whoever had them on their side. No doubt the garrison developed strong bonds with the Captains of Calais, but their loyalty to the king came first. Warwick had worked hard to win them over. His decision to base himself in Calais went a long way towards gaining their trust and their respect, but if he thought he had himself a private army unequalled in England, he was mistaken. Led by Sir Andrew Trollope, a sizeable number of the garrison quit their Captain during the night of 11–12 October, taking with them all they knew of York's battle plans. Faced with almost certain defeat and death, York, Warwick and Salisbury had no choice but to abandon their men and flee.[18]

> The duke thus keeping his field upon the one part and the king with his people upon the other, on the night preceding the day that both hosts should have met … Andrew Trollope, with all the chief soldiers of Calais, secretly departed from the duke's host and went to the king's, where they were joyously received. When this thing to the duke and the other lords was ascertained, they were therewith sore dismayed, and especially for the said lords had to the said Andrew showed the whole of their intents, which then they knew well should be clearly discovered unto their enemies, wherefore after counsel for a remedy taken, they concluded to flee and leave the field standing as if they had been present and still abiding.[19]

They split up, for in this instance there was no safety in numbers. York travelled west with his second son, Edmund, earl of Rutland and a small band of men whose loyalty could absolutely be depended on. Warwick, Salisbury and York's oldest son, Edward, earl of March, along with Sir John Wenlock and Sir James Pickering, made their way south into Devon. The plan was to take ship as and when they could and cross to Ireland. With Somerset newly appointed Captain of Calais, they expected him to secure the outpost as swiftly as possible.[20]

A letter was sent to the treasurer and chamberlains of the exchequer ordering sums totalling a little more than £450 to be paid to Somerset, lord Rivers, Gervase Clifton and Thomas Thorpe for soldiers' wages, supplies and a ship to get Somerset to Calais as quickly as possible. The king was impatient, demanding 'that herein be no excuse nor delay in no wise'.[21]

By this point, it must have been clear the countess of Salisbury was also to be attainted. Any letters that flowed between Middleham and Ludlow have not survived, but it is not difficult to imagine Salisbury writing to his wife advising her to make plans to leave England as soon as she could and join the exiles in Ireland. Her life, at least, would be as safe as they could make it. There was nothing he could do for his younger sons imprisoned in Chester Castle but pray.

> Upon the morrow, when all this coven was known to the king and the lords in his party, there was sending and running with all speed toward every coast to take these lords but none might be found. And forthwith the king rode into Ludlow and despoiled the town and the castle.[22]

Despite popular belief, there is little in the historical record to suggest York abandoned his duchess along with his army. There is one brief reference, in one chronicle, to the king in Ludlow sending the duchess and her children into the care and custody of her sister Anne, duchess of Buckingham. Other references place Cecily's supplication to the king later in time and in Coventry. There is certainly no evidence that she was physically harmed in the orgy of rape and pillage that followed the departure of the duke.

> The misrule of the king's gallants at Ludlow, when they had drunk enough wine that was in taverns and other places, they full ungodly smote out the heads of the pipes and hogsheads of wine, that men went shod in wine, and then they robbed the town and bore away bedding, clothes and other stuff and defouled many women.[23]

After taking out their frustration and anger on the town of Ludlow, the royal army moved back to Worcester, 'harrying all in its path for no very obvious reason'. The rebels had vanished. There was to be no swift battlefield justice. Henry VI and his lords returned to Coventry to await the gathering of Parliament and the final destruction of the duke of York and the Nevill earls.

# PART 3

# THE NEVILLS
# IN EXILE

.

# 20

# *Somnium Vigilantis* and the Parliament of Devils

hen Parliament met in Coventry in November 1459, Bishop George Nevill sat among his fellow lords spiritual. He could do nothing but listen as an act of attainder was passed against his father, his mother and all three of his brothers. His family was in disarray. Warwick and Salisbury had fled the country. Thomas and John were prisoners in Chester Castle. George's mother, the countess of Salisbury, was homeless and in fear of her life. If she was not already with York in Ireland, she soon would be, making the perilous journey with little protection.

It had all fallen apart so very quickly. The events of late 1458 and early 1459 are obscured by the fogs of history but suspicion had, once again, fallen on the duke of York and his Nevill allies. They were accused of plotting against the life of the king, planning to do away with him at Kenilworth Castle, along with the queen and the Prince of Wales. Despite his instinct to forgive, the king was urged to take a hard line against them. This time there was to be no pardon, no welcome back into the fold. George, his sisters and sisters-in-law might be safe, but he would have to be careful if he wanted to stay that way. In 1454, he had been promised the next available bishopric.

> It was also advised and assented, considering the blood, virtue and cunning that master George Nevill, son to the earl of Salisbury, chancellor of England, that he should be recommended to the ... Holy Father to be promoted to the next bishopric that shall void within this realm.[1]

In 1455, the see of Exeter had become vacant. Edmund Lacy, Bishop of Exeter, died in September 1455. Forgetting his promise to the Nevills, Henry VI appointed John Hales, confessor to Margaret of Anjou, as his successor. This received the approval and assent of Pope Calixtus III. When reminded of his earlier promise, the king had to write another letter to the pope rescinding his previous recommendation. Calixtus took some convincing. George was too young and Hale's appointment had already been made, but Henry was insistent. There was trouble in the West Country, the Bonville–Courtenay feud was in full swing and a strong leader was needed. The pope gave in. George would be the next Bishop of Exeter but he would have to wait till he reached canonical age to be consecrated. That finally took place in November 1458, after the death of Calixtus.[2]

> Mandate to the escheator in Devon and Cornwall to deliver the temporalities of the bishopric of Exeter to master George Nevill, whom the pope has provided to be the bishop in the room of Edmund, deceased, and of Master John Hale, archdeacon of Norwich, who was provided by the late pope and has withdrawn.[3]

Despite Henry's hope that he would be a calming and stabilising presence, George spent little time in his diocese, appointing others to take care of administrative tasks. In late 1459, however, Exeter offered something of a safe haven where the bishop could keep his head down and stay out of the public eye. From here, he no doubt reported what he could to his father and brother in exile.[4]

George could do nothing else to help his family. He had no authority, no wide affinity of friends and allies and no power base. While no suspicion attached to him, he was wise to draw no attention to himself. The family's property, including his mother's, was forfeit. He had no home now but his palace at Clyst.

If tried for treason, Alice Montagu faced death by burning at the stake. Perhaps this would be commuted to life imprisonment, as it had been for the duchess of Gloucester. That thought would have brought little comfort to her youngest son. What may have is the news that she was in Ireland, for the moment out of immediate danger, but for all intents and purposes, George was on his own. He had brothers-in-law who had already demonstrated, from the family's point of view, they could not be relied on, and his sisters had no authority of their own. Any letters from the exiles have not survived but 'keep your head down' may have been the best counsel he could hope to receive.

Alice may have accompanied her husband to Ludlow and crossed to Ireland with the duke of York. If she did not, we do not know how she made her way to the coast or who accompanied her for protection and guidance. The potential dangers to a woman travelling on her own in the depths of winter should not be underestimated. While she must have had some protection and help along the way, it would have been a small party that left Middleham, both because few armed men were available and for the sake of speed and secrecy. She had to get to the coast as quickly as she could to either meet a ship sent by York or find a captain willing to take on board such a dangerous passenger.

Despite the strong stand made by the king at Leominster and Ludlow, there were concerns his conciliatory nature could derail the planned attainders. He must have shown signs of wavering for a document was drafted designed to stiffen his resolve and show him just what was at stake. *Somnium Vigilantis* was written in the form of a dialogue. One voice defended the actions of the rebel lords, urging the king to clemency; a second advised him to condemn them utterly for the good of his realm and his crown. The authorship is uncertain. Sir John Fortescue, then chief justice of the king's bench, most likely had a hand in it, as did Lawrence Bothe, the queen's chamberlain, guardian of the Prince of Wales and keeper of the privy seal, who succeeded Robert Nevill as Bishop of Durham. Bothe had little love for the Nevills and would have relished the chance to contribute to their downfall.[5]

Attainder was the most serious punishment that could befall an individual, short of execution, which frequently swiftly followed. It was certainly the most serious punishment that could befall a family. Not only were all possessions forfeited to the crown but the original stain was carried by all the attainted party's direct descendants. From the legal, property-owning perspective of the fifteenth century, the family no longer existed.[6]

The destruction of a family subject to attainder was not always final, however. No king could afford to squander his ruling elite without good cause. There was a constant churning of society. Families such as the Pastons rose from peasant farmers to wealthy and influential lawyers. The Nevills rose from land-owning gentlefolk to the highest orders of the nobility. The time and money invested in military training, the depth of experience in estate management and the fulfilment of quasi-inheritable public offices made the nobility a valuable resource not to be wasted. Attainders in one generation could be overturned in the next. Both the late earl of Northumberland (who died at St Albans in 1455) and Alice Montagu's father benefited from this practice. Thomas Montagu, who was just 12 when his father died, was the recipient of grants from the confiscated estates throughout his childhood. When he came of age in 1409, he was given control over his late father's land. In 1410, the earldom of Salisbury was restored to him by Henry IV, and Henry V benefited from this policy of rehabilitation and restoration. Thomas Montagu was one of the finest military minds of his generation and did much to support Henry V's conquests in France. There was always a chance, assuming they were not captured and beheaded, that the attainders against York and the Nevills would be reversed at some time in the future.[7]

Attainder was a terrifyingly quick and easy process. In 1459, it took just a month from the first reading of the bill of attainder to its passing. The final hurdle, and not usually one that was a cause of delay or defeat, was agreement by the king. In the case of Henry VI, this could not be guaranteed.[8]

*Somnium Vigilantis*, unlike past and future writings by and on behalf of York and his associates, was not meant for public consumption. Unlike York in the 1450s and Warwick more recently and in time to come, the Lancastrian government saw no need to appeal to the popular element. Neither 'the people' nor 'the commons' were considered a suitable audience for writings emanating from court circles. In fact, it is clear from the text of *Somnium Vigilantis* that the commons were an unruly mob and the people's voice was not one that could be relied upon or need be listened to. The document, written to justify the attainders and the use of absolute and final force against the rebels, was not designed to win over popular opinion but to stiffen the resolve of the king.[9]

Warwick's appeal to the good of the people was viewed with suspicion. Not only were the people incapable of an informed opinion on political events, but they were utterly incapable of holding firm to whatever opinions they did have from one day to the next. This was the view put forward in *Somnium Vigilantis*. Popularity was no measure of a man's worth, for everyone knew of 'the great variableness of the people and of the uncertainty of their opinions'. There was little point trying to get the commons on side, so quick were they to turn. It was representatives of 'the people' who killed Suffolk; unruly and bloodthirsty mobs that murdered three of Henry VI's counsellors before and during Cade's rebellion. The idea that 'The people favour them, ergo they be good' was no argument to show mercy to rebels and traitors.[10]

Appeals to the 'common weal' and calls for the eradication of corruption in government were strong recurring motifs in all Yorkist writings of the 1450s. The writers of *Somnium Vigilantis* allowed the defence to put this argument forward:

> first, they intend the common good of all the realm, for the which it is reasonable and worshipful to expose themselves to jeopardy of goods and life; second, considering the great perplexity where in the realm stood at that time and nobly employing themselves to the reformation thereof, ought to be ascribed to virtue and magnanimity than to rebellion and so to have rewards and thankings and not to be put to exitial destruction.[11]

This argument was, of course, neatly knocked down. If the interests of the common good of the kingdom were to be served, then it must be through 'faithful and voluntary honour', not attempts to take the law, or the government, into their own hands. Any 'controversies and debates, civil and criminal, real or personal' should be determined according to the king's laws.

> God knows what token of subjection was it to exalt themselves against the will of the sovereign, to gather his people, to prove and to stir themselves expressly against their profession to bear arms in any wise against the king, without he were obstinately repugnant to the faith.[12]

Old wounds were picked at: the confrontation on Black Heath, the battle of St Albans, 'where they did such an offence against the sovereign the which … was inexplicable and sufficient to be repelled from the mercy of any man'. More recent was the battle of Blore Heath and the death of Audley. Did any of this promote the common good?[13]

As for the reformation of a corrupt government, 'what authority and power had they to reform it, the king present and not giving them commission thereof?' If that was indeed their intention, York and his allies sought to usurp the king's power in order to carry it out. There was no choice for Henry but to 'punish them and exterminate them without mercy'.[14]

But, the defence was allowed to say, they meant no harm. The only people harmed were those 'odious to God and to the people for their misrule'. If anyone else died, such as Audley, 'it was not their intent but happened casually and against their will'. Punishment for such unfortunate, unforeseen and unwanted consequences would be both 'uncivil and unreasonable'.[15]

Actions, said the prosecution, can only be judged on the merits of their results. It was no defence at all to claim 'that they intended but good'. The deaths of Somerset, Northumberland, Clifford and Audley could not be swept away so easily. Even if the claims of misrule were true, 'who made them judges?'

> They made an end of many better knights than ever they were at that execrable journey of St Albans, the which were as high in state as they … you say that all the world cried upon them the which they slew; and I say that they were principal cryers and stirrers of others. Was it then no harm so to pervert the process of rightwiseness and justice?[16]

It would be a mistake, the defence put forward, to destroy those England relied on for protection, 'considering the multitude of the enemies that in every side environ this realm', especially those of 'old noble ancestry'. No offence they might have committed was so great that it was worth losing such assets to the kingdom. They may yet in the future do some great good for England that would far outweigh any previous harm.[17]

A nation 'stands much in the multitude of good knights', conceded the prosecution. But these knights had to put aside the concerns of their own will and act only on the commandments of the king. Their high and exalted status came to them 'of the king's large munificence', which gave them 'greater cause of more and lowlier subjection to their sovereign and the more unkind they were of doing of the contrary'.[18]

As for any good they might do if they were pardoned and returned to the king's confidence and trust, 'your lords are so habituated in their malice that they have exercised by so many repeated actions that it is impossible of nature that ever they might be good'. To trust them again would be a grave mistake. 'If they are reconciled again they will work much harm and more than ever they did, and shall achieve better than before for various skills that may be reasonably conjectured.' The defence case concluded with a warning. York and the Nevills 'have friends in this land and shall have whoever says nay'. If they were not offered mercy at this time, when they were prepared to accept it, 'it is to be doubted another time they will ask for none'.[19]

They may well have friends, the prosecution argued, but no matter how many deluded people might give them aid and support, 'there are as many more without comparison that abide in their loyalty and faithfulness'. They may well have 'secret favour and latent support', and it may well be impossible to 'change such men's hearts as are of that alliance', but that made swift and terrible punishment all the more necessary. '[I]t is of no need to give them pardon or mercy, but the rather to exercise against them all the points of rigour that may be brought to their irreparable destruction.'[20]

These arguments against mercy, forgiveness and reconciliation did their job. Reluctant the king may have been, but the logic and sense of the case put forward in *Somnium Vigilantis* was, from the perspective of the Lancastrian government, difficult to set aside. That Henry VI required such persuasion demonstrates how easily the course of events could have been changed. If York had been left to stew, as he had after his second dismissal as Protector, or been allowed to take control of the agenda and engineer another exculpation, as he had after the battle of St Albans, the next few years may have been very different. However, *Somnium Vigilantis* did what its authors had set out to do. The king was convinced by its arguments and allowed a petition to be presented to Parliament calling for the attainder of 'Richard duke of York and others'.[21]

York had been greatly trusted and much favoured by the king. He was appointed Henry's lieutenant in France and Normandy; his two oldest sons were ennobled as earls. All this should have given York more cause to be 'a true, obedient and diligent' servant to his king than he turned out to be. The tone of the petition was uncompromising. Those who heard it, including and especially Henry VI, must have been left with no choice. York was ungrateful, disloyal and dangerous.

> [H]ow falsely and traitorously he has acquitted himself to your highness, against God, nature, all truth, humanity and contrary to his allegiance, howbeit your grace chooses not to take displeasure thereof; yet it is openly known to your liege people his subtle and … his false imaginations, conspiracies, feats and diligent labours bourn up with persuasive lies, contrived by the most unheard means that ever did any subject to his sovereign lord.[22]

All of York's past actions were raked over, including the rumours from 1450 that Jack Cade was planning to make him king in Henry's place. York's return from Ireland; his attempts 'in divers parliaments' to undermine Henry's rule; the confrontation at Black Heath; and the solemn oath of loyalty of York at St Paul's, 'upon the holy cross and also upon the holy evangels … which oath … was subscribed with his own hand with his sign manual, and also sealed by him with the seal of his arms, and so down by his hands delivered to you'. All this was remembered.[23]

York's word, his most solemn and sacred oath, could not be trusted. The more recent oath sworn in Worcester cathedral meant nothing. The words of assurance in Warwick's letter meant less. He and his father had burned their bridges, they had chosen York over the king and they must live, and die, by that decision.

George Nevill left nothing that recorded his feelings as he sat on the benches with his fellow lords spiritual listening to the recitation of his family's treasons. Both Warwick and Salisbury had been given favourable and preferential treatment by the king. Warwick was made pre-eminent earl. Not only was Salisbury appointed warden of the west march, but he had 'surety of payment by patent, not accustomed before'. He was a trusted royal servant with control over much of the north of England, and now he and Warwick were confederated with York. Traitors all.[24]

The king was reminded of the lives lost at St Albans,

> where you … were present and your banner displayed there, and there they falsely and traitorously reared war against you, by the which your royal person was sore hurt and in great peril of your life, and there they slew divers lords of your blood … with other your liege people and many of them hurt, robbed and despoiled. And the hurting of your most royal person can never out of the hearts of your true liege people.[25]

Yet they had been forgiven, pardoned in Parliament, bound by a negotiated settlement of peace and amity. Buckingham had done his best to 'make the said duke of York to understand of what demeaning he had been'. York had only the king's grace to lean on and now he had squandered it. Henry was reminded of the decisions taken at the council meeting in Coventry, after Buckingham and all the lords fell to their knees, begging him to show no more mercy to those who upset the peace. York had sworn on the gospels and signed his oath, as had Warwick, by 'signet of his hand and sealed with his seals … of true and faithful obedience to you and your succession'. How many more times could they be pardoned? How many more oaths must they swear and break? There must be no weakening, no forgiveness.[26]

The rebels' purpose, the destruction of the king and his family, was inferred by the speed with which the three men came together, Warwick from Calais and Salisbury from Middleham. They meant, the petition claimed, to take Henry by surprise at Kenilworth but the king had been forewarned, sending his loyal lords out to intercept Salisbury.[27]

Blore Heath was the pivotal point. Without that battle, things might have ended very differently. Warwick's letters, the oaths taken in Worcester Cathedral, the reassurances of peaceful and loyal intent may have rung a little truer. As it was, Salisbury took the field against the forces of the king and Audley was killed. This section of the bill of attainder is both long and detailed. All the noble commanders were charged with treason, not only Salisbury and his sons but John Conyers, Thomas Parr, Thomas Harrington, Thomas Merring and William Stanley. To compound their crimes, the rebels were now gone from the kingdom. After great hardship, inclement weather and floodwaters blocking his path, the king had come to Ludlow, set up camp and field, ready to face them in battle.[28]

> And they, intending the destruction of your most noble person, the same Friday and town, in the field there falsely and traitorously reared war against you, and then and there shot their said guns as well at your most royal person, as at your lords and people with you then and there being … But Almighty God, that sees the hearts of people, for whom there is nothing hid, smote the hearts of the said duke of York and earls suddenly from that most presumptuous pride to the most shameful fall of cowardice that could be thought, to that about midnight that next night they stole away out of the field, under pretence they would have refreshed themselves a while in the town of Ludlow, leaving their standards and banners in their battle directly against your field, fled out of the town unarmed, with few persons into Wales.[29]

If there was any doubt in the king's mind that he had escaped deposition and death, a captive, one Robert Ratcliffe, before being put to death, confessed the true and full intentions of his masters, 'that both the crown of

England and duchy of Lancaster they would have translated at their will and pleasure'.[30]

While it is likely Ratcliffe's confession cannot be taken at face value and this was not, in fact, York's intention, the disingenuousness of Warwick's manifesto and letter should also be questioned. York did mean to seize power, albeit as Henry's chief councillor. He did mean to dispose of Somerset, one way or another, and in this he had the unquestioned support of Warwick. He did not intend to endanger the life of the king or his family. Of the three, Salisbury was the least likely conspirator in regicide. He was with his son and brother-in-law because their names were now inextricably linked and because he was nothing if not a wholehearted supporter and protector of his sons.

The countess of Salisbury's attainder was dealt with briefly. According to the bill, at Middleham on 1 August, she 'falsely and traitorously imagined and compassed the death and final destruction' of the king. Her name was linked with Thomas Vaughan and William Oldhall, whose treason related to their actions in London on 4 July. One thing this link might suggest is a coordinated effort between the three to purchase and take delivery of arms or supplies for Salisbury's men, which were used against the king's forces at Blore Heath.[31]

The countess, Vaughan and Oldhall 'laboured, abetted, procured, stirred and provided the said duke of York and the said earls of Warwick and Salisbury to do the said treasons, rebellions, gatherings, ridings and rearing of war against your most royal person at the said town of Blore and Ludlow'. None of the other Nevill women were implicated. Apart from Salisbury's countess, nothing in the act of forfeiture was to extend to the wives of the named traitors. Sound provision was made for their ongoing financial support 'that they may have and enjoy after the decease of their said husbands all such honours, castles, lordships, manors, lands and tenements, rents, reversions, annuities, fees and offices or any other possessions which they or any of them had or held jointly with their said husbands'.[32]

The bill of attainder was a long and damning document, a wall of words that rang through the Parliament chamber. There were no dissenting voices, no attempt at defence. The lords assented; the commons assented. In the end, the king also assented, but he would not be denied his right and 'prerogative to show such mercy and grace' as should please him. One of the first to benefit from this was Sir Thomas Stanley.[33]

The case against Stanley was circumstantial. Unlike his brother William, he made no open move to support Salisbury at Blore Heath, though the petition calling for his impeachment mentions the letter he sent to Salisbury at Market Drayton. The petitioners claimed that Stanley declared he would 'live and die with the said earl, against his resistors'. At least one of his servants had fought under William Stanley's command. Three other servants of Sir Thomas confessed 'the day before their death … that they were commanded in the name and behalf of the said lord Stanley to attend to await upon the said William Stanley, to assist the said earl [of Salisbury] in such matters as he intended to execute'.[34]

The king declared early in December that anyone who came to him within eight days would be granted his grace and pardon. Given that no further action was taken against Thomas Stanley, it would seem safe to assume he took advantage of Henry's clemency. He had certainly been as ready as Salisbury's other sons-in-law, as was the Bishop of Exeter, to take the oath required of all the lords in Parliament.[35]

This oath not only bound those who took it to allegiance to the king, the queen, the Prince of Wales and the Lancastrian succession; it also bound them, with their 'body, goods, might, power, counsel and advertisement to resist, withstand and subdue all them that would in any wise presume to do contrary to the premises [of the oath] or any of them'.

George Nevill, the earl of Arundel, lords Fitzhugh, Bergavenny, Bonville, Sir Thomas Stanley, lords Berners, Grey of Ruthyn and Greystoke – who all had close family connections to the Nevills – swore to uphold the king's rule and, if it came to it, to do all in their power to destroy their kinsmen. Before two years were out, all had broken their oath.[36]

# 21

# WIVES AND SISTERS LEFT BEHIND

he duchess of York loved her husband. In the course of their thirty-year marriage, they had rarely been apart. When he was sent to France and Ireland, Cecily went with him. Of their seven surviving children, only three were born in England. When the duke was out of favour with the king, Cecily wrote letters to the queen pleading her to intercede on his behalf. Now he was a long way away, a declared and attainted traitor, and she had to intercede again, this time with the king himself.

Apart from her husband, Cecily had other immediate concerns. The provisions in the act of attainder concerning the traitors' innocent wives did not apply to her, as no jointure had been settled on them at the time of their marriage. Cecily had her three youngest children, George, Margaret and Richard, to take care of, with no means of support and no home.[1]

In Coventry, on or about 6 December, she made a personal appeal to the king, 'and submitted herself unto his grace, and she prayed for her husband that he might come to his answer and to be received unto his grace, and the king fully humbly granted her grace and to all that would come with her'. Two weeks later, as she had not herself offended the king, the duchess was granted 1,000 marks yearly from revenues from her husband's forfeited estates, 'for the relief of her and her infants'. She was not, however, free to go where she chose. Innocent she may have been but there was always the risk she would find a way to leave the country and join her husband in exile. Having their wives and children under close watch might make the Yorkist lords think twice before taking further action. There were loyal lords enough around the king to assist with this.[2]

The duchess of York was taken to the duke of Buckingham and his lady, for they two were sisters and there she was till the field was done at Northampton, and she was kept full strait and many a great rebuke.[3]

Four years older than Cecily, Anne, duchess of Buckingham was the closest to her in age. We do not know what form the 'great rebukes' took, nor who delivered them. The private lives of fifteenth-century women, their relationships with sisters and other women, are not easy to tease out. Ralph Nevill's two youngest daughters may have been close or they may not; the rebukes may have been delivered by Anne or by her husband. They were most likely on the subjects of obedience and fealty. Caught as she was – as were the wives of all rebels – between loyalty and love for her husband and expectation of a higher allegiance to the king, Cecily had little choice but to accept whatever support she was offered and submit to whatever strictures were imposed.

Cecily at least had a roof over her head and sufficient funds to keep her and her children in a reasonable level of comfort. Maud Stanhope was not so fortunate. It is unclear just when Maud and Thomas took possession of her dower property at Eresby, but by 1459 it was their principal home. Once again, some time late in the year, or early in the next, she was turned out and her property and personal effects seized. Named in the commission to 'confiscate into the king's hands the possessions late of [among others] Thomas Nevill, knight, in the county of Lincoln' was Richard Welles. As the husband of Maud's stepdaughter Joan Willoughby, he may have been using the opportunity to put Eresby back into his wife's hands. If this was the case, he did so illegally.[4]

Maud may have appealed to several lords who stood in favour with the king but it was John, viscount Beaumont, her husband's uncle by marriage, who served as her champion on this occasion.

Grant to John, viscount Beaumont, of 200l yearly from the lordships, manors and lands whereof Maud, lady Willoughby, wife of Thomas Nevill, knight, now in prison waiting the king's grace, is dowered by the feoffment of Robert, lord Willoughby, sometime her husband, to hold to the use of Maud until she have redelivery of the said possessions, now in the king's hands; grant also to her of all clothing and goods seized of late in the king's name.[5]

During this difficult time, Maud may have taken shelter at Tattershall Castle, which she shared with her sister Jane. It is unlikely she made her way to Middleham. That she made the long and difficult journey to Chester to be near her husband is, of course, a possibility but nothing is recorded to that effect. Maud may also have taken refuge at Clifton Hall, home of the legitimate branch of her old friend Gervase Clifton's family.

Like Maud, John Nevill's wife, Isobel Ingoldisthorpe was a woman of independent means. Both were heiresses of considerable fortunes; both had sizeable jointures settled on them at the time of their marriage. Maud also had her dower property at Eresby. This was seized in error after her husband's capture, and the error caught in February 1460. It may, however, have taken some time to rectify the situation. £200 a year was not much to live on for a woman used to more than twice that, but it was better than nothing and would have to suffice for the time being.

As no personal letters either between the two women and their husbands, or to and from relatives and friends survive, it is difficult to judge their emotional state of mind. Everything we know about John and Isobel's marriage, which is little enough, would suggest a strong bond existed between them. Isobel was young, 16 or 17 in 1459. She had at least one child to take care of. Not knowing when, or if, her husband would be released, worrying the next step might be taken from attainder to execution, simply being without him, cannot have been easy. Since she had no sisters, Isobel may have turned to her mother for emotional support. Her sisters-in-law would have had little to offer in the way of comfort. All of them had troubles enough of their own.

Joan, countess of Arundel had, by 1460, been married for more than twenty years. Her husband William seems to have been devoted to her. Certainly, after her death, he withdrew almost entirely from public and political life. Indicted after the rout at Ludford, Arundel soon received a pardon. Joan had been living away from her family in the south of England for close to two decades. Married at 15, she likely did not leave home immediately, for her parents were conscious not to let their daughters consummate their marriages and risk pregnancy and childbirth at so young an age. As it was, Joan was 26 when she had her first child, Thomas, heir to her husband's earldom.[6]

Arundel's part in his father-in-law's battle at Blore Heath is not clear. He was with them at Ludlow, but his name was not on the list of those indicted for taking the field against the king. Along with the other lords present in Parliament, he took the oath of loyalty on 11 December. Just days later, he was rewarded for 'assistance against the rebels' with the office of justice of the king's forests south of the Trent for life. In January 1460, he was included in a commission of array to 'resist the rebels, adherents of Richard earl of Warwick'. In March, he was granted a reward of 100 marks a year for 'good service against the rebels'. In June, he was among those commissioned to 'arrest and commit to prison all adherents of Richard duke of York, Richard earl of Warwick and Richard earl of Salisbury and their accomplices … to go against the said rebels and all who resist them herein'. If Arundel's natural sympathies lay with his wife's family, and his later actions would suggest they did, there was nothing he could do to help them in the first six months of 1460.[7]

One son-in-law of Salisbury whose sympathies were always difficult to pin down was Thomas, lord Stanley. Despite the very real aid and support given to Salisbury at Blore Heath by his brother William, lord Thomas was very quick to distance himself, disavowing all involvement and seeking a pardon. Despite a determined effort in Parliament and a petition that, on the face of it, was decidedly damning, Thomas, unlike his brother, escaped attainder and all that went with it.[8]

Stanley's wife was Salisbury's third youngest daughter, Alianor. Of all the Nevill sisters, she was the one close enough to visit or, at least, provide aid and support for her brothers in Chester Castle. Cheshire was Stanley country and though they did not control the castle in 1459, they were powerful and influential enough to ensure decent, perhaps favourable, treatment for the prisoners.

This power and influence had been built up by Thomas Stanley's father over decades. In 1439, Stanley was controller of the king's household. He had custody of the disgraced duchess of Gloucester during the last ten years of her life. When York returned from Ireland in 1450, Stanley had been one of those sent with troops to try and prevent him landing and moving towards London. After the failure of Cade's rebellion, Stanley led a punitive expedition into Kent. He was caught up in the turmoil of Suffolk's arrest and exile, and there were demands he be removed from the king's household. This did not last long and in 1454, during Henry VI's illness, he was appointed to council and gave York much-needed assistance in putting down the Exeter–Egremont rebellion.[9]

In December 1454, Sir Thomas's son married Alianor Nevill. Nevertheless, and despite York's expectations, Sir Thomas failed to come to his side at the battle of St Albans. He also failed to come to the king's side, arriving in St Albans the following day, and thus setting a trend his sons were to follow almost compulsively in the following decades. Restored to the household and raised to the peerage in 1455, he had little time to enjoy his new status. The first lord Stanley died in February 1459, leaving vast landholdings for his son to inherit.[10]

The second lord Stanley's action – or inaction – before and during the battle of Blore Heath attracted considerable suspicion. Though he had been sent letters by both king and queen commanding him to join them in opposing Salisbury, he kept the bulk of his troops back, though some may have fought under his brother William on Salisbury's side. Suspected of treason, he was not initially summoned to Parliament but managed to secure a pardon in time to take his seat. Like the other lords in the chamber, he took the oath of loyalty to Henry VI. Unlike other lords who had been under suspicion, he was not included in any commissions against the exiled rebels.[11]

William Bonville, lord Harrington was too young to take his seat in Parliament; his grandfather lord Bonville attended and took the oath along with the others. Harrington, married for about two years to Katherine Nevill, Salisbury's second youngest daughter, was neither involved nor implicated in his father-in-law's treason. Katherine was in the early months of her first pregnancy. Both she and her husband were 18 years old and living at Shute Barton, principal seat of the Bonvilles in Devon.[12]

No lasting suspicion seems to have fallen on Harrington or his father. In February 1460, Bonville was commissioned to

> call together all lieges of Somerset, Devon and Cornwall, to resist [the exiles]
> if they should presume to enter the said counties; and to take the muster
> of the men at arms and archers of those counties, and to cause wards and
> watches and beacons to be appointed and set in the usual places, and to
> arrest all suspected persons of those counties and commit them to prison till
> further order.[13]

Bonville's sole co-commissioner was Thomas Courtenay, earl of Devon since his father's death the previous year, murderer of Nicholas Radford and an unwanted confederate. In March, Bonville was commissioned, again under Devon's command, to find out what goods and chattels the rebels held in Cornwall. Again in March, he was commissioned to arrest several men who were to be brought before the king or his council to answer unspecified charges.[14]

Like all her sisters, Katherine could do nothing for her father and oldest brother, and little for Thomas and John. If Warwick left word with anyone in England before he took ship on the south coast of Devon, it would most likely have been Katherine. She faced the very real probability of giving birth to her first child while both her father and mother were out of the country and unable to return without risking their lives.

The son-in-law who had always been the least likely to join Salisbury's cause, and the one most extravagantly rewarded for holding firm to the king, was Henry, lord Fitzhugh.

Prior to setting out from Middleham in October, Salisbury had not set-tled his property in the hands of feoffees. Both Thomas Harrington and Sir John Conyers had. This was not an unusual practice for a property owner about to go into battle or undertake a potentially dangerous journey. Enfeoffment did two things. It kept an estate, particularly an extensive, scat-tered estate, safe from plunder and alienation during its owner's absence; and it prevented that estate from being subject to forfeiture should the owner be attainted for treason. The feoffee would hold the property and enjoy its benefits in return for a fee, either in the form of cash or services to be rendered to the owner of the estate. That Salisbury did not take this precaution, nor Warwick or York, would suggest he saw no danger to himself, either physically or legally, when he left his home to meet his son and brother-in-law.[15]

The result of this was the carve up of Salisbury's estate, including the property he held by right of his wife, and the redistribution of offices. Fortunately, a good part of it ended up in the hands of Fitzhugh.

> Grant for life to Henry lord Fitzhugh for good service against the rebels of the offices of steward of the liberty and lordship of Richmond, and master forester of the New Forest, Arkylgarthdale and 'le Hope' in the king's hands by the rebellion of Richard earl of Salisbury, to hold himself or by deputies, with the usual wages, fees and profits as Richard had.[16]

This included Middleham Castle, lady Fitzhugh's childhood home. Alice Fitzhugh had at least five children by 1459, the oldest, also Alice, being 10 or 11 years old. It makes sense that her youngest sister, Margaret, then about 14, was left in her care and custody when their mother took flight. Though the future looked bleak for their parents and three of their brothers, the sisters were spared the heartbreak and ignominy of seeing Middleham in the hands of their family's enemies.

Salisbury would have been somewhat relieved to hear Middleham and Richmond were in Fitzhugh's hands. A strong family interest would serve to keep the estates solvent and intact. That would not have been Henry VI's only concern when considering who should be granted the forfeited lands. With Salisbury no longer a presence in the north, there was a risk Northumberland and his allies would try to fill the power vacuum left behind. Fitzhugh had taken full part with Salisbury and his sons against the Percies in the past, being present at both Heworth and the meeting near Topcliffe in 1453. Granting him at least part of Salisbury's Yorkshire holdings would keep the Percy affinity in check.[17]

Fitzhugh was not to enjoy all the revenues of Middleham, however. Northumberland was to receive just over £200 a year to pay wages arrears. Clifford was appointed warden of the west march while Northumberland retained wardenship of the east. Neither man was given the powers Salisbury had enjoyed.[18]

The political disruption caused by the attainder of three prominent landowners could not be avoided but a disruption to the English economy could. It was important that the transfer of property was smooth. The best way to achieve this was through continuity of administration, the collection of revenues, the authorisation of expenditure on repairs, maintenance and supplies, and the collection and sale of resources. The ownership of a manor or castle might change but the management team and workforce, by and large, did not. Many of Salisbury's retainers and associates sued for pardons in the eight days allowed them by the king, including Sir Christopher Conyers and his son Richard, and the sons of Thomas Harrington and Scrope of Bolton. While this might seem a sign of disloyalty to their good lord, it was to Salisbury's benefit they did so. Salisbury might have been an attainted traitor in exile, but he had no intention of staying that way. Keeping the Nevill affinity as together as was possible, though no doubt closely watched, would serve him better in the long run than if they refused to submit to the king and were imprisoned, executed or outlawed.[19]

As for Warwick's estates, the Beauchamp properties were shared between the countess's half-sisters and the rest parcelled out to Henry VI's most loyal servants.[20]

Life was not easy for those left behind. Some suffered economic hardship following the illegal seizure of property. Some had their movements severely restricted. All would have spent much of their time worrying about their husbands, sons, brothers and good lords. As difficult as it was, life had to go on. They were expected to keep things together, whether that was family, home or a slice of a large estate. Wives must take care of temporarily fatherless children. Brothers must do nothing to endanger their own freedom. Servants, councillors and retainers must keep the faith and ensure their lords had prosperity and continuity waiting for them on their return. For return they surely would. There was only temporary safety in exile, and unfinished business awaited York, Warwick and Salisbury in England.

# 22

# LORD OF THE CHANNEL

nother wife who was left behind, though not in England, was Anne, countess of Warwick. When her husband left Calais in September, Anne and their daughters did not go with him. This suggests Warwick expected to conclude his business in England quickly and return to Calais its Captain, a free man and exonerated. An armed face off against the king, charges of treason, attainder and expedited flight were likely not among his plans.

Since setting up their first household together, the countess and earl of Warwick had spent little time apart. Warwick was not in the habit of leaving his family for extended periods of time. They left no personal letters behind and it is difficult to establish just how they felt about one another. The relocation of Anne and the children to Calais, when Warwick decided the best way to carry out his duties as Captain was to take up permanent residence, might suggest a certain level of fondness. On the other hand, the births of their two daughters had been a long time coming and five years apart. There are hints of at least one other unsuccessful pregnancy in 1453, and they may have taken the decision to live together as much as possible to maximise the chances of conceiving a much-needed son.

In Calais, in the last weeks of 1459, Anne had no idea what had become of her husband. She would have got news of the outcome of the Parliament of Devils and no doubt heard rumours of his disappearance from Ludlow. She would also have known that Somerset had been appointed Captain of Calais in Warwick's place and that he was surely on his way to take possession. With just a thin remnant of the garrison remaining in Calais, and their support of Warwick questionable given their fellows' desertion of him at Ludford, Anne's security and that of her daughters could not be guaranteed. Warwick's uncle Fauconberg was still in residence and in charge during his absence. While his presence was no doubt reassuring, more reassuring still would have been news Warwick was alive and well. There could be little hope he would return to Calais. Anne had to face an uncertain future without him.

Anne would likely have been getting reports of any sails seen in the Channel that might signal Somerset's arrival. There was little love lost between Anne and her sister the duchess of Somerset and if she were removed from Calais and, like the duchess of York, consigned to her sister's custody, her life was unlikely to have been particularly pleasant. The best Anne could do was keep her little family safe and together and wait for news, fearing it would be ill, hardly daring to hope it would be good.

Nothing remains of Calais Castle but it was a strong fortress in its day. The countess and her daughters lived there in some comfort and security, but Calais was still a garrison town, full of soldiers and sailors. She did not much like living there. As one observer, possibly the master of a merchant ship, reported, 'My lady Warwick comes but little abroad but keeps her always in the castle.' Though she was described by Rous to be 'free of her speech with every person familiar, according to her and their degree', the wives of the merchants of the staple and the town's petty bourgeoisie were unlikely to become her intimate friends. She had the women of her household, of course, the company of her daughters and her husband, when he was in Calais and was not busy with more important matters, but Calais Castle was not Warwick and the Pale of Calais was not England.[1]

Isobel Nevill, the Warwicks' older daughter, was now 9 years old, an age where she may have picked up some of the tension, if she did not understand entirely what was going on. At just 3, the younger daughter Anne was less likely to have noticed anything was wrong. The countess, Isobel and Warwick's daughter Margaret would have prayed for his safe return, trusting to God to keep the little family intact.

Anne may well have taken comfort from the continuing presence of Fauconberg. An experienced soldier, he could be relied upon to do all he could keep the town secure, his nephew's family unharmed and the morale of the remaining soldiers high.

On 1 November, when sails were sighted approaching Calais harbour, there were murmurs it could be Somerset, come at last to take possession. They had feared this for weeks. Fauconberg was among those who went down to the docks to see who had come and, to the great relief of all, familiar faces were seen: 'so distinct were the eleven on board the ship among the mariners, those in Calais who saw them coming were joyous and amazed, joyous especially for the news of others about whom they had no report'.[2]

Warwick was not alone. With him were Salisbury and the young earl of March. Fauconberg, the countess and her daughters were overjoyed. All of Calais turned out to greet their Captain. After a pilgrimage of thanks to Notre Dame de St Pierre, the mayor, the soldiers, the merchants of the staple all came to welcome Warwick back to Calais, and 'they had that night very good cheer'. Somehow, Warwick had taken disaster and turned it into triumph.[3]

When he left Ludlow with his father and his young cousin Edward, earl of March, it was most likely Warwick's intention to find a ship that would take them to Ireland. With Somerset appointed Captain in his place, and the loyalty of the garrison in some question, Calais was unlikely, at this point, to have been considered an option. Ireland was where York was bound. He would be sure to find a welcome and a refuge there. Once Warwick, Salisbury and March joined him, they could make real plans for their return and yet another rehabilitation. Contrary winds, a friendly face on the coast of Devon and the failure of Somerset to secure his prize changed all that.[4]

The most coherent account of Warwick's journey to Calais comes from the chronicler Waurin. Obtained first hand from Warwick himself, it has a decidedly positive and heroic spin, but is built around a thread of authenticity. Waurin seems to conflate two voyages into one. The first, from the coast of South Wales to the north Devon coast, may have been in a ship easily procured by Warwick as local lord. Initially telling the crew he intended to sail to Bristol, it was not until they were in the Bristol Channel that he asked them if they knew the route to the west. Neither the master nor his mariners had ever sailed west and did not know the seas. This caused a good deal of dismay.[5]

> When the earl of Warwick saw his father and all the others were afraid, to comfort them he told them that with God's pleasure and St George's he would get them to a safe harbour, he stripped to his doublet so he could take the tiller, he set the sail so the wind pressed against them hard until they arrived at the island of Jersey.[6]

This is where Waurin seems to have conflated the two voyages. Sailing west from the Bristol Channel would have taken them towards Ireland, which was likely Warwick's original destination. It was also the direction they had to take if Warwick planned to navigate around Cornwall and into the English Channel. This seems a less probable course of action. Since Somerset was likely to be waiting for him in Calais and the loyalty of the remaining garrison uncertain at best, attempting to sail to and take Calais was, on the face of it, both an unnecessary and untenable risk. Warwick, of course, may well have taken charge of both legs of the journey, stripping to his doublet, taking the tiller and setting the sails.

The ship never made it to Ireland; adverse winds blew it onto the coast of north Devon. Here, the young earl of March had a friend, John Dynham. He was around 26 in 1459, the oldest son of one of the wealthiest men in the county. Perhaps Dynham gave Warwick the news that Somerset had not yet sailed for Calais. Conscious of his wife and children, and not wanting to leave them open to danger, this news would have given Warwick hope that, if he was quick enough, he might reach Calais first. Suddenly, the risk that had been untenable when he left Ludlow was now worth taking. With properties in both north and south Devon, Dynham would have known the quickest way to cross the peninsula, and where they might change horses in order to maintain their speed. As it was, it likely took them two days of hard riding.[7]

John's widowed mother Joan lived at her dower property of Nutwell Manor on the Exe Estuary, just 23 miles from Warwick's sister Katherine in Shute Barton. Joan Dynham was a formidable woman, wealthy in her own right and decidedly comfortable in widowhood. John, her oldest son, was the only one of her children living in his own household. Her remaining eight children were as yet unmarried and still living at home. Joan managed the part of her estate centring around Nutwell and employed a woman as reeve. While her son purchased a ship for Warwick's use, loaning him 220 nobles for the purpose, Joan set about organising a master and crew, probably from among her own tenants and servants. When the ship was ready to sail, John Dynham took his place on board.[8]

Once in the Channel, whether Warwick took command of the vessel or not, they made good time to the Channel Islands, where Warwick's old servant John Nanfan was governor. Here, they had to wait eight days for the right wind to take them the rest of the way to Calais.[9]

In the meantime, Somerset was making preparations to take possession of Calais. Along with lord Rivers, he set sail from Sandwich, but was forced back to shore by contrary winds, giving Warwick yet more breathing space.[10]

The run from Guernsey to Calais was trouble-free and quick, and Warwick beat Somerset to the post by just a few hours. Those left behind in Calais, from the countess of Warwick and Fauconberg to the soldiers, merchants and townsfolk, had daily expected, and dreaded, Somerset's arrival. Warwick's appearance was greeted by everyone with great joy.

> [T]hen after the joyful reunions they all went on pilgrimage to Notre Dame de St Pierre and when they returned to Calais those of the staple came to meet them, the mayor of the town and all the soldiers who were on their side, so they had that night very good cheer as for a long time they were expecting to find their enemies facing them in Calais.[11]

Warwick arrived just in time. Later that night, Somerset sent his herald to Calais to carry his credentials to the town, 'to which the watch answered that they well understood and that they would go and talk to the earl of Warwick who was their captain, and told the herald he would bring him Warwick's response'.[12]

The news that Warwick had beaten him to the prize incensed Somerset, who was 'so distressed that little could console him'. He vowed, then and there, that he would bring Calais to heel and make the townspeople obey his commands. He turned on Rivers, blaming him for the situation and 'demanded of [him] what he was going to do about it because he knew well these things happened because of his negligence'.[13]

Warwick was in a far better position than he could have dreamed when faced with defeat, disaster and probable death at Ludlow. Thinking on his feet, changing his plans as one opportunity closed off and another opened up was a character trait that would stand him in good stead well into the future. He also commanded great personal loyalty from his supporters and friends. The garrison was depleted but those who were with him, as they reported to Somerset's herald, 'wanted no other captain but the earl of Warwick'.[14]

Andrew Trollope landed at Scales Cliff and made his way to Guines, some 7 miles south of Calais. There, he persuaded the constable of the castle to admit Somerset and his soldiers on promise of payment of long overdue wages. In the meantime, Somerset's fleet was battered by a tempest and 'a wind so strong that whether they wanted to or not they were forced into Calais'. Waurin tells us that 'a tempest' blew the other ships into Calais harbour; other sources say that the ships' captains decided to sail in. The only one of his ships to reach its original destination was the one carrying Somerset himself.[15]

Warwick was delighted to find himself in possession of the horses Somerset had brought from England, arms and harness for his soldiers and, once again, his flagship *Trinity*. His delight, however, did not stop him from wreaking a bloody revenge on those members of the garrison he considered traitors. Like Somerset and other Captains before him, the success of Warwick's command depended to a great extent on developing a sense of personal loyalty among the soldiers. The limits of that loyalty when faced with the prospect of raising arms against the king seemed to come as something of a surprise to Warwick at Ludford. The men were taken from their ships and their loyalty questioned. Warwick was not interested in those who had not previously served in Calais and who professed their loyalty to the king. These were free to go, to make their way to Guines and the duke of Somerset. Those who had 'given him their oath in the past' were imprisoned and further interrogated before 'they were brought back before the lords where their heads were cut off before the people of the town, as punishment for the treason which they had committed against the earl of Warwick'.[16]

Though he was on the front line, sole responsibility for neutralising or even killing Warwick did not rest on Somerset's shoulders alone. The bulk of Warwick's fleet was in Sandwich, and steps were taken to secure it and to protect the town from threat of invasion. Rivers and his son Anthony Wydeville were sent to Sandwich, along with Gervase Clifton, to ready themselves for an expedition to Calais to rout the rebels. In Ireland, York was untouchable. Henry VI's best chance of bringing a decisive end to his current troubles was to deal with Warwick once and for all. In Calais, Warwick was in possession of the strongest card in the rebels' hand. He must not be allowed to play it. All that could be done was to keep him bottled up in Calais and to lay siege to the town from the sea and from Guines.[17]

Between December 1459 and March the following year, a stream of commissions was issued ordering the arrest, victualing and crewing of ships. Merchantmen setting sail for Flanders were ordered to keep clear of Calais. All those sent out to keep the seas and resist the king's enemies were ordered to make sure 'that no victuals, men, arms, horses, fuel or any other thing be taken in such ships for maintenance, victualing, fortification or the relief of Calais'.[18]

These attempts to shut up the Yorkists in Calais failed. They had a high level of support in Kent and Sussex, and not only did a steady stream of men and ships make their way across the Channel but, crucially, they brought accurate and up-to-date news of Henry's moves. The merchants of the staple, faced with a lengthy siege and financial ruin if things continued as they were, chose their side and threw their support, and money, behind the rebels. A sizeable loan was secured to pay the garrison. It was clear to the members of the staple their only hope of being repaid was if the Yorkists triumphed and took control of the government.[19]

Almost on a daily basis, Somerset sent men the few miles south to Calais to attempt to gain entry. He 'found a way to make alliance on this side of the sea', trading silver for horses and armour. Thus equipped, 'he and his people began to make strong war against those of Calais, patrolling daily and guarding the approaches, so that no other supplies were getting to their enemies'.[20]

Warwick was not the lone authority in Calais. The idea that from this point, Warwick's rising star eclipsed that of his ageing father might be attractive but it is not quite sustainable. Every action taken in Warwick's name as Captain of Calais was decided on by a council. Though the chroniclers name no names, it is likely this council consisted of Warwick, Salisbury, Fauconberg, Edward, earl of March, officers and officials of the garrison, representatives from the staple and the town as well as men like John Dynham who had proved themselves of use and value. Salisbury was no spent force trailing along in his son's wake. His military experience and expertise were invaluable. He was no passive passenger, in Calais or afterwards. One chronicler in particular stresses the collaborative nature of the decision-making.[21]

If there was any hope of returning to England in strength, Warwick needed to get his hands on the ships gathered at Sandwich. To this end, in January, Warwick's council took the bold decision to send Sir John Dynham and Sir John Wenlock across the Channel 'with a great fellowship'.[22]

The decision to gather a fleet in Sandwich had not, on the face of it, been a bad one. Had Rivers and Gervase Clifton managed to hold on to the element of surprise, they may well have launched a successful raid on Calais, especially if it had been coordinated with a similar assault from Guines. As it was, it turned more to Warwick's advantage than the government's.

As luck would have it, at this point a man turned up in Calais, well known to the earl of March, who was able to tell them just what they wanted to hear. They could take the ships from Sandwich with ease, 'because they knew well that those in Sandwich would not take up arms against them and they had no men of arms, being anchored on the sand among the flat country as they had no quays and they had only the lord Rivers who lodged at the friary'.[23]

So Dynham and Wenlock set sail with 700 men between them. The ships at Sandwich were, indeed, taken with ease and the collusion of their masters. Rivers, asleep in his bed, was taken along with his son Anthony. Dynham and Wenlock returned to Calais with the bulk of the assembled fleet, masters and mariners, and two prominent prisoners. The raid had been a spectacular success. The only thing that might have disappointed Warwick was the failure to take the *Grace Dieu*, the finest ship in the fleet, 'which might not be had as she was broke in the bottom'. Dynham did, however, manage to get hold of her tackle and this, too, was carried away to Calais. One source reports that Dynham was 'sore hurt … in the leg and halted while he lived after', though this would seem to relate to a later raid.[24]

In Calais, the prisoners were subjected to an extraordinary piece of theatre. Lit by more than 100 torches, presumably with an enthusiastic and receptive audience, the two Wydeville men were soundly rated by the Calais earls for their lowly origins and for daring to call such lords as they 'traitors'. Warwick, Salisbury and March were 'of the king's blood', whereas Rivers was 'but a squire', a 'knave's son' and 'made by marriage'.[25]

If this story, related by William Paston to his brother John, is true, it shows the Nevills in a most unflattering and arrogant light. Writing from London towards the end of January, William Paston gives no information about his source. It may have been gleeful pro-Yorkist gossip or it may have come from a witness to the event. What it suggests is that Warwick, his father and cousin benefited far more from the admiration of the people of London than did Rivers. The city's sympathies lay with the Yorkists, not the government.

Rivers, once the duke of Bedford's chamberlain and long associated with Calais, was not a popular figure among the garrison. By March 1434, he had secretly married Bedford's widow and the couple went on to have more than a dozen children. While it might be thought somewhat ironic that two men who owed their titles to their wives would berate someone for marrying 'above them', neither Salisbury nor Warwick would have seen it this way. Though Ralph Nevill, first earl of Westmorland was the first member of the family to be elevated to the higher peerage, the family had been barons for several generations. Richard Wydeville's rise through the ranks was entirely different, certainly different enough to arouse the spite of the Nevills. It could be argued that the Nevills had come from equally obscure beginnings, but time, and the blood of Edward III, allowed them to reshape their thinking. They were lords by inheritance and right. In that cold January morning, under the blaze of torchlight, Richard Wydeville and his son were upstarts who dared to insult their betters by calling them traitors and daring to think they could stand against them. Along with the new lord Audley, who had been captured in an attempted raid, the two Wydevilles were kept in Calais Castle, 'where they were long time prisoners'.[26]

In March, with a fleet at their disposal, Somerset bottled up in Guines, Rivers neutralised and little danger of an attack on Calais itself, Warwick and his council felt secure enough for him to leave for a time. He would to go Ireland and consult with York as to the next stage of their plans to return to England in force.

The fall of Normandy and Gascony had brought a stream of French refugees to England, including Gaillard de Durefort, lord of Duras and Blanquefort. He had entered Warwick's service in 1457, bringing around thirty men with him. In 1460, his loyalties were somewhat torn. He was only, he declared, prepared to help the Calais earls 'maintain their war on sea and on land so long as there was nothing done against the person of the king'. This was readily agreed and Duras was appointed admiral for the voyage to Ireland.[27]

Fauconberg was once again left in charge. Warwick was urged by the people of Calais 'to return as early as possible, which he promised them as much as it was in his power to do'. Though this time she at least knew where he was going, and Calais was much more secure than it had been just four months earlier, the countess of Warwick was once again to be without her husband for a time.[28]

By March, the *Grace Dieu* was repaired and fitted with new tackle. Exeter, as Admiral of England, was commissioned to go to sea 'to resist the king's enemies', the *Grace Dieu* granted to him for the purpose. He was also granted 2,500 marks, to be raised from loans. 'Then were the king's privy seals directed to all manner of bishops, abbots, priors and to all the great men of the spirituality and temporality for to give the king money without delay for to wage men to keep the sea coasts, that the said earls should not arrive on any side.'[29]

A further 2,000 marks were granted to Sir Baldwin Fulford and on 3 February he was indented to serve 'upon the sea, at such places convenable as we shall assign him, if wind and weathers will serve, for the resistance of our enemies and the repressing of their malice'. Fulford's ships were to be 'furnished of gunpowder, bows, arrows and strings'. A letter to the chamberlains of the exchequer, so recently Sir Thomas Nevill and his brother-in-law Sir Humphrey Bourchier, sets out the rewards and wages to be enjoyed by Fulford and his men. However, there was not sufficient ready money in the treasury, and Henry VI had once again to turn to his loyal supporters for funds. These loans were to be passed on to Exeter and Fulford as they came in.[30]

Still the king needed ships to replace those commandeered by Dynham at Sandwich. An attempt was made to persuade Genoese and Florentine merchantmen to join the hunt for Warwick, with large offerings of money and pardon for any illegal goods that might be aboard their ships. Not prepared to let themselves get caught up in another country's woes, the Italian merchants preferred to weigh anchor and return home.[31]

Warwick's outward journey to Ireland was without notable incident. Once there, York greeted him 'with great joy', for not only had he had no knowledge of Warwick's whereabouts, he had had no news of his son since they parted at Ludford the previous year. Waurin had a low opinion of Ireland, writing that 'the reception they gave [Warwick] and those with him was very grand, according to the ways of that savage country'.[32]

That very night, they held a council, swearing to 'any lords that wanted to help' that 'they were not going to go against the king but to wage war against the duke of Somerset who made very great war against them in Calais and everywhere he had power, which they needed to remedy'. A plan came together during Warwick's time in Ireland. York would gather what men at arms he could, and 'if [Warwick] could enter England through the county of Kent[, York] would descend from the north and he would most likely have enough men and ships; so it was decided that this was what the lords of York and Warwick would do'.[33]

All the chroniclers agree that Warwick found his mother in Ireland. Whether he had known she was there or not is not something anyone saw fit to mention, or perhaps they did not have access to this level of detail. Waurin, who was in the best position to know, says nothing but that 'he set off, with him madam his mother'. As Waurin also believed the duchess of York and her children were in Ireland, he may have been relying on uncertain memories of conversations, or filling in gaps left by other writers, or simply made the assumption that because the countess of Salisbury was in Ireland, the duchess of York must have been there too. However she came to be there, Alice Montagu must have been delighted to see her son and at the prospect of reunion with her husband in Calais.[34]

Meanwhile, in Calais, Fauconberg, Salisbury and March faced their greatest threat yet. Somerset, hoping Warwick's absence had weakened the defences and the resolve of those left behind, launched an attack on Newnham Bridge, the western approach to the town of Calais. No details survive, except it was a decisive defeat for Somerset and caused him heavy losses. Fauconberg would not have gone out to face this attack alone. With him were his brother Salisbury and the young earl of March. This would have been March's first taste of real battle, under the command of two of England's most experienced and skilled soldiers. Sadly, the chroniclers' lack of detail does not allow confirmation of his presence at Newnham Bridge or an assessment of his conduct.[35]

It was on his way back to Calais that Warwick faced the greatest and most immediate threat to his life and freedom. Not, as might be thought, from Sir Baldwin Fulford, outfitted at great expense by the loans raised by the king. He was nowhere to be seen, having declared 'that on pain of losing his head he would destroy the earl of Warwick and his navy, if the king would grant him his expenses, and he received therefor a thousand marcs and when he had consumed and wasted all that money, his voyage was done and he went home again'.[36]

Fulford had been indented in February for three months, and now his time was up. He had failed entirely to do what he had set out to do. That the king had agreed to fund him and outfit his ships in the first place shows the level of the government's desperation after the loss of the fleet at Sandwich and the capture of Rivers. No doubt Fulford set sail in good faith but one ship, even with 1,000 well-armed men aboard, was never going to survive an encounter with Warwick at sea, nor an attempted assault on Calais. Going home was the wisest thing Fulford could do under the circumstances.

Warwick came up against Exeter who, on hearing Warwick had put to sea, set sail himself, declaring 'that he had vowed to God and to the king that the earl would never see Calais'. Warwick was in the habit of sending a caravel ahead of his fleet as a scout. When a great ship was sighted in the distance, this caravel returned to lord Duras's ship and signalled there was trouble ahead. Understanding how swiftly news travels along the coast, a fisherman was picked up and questioned. The great ship sighted by the crew of the caravel was none other than the *Grace Dieu*, under Exeter's command. Fourteen other ships were with him, the fisherman said, and three great carracks.

> Then the earl of Warwick called his admiral and all the ships' masters, he asking what would be the best way forward, to which with one voice they responded that they wanted to fight because they were strong enough, and when the earl heard the response they made and their sincere desire, he was

very joyful and so armed his men and made all ready, in the same way, he took up his arms and went down the side aisle, walked down the length of the ship and prayed quietly to all his men that they would serve him loyally that day because he had faith in God that He would give them the victory, to which they responded that they all wanted to do this, for which he thanked them.[37]

At first, when Exeter saw Warwick's ships, he thought they were running from him and would be easy pickings if he gave chase. '[B]ut when they saw that the earl came to fight them they retreated into Dartmouth harbour', leaving Warwick free to return to Calais unhurt and undamaged.[38]

Despite running short on provisions and his crews exhausted, Warwick's fleet made quick time to Calais, arriving the following day on a west wind that blew just when it was needed. Once again, Warwick's arrival in Calais was greeted with joy 'because they believed his coming would make things better'. There was a great cheer from those Somerset had set to keep watch on the sea as well, for they thought the ships were a relief force, sent from England, 'which they had been promised several times'. When they realised the ships carried Warwick, those cheers died away. Things were becoming grim in Guines; every time there was a spark of hope it was ground out. Everything attempted by Henry VI's government not only failed to dislodge the Calais earls, it served to put them in a stronger position than before. Here was Warwick, returned to Calais safe with his great fleet. It must have looked like nothing could stop him.[39]

The countess of Warwick had her husband home and safe again. His mother, who had had adventures enough of her own, even if no chronicler saw fit to note them down, was delighted to be on dry land again. While all of Calais celebrated their Captain's safe return, the countess of Salisbury saved her 'great joy ... principally for her husband, who she had not seen in a long time'.[40]

The Calais earls now turned their minds from survival and defence to invasion. Pleading letters were coming from Warwick's supporters in Kent, urging them to 'in all haste possible come and save them from their enemies, promising they would assist them with all their power', and Fauconberg was sent across the channel to see the truth of this for himself. He was soon joined by people from Kent and 'other shires about ... in great number' and sent news of this back to Calais. Whatever else awaited them in England, they had supporters enough in the south-east. There was also news of yet another attempt to gather a force in Sandwich, under Sir Osbert Montford. Once again, John Dynham was despatched to Sandwich to deal with the threat.[41]

Mountford, like Andrew Trollope, was an old soldier, and their paths had crossed many times over the years. Sometimes they served the same lord, Mountford as a military administrator and Trollope in the field. Both had long-standing connections to the Beaufort earls and dukes of Somerset. In 1449, they drew even closer when Trollope married Mountford's sister. Shortly after this, when Mountford was captured by the French and Trollope was forced to surrender the town of Fresnay, he made sure his brother-in-law's release was included in the terms of surrender. When Somerset took over as Captain of Calais, he appointed Mountford to the post of marshal and Trollope master porter. Now Mountford was to lead a last-ditch attempt to keep the Calais earls out of England. In some desperation, 'the king's council … ordained a garrison at Sandwich, to abide and keep the town, and made one Mountfort captain of the town, and warned that no man, nor victuals, nor merchant that should go to Flanders should go into Calais'.[42]

Dynham once again successfully completed his mission, though he was badly wounded in the leg in the attempt. He 'assailed the town by water and by land and got it'. Once Sandwich was under Dynham's control, he had little trouble securing the person of Mountford, who was taken to Rysbank Tower, built on an island in Calais harbour, 'and there [his captors] smote off his head'. By this act, the Calais earls ended all organised resistance on the Kentish coast. Nothing now stopped them crewing their ships and packing them with arms, horses and soldiers. The final act of rebellion – the invasion of England – was about to begin.[43]

# PART 4

# THE NEVILLS
# IN POWER

# 23

# INVASION AND TRIUMPH

ames Ormond, earl of Wiltshire had something of a reputation for cowardice and vanity. After the first battle of St Albans in 1455, he 'fought manly with his heels, for he was afeared of losing his beauty, for he was named the fairest knight of this land'. Flight was a sensible course of action for those nobles on the losing side of a battle and was often reported in chronicles and letters without negative comment. The difference in tone and the reason given for his flight – not to fight another day but to protect his looks – suggests that Wiltshire was not well regarded. He certainly found no admirers among the more partisan Yorkist chroniclers. After York's flight from Ludford, Wiltshire, the elderly lord Scales, father-in-law of Anthony Wydeville, and lord Hungerford used their commission from the king to harry York's town of Newbury in Berkshire,[1]

> and there made inquisition of all them that in any wise had showed any favour or benevolence to the said duke, or to any of his [supporters]; whereof some were found guilty and were drawn, hanged and quartered, and all other inhabitants of the foresaid town were spoiled of all their goods.[2]

Later, on hearing the Yorkist lords were preparing to land in force in Kent, Wiltshire went to Southampton, declaring that he was going to sea to intercept Warwick:

> but specially for to steal privately out of the realm as it proved afterwards, he armed and victualed five great carracks of Genoa that were at that time in the port of the said town, and stuffed them with soldiers of Englishmen, taking victuals of the king's price without payment, as he should have made a voyage for the king, and put a great part of his treasure into the said carracks, and soon after he passed out of the port and sailed about in the sea, dreading the coming of the foresaid earls of Warwick and Salisbury, and at last arrived in Holland and sent his soldiers into England again.[3]

The English government was in chaos. All efforts to dislodge the rebels from Calais had not only failed but served to put them in an even stronger position. Now the treasurer fled. Henry VI still had a core of loyal lords who stood by him, but his fear – for his life, his crown and his kingdom – could only grow stronger the closer the threat came, and the threat was about to come very close indeed.[4]

From Calais, late in June, the earls issued yet another manifesto, which must have been written at least partly in collaboration with York while Warwick was in Ireland. At around the same time, a ballad of unknown origin was 'set upon the gates of Canterbury'. The ballad, like the manifesto, lists the ills that had befallen England. It also celebrates the homecoming of York (who was yet to come home) and the Calais earls.[5]

Send home, most gracious Lord Jhesu, most benign,
Send home thy true blood unto his proper vein,
Richard, duke of York. Job thy servant assign,
Whom Satan not ceases to set at care and disdain;
But by the preserved, he may not be slain,
Set him at sedeat in principibus, as he did before,
And so to our new song, Lord, thine ears incline,
'Gloria, laus et honour tibi sit, Rex Christe Redemptor!'

Edward, earl of March, whose fame the earth shall spread,
Richard, earl of Salisbury, named prudence.
With that noble knight and flower of manhood
Richard, earl of Warwick, shield of our defene,
Also little Fauconberg, a knight of great reverence;
Jhesu tem restore to theor honour as they had before,
And ever shall we sing to thine High Excellence,
'Gloria, laus et honor Tibi sit, Rex Christe Redemptor!'[6]

Warwick's latest manifesto repeated much that had been said before. England was under bad governance, the king was living beyond his means, covetous and greedy lords took what they wanted without payment. The loss of English territory in France, 'won and got by his father of most noble memory, and other his noble progenitors to be shamefully lost or sold', was still a sore point and blame could be assigned to others besides the king. By their greed, the merciless taxing of the commons 'to their great impoverishment, whereof little good has grown to the king or to the said land', England suffered.[7]

York, Warwick and Salisbury were beset by enemies who wanted to silence them, destroy them utterly so they might claim their 'livelihood and goods'. The blame was set squarely upon the shoulders of three men: the earls of Shrewsbury and Wiltshire and viscount Beaumont. Buckingham's name was added to this list some time later. Two of these men were married to sisters of Salisbury and the third, Shrewsbury, to a half-sister of the countess of Warwick. The ties of blood and marriage that were supposed to keep the nobility stable and united had failed. Beaumont may have been due some recognition for his support of Thomas Nevill's wife Maud, but his long association with and staunch support of Queen Margaret set him irrevocably in the list of 'enemies'.

These men, the manifesto asserted, had robbed and despoiled 'all our places and our tenements, and many other true men; and now proceed to hanging and drawing of men by tyranny; and will therein show the largeness of their violence and malice as vengefully as they can'. They would continue to behave in this way until they were stopped. The king, the earls conceded, neither knew of any of this nor consented to it. For fear of 'the charge that would have been laid upon them of the misery, destruction and wretchedness of this said realm', these lords conspired to keep the king in ignorance. They whispered in his ear, poisoning his mind against those who most had his well-being and the good of England at heart. They would not 'suffer the king's said good grace to receive and accept us as he would have done might he have had his own will'. The king himself was 'as noble, as virtuous, as righteous and blessed of disposition, as any prince earthly'.[7]

Ever since the arrest and death of Humphrey, duke of Gloucester, 'the king's true uncle',

> it has been laboured, studied and conspired to have destroyed and murdered the said duke of York and the issue that it pleased God to send me of the royal blood; and also of us the said earls of Warwick and Salisbury, for none other cause but for the true heart that God knows we ever have borne, and bear, to the profit of the king's estate, to the common weal of the said realm, and defence thereof.[8]

There is something new in this manifesto, however. York, his sons and the Nevills were attainted traitors. They were non-persons and their lives forfeit should they fall into the hands of the king. It was the crown's responsibility, whether attainder was objectively justified or not, to bring traitors to justice. From the government's point of view, removing York from Ireland, and Warwick and his party from Calais, was essential to the restoration of stability. If territories sheltering rebels, such as Ireland and Calais, must suffer for this to be achieved, or punished after the fact for providing shelter and support, from a purely political perspective, that was an unfortunate but necessary consequence. York and Warwick, however, saw things very differently: 'various lords have caused his highness to write letters under his privy seal to his Irish enemies ... whereby they may have comfort to enter into the conquest of the said land'. York had seen copies of these letters 'and marvelled greatly that any such letters should be to them sent, speaking therein great shame and villainy of the said realm'. Other letters, 'by excitation and labour of the same lords', were written to the king's 'enemies and adversaries in other lands, that in no wise they should show any favour or good will to the town of Calais, whereby they had comfort enough to proceed to the winning thereof'.[9]

The embargo on Calais left the outpost in danger of being lost to external enemies. From the earls' own perspective, as ever Henry's most loyal and true liegemen, the ordinance that 'neither victual nor any other thing of refreshing or defence should come out of England' to Calais and the letters to the king's enemies in Ireland were nothing short of attacks on English subjects. The covetous lords who surrounded the king, who had thought of little for years but ridding the world of the duke of York, thought nothing of endangering English lives and English territory in the process.[10]

This connects neatly to an argument in *Somnium Vigilantis* where the defence is allowed to speak of the dangers to the defence of England if York and his allies were declared traitors. Though neatly countered, the argument clearly had merit for York's supporters. The time, money and effort expended – and wasted – in attempting to dislodge Warwick from Calais would have been sorely missed had France or Burgundy attempted an assault. On the other hand, it is intriguing to speculate, though impossible to state with any certainty, how Henry VI's attitude towards Warwick, Salisbury, Fauconberg and March might have changed in the face of imminent attack. They would surely not have abandoned Calais but, under such circumstances, their attainders may well have been swiftly reversed.[11]

As it was, their view of the sheer injustice of the attainders was evident, their rage maintained. Brought about by malice and spite, they would surely be overturned if the king would but listen to them. They wished only to come into the king's presence to talk about these things, to 'sue in as reverent and lowly wise as we can to his said good grace and to have pity and compassion upon his said true subjects and not to suffer the same mischiefs to rain upon them'.[12]

The purpose of this, as of every manifesto, was not simply to keep the king informed of their thoughts and actions; it was meant to be published and widely read. Reaching London, gaining admittance to the city, winning the people's support and confidence, was the next crucial step. The manifesto was to pave the way.

On 26 June 1460, the earls of Warwick, Salisbury and March crossed the Channel, 'having wind and weather at their pleasure', and landed at Sandwich. Here they were met by Thomas Bourchier, Archbishop of

Canterbury, lord Cobham and 'a great multitude of people'. They heard mass in the cathedral and, gathering more supporters and followers as they went, the archbishop with the Cross of Canterbury carried before him, they took the road to London.[13]

The people of London were not quite clamouring for the earls to be given entry. The mayor, in particular, feared for the safety of the city. The king had commanded him to keep them out and this he was determined to do. With 500 mounted knights and anything up to 40,000 men following on foot, the Yorkist army was a terrifying prospect. Camped at St George Bar outside the city, the earls received a visit from the mayor and the recorder, both urging them not to

> approach to enter into the city but take their course another way for displeas-
> ure of the king and his council which had given by the advice of his council
> commandment to the mayor to resist them and had willed and sent to the
> mayor the lord Scales and others to help the city to withstand the said lords
> and put them back.[14]

Scales was particularly adamant that they not be given welcome. His presence there was not entirely to everyone's liking. The mayor and his aldermen 'considered that the city was mighty and of power with itself to resist the said lords and their power', especially as it was understood, by the commons of London at least, that the Yorkists intended only 'the worship and well-being of the king and his commons'. The mayor was urged by '[t]hey that were not friendly to the earls', to turn the city's guns on the Yorkist army.[15]

Since argument within the city risked ending in violence and bloodshed, it was finally agreed the rebel lords should be allowed to enter, which they did on 2 July. They took up lodgings in Greyfriars, sending their men to camp in St John's Field, and undertook to be on their way as quickly as possible. Scales, along with lord Hungerford, Sir Gervase Clifton and other prominent Lancastrians, retreated to the Tower, which was soon 'besieged by land and by water; that no victuals might come to them that were within'.[16]

The duchess of Exeter is listed among those who took refuge in the Tower. While Warwick was no friend to her husband, it could hardly be said that she herself was. If Warwick's presence in London caused her any fear, her brother was in his party and would surely have offered her protection. It is entirely possible she did remove to the Tower by choice. Exeter was Constable of the Tower at the time. However reluctant she may have been, his men may have thought it prudent to take the duke's wife to a place of safety, regardless of many of her blood kin being in the Yorkist party. How long she remained with the refugees in the Tower is not recorded.[17]

Among the mix of hostile, suspicious and friendly faces was one that would have delighted both Salisbury and Warwick. George Nevill, Bishop of Exeter was in the city. He had no doubt left the safety of his see the moment he heard of their coming. He was among the 'convocation of the clergy' at St Paul's before whom Warwick 'recited … the causes of their coming into the land'. There Warwick, his father, cousin and uncle 'made an open oath upon the Cross of Canterbury that they had ever borne true faith and liegiance to the king's person, willing no more hurt to him than to their own persons; whereof they took God and his mother and all the saints of heaven to witness'.[18]

A council of war met at Greyfriars and the following day 'they went to the Guildhall and there was indicted many persons and put in prison'. Soon after this, with Salisbury, Wenlock and Cobham staying behind to deal with the lords in the Tower, Warwick, March and Fauconberg, along with the Archbishop of Canterbury and the Bishops of Exeter and Ely, rode out of London in a bid to intercept the king. To speed their way, horses and carts were provided and a loan of £1,000 secured, underwritten by the bishops.[19]

In the meantime, Henry and his loyal lords attempted to reach the relative security of the Isle of Ely. At that time surrounded by fens, it offered both safety and a means of escape should things go badly. It was imperative the Yorkists reach him before he reached the Isle. To this end, the Yorkist army split into two before leaving London. The first group, which took the route north through St Albans, was commanded by Fauconberg; the second, heading for Ware, by Warwick and March. Unable to reach the safety of the fens, the king's army set itself in a field just outside the walls of Northampton along the banks of the Nene.[20]

Edmund, lord Grey of Ruthyn had distant family connections to the Nevills through both the Montagus and the Bonvilles. He had been caught up in the Ampthill dispute between Cromwell and Exeter, which was resolved on Cromwell's death when Grey purchased the property from the executors. Prior to this, he had been involved in the murder of the then speaker of the commons, William Tresham. At the battle of Northampton, Grey of Ruthyn commanded Henry VI's right flank.[21]

The battle itself was preceded by some hours of fruitless negotiation with Buckingham, conducted first by a party of bishops led by the Bishop of Salisbury then by Warwick Herald. Buckingham refused to allow the Archbishop of Canterbury to act as mediator on the grounds he was too firmly aligned with the Yorkists. To the bishops, Buckingham declared: 'You come not as bishops for to treat for peace but as men of arms.' The bishops responded that they only came with an armed escort for their own safety, as 'they that be about the king be not our friends'. Warwick, Buckingham said, 'shall not come to the king's presence, and if he come he shall die'.[22]

In response, Warwick

> … sent a herald of arms to the king, beseeching that he might have hostages
> of safe going and coming, and he would come naked to his presence, but he
> might not be heard. And the third time he sent to the king and said that at two
> hours after noon he would speak with him or else die in the field.[23]

Sometime prior to the battle, either during the negotiations or through a message sent to Warwick's camp, Grey of Ruthyn indicated his intention to throw in his lot with the Yorkists. If it came to battle, he would choose his moment and change sides. To this end, Warwick informed his captains 'that they should tell their men that all who bore the black ragged staff were to be saved'.[24]

Just why Grey of Ruthyn came to such an understanding with Warwick is not clear. His brother Thomas remained loyal to Henry VI, losing his life after a battle yet to come. Edmund Grey was not notably rewarded in the years immediately following the Yorkist triumph, so it is unlikely his actions were prompted by promises of future benefit. He may simply have assessed the situation and decided to throw in his lot with the rebels 'in an inspired gamble'. Whatever his reasons, his actions were decisive and brought the battle to a swift end, 'which caused salvation of many a man's life'.[25]

With Warwick, March and Fauconberg in command of the three flanks, the Yorkists attacked at 2 o'clock, as Warwick had promised. In the pouring rain, the royalist guns were useless, some bogged in the mud, all too waterlogged to fire. Grey of Ruthyn held good to his word, 'for as the attacking squadrons came to the ditch before the royalist ramparts and wanted to climb over it, which they could not quickly do because of the height … lord Grey with his men met them and, seizing them by the hand, hauled them into the embattled field'.[26]

Once in the king's camp, the fighting was brutal, swift and uncompromising. The duke of Buckingham, 'standing still at his tent', the earl of Shrewsbury, viscount Beaumont and Thomas Percy, lord Egremont were all slain. In less than an hour, it was all over. In the confusion and rout that followed, many men were drowned in the swollen River Nene.[27]

An extraordinary event now took place. With the bodies of his most trusted advisers and staunchest supporters lying in the heavy rain, the king was confronted in his tent by the victorious earls of Warwick and March. According to one chronicler, they fell to their knees, declaring their love and loyalty, noble and conciliatory words pouring from their mouths.[28]

> Most noble prince, displease you not, though it has pleased God of His Grace to
> grant us the victory of our mortal enemies, the which by their venomous malice
> have untruly steered and moved your highness to exile us out of your land and

would have us put to final shame and confusion. We come not to that intent for to inquiet nor grieve your said highness, but for to please your most noble person, desiring most tenderly the high welfare and prosperity thereof, and of all your realm, and for to be your true liegemen, while our lives shall endure.[29]

The chronicler records that the king was 'recomforted' by these words, though one might be forgiven for wondering at such a notion: his party had been attacked; he had been betrayed by the commander of his vanguard; and Buckingham, Shrewsbury, Beaumont and Egremont were all dead, along with countless others. Henry had little choice but to submit, allowing himself to be taken in a procession of great state into Northampton, where he was allowed to rest for three days.[30]

Word was immediately sent to Chester Castle ordering the release of Thomas and John Nevill and Sir Thomas Harrington. They would surely have known of their father and brother's arrival in Sandwich, eagerly awaiting to be freed. News from Northampton would have been greeted with mixed feelings, pride in Warwick's victory and regret they had not themselves been there to share it. On their release, they travelled to London, where they were reunited with family members they had not seen for nine months.

Queen Margaret and the Prince of Wales, who were not at Northampton with the king, headed for the shelter of Harlech Castle. Along the way, the queen fell into an ambush and was 'robbed and despoiled of all her goods to the value of 10,000 marks' and 'put her so in doubt of her life and her son's life also'. She later made her way to Scotland, where she and her son became a rallying point for the Lancastrian resistance.[31]

Margaret's popularity, already fairly marginal, plunged from this point. Rumours would soon abound about the paternity of her son and her promises to the men who held loyal to her.[32]

> Not long before this battle it was proclaimed in Lancashire and Cheshire that if so were that the king had the victory of the earls, that then every man should take what he might and make havoc in the shires of Kent, Essex, Middlesex, Surrey, Sussex, Hampshire and Wiltshire; but God would not suffer such false robbery.[33]

From Northampton the king was taken to London, again in great procession with Warwick bearing his sword, reaching the capital on 16 July. On hearing of the Yorkist victory at Northampton, the people of London 'gave to Almighty God great laud and thanking'. The king was lodged in the Bishop of London's palace and Warwick's attention turned to the ongoing siege of the Tower.[34]

Salisbury, Cobham and Wenlock had not had an easy time of it while the others were fighting in Northampton. The Tower's cannons bombarded the city, wildfire set houses alight and citizens were killed or seriously injured in their homes and in the streets. Cobham responded with like force and cannon fire also came from across the river, the citizens of London taking matters into their own hands. With Wenlock and his men holding St Katharine Docks and Warwick's ships controlling the river, the Tower was blockaded.[35]

On the day of the battle, a party of men led by one Thomas Browne broke through the blockade in an attempt to bring aid to those within. With the mayor and sheriffs now fully cooperated with Salisbury to prevent further deaths and destruction, anything that prolonged the siege was bound to be viewed in a dim light.[36]

On 19 July, with the guns in the Tower still sounding, the king heard mass at St Paul's before riding in procession through the city. That same day, 'for lack of victuals', Scales and Hungerford 'yielded up the Tower and came out'. Sir John Wenlock and a mercer by the name of Harowe were sent to the Tower to arrest those who needed to be arrested and, quietly, allow the lords to make their way to safety. Hungerford was later given permission to leave England to go on pilgrimage and Scales made his way by river to Westminster sanctuary, but 'that was perceived by the shipmen, and they laid watch and took him and slew him and laid him naked in St Mary Overy churchyard'.[37]

Scales had been something of an English hero, having spent much of his life fighting in France. Over the years, he had been closely associated with York, acting as godfather to his son Edward, and with Suffolk. Alongside Suffolk's widow, he took charge of the duke's estates after his murder to hold in custody until his son came of age. Scales's daughter Elizabeth married, as her second husband, Anthony Wydeville, eldest son of lord Rivers and the dowager duchess of Bedford. Scales's death was deeply regretted. Warwick immediately issued a proclamation condemning the murder and he and the earl of March both attended Scales's funeral.[38]

While the lords who had held out in the Tower were not to be punished, the same did not apply to Browne and his accomplices. Arraigned for treason, they were found guilty 'and were drawn and hanged, and their heads smitten off'.[39]

On 20 July, letters were sent summoning the lords and commons of England to a Parliament to be held on 20 October. On the 25th, at the Bishop of London's palace, the great seals were transferred from Thomas Bourchier to George Nevill. The bishop, who had spent much of the last year in his see of Exeter, was destined never to return there, his new responsibilities making it increasingly difficult. In London, he took up residence in a house belonging to the diocese and while he remained bishop he continued to meet his responsibilities, albeit through an able and experienced deputy. He gave considerable gifts to Exeter cathedral and contributed substantially to building works, including the great east window.[40]

Salisbury was appointed Great Chamberlain of England and set about ridding the royal household of corruption. John Nevill's appointment as chamberlain of the king's household gave him authority over who was allowed into the royal presence. Besides several lucrative stewardships and constabularies, Thomas became joint keeper of the royal mews alongside his father. Among their responsibilities was the acquisition of 'the king's right prizes of falcons, goshawks, sakers, sakerets, lancers, landerets and gyrfalcons for sale through the realm, paying 20s for a falcon, 10s for a tercel gentle, 13s 4d for a goshawk and 6s 8d each for the tercel of a goshawk, saker, lancer and lanneret'.[41]

Securing his position as Captain of Calais, renewing his indenture as keeper of the seas for a further three years and being appointed warden of the Cinq Ports, Warwick was effectively Henry's chief councillor. Several foreign governments, pleased with the change of regime, recognised his pre-eminence in England. 'Thus one may say that today everything is in Warwick's power and the war at an end, and that he has done marvellous things. God grant him grace to keep the country in peace and union!'[42]

August was a busy month for Warwick. He had one final loose end to tie up. Not only must he bring his mother, wife and daughters home from Calais, he had Somerset to deal with. On 2 August, he accompanied the king to Canterbury before crossing the Channel to Calais five days later. A meeting with Somerset was arranged for the following day and the two men kissed in a gesture of peace and reconciliation. Somerset undertook not to take up arms against Warwick in the future and was allowed, along with lord Roos and Andrew Trollope, to make his way to Dieppe, whence they were later to return to England.[43]

The disaster at Ludford had been comprehensively overturned and the change of the Nevills' fortune was absolute. Every setback along the way had been turned into triumph. From the failure of the boatmen in the Bristol Channel to sail Warwick's ship to Ireland, Somerset's appointment as Captain of Calais and his delay in taking possession, the gathering of the fleet in Sandwich to the appointment of Grey of Ruthyn as battle commander, everything had fallen Warwick's way. He must have felt himself blessed by God, incapable of failure. Now all he had to do was hold England together and wait for York to arrive from Ireland. 'Warwick was now the principal Neville and the whole country was lost without him.'[44]

Warwick Castle.

Raby Castle.

Middleham Castle.

Towton Battlefield memorial cross.

Battle of Barnet Memorial.

Tattershall Castle.

Alnwick Castle.

Bamburgh Castle.

Gatehouse Dunstanburgh Castle.

Garter stall plate of Richard Nevill, earl of Salisbury.

Effigy of Joan Nevill.

# 24

# SIR THOMAS NEVILL
# AND THE DUKE OF YORK

ir Thomas Nevill found his uncle York busily preparing for his coronation. It would be held, the duke had decided, in two days on St Edward's Day. He was in the king's apartments at Westminster, refusing to back down and refusing to move. The king had moved to other quarters, not wishing to be embroiled in a physical confrontation.[1]

York would not deviate from the plan he and Warwick had discussed the previous month in Shrewsbury, where they met in council for four days. York would make his slow way to London, gathering support on the way, orchestrating 'spontaneous' clamour for him to take the throne. Warwick was to put the idea to the lords gathering in London for the upcoming Parliament. That the idea was at least in York's mind when he and his second son returned from Ireland is evident. He displayed the arms of his ancestor Lionel, duke of Clarence, second son of Edward III. In dating his letters, he made no reference, as was customary, to the years Henry VI had been on the throne. He sent for his duchess, asking her to meet him in Hereford. If he was to be king, he wanted the woman who would be his queen by his side.[2]

Just how much Warwick collaborated with York is open to speculation. He would hardly have missed the signs and it is unlikely York said nothing of it during their four days together in Shrewsbury. Warwick's most crucial task was to bring the Archbishop of Canterbury on board. York could not be crowned without him, but this Warwick failed to do. While York travelled in great state, with 'trumpeters and clariners to bring him into London', he failed utterly to win over the citizens. They were unsettled, to say the least, at York's display. They feared it would bring more trouble, just when they thought things had settled at last.[3]

The duchess of York, only just arrived in London, left immediately she got her husband's letter. Leaving her three youngest children in a house borrowed from John Paston, she 'met with [York] in a chair covered with blue velvet'. Her oldest son, Edward, earl of March visited his younger siblings every day in her absence. The duchess had spent some months living in the house of her sister the duchess of Buckingham. With Buckingham's death and the Nevills firmly in control of the government, the dynamic between the sisters must have gone through something of a shift. Cecily had no difficulty leaving Anne's custody once news of her husband's arrival reached her.[4]

Parliament was already sitting when York arrived. The new chancellor, George Nevill had opened the session on 7 October. The king attended 'sitting on the royal throne in the painted chamber'. With some difficulty, a speaker of the commons was elected and the first act of business was the repeal of the whole of the preceding Parliament. Malicious lords had urged the king to call it so they could 'destroy certain of the great, noble and faithful true lords and estates of your blood'. Not only that, it had been improperly called, several of its members 'returned and accepted, some of them without due and free election and some of them without any election'. The Parliament of Devils must be made 'void and taken for no parliament ... all acts, statutes and ordinances ... reversed, annulled, ceased, invalidated, repealed, revoked, void and of no force nor effect'.[5]

With four words – 'Le roy le voet', the king wills it – the attainders of York, the Nevills and their supporters were reversed.[6]

The king was not in the chamber when York arrived with great ceremony. He 'took the king's place, claiming it for his right and inheritance, and said that he would keep it to live and die'. This caused great consternation among the assembled lords, who did not, as York must have been counting on, leap to their feet and proclaim him king with one voice. If Warwick had managed to warn him that things were not going quite to plan, this warning was ignored. Frustrated, the duke broke down the doors of the king's chambers to take up lodging. 'And the king hearing the great noise and rumour of the people, gave him place and took another chamber.'[7]

There followed several days of negotiation, the lords in Blackfriars and York refusing to move from the royal apartments at Westminster. A solution to the impasse must be found if trouble were to be averted. York may have enjoyed a certain popularity with the people of England, but they were not at all happy with the idea of deposing Henry VI in his favour. After Thomas Nevill's first fruitless attempt to talk his uncle out of claiming the throne, the lords met for further discussions. Attempts were made to get the earl of March to go to his father to let him know how restless the city grew. March refused the commission. The Archbishop of Canterbury also refused to attempt to mediate. Instead, a party of bishops went to talk to York, but he still would not back down. On 12 October, Thomas Nevill was sent once more to talk with him.[8]

No one knows what was said but, finally, Thomas's words got through to the tenacious duke. Perhaps he talked to him of the dangers of civil war, reminding him of those who had died at Northampton, and telling him bluntly that he did not enjoy the universal love and support of the commons. Perhaps he reminded York of the oaths his brother and father, and York's son, had made on the Cross of Canterbury, or of the nine months of imprisonment he and John had suffered in York's service. Perhaps he was authorised to threaten the withdrawal of Nevill support if the duke persisted in his course. The merchants of London had come to Warwick in protest. They would not support the deposition of Henry VI. York, doggedly following a course of action that could not be peacefully concluded, was on his own. Whatever was said – and however it was said – Thomas's words had some effect at last. York would put his claim to the throne to the lords for their judgement. He would not, however, leave the king's apartments.[9]

That Thomas, York's nephew and a man of far lesser rank and status, could speak with him to such effect throws up a number of interesting possibilities. Either the force of his argument itself left York with little choice but to back down to the degree he did or there was something in their relationship that allowed Thomas greater candour than others might have dared. Warwick himself did not go, nor did Salisbury. Thomas Nevill had already shown both, through the feud with the Percies and his response to Cromwell's changed will, that he was not one to accept any situation as impossible or unchangeable. We do not know how long the two men spent in discussion, or argument, any more than we know what was said. We do know that in Sir Thomas, York met his match.

In 1454, during York's first protectorate, both Thomas and John Nevill had been pivotal to his success. Their capture of the Percies in Yorkshire ended not only the feud, for the time being at least, but brought the rebellion to a decisive end. A working relationship may have developed then between the two men that allowed Thomas to speak freely and frankly when the need arose. It would seem that a combination of factors – the urgency of the situation, the need to avoid more bloodshed and strife, the slim chances of York gaining popular support for his plan and Thomas's willingness to pull no punches – produced a workable outcome. York's claim would be examined and he would abide by the decision reached.

York's claim to the throne rested on his descent through his mother from Lionel, duke of Clarence, Edward III's second son. Henry VI was descended from John of Gaunt, fourth son of Edward III. The 'violent intrusion' of Henry IV had 'displeased and diseased' York from his rightful inheritance. After much discussion, York's claim was upheld but Henry VI was not to be deposed, or asked to resign, in his favour. Instead, his son was to be set aside from the succession and York named heir apparent. Should Henry choose at some time in the future to abdicate, he would resign his crown to no one but York. If York predeceased Henry, the crown would go to his oldest surviving heir.[10]

This agreement, known as the Act of Accord, was reached on 30 October 1460, York and his sons March and Rutland having sworn yet another oath to uphold and protect the life of the king. That same night, Henry was removed from Westminster to the Bishop of London's palace, where he was visited by York 'by torchlight'. York seems to have been less than magnanimous on this occasion, reminding Henry that *he* was the rightful king, and may have attempted to persuade him to abdicate.[11]

None of this pleased Queen Margaret. Already, rumours were spreading about the paternity of her son and now he had been disinherited and removed from the succession. His father had been able to do nothing to protect his rights. If they were to be restored and upheld, it was up to his mother to do something. The Queen of England found herself in the unlikely position of king's rebel. Her son's seventh birthday was spent away from the court, his father, everything he knew and in a state of uncertainty. Just six months earlier, he had taken the first steps along the long road to manhood. When his governess Alice, lady Lovell sought to retire due to 'grave infirmities in body and sight', the prince was taken from the care of women 'because he is now so grown as to be committed to the rules and teaching of men wise and strenuous, to understand the acts and manner of a man befitting such a prince'.[12]

Prince Edward had just turned 7 and was now living a very different life, sleeping in armed camps and distant Welsh castles. No longer Prince of Wales and heir to the throne, he was now a rebel and could look only to his mother and the men she chose to trust for his survival. Queen Margaret and her son took refuge with Jasper Tudor in Harlech Castle with only a handful of supporters for protection, 'for she dare not hide in no place that was open'. Desperate attempts were made to lure her back to London, with false tokens purported to come from the king himself. Margaret, however, was not so easily fooled, 'for at the king's departing for Coventry towards the field of Northampton, he kissed her and blessed the prince and commanded her that she not come to him till that he send a special token to her that no man knew but the king and she'.[13]

She sent for Somerset, now back in England and staying at Corfe Castle in Dorset. She arranged to meet him in Hull, along with Exeter, Devon and lords Roos, Clifford and Greystoke. Lord John Nevill, brother of the earl of Westmorland, was in her party. One source claims that she had Salisbury's brother Latimer with her, though this seems unlikely as Latimer had suffered a mental breakdown twenty years earlier and never fully recovered.[14]

Many of these lords, and others, faced not simply a choice between submitting to the new authority of York or remaining loyal to the queen and Prince Edward. In standing with Margaret, bizarrely, they put themselves in opposition to orders and commandments issued in the name of the king. They saw Henry as a captive of York and the Nevills, however, in need of rescue. To that end, Northumberland set about raising an army in Yorkshire.[15]

Margaret's gathering of lords and men in the north of England caused alarm in London but it was not the only cause for concern. March was sent to Shrewsbury in hopes that he could prevent Jasper Tudor, earl of Pembroke joining the queen in Yorkshire. Commissions were sent out to various lords, knights and squires, some whose loyalty to the new regime was not yet confirmed, to deal with lawlessness and rebellion wherever they found it. York himself, accompanied by Salisbury and their sons Rutland and Sir Thomas Nevill, set off for the north on 2 December. With them were three generations of Bonvilles – Salisbury's son-in-law, his father and grandfather. Sir Thomas Harrington, ever a staunch supporter of the Nevills, rode with them. Warwick and John Nevill remained in London. Edward, earl of March was on his way west.[16]

York and Salisbury did not know that they were riding to face an organised army led in spirit by Queen Margaret and in fact by Somerset. They went primarily with the aim of punishing 'rebellious malefactors, oppressors, extortioners and thieves', and bringing a quick end to the 'malice and insurrection intended by the queen, the prince' and their supporters. They left London with 400 men between them, expecting to be reinforced along the way. They had planned to go armed, 'one called Lovelace, a gentleman of Kent, followed them with great ordinance of guns and other stuff of war', but bad weather forced the artillery to return to the city. The lack of urgency was marked not just by the size of this small force but the slow pace of their journey. They arrived in Sandal some time between 21 and 24 December.[17]

The north of England, however, was far more set against York than had been realised. A failure of intelligence, and probably a sign that York was so unaware of the scale of the opposition that he did not vigorously seek intelligence, led to the loss of a party of scouts at Worksop, some 38 miles south of Sandal. It was this skirmish that finally gave York some useful intelligence about the size of the enemy's forces and their level of organisation.[18]

Somerset and York both learned something from the encounter at Worksop and both changed their plans because of it. It is highly unlikely that men of York and Salisbury's experience would forget to make sure their destination was properly supplied and Sandal Castle was not. They may have originally been heading for Pontefract in an attempt to subdue those who held it and impose law and order. At Sandal, they could wait for reinforcements. Somerset seems to have been heading for Hull and his change of plans took him to Pontefract.[19]

At Sandal, the men kept a quiet Christmas, away from their homes and families. If they wrote letters to wives and mothers, brothers and sons, they left no trace. Given the season, it was necessary for both Somerset and York to send out parties to forage for supplies where they could find them. The two armies were barely 12 miles apart and competing for the same scarce resources, so there was always danger of a confrontation. One widely held view, though now becoming less popular, is that York heard his foragers were under attack, and rashly issued forth from Sandal to rescue them, only to find himself confronted by Somerset's waiting army.[20]

Somerset and his men left Pontefract on 29 December, marching towards Sandal. The circumstances that led to the battle are still very much in dispute. It seems likely it was the result of a combination of two factors – the need to collect supplies and the arrival of lord John Nevill, Westmorland's brother, with 8,000 men. The timing of both Nevill's arrival and his offer to join York with his men is also uncertain. While he may have arrived at Sandal unannounced, it is also possible he was in communication with York and Salisbury before they themselves reached the castle. What is not in dispute is that Nevill's intentions were not what he declared them to be. Like Grey of Ruthyn at Northampton, Nevill had already decided to turn on his kinsmen when the opportunity arose. This opportunity seems to have presented itself when a group of York's foragers was attacked while returning to Sandal. Without Nevill's extra troops, York could not have made an attempt to rescue the foragers without putting himself and everyone with him in danger.[21]

Whatever the cause, the battle was over quickly. York's forces were encircled by an army that had declared itself on his side. He died in the battle, as did Sir Thomas Nevill, Salisbury's son-in-law William Bonville along with his father, and Sir Thomas Harrington. Salisbury survived the battle but was taken prisoner, along with others, and held overnight in Pontefract. The young earl of Rutland is reported to have been killed fleeing across Wakefield Bridge by Clifford, possibly during the rout.[22]

At first it was agreed Salisbury would be freed on receipt of a large ransom but he was dragged from his quarters. 'But the common people, which loved him not, took him out of the castle by violence and smote off his head'. Robert Bastard of Exeter, older half brother of the duke of Exeter, was subsequently held personally responsible for the murder. Salisbury's head, along with those of his son, York, Rutland 'and others of note who fell in the battle', was taken to York and prominently displayed on the city gates, 'a paper crown placed in derision on the head of the duke of York'.[23]

# 25

# THREE BATTLES THAT MADE A KING

In the uncertain days after the disaster at Ludford, in a small ship in the Bristol Channel, Warwick had comforted his father, seizing the tiller and the initiative, and bringing him safe to harbour. Warwick owed everything to Salisbury. His careful husbandry of the Warwick inheritance during the brief life of Henry Beauchamp's daughter and the swift action taken after her death secured the young Richard Nevill an earldom and a fortune.

Warwick and his brothers had learned much from Salisbury, not just how to be men of property and war but husbands and fathers. The evidence is scant and circumstantial at best, but what there is points to the Salisburys enjoying a strong marriage, the kind of partnership noble couples aspired to. To her personal cost, Alice Montagu had not hesitated to support her husband in 1459. Attainted and forced into exile, enduring long months without knowing if the other lived or died, their mutual joy when they were reunited in Calais points to a couple who shared a genuine affection. Now, after forty years of marriage, he was gone.

Salisbury had supported his children all their lives. In choosing husbands for his daughters, he had taken their future happiness into account as well as the benefits his sons-in-law would bring to his affinity. He worked hard to advance his sons, providing both Thomas and John wealthy young wives, sharing with them his lucrative and important posts in the north of England, backing them every chance he got. In return, he expected them to come when they were summoned, to ride with him to battle and to support the cause he chose even at the risk of their lives and freedom. Richard Nevill and Alice Montagu headed a strong family unit that understood their mutual dependence and responsibility. Now Warwick had to find a way through his own sorrow to step into his father's shoes. If his grief struck him physically, it is hardly to be wondered at.[1]

Compounding the loss of their father, Warwick, John and George had to deal with the death of their brother Thomas. John, in particular, must have felt this deeply. He had shared his greatest triumphs and his deepest despair with Thomas. The violence of the feud with their cousins, the capture of Egremont and Richard Percy at Stamford Bridge, their months of confinement in Chester Castle after Blore Heath had forged a strong bond that only death could break. Thomas's death robbed Warwick of a more than able lieutenant and John a companion in arms.

George owed his father far more than filial respect and love. It was Salisbury's dogged support that saw him appointed to the see of Exeter. After his short tenure as chancellor in 1454, Salisbury would have been a valuable support to George in the first few weeks after Northampton, when he was appointed to the post. In the early days of 1461, George transferred, irrevocably and without hesitation, the whole of his allegiance to his brother Warwick.

The brothers, and their mother, were together in London where they might draw comfort and strength from each other. Salisbury's daughters were scattered across England and one of them had an even greater grief to bear. The news of the deaths of young lord Harrington and his father would have reached Shute Barton soon after it reached London. Katherine Nevill was widowed at just 18 and her six-month-old daughter Cecily, heir to his title and sizeable fortune, would never know her father.

The deaths at Wakefield galvanised the earl of Arundel into unaccustomed action. Husband of Salisbury's oldest daughter Joan, Arundel narrowly avoided attainder after Blore Heath. Joining the other lords in the oath of loyalty to Henry VI sworn at the Parliament of Devils, he now abjured this and joined Warwick in London. In Chester, the Stanleys made no move, either to join the surviving Yorkists or to support Queen Margaret. Alianor, who had been closest to her brothers Thomas and John during their imprisonment, close enough perhaps to visit or send gifts, was far from the comfort and support of her family.

It was Alice Fitzhugh, far away in Yorkshire, who arguably faced the greatest difficulty. Her youngest sister Margaret may still have been in her care or she may have been despatched to London shortly after their mother's arrival the previous August. Alice is likely to have been the first to hear the news from Wakefield. Her husband remained true to the oath he made in Parliament and was with Somerset's army, though there is no record of him taking the field against his father-in-law. He may have held back or he may have been deliberately kept from the field.

In the months to come, both Fitzhugh and Ralph, lord Greystoke would be viewed with some suspicion. Their family connection to Salisbury, and their years of service as his loyal retainers, made them suspect in the eyes of Queen Margaret. In January 1461, at the queen's council of war in York, things came to a head. Such were the doubts as to Fitzhugh and Greystoke's loyalty that they were required to renew their oaths to the king, the queen and their son Prince Edward. It has been speculated that Greystoke, at least, may have been playing a double game. If this was the case, he had been unable to warn York and Salisbury of the treacherous plans of lord John Nevill.[2]

On paper at least, a fifteenth-century nobleman's wife was expected to respect her husband's decisions, obey his commandments and do all she could to support and help him achieve his goals. In practice, however, things may have been a little different. We cannot know whether Alice Fitzhugh attempted to influence her husband, as such details were rarely recorded. On the other hand, it is difficult to imagine a woman of Alice's character remaining silent while her husband ranged himself and his men against her family. Fitzhugh owed the Nevills a good deal, she might have reminded him. Her brothers were his friends – four of the five Fitzhugh sons were named after them – and her father had been his good lord at least since their marriage. Few of Salisbury's affinity had deserted him after his return from Calais. That Fitzhugh was one could not have sat comfortably with his wife. Now her father and brother were dead and she could not call on the man with whom she shared her life to exact vengeance.

Compounding all of this, of course, was the death of the duke of York. The hard work of the last few months, the return of the Calais earls, the taking and keeping of London, the battle at Northampton and the hard negotiations that resulted in the Act of Accord, was all for nothing. Without York, the Yorkist cause may well have collapsed. What saved it was the existence of York's son the earl of March and the determination and hard work of the earl of Warwick.

March was in Wales when he learned of the deaths of his father and brother. He was just 18 years old, enjoying his first independent command, and a long way from family. Under the terms of the Act of Accord, he was now heir apparent to the English crown. He had been away from his father's influence for almost a year, serving as an equal in Warwick's council in Calais and returning to England in the company of the Nevills to great acclaim and praise. He had acquitted himself well at Northampton, under the command of Warwick and Fauconberg. During his mother's brief absence from London, he showed himself to be a good and conscientious brother to his younger siblings, visiting them every day until their parents' arrival in the city. Whatever the future he saw for himself in late 1460, his brother Edmund would have played a large part in it. Though apart for the best part of a year, the two had grown up together in their household at Ludlow Castle, at times forming a united front in the face of adult tyranny and unfairness. As they grew into adulthood, Edmund would have formed the core of his older brother's affinity. Now Edward had to forge his own future, as duke of York and heir to the throne. March spent Christmas in Gloucester and set off for London on receipt of the news from Wakefield.[3]

It was news that sent London into a panic: 'all this season was great watch made in the city of London, for it was reported that the queen with the northern men would come down to the city and rob and despoil the city and destroy it utterly, and all the south country.' Warwick had no choice but to set his grief aside and get on with the business of governing. In two letters, both dated 11 January 1461, we catch a glimpse of how difficult this must have been. In almost offhand reassurances to Pope Pius II and the duke of Milan, he wrote of 'the destruction of some of my kinsmen in the battle against our enemies' and urged both duke and pope to 'be of good cheer' as 'all will end well'.[4]

Warwick was not writing to elicit sympathy for the deaths of his father, brother, uncle, cousin and brother-in-law. These were not personal letters to friends but from one statesman to another. He had to present both himself and his government as strong and enduring and his enemies as malicious and vulnerable. To the pope, he wrote 'do not desert me and the others you formerly received as sons, for eventually you will see us end well and devoutly'. And to the duke of Milan: 'We are devoted to the pope and to the commonweal of his Majesty and the realm, which our adversaries endeavour to destroy.'[5]

In Wales, March knew nothing of this. He knew he must return to London as quickly as he could but he could not easily abandon his original mission. He had been sent into the west to raise troops, keep the peace and prevent the earls of Richmond and Pembroke, Edmund and Jasper Tudor, and their father Owen, from linking up with the queen's army. When Wiltshire landed in South Wales with an army of mercenaries from Brittany, France and Ireland, joining Jasper and Owen Tudor and heading towards Hereford, March had no choice but to stand and fight. A rare atmospheric phenomenon seen by all he interpreted as a good omen.[6]

And the Monday before the day of the battle, that is to say in the feast of purification of our blessed lady, about ten at the clock before noon, were seen three suns in the firmament shining full clear, whereof the people had great marvel and thereof were aghast. The noble earl Edward them comforted and said, 'Be of good comfort and dread not; this is a good sign for these three suns betoken the Father, the Son and the Holy Ghost, and therefore let us have a good heart and in the name of Almighty God go we against our enemies.'[7]

The two armies met at Mortimer's Cross on the morning of 2 February. For some hours, nothing happened, no one made a move. Then, at midday, the whole of the Lancastrian line advanced, Pembroke's and Wiltshire's divisions engaging with Edward's army. Owen Tudor attempted a flanking movement, hoping to attack Edward from the rear. This turned out to be a miscalculation, as Wiltshire's line broke and Pembroke's men yielded ground. Owen Tudor was out of position and Edward's army slammed into his flank. All attempts to turn, rally and reorganise them failed. Wiltshire's mercenaries, knowing that a defeated army does not get paid, left the field to try their luck elsewhere. Wiltshire himself, and Pembroke, managed to escape. Owen Tudor was not so fortunate.[8]

Edward's victorious men chased Tudor and his forces as far as Hereford, where he was captured and executed in the marketplace.

> This Owen Tudor was father to the earl of Pembroke and had wedded queen Katherine, king Harry VI's mother, believing and trusting always that he should not be headed till he saw the axe and the block, and when that he was in his doublet he trusted on pardon and grace till the collar of his red velvet doublet was ripped off. Then he said, 'That head shall lie on the stock that was wont to lie on queen Katherine's lap' and put his heart and mind wholly unto God and full meekly took his death.[9]

In his first independent command, Edward, earl of March managed a stunning victory. Two of the enemy commanders got away, but the third was dead and their armies scattered. Though not quite a fatal blow to Lancastrian hopes, it was something of a setback. It was still crucial that Edward make his way to London to support the beleaguered Warwick but for reasons that remain unclear, he tarried a while in Wales.[10]

Queen Margaret's army, fresh from victory at Wakefield, marched south towards London, much to the consternation of its citizens. Her army was largely untrained, inexperience and ill-disciplined. A good many deserted on the way south and there was a great deal of looting and destruction of property along the route. Londoners were terrified and feared the worst. Some barricaded themselves inside their houses; others buried valuables. Everyone stayed off the streets.[11]

Warwick left London with King Henry on 12 February, along with Norfolk, Suffolk and Arundel. His brother John, newly ennobled as lord Montagu, his uncle Fauconberg, lord Berners and Sir John Wenlock were also in his company. Lovelace, commander of York's artillery, survivor of Wakefield and historical mystery, was also said to have accompanied Warwick. In total, the Yorkist army consisted of some 25,000 men. Hoping to halt Queen Margaret's advance on the capital, Warwick chose his ground, deploying his troops in and to the north of St Albans.[12]

Queen Margaret also had around 25,000 men with her, under Somerset's command. With her also were the duke of Exeter, the earls of

Northumberland and Shrewsbury, and lords Roos, Grey of Codnor, Clifford, Greystoke, Wells and Willoughby. Somerset had more to consider than the eradication of the Yorkists. His brother Edmund was captive in Carisbrooke Castle on the Isle of Wight. Captured the previous December by Sir Geoffrey Gate, a long-serving retainer of Warwick, he was vulnerable and this must have been in the back of Somerset's mind. The execution of Salisbury marked a new twist in the conflict. Aware of the bloody revenge Warwick had meted out on those of the Calais garrison who deserted him at Ludlow and aware of the execution of Sir Osbert Mountford, Somerset must have been concerned for his brother's life. That he did not order Edmund Beaufort's immediate execution, more particularly after the news of his father's murder, suggests that Warwick was well aware of Beaufort's value as a hostage.[13]

The chaotic second battle of St Albans was a mixture of over-thinking; experimental tactics, defences and weapons; a failure of intelligence; and poor communication. It is also important to remember that Warwick was expecting the arrival of March and his men, which may help explain why he relied so heavily on defence. Keeping Queen Margaret's army from London was crucial and Edward's delay is not easily explained, though it may simply have been a case of excessive caution. London was in safe hands but Richmond, Pembroke and Wiltshire were still alive and at large. Edward's slow progress from Wales may simply reflect his priorities and his confidence in Warwick's ability to defend the city.[14]

Those troops that saw action on the Yorkist side at St Albans fought hard but early mistakes and assumptions doomed Warwick to failure, almost from the start. The crucial event was the change in the line of march of Queen Margaret's army; everything else flowed from this.

Everything Warwick knew, and every report he received, told him the Lancastrian army would come directly south along the Great North Road, and it was in this line he arranged his troops. A squad of Montagu's archers was positioned in St Albans itself with the rest of his men on Barnard's Heath just north of the town. The centre and reserve, commanded by Warwick, was a little further north, near the village of Sandridge. Norfolk's troops were further north still on Nomansland Common.[15]

Had it just been a matter of redeploying his armies to align with the Lancastrian approach, things may well have turned out differently. Warwick, however, had set elaborate defences that could not be repositioned easily or quickly. Long anti-boarding nets, more usually hung over the sides of ships, were spread out along the road, 'and every two knots there was a nail standing upright, that there could no man pass over it by likelihood but he should be hurt'.[16]

As well as this, Warwick's Burgundian handgunners had elaborate pavises, shields they could fold up and carry with them. There was a window through which they could shoot fearsome new guns 'that would shoot both pellets of lead and arrows of an ell of length with six feathers, three in the middle and three at the other end, with a great mighty head of iron on the other end, and wild fire withall'. These weapons were useless in wet weather however and, as often as not, 'the fire turned back upon them that would shoot these three things ... And when their shot was spent and done they cast the pavise before them, then there might no man come to them over the pavise for the nails that stood upright, but if he would mischief himself.'[17]

Warwick was thinking defensively, as perhaps had become habit during his time in Calais. Three days were spent deploying the nets, boards 'full of nails' and the many caltraps strewn along the road. Had the queen's army been forced to attack only from one direction, they might have worked. The Lancastrians seem to have had more reliable intelligence than the Yorkists, however, for they changed their line of march to avoid attacking Norfolk's troops, aiming to approach St Albans from a different, less vigorously defended direction.[18]

The Lancastrians made for Dunstable, where there was a small forward party of some 200 Yorkist soldiers under the command of a retainer of Norfolk's, a knight by the name of Poynings. This group was neutralised very quickly, all the men killed or captured. A report filtered through to Warwick but was lost in a sea of conflicting reports brought by panicked refugees pouring down from the north, and insufficient credence was given to it.[19]

Adding to the confusion, Somerset and Trollope led their men on a night march along Watling Street, arriving in St Albans far sooner than might have been expected. Trollope arrived first, leading a small group of men into the town in the early hours of the morning of 17 February. Despite Warwick's attention to defence, St Albans itself was not well defended. Barriers and gates were left open and unmanned, such was his confidence that Somerset would attack from the north. Though taken by surprise, Montagu's archers stationed near the marketplace organised themselves quickly and were able to push Trollope's forces from the town. Trollope immediately searched for a second way in.[20]

This he found in St Catherine's Lane, again unguarded and undefended. Now attacked from two directions, Montagu's archers put up a spirited resistance before being overcome, distressed survivors fleeing the town centre. The Lancastrians were now in control of St Albans. Trollope's men rested a short while, waiting for the bulk of their forces to catch up, before moving to Barnard's Heath around midday to face Montagu's men.[21]

In Warwick's battle plans, his brother Montagu commanded the rearguard. In the rapidly changing situation, he now found himself in the van. This was Montagu's first solo command of a sizeable force. Up until now, he had either fought alongside his brother Thomas or under the direction of his father. Now, with little warning, he had to deal with an enemy coming in force from the wrong direction. He had no time to reposition his guns and barely enough time to ready his men.[22]

Outnumbered, Montagu sent increasingly desperate messages to his brother Warwick for reinforcements and fought on. The battle on the heath raged for several hours with no help in sight. Just why it took so long for the message to reach Warwick is unclear but might be explained by the topography of the extended battleground. Warwick was not in his tent and proved difficult to find. When at last the message was delivered, Warwick responded immediately, gathering his men together and leading them across country to bolster his brother's exhausted army.[23]

It was at this point, according to Yorkist sources, that treachery once again played a role in the outcome of a battle.

> And at that last, through the withdrawing of the Kentishmen with their captain, called Lovelace, that was in the vanguard – the which Lovelace favoured the north party, forasmuch as he was taken by the northernmen at Wakefield when the duke of York was slain, and made to them an oath for to save his life, that he would never be against them – and also by indisposition of the people of the king's side, that would not be guided nor governed by their captains, king Harry's party lost the field.[24]

This Kentish Captain Lovelace is something of an enigma. He is mentioned in few sources and may either have never existed or died at Wakefield only to be resurrected as a convenient scapegoat for the Yorkist defeat. Several chroniclers writing close to the event do not mention him, nor is he mentioned in letters written by chancellor Nevill in the weeks after the battle. There may well have been a group desertion of Kentishmen, especially when it became clear that reinforcements, if they were on their way, would not arrive in time. This mutiny seems to have been exaggerated and the name of the dead (or non-existent) Lovelace attached some time after the fact.[25]

Warwick did not reach his brother in time. While he was still on his way, a stream of men fleeing the field gave him the news of the defeat of Montagu's army, and the arrest of both Montagu and lord Berners. There was nothing Warwick could do but get word to his captains, disband his armies and leave the field with around 4,000 of his men.[26]

The Yorkists lost around 4,000 at the second battle of St Albans and the Lancastrians around 2,000. One of these was Sir John Grey of Groby, a young husband and father of two small boys. Like many of the dead, his name might well have been forgotten over the years but for the glittering, and dangerous, future his widow Elizabeth Wydeville forged for herself some three years later.[27]

King Henry was left in his tent, guarded by lord Bonville, whose son and grandson had been killed at Wakefield, and Sir Thomas Kyriell. Found by one Thomas Hoo, according to the chronicler Whetehamstede, Henry was taken to where Queen Margaret and their son waited in Clifford's tent. Here there was an emotional reunion. Henry knighted his son, who, in turn, knighted some thirty men including Andrew Trollope. The young prince then sat in judgement of the prisoners, condemning them to death. Both Bonville and Kyriell were beheaded, despite the king's earlier reassurances their lives would be spared.[28]

Montagu and Berners were more fortunate. Some sources suggest that King Henry personally intervened to save Montagu, as he had been his chamberlain since the battle of Northampton, but it is more likely to have been prudence on Somerset's part than pity on the king's. Had Montagu been executed, Somerset could have expected swift retaliation from Warwick, and the death of his brother Edmund. Lord Berners's brother Henry, viscount Bourchier was married to York's sister Isobel. This connection to the earl of March may have prompted similar fears for Edmund Beaufort's life. Montagu and Berners were taken to York, where they were held for several weeks.[29]

The town of St Albans was violently sacked by Queen Margaret's victorious army, despite pleas from the abbot and a proclamation from the king. Warwick, Norfolk and Arundel escaped with their lives and liberty, though the field was lost. Expecting Queen Margaret to be given entry into London, Warwick turned west to meet up with the earl of March.[30]

On hearing of Warwick's defeat at St Albans and the queen's march on London, and fearful for the lives and safety of her youngest sons George and Richard, the duchess of York sent them into the care of the duke of Burgundy, 'the which were of the said duke notably received, cherished and honoured; and afterward sent home with many great gifts to London again'.[31]

London, however, was not ready to welcome Margaret's unruly northern forces. The mayor wanted the queen's assurances that there would be no trouble; the commons wanted them kept out. A deputation was sent.

> [T]he duchess of Bedford and the lady Scales, with divers clerks and curates of the city, went to St Albans to the king, queen and prince, for to entreat for grace for the city. And the king and his council granted that four knights with three hundred men should go to the city and see the disposition of it, and make an appointment with the mayor and aldermen.[32]

Hoping that a swift and favourable response to the queen's demand for money and supplies would be sufficient incentive for her to remove her army from the city's outskirts, 'certain carts were laden with victuals to have gone to St Albans' but 'the commons of the city would not suffer the carts to depart'. Instead, urged on by one John Bishop, sir John Wenlock's cook and a 'great doer in this matter', the commons seized the carts and divided the spoils among themselves.[33]

By then, news had arrived that Warwick had met with March in Oxfordshire and they were on their way back to the city. Rather than press the point with the mayor and citizens of London and risk another battle with a refreshed and reinforced Yorkist army, Margaret ordered her army to make the long trek back north. Just what was said when Warwick met up with March is a matter of much conjecture. Warwick had lost not only a battle but custody of the king. Now they could no longer claim to be acting in his name or interests, which rendered the Yorkist government illegitimate. They were rebels once again.[34]

London's refusal to give Queen Margaret either entry or aid gave Warwick and March confidence they could take things a step further. Since the Act of Accord, York and his sons had been heirs to the throne. If Margaret managed to get the king and his supporters back into the capital, it would be only a matter of time before the accord was overturned and Prince Edward was restored to the succession. The Yorkists would find themselves attainted once again. To circumvent this, perhaps Edward, earl of March's claim could be promoted, and Henry VI sidelined altogether. The plan to have March declared king must surely have been made before the two reached London.

This was yet another example of Warwick's remarkable ability to take disaster and turn it to his advantage. If he had lost physical custody of the king then there was another younger and more vigorous man, already heir apparent, who could take his place. The capture of Berners might even push the Bourchiers into more open support of the Yorkists; March might have more luck than his father convincing the Archbishop of Canterbury to agree to a coronation. It was well worth the attempt but had to be more carefully planned and executed than York's had been.

On 27 March, Warwick and March entered London to great rejoicing and acclaim. Almost immediately, the plan was put into motion. York's mistakes would not be repeated. For March it would not simply be a matter of demanding to be made king and expecting the unanimous acclamation of the lords. There was a lot to be done and not much time in which to do it. Robes and regalia had to be found and made ready; arguments had to be researched; sermons and speeches written. Chancellor Nevill was pivotal to the whole undertaking and it was his speech in St John's Field, in front of a carefully chosen audience of staunch Yorkist supporters, that set the whole thing in motion.[35]

March's claim rested on the principle of inheritance, the same argument that underpinned the Act of Accord. Since his father's death, he was king by right. The anomaly of the Lancastrian kings could now be corrected and the crown of England returned to its rightful owner. Forgotten was the part Ralph Nevill played in the accession of the first of those kings, Henry IV. Forgotten also were the oaths Warwick and March had sworn on the Cross of Canterbury to uphold the rights and life of Henry VI and the heirs of his body.[36]

On 1 March in St John's Field in front of a crowd that could reliably be expected to agree with him, George Nevill read 'certain articles and points that king Henry had offended in'. 'And then it was demanded of the people whether the said Harry were worthy to reign still and the people cried nay; and then was asked if they would have the earl of March to their king and they cried yea.'[37]

Public acclamation was not quite enough, however, and representatives of this carefully chosen crowd next took themselves to Baynard's Castle to inform March 'that the people had chosen him for king and he thanked them and by the advice of the bishop of Canterbury, the bishop of Exeter and the earl of Warwick with other grant it to take it upon him'.[38]

On 3 March, great council met and formally elected Edward, earl of March king. With the lords temporal and spiritual divided, this council was a small group of those already committed to the Yorkist cause, the same lords York had been counting on the previous year. In the circumstances, this hardly mattered: the opinions, advice and approval of those lords who stood with Henry VI and Queen Margaret were far from required. Indeed, these lords would have to be neutralised before Edward could truly consider himself king. The only way either he or Henry could be secure in their king-ship was through the defeat, capture or death of the other. That each had the support of the lords in their party was sufficient for current purposes.[39]

The following day, Edward went in procession 'with all the lords in goodly array' to Paul's Cross, where George Nevill preached a sermon, the content of which is sadly lost.

> [A]t the end of the sermon he declared the earl of March's right and title to the crown and demanded the people if they would have him to their king as his right asked and they cried yea; then all the people were prayed to go with him to Westminster to see him take his possession and so the people did.[40]

Edward took two oaths that day, one in the privacy of the chancery before the lords of his council and the other more publicly in Westminster. The first was in line with ancient practice, according to which the lords of England exercised their right to gather in the hours before a coronation to consult on certain matters, including 'the establishing of laws and customs'. This oath may have bound Edward to more than that of his later public coronation. Perhaps he was required to swear he would not seek to end the life of Henry VI. If this was the case, it was a bond he was able to keep throughout the first half of his reign.[41]

Now, dressed in the robes and cap of estate, St Edward's sceptre in his hand, Edward took the king's seat in Westminster, again to great acclaim. In the abbey, he made offerings at the high altar and St Edward's shrine. Edward, earl of March was now Edward IV.[42]

> And upon the morrow following were proclamations made in accustomed places of the city, in the name of Edward IV then king of England. Upon which day the king came to the palace at Paul's and there dined, and there rested him a season, in making provision to go northward for to subdue his enemies.[43]

It was surely not modesty that prompted chancellor Nevill to underplay his role in the events recounted in his letter of 7 April.

> Meanwhile Prince Edward, then commonly called earl of March, was lead-ing an army of 30,000 men towards London, where he made his entry with my brother the earl of Warwick (who had escaped to him from the former battle) on the 3rd kalends of March [27 February]. He was received joyfully by the entire population, and at Westminster on the fourth of the nones of the month [4 March], at the demand, nay, by compulsion of well nigh all present, both lords and commons, he was appointed King; the ceremony of his coronation, for important reasons, being alone deferred.[44]

On 6 March, Edward IV issued a proclamation offering 'pardon of his life and goods' to any who would leave the king's party within ten days. There was a long list of exceptions, however, including Andrew Trollope, Gervase Clifton, Dr Morton and 'both bastards of Exeter'. A reward of £200 was offered to 'whatever persons shall effectually destroy and bring out of life Andrew Trollope, the bastards of Exeter' and five others named. There was to be no mercy for the man who betrayed the Yorkists at Ludford or those responsible for the death of Warwick's father. Just over a week after the Yorkist coup, their combined armies left the city.[45]

Norfolk was the first to leave, travelling to East Anglia to raise troops on 5 March. Two days later, Warwick travelled to his estates in the Midlands for the same purpose. In Coventry, he found Exeter's illegitimate brothers and oversaw their summary execution. Fauconberg left on the 11th and Edward IV two days later, with his brother-in-law the duke of Suffolk.[46]

The movement of a large army was no simple matter, but supervised by men who knew what they were doing it could at least be achieved relatively swiftly and in good order. Discipline was key, for which morale must be high. And for good morale, the soldiers needed to feel secure – of food and other supplies, of rest and good leadership. Though some disturbance of the country they passed through was inevitable, none of the Yorkist leaders wanted their armies to behave as Queen Margaret's had done, even if the claims were exaggerated. The armies must travel with their own supplies, though some foraging would still be necessary, especially out of season. Many of the towns, villages, farms and settlements had already suffered – twice – the passing of the ill-disciplined Lancastrians. If anything, the new King Edward had to be more careful still. Alienating his new subjects just days after he was proclaimed king was not a good idea.

Warwick and Fauconberg, their armies swollen with fresh recruits, caught up with Edward as he crossed the Trent. Norfolk, who was suffering from an unspecified illness, was delayed but sent word he was on his way. They marched north to Pontefract Castle, Warwick and the vanguard arriving on the evening of 27 March.[47]

This was the place Warwick's father had been murdered just months earlier. Warwick had already had the satisfaction of dispatching two of the men responsible. Now, perhaps, he could take a moment to pray for Salisbury's soul. There was time for little else, with Somerset's army encamped some 16 miles away, roughly halfway between Pontefract and York. The men needed to eat and rest while their commanders discussed what must be done the following day.[48]

The first priority was to find a way to cross the River Aire. There were two crossing points near Pontefract, one at Ferrybridge and the other just a few miles away at Castleford. Somerset had ordered the bridges destroyed behind his army as he headed north. The following day, lord Fitzwalter was sent with a party of men to repair and occupy the crossing at Ferrybridge.[49]

Repairs were successfully made and the crossing held. If Somerset had left men behind to guard it, they were soon seen off. Fitzwalter's men settled down for the night and either no guard was posted, which seems unlikely, or they were asleep at their posts for, just before dawn on 29 March, Clifford launched a surprise attack with 500 men behind him.[50]

The lord Fitzwalter hearing the noise suddenly rose out of his bed and unarmed, with a pollaxe in his hands, thinking that it had been a fray amongst his men, came down to appease the same but before he either began his tale or knew what the matter mean, he was slain and with him the Bastard of Salisbury brother to the earl of Warwick, a valiant young gentleman and of great audacity.[51]

News of this attack soon reached Pontefract, brought by panicked survivors. Edmund Hall, writing some seventy years later, puts a stirring speech into the mouth of Warwick, and attributes to him an extraordinary gesture.

> When the earl of Warwick was informed of this feat, he like a man desperate mounted on his hackney and came blowing to king Edward saying: Sir, I pray God have mercy of their souls, which in the beginning of your enterprise, as lost their lives, and because I see no succours of the world I remit the vengeance and punishment to God our creator and redeemer, and with that lighted down and slew his horse with his sword, saying: Let him flee that will, for I surely will tarry with him that will tarry with me, and kissed the cross of his sword.[52]

Warwick was certainly a man of great wealth with an enviable stable of warhorses, but he knew their value and was unlikely to have wasted the life of one simply to make a dramatic gesture. As both he and Edward IV fought on foot at Towton, it seems far more probable that if he made a declaration to that effect, he did so in order to stiffen the resolve of his men. He would take the same risks they must take with no easy means of escape. Reassured that their commander would not fly the field as he had done at St Albans, a stout force followed Warwick back to Ferrybridge to wrest it from Clifford's hands. Archbishop Nevill gave a detailed and stirring account of this battle. 'The enemy had broken the ferry-bridge, and, occupying the narrow raft which our people had made after its destruction by handicraft, they stoutly disputed its passage, but we carried it sword in hand.'[53]

In the meantime, Edward ordered Fauconberg to the alternative crossing at Castleford in an effort to outflank Clifford. The fight at the bridge was no trivial skirmish and Warwick sustained an arrow wound in his leg. With Fauconberg's approach threatening to catch him in a trap, Clifford chose to withdraw and retreated back towards the main Lancastrian camp with Fauconberg in close pursuit.[54]

A forward party caught up with Clifford and his men almost within reach of the main Lancastrian force, where

> they met with some that they looked not for and were entrapped before they were aware. For the lord Clifford, either for heat or pain, putting off his gorget, suddenly with an arrow (as some say) without an head, was stricken into the throat and incontinent rendered his spirit, and the earl of Westmorland's brother and all his company almost were there slain, at a place called Dintingdale not far from Towton.[55]

The deaths of Clifford, reportedly responsible for killing Edward IV's brother at Wakefield, and lord Nevill, whose treachery had won the battle for Somerset, affected the morale of both armies. So close was Dintingdale to the Lancastrian camp that the men there may have witnessed the fight, and even Clifford's death.[56]

All this happened within a few short hours and, at around nine in the morning, the bulk of the Yorkist army had reached Towton; Norfolk was still on his way. Though outnumbered, and boasting far fewer noble commanders, the morale of Edward IV's men was high. They were led by a young and energetic king, an experienced soldier who had fought with honour in France and the man who had brought the Yorkist cause back from the brink and held England together for the past year. They faced an army steeped in treachery and brutality that had marched its way to London, looting and destroying all in its path, led by a king who no longer had the confidence of a sizeable percentage of the population and a queen whose popularity, never particularly high, had plummeted in recent years. Whether these perceptions were entirely justified or not, they were upheld by the leaders of the Yorkist faction, already proven masters of propaganda and spin. There were no signs from God at Towton but there was no need of them. They had Edward IV, Warwick and Fauconberg to lead them, and they had right on their side. God had surely forsaken the Lancastrian cause.

The Lancastrian army would not, of course, have conceded this point. They considered Henry VI the rightful king. Edward and his followers were rebels and usurpers. He was an untried general, Fauconberg was old and weary, and Warwick was marked by his recent failure. Apart from Suffolk and Norfolk – one as young and inexperienced as the man who called himself 'king' and the other in the grips of illness and still on the road – most of England's lords had chosen Henry's cause over Edward's. Somerset, Exeter, Northumberland, Devon, Wiltshire, Shrewsbury, lords Dacre, Rivers and Scales, all of them as sure as their opponents that their cause was the just one and that God would uphold their right.[57]

With the executions of the bastards of Exeter and the deaths of Clifford and lord John Nevill, Warwick, not unknown for his ruthlessness and his affinity with vengeance, had achieved a certain retribution for those killed at Wakefield. In among the vast horde that faced him was another who needed to be dealt with. This day must see an end to the life of Andrew Trollope, once Warwick's trusted master porter of Calais. His long military experience was an incomparable asset to the Lancastrian army and Somerset would have relied on Trollope's counsel in much the way Edward IV relied on that of Fauconberg and Warwick. His death would deliver a body blow to Lancastrian hopes. For Warwick, though, it was more than that, it was deeply personal. His order to his men was simple: find Trollope, kill Trollope. Perhaps similar orders worked their way through the Lancastrian ranks, to hunt down and kill the traitor of Northampton, lord Grey of Ruthyn.

Neither Fitzhugh nor Greystoke took the field at Towton. Both may have been reluctant, making excuses and holding back. Both may have been so mistrusted, despite the renewal of their oaths of allegiance, that they were held back for fear they might turn traitor and change sides. They were close by, perhaps left behind in York, but not close enough to come to anyone's rescue.

At Towton, there were no pre-battle negotiations, no heralds trudged between the two armies, carrying messages of conciliation or defiance. With 40,000 on one side and 36,000 on the other, this was to be a battle to the bitter end. Whoever left the field in victory must leave no hope behind for the defeated. After Wakefield and, more particularly, after St Albans, all knew the fate that awaited any who were captured. It was die on the field or hope to flee. Edward and Warwick, in what was far more than a mere gesture, left their horses behind and joined their men-at-arms on foot. The message to their men was clear: they would win this fight or they would die. Fauconberg commanded the van, Warwick the centre and Edward the rear and reserve. Opposite them, Northumberland and Trollope commanded the van, lord Dacre the centre and Exeter and Somerset the rear.[58]

The weather, already cold, gloomy and overcast, steadily worsened as the day wore on. By the time the Lancastrian army made its opening moves, snow was falling, the wind driving into the faces of Northumberland's archers:

> The lord Fauconberg, which led the forward of king Edward's battle … being a man of great policy, and of much experience in martial feats, caused every archer under his standard to shoot one flight … and then made them to stand still. The northern army, feeling the shot but by reason of the snow not well viewing the distance between them and their enemies, like hardy men shot their sheaf arrows as fast as they might but all their shot was lost and their labour vain for they came not near the southern by 15 tailor's yards. When their shot was almost spent, the lord Fauconberg marched forward with his archers, which not only shot their own whole sheaves but also gathered the arrows of their enemies, and let a great part of them fly against their own master, and another part they let stand on the ground which sore annoyed the legs of the owners when the battle joined.[59]

His archers rendered useless either by the wind and heavy casualties, Northumberland gave the order for the infantry to move forward. It was at this point, according to Waurin, having receiving the unanimous support of his men, Edward IV 'told them, sword in hand, that on this day he would live or die with them in order to give them courage'. The Yorkist archers were almost out of ammunition by this time but continued to shoot what they had into the advancing Lancastrian army until they were ordered to retire. Then the two forward divisions met, the Yorkists running to meet the charging Lancastrians.[60]

For hours the battle raged. As men fell, others stumbled over their corpses. From time to time, those who could retired to rest before rejoining the fight with renewed vigour. First the centres joined the fray, then the rearguard, until the entire battlefield was a seething mass of men fighting for their lives. Though they had vowed to fight afoot and not fly the field, both Edward and Warwick must have kept horses close by so they could mount from time to time to bring orders and messages behind the lines. Warwick must have been in some difficulty, having sustained an arrow wound earlier in the day. Not serious enough to keep him from the fight, it is likely the pain and weakness would have tired him more quickly than he was used to. Still, there was no question of watching and commanding from the sidelines. Fight with his men he had vowed to do and fight he did.[61]

Slowly, the Yorkist line gave ground, pushed back by the sheer weight of numbers, exposing ground littered with the dead and dying. Just why the Yorkists were pushed back is a matter for conjecture, including the possibility of a carefully set ambush of spearsmen concealed in a densely wooded area. Edward's men were tiring, and the Lancastrians' steady advance would have buoyed up their spirits and energy. Edward and Warwick worked hard to bolster morale and shore up their troops. Chancellor Nevill gives us a glimpse of this in a letter written after the battle. 'Of the behaviour of the king, the valiant duke of Norfolk, my brother and my uncle in this battle in fighting manfully, in guiding, encouraging and re-forming their forces, I would rather your lordship heard it from others than me.'[62]

Edward committed the reserve. He and Warwick worked hard behind the lines as they fought alongside their men, urging their soldiers on, plugging gaps here and shoring faltering lines there. The exhausted men were close to breaking point when two events in quick succession proved too much for the almost jubilant Lancastrians. With the end almost in sight, the Yorkists rallied, fresh troops slamming into the Lancastrian flank, and lord Dacre, who was resting a while, his helmet off, was felled by an arrow. Then, around midday, Norfolk arrived at last. Too sick himself to take the field, he commanded as he could from his tent, leaving the more practical decisions to his lieutenants and captains.[63]

It was not long before cracks appeared in the Lancastrian line as more and more men turned tail and fled, disheartened by the thought of hours more fighting, bitter that the victory they could almost taste was snatched away and fearing the death they had avoided so far was soon to catch up with them. It took time for the Lancastrian army to collapse but, at last, there was nothing but a stream of running men, fleeing for their lives. The Yorkist horsemen found their mounts and gave chase. Exhausted foot soldiers took a moment to rest before turning their attention to the dead, looting arms and armour, the small items they carried and the rings on their fingers.[64]

Many men lost their lives in the rout, drowning as they attempted to cross streams and rivers, hunted down and hacked to pieces. Chancellor Nevill paints a grim and brutal picture of the closing stages of the battle.

> Of the enemy who fled, great numbers were drowned in the river near the town of Tadcaster, eight miles from York, because they themselves had broken the bridge to cut our passage that way, so that none could pass, and a great part of the rest who got away who gathered in the said town and city, were slain and so many dead bodies were seen as to cover an area six miles long by three broad and about four furlongs.[65]

The chancellor numbered the dead at 28,000 ('Alas! we are a race deserving of pity even from the French …'). These numbers, and the names of the dead, were collected and collated in the hours after the battle. This was the time for mass burials, tending to the wounded, offering up prayers of thanks and for the souls of the fallen.[66]

Lords Clifford, Dacre and Nevill were among the dead but most of the Lancastrian command had got away with their lives. If Edward IV wanted to avoid another battle on a similar, or perhaps greater, scale, these men had to be found and dealt with. Both Clifford and Northumberland's sons were found alive after the battle and taken into custody, their lives spared. Northumberland himself had died in the field, as had Andrew Trollope. Others who got away, Somerset, Exeter, Shrewsbury and Wiltshire among them, were not caught in the rout so must have made their escape before the irrevocable collapse of their armies. The earl of Devon was found alive but in a bad state. He was taken to York soon after the battle and executed. At some point, either that night or in the following days, both Fitzhugh and Greystoke submitted to the new king, pleading their allegiance and shaking off old and uncertain loyalties.

Rivers and Scales also submitted to Edward IV. Their decision to do so cannot have been made lightly. Rivers's wife, the duchess of Bedford, had a long and close relationship with Queen Margaret. The memory of their torch-lit humiliation in Calais, where this new young king had berated them soundly for their low birth and presumption, may have been fresh in their minds but pragmatism overwhelmed their inclination to hold a grudge. The Wydevilles were a large and far from wealthy family. Perhaps they thought it better to take their chances with the new regime, offering their services and securing an income. Rivers had lost his post in Calais when Warwick took over as Captain and he had a far better chance of winning that back, or perhaps being offered something better, from King Edward than from the defeated and retreating King Henry.[67]

In York the following day, the heads of the duke of York, the earl of Salisbury, the earl of Rutland and Sir Thomas Nevill were removed from display and carried to Pontefract to be buried with their bodies. Warwick and chancellor Nevill were reunited with their brother Montagu. Still there was no time to pause, to mourn the dead and celebrate their achievements. Henry VI, the queen, the Prince of Wales, Exeter, Somerset, Shrewsbury and Wiltshire were all still at large. Immediately after the battle, Henry and his party had quit York and headed north. There was nothing to be done but follow them. Edward and Warwick might have fought the greatest battle of their lives, the largest battle, it is often said, on English soil, but they had by no means cemented Edward's hold on the throne.

# 26

# RESISTANCE AND CONSPIRACY

n 5 January 1463, the Scots army, led by Piers de Breze and the earl of Angus, arrived at Alnwick Castle. Warwick had known they were on their way for days. Those who held out inside the castle were on the edge of surrender, unaware relief was almost in sight. Had they known de Breze and Angus were on their way, it would have given them heart and hope. The morale of their armies dangerously low, the Yorkist defenders must press home the advantage.[1]

Warily watching the approach of the Scots alongside Warwick were his brother Montagu and the duke of Somerset. Warwick pulled his exhausted men back, fearing a trap. The Scots army halted, not ready to trust they were not walking into danger. Had Warwick given the signal to attack, he might have destroyed the Scots but his men were weak from cold and fatigue; he might have lost more than he could afford.[2]

While both armies remained motionless, the gates of the castle opened and the garrison came out, led by lord Hungerford. They were exhausted, filthy and on the edge of starvation. Under the watchful gaze of the Yorkist army, they joined the Scots, who then turned and began the march back north.[3]

Alnwick was the last of the castles to fall. Just days before, Warwick and Montagu had accepted the surrender of Bamburgh and Dunstanburgh to the north. It had a been a long winter siege and had de Breze and Angus come to fight, 'they might have taken and distressed all the lords and commoners, for they had lain there so long in the field and were grieved with cold and rain that they had no courage to fight'. Bamburgh capitulated first on 26 December 1463 and Somerset's men were allowed to walk away with their lives, their weapons left behind. Dunstanburgh, garrisoned by Sir Ralph Percy, fell two days later. Both Somerset and Percy were taken to Durham to face Edward IV. Both swore allegiance to the new king and were soon put into positions of trust. When Warwick returned to Alnwick to witness the final act, Somerset went with him.[4]

Somerset's change of heart was probably genuine at the time, though fuelled by exhaustion and despair. For years, he had been the core of the Lancastrian cause. Since his father's death at the first battle of St Albans in 1455, he had been an implacable enemy of the Nevills and the house of York. Though ultimately unsuccessful, his attempts to dislodge Warwick from Calais in 1460 had won him respect both in England and on the continent. After coming to terms with Warwick, Somerset had found shelter and support in France, Charles VII giving him both a place to stay and financial aid. He also developed a strong friendship with the son and heir of the duke of Burgundy, Charles of Charolais. Charles VII backed Somerset's return to England in October 1460 and he was able to reach Corfe Castle, where he had set plans in motion, with the earl of Devon, to raise the West Country in support of Queen Margaret. When the duke of York marched north, these plans changed and Somerset followed him, engaging with York's forces at Wakefield, where the duke lost his life.[5]

Somerset developed a strong partnership with Andrew Trollope and together they achieved stunning victories at Wakefield and St Albans. Trollope's death at Towton was a savage blow and Somerset never quite recovered from it. After the battle, he fled to Scotland with Henry VI and Queen Margaret. From there, he was sent on an embassy to France but Charles VII had died and the new king, Louis XI, was not quite as ready as his predecessor to support the Lancastrian cause. Somerset was imprisoned for two months and it was only the intercession of Charles of Charolais that freed him. He then lived for some six months in Bruges before returning to Scotland in March 1462. His first tentative steps towards reconciliation with the Yorkist government may have been taken that same year. '[I]t is said that my lord Warwick had sent to the king and informed his highness that the lord Somerset had written to him to come to grace.'[6]

Though the decision did not rest with him, one man who likely viewed Somerset's change of sides with deep suspicion was Montagu. He and Somerset had come close to open war on several occasions in and around London in the late 1450s. Both were soldiers rather than politicians and neither could forget the harm wrought by the other at the first battle of St Albans and at Wakefield.

Montagu had been in the north almost continuously since his release from captivity in York in March 1461. At some point in the early 1460s, he purchased Seaton Delaval Hall, some 32 miles south of Alnwick Castle. Here he settled his wife Isobel and his growing family. He purchased other properties in Northumberland and Yorkshire, building up a sizeable estate in the north of England, where he saw his future. Montagu was always more comfortable in the north, though he was no unsophisticated provincial.

His marriage to Isobel had brought him a reliable though by no means large income. His elevation to the barony brought him status, a summons to Parliament and, from at least March 1463, a seat on Edward IV's council.[7]

On 22 April 1461, Edward IV and his party arrived in Durham, where Edward hoped to gain the support of Bishop Lawrence Bothe. As Bothe was closely connected to Margaret of Anjou, this was no easy task. From there, they travelled to Newcastle, where they oversaw the execution of the captured earl of Wiltshire and other prisoners. After two days at Middleham Castle, the king then returned to London to make ready for his coronation in June, making a royal progress through Lancashire, Cheshire and the Midlands. He left the problem of Lancastrian resistance in the north, particularly in Northumberland, in the hands of the Nevills. Warwick was appointed warden of both the east and west march, with Fauconberg and Montagu as his lieutenants. The Nevills had been instrumental in Edward winning the crown and they were determined he would keep it.[8]

Sir Ralph Percy, brother of the late earl of Northumberland and veteran of the Nevill–Percy feud, had quickly organised the family retainers to occupy four important castles on the coast between Newcastle and Berwick. With these in Lancastrian hands, supplied from Scotland by land and sea, the resistance could hold out for some considerable time. With a secure base of operations, supplies and men could be gathered and a full-scale assault launched. Taking these castles was an immediate priority.[9]

More immediate still was the Scots siege of Carlisle and a simultaneous attempt by the new lord Dacre, with lord Roos, to seize Brancepeth Castle in Durham. While Warwick saw off Dacre and Roos, he sent Montagu to Carlisle.[10]

Margaret of Anjou had negotiated the support of the Regent of Scotland, queen mother Mary of Guelders. The sudden death of her husband James II in 1460 propelled Mary into the spotlight. Seizing the initiative, she had her 8-year-old son crowned within a week of his father's death and took control of several important castles. The aid she gave the deposed King of England and his queen was not motivated by ideology or pity but by material gain. Margaret of Anjou ceded Berwick to the Scots and offered up Carlisle, if it could only be taken.[11]

The citizens of Carlisle were not happy with the idea of their town being handed over to a foreign power and resisted vigorously. Learning that Montagu and his army were coming to the citizens' aid, the Scots army sent to take the town broke off the siege after six weeks and returned across the border. In London, Edward IV prepared to bring forward the date of his coronation and travel back to the north, 'howbeit, blessed be God, that he has now good tidings, that lord Montagu has broken the siege and slain of Scots 6,000 and two knights, whereof lord Clifford's brother is one'.[12]

The coronation went ahead as planned on 28 June. Edward then turned his attention to quelling the pockets of resistance in Wales led by Jasper Tudor and the duke of Exeter. Edward's Welsh allies William Herbert and Sir Walter Devereux were in charge of military operations in Wales and, in August, Edward left London on a progress through several towns on the south coast. It may have been his intention to travel as far as Hereford but he halted his journey in Bristol. After pronouncing sentence over the captured Sir Baldwin Fulford and witnessing his execution, he turned back towards London. With the opening of Parliament just a few months away, the Lancastrian rebels in the field would have to be left to his trusted military commanders.[13]

Now the attention of the Nevills could be turned to the northern castles of Warkworth, Alnwick, Bamburgh and Dunstanburgh. By late September, Alnwick had fallen to Warwick and early the following month Ralph Percy surrendered Dunstanburgh. When Percy proved willing to swear an oath of allegiance to the new king, Warwick was instructed to retain him as captain of the castle and return him to his post.[14]

Edward IV's first Parliament was to sit in November and Warwick, Montagu and Fauconberg were all required in London. There was also another event to attend. Some time before February the following year, Katherine Nevill married William, the newly created lord Hastings. Though he was now head of the family, as a widow, Katherine did not need to seek Warwick's approval to remarry, though it is likely he had a hand in bringing the marriage about. Hastings had been appointed chamberlain of the royal household early in Edward's reign and accompanied him north after Towton. Perhaps the king himself came to Warwick with the proposal of a marriage between Hastings and Katherine. Though Hastings was of lowly stock and only recently elevated to the peerage, the benefits to Katherine and her baby daughter were considerable. Cecily Bonville was barely eighteen months old and would find in her stepfather, a man already high in the king's confidence and trust, a competent and capable protector of her considerable inheritance. For Hastings, the marriage was a stamp of approval, cementing his place in the close circle about the king. Of course, the marriage may have been Katherine and Hastings's idea in the first place, though there is no evidence of this. The couple were granted lands in Leicestershire forfeited by the late earl of Wiltshire, including Ashby-de-la-Zouche, which was to be the family's principle home for the next twenty years. Whenever the wedding took place, there was little time for a honeymoon. Parliament opened on 4 November and there was a good deal of business to get through.[15]

Sir James Strangeways, a retainer of Warwick, was elected speaker of the commons and gave a stirring speech of thanks to the new king.

Most Christian king, right high and mighty prince, and our most dread sovereign and natural liege lord; we your humble and true subjects, the commons of this your noble realm, come to this your high court of parliament by your high commandment, have as great cause to call, and call to the tenderness of our mind, as ever had people living under any Christian prince, the honourable and noble endeavour that it has pleased your highness to put the same in, of princely and knightly prowess and courage, for the redemption of your said realm and subjects from the persecution and tyranny of your, and their, great and insatiable enemies.[16]

Strangeways enumerated three things in particular for which the nation had cause to thank Edward. The first was the defeat of the Tudors, and 'their malicious intent and purposes', at Mortimer's Cross. The second was his return to London when the city was threatened by Queen Margaret's army. The third was the victory at Towton and the flight of Henry VI and his supporters.[17]

After a restatement of Edward's claim to the throne, Strangeways declared the commons would 'take, accept and repute, and will ever take, accept and repute, the said Edward IV their sovereign and liege lord, and him and his heirs to be kings of England, and none other, according to his said right and title'.[18]

The commons then introduced a bill of resumption which was passed, after the usual rounds of exemptions for colleges, religious houses, institutions and foundations. There were also exemptions for Alice Chaucer, dowager duchess of Suffolk, the duchesses of Bedford, Somerset and Buckingham, and the countesses of Richmond and Shrewsbury. Some of these women had lost husbands and sons at Northampton or Towton. Others were married to active rebels still at large in Wales and Scotland. An annuity of £400 was also confirmed for the king's mother Cecily, duchess of York. There was a raft of exemptions for various knights, clerks, chaplains and merchants. Sir Geoffrey Gate, who had captured Somerset's brother the previous year, was confirmed in his post as Lieutenant of the Isle of Wight. Ralph Hastings, William's brother and esquire of the body to the king, was to retain his post 'of the office of keeping lions, lionesses and leopards within our Tower of London'.[19]

The attainder of Edward's paternal grandfather Richard, earl of Cambridge was overturned, his plotting against Henry V recast as loyalty to the deposed Richard II rather than a desperate, and doomed, attempt to murder and replace the king from what were essentially self-serving motives. With this, Edward was not only honouring his disgraced grandfather but also his father. The house of York must not only be restored to its rightful place as the ruling dynasty of England, the dark blots on its copybook must be erased.[20]

Also overturned were the attainders of both the earl and countess of Warwick's maternal grandfathers, John Montagu, earl of Salisbury and Thomas Despenser, earl of Gloucester. Their adherence to the cause of Richard II and his heirs was lauded, as was their resistance to the usurpation by Henry IV. Montagu and Despenser had been 'murdered with great cruelty and horrible violence' by 'persons of evil, riotous and seditious dispositions'. All property then forfeited, and not already restored during the subsequent three reigns, was to be returned to Warwick and his countess. No mention was made of the long years of service rendered to the Lancastrian kings by the countess of Warwick's father, let alone his close friendship with Henry V. Nor was there mention of the support given to Henry of Bolingbroke, later Henry IV, by his brother-in-law, Ralph Nevill, grandfather to both Edward and Warwick. The reversal of these two attainders might reasonably be interpreted as an attempt on Edward's part to reward Warwick for his invaluable support rather than the rehabilitation of two men who had died for their 'continued … faith and allegiance' to the cause of Richard II and his heirs.[21]

Though the reigns of Henrys IV, V and VI were to be considered unlawful and 'pretenced', the acts, grants, appointments and payments made by them were, by and large, confirmed. Quite apart from the nightmare of unpicking and unravelling the last sixty years, there was no need to do so.

Next came the grimmer business of attainder. It was a long bill, with lists of over 100 knights, squires and gentlemen, among them Sir Andrew Trollope and Baldwin Fulford, both deceased. Henry VI was attainted for breaking the Act of Accord and stirring his followers to murder the duke of York, the earl of Salisbury and the earl of Rutland at Wakefield. Queen Margaret was attainted for 'intending to the extreme destruction of the … realm', and allowing her men to rob churches and rape 'religious women, widows and maidens'. There was one oddly specific charge of 'unmanly, unnatural and beastly cruelty to draw women being in childbed from their beds naked and to spoil them of all their goods, a piteous desolation'.[22]

Also attainted were the late Viscount Beaumont and the earls of Northumberland and Devon. Somerset and Exeter were attainted, as were various lords, living and dead. Clifford, who was said to have killed Rutland with his own hands, and lord John Nevill, who betrayed his Nevill kin and York at Wakefield, were posthumously attainted, along with Robert and William Holland, the Bastards of Exeter.[23]

Missing from the list was Sir Gervase Clifton. The previous March he had been named in a proclamation as one of several men who were never to be offered pardon. In July, he nevertheless managed to secure a pardon for 'all offences committed by him before 20 July'. On 12 March 1461, Warwick had been commissioned to 'receive deserters from the party of

Henry VI'. It was presumably to Warwick that Clifton made initial overtures that led to the offer of pardon. Before deserting the Yorkist cause at Ludford, Clifton had been treasurer of Calais under succeeding Captains, including Warwick. There was another reason Warwick may have been prepared to champion Clifton's cause, which will be explored in a following chapter.[24]

With Christmas fast approaching and much business still to be done, Parliament was prorogued on 21 December until 6 May the following year. Before the lords and commons were dismissed, Edward IV wrapped up current business with several acts mainly to do with matters of law and order. This included a prohibition on 'dicing or playing at the cards ... out of the 12 days of Christmas'. Edward's closing words were an ominous reminder, if one was needed, that he would brook no backsliding. Anyone who had obtained pardon 'for being against his royal person in any field or fields', and subsequently abjured their oaths of loyalty, 'shall never hereafter be accepted to his said grace, nor be pardoned, but utterly punished according to their demerits, without remission or favour'.[25]

In February 1462, while Edward IV and Warwick were preparing to return to the north, a conspiracy was uncovered that, had it succeeded, would have brought down the fledgling Yorkist dynasty. The earl of Oxford, who had until then remained apolitical and uninvolved, sent one of his servants with letters to King Henry in Scotland. The servant got as far as York before turning to London and handing the letters over to King Edward. The letters were copied and resealed, the servant sent off to deliver them and wait for a reply. When Henry VI's response was shown to the earl of Worcester, now Constable of England, Oxford, his son Henry, lord Aubrey and other conspirators were arrested.[26]

> Their plan was to follow the king as his servants towards the north, as his majesty was not going to take more than a thousand horse and their two thousand and more, and once among the enemy they were to attack the king and murder him and all his followers.[27]

At the same time, Somerset, then in Bruges, was to 'descend upon England, and King Henry was also to come with the Scots and the earl of Pembroke from Brittany'.[28]

A letter to John Paston in early February would seem to confirm that some kind of conspiracy was in the wind.

> [P]lease your mastership it has been let me know in right secret wise that a puissance is ready to arrive in three parts of this land, by the means of king Henry and the queen that was, and by the duke of Somerset and others, of 120,000 men; and here they, if wind and weather had served them, should

have been here soon upon Candlemass or soon after, one part of them, and another part coming from Wales, and the third from Jersey and Guernsey. Wherefor it is well done you inform my lord Warwick, that he may speak to the king that good provision be had for withstanding their malicious purpose and evil will, which God grant we may overcome; and so we should, I doubt not, if we were all one.[29]

It may have been this threat of invasion, though the conspiracy was well blown by then, that had Warwick in Sandwich in late February, arming the fleet and sending it out into the Channel.[30]

Though one source has Aubrey betraying his father, this seems unlikely, especially as Aubrey received neither pardon nor reward but shared his father's fate. Given his recent marriage to the late duke of Buckingham's oldest daughter, Anne, and a report that 'he is great with the queen', it may well have been Aubrey who was at the centre of the conspiracy. Whatever the circumstances, both were tried by the Constable and found guilty. Oxford was executed in the Tower on 26 February and Aubrey on 5 March.[31]

Oxford's second son, John de Vere, was not implicated in the plot. His marriage to Warwick's youngest sister Margaret later that year or early in the next helped to confirm his rehabilitation. Soon after his twenty-first birthday in 1464, John succeeded to the earldom of Oxford and was not considered a threat to Edward's reign.[32]

Before Warwick, Montagu and Fauconberg returned to the north, accompanied by Hastings, they had word that the northern castles had changed hands. William Tailboys, one of those attainted by Parliament, had seized Alnwick. Having second thoughts about his change of allegiance, Ralph Percy had opened the gates of Dunstanburgh to Tailboys and his followers. At around the same time, Dacre occupied Naworth Castle in Cumbria.[33]

It was becoming increasingly clear that as long as the Lancastrians had a safe haven in Scotland, and military and monetary support from the queen mother, resistance to Edward's rule would continue. It was now imperative to break the ties between Margaret of Anjou and Mary of Guelders. In April 1462, while Queen Margaret was in France in talks with Louis XI, Warwick travelled to Dumfries for peace talks with the Scots. Nothing came of them and Warwick returned to Middleham, from where he orchestrated raids deep into the Scottish Lowlands. Along with an escalation of internal strife in Scotland and Edward IV's attempts to persuade the duke of Burgundy to help shift Mary of Guelders' pro-Lancastrian stance, talks were soon reopened. The result was a short truce to run from June 1461 to August the following year.[34]

In mid-July, lord Dacre surrendered Naworth Castle to Montagu. After a siege led by Hastings and Sir Ralph Grey, Tailboys surrendered Alnwick soon after.

> This second year of king Edward, sir Piers de Breze ... came out of Scotland in the favour of king Harry, and stole by treason the castle of Alnwick, whither were sent against him sir William Hastings and with him were sir John Howard and divers lords and gentlemen, and with a strong power besieged the castle; in the which time the said sir Piers had many injurious words against these lords, the which, notwithstanding, he was fain to fall to agreement. Whereupon such appointment made, he and his Frenchmen and Scots departed the 30th day of July.[35]

When Bamburgh was captured and occupied, all three of the castles were once again under Yorkist control.[36]

When Parliament regathered on 6 May, it was immediately dissolved by the Archbishop of Canterbury on the king's behalf. Edward was not present, citing 'certain reasons personally concerning us' for both his absence and the abrupt dissolution. Chancellor Nevill thanked the lords and the Commons for their attendance and for their 'efficiency and hard work'. Whatever personal business it was that detained the king in May, in October he was on his way north again as the situation in Northumberland had deteriorated once more.[37]

A long siege lay ahead and a dangerous illness for the king. By Christmas 1462, the castles were back under Yorkist control. Early in the new year, Somerset was standing shoulder-to-shoulder with both Warwick and Edward IV.

# 27

# JOHN NEVILL'S WAR

In November 1462, Henry VI, his queen and their son left the shelter of Bamburgh Castle with Piers de Breze and set sail for Berwick. They had with them 400 French soldiers and their personal belongings, including a substantial sum of money given to them by the French king. Bamburgh Castle had opened its gates to them only days earlier. Alnwick and Dunstaburgh, held by Sir Ralph Percy, followed suit soon after.[1]

Margaret had stopped her journey at Bamburgh to collect her husband and deliver Somerset, who had travelled with her from France to take charge of the Lancastrian forces. Bamburgh was not safe for a deposed king. Not only had Warwick recently returned to the north but Edward IV was on his way with a large and well-supplied army. On hearing this, Margaret immediately ordered the fleet readied so they could return to Scotland.[2]

A tempest blew up, battering and scattering Margaret's fleet, threatening to send the Lancastrian royal family to a watery grave. Fortunately, they were picked up by a fisherman and taken to Berwick but their carvelle, and all it carried, sank in the storm; their French retinue too was lost.

> And the same day four hundred Frenchmen or there about, being of her host, were driven to land about Bamburgh; where as when they saw they might not have away their ships for the tempest, they set fire in them and burnt them; and so went into an island of Northumberland, where they were encountered with one Manners, a squire, and the Bastard of Ogle with 200 men, which slew and took prisoner the said 400 Frenchmen.[3]

This was more than a setback: they had lost an entire fleet of ships, all Queen Margaret's treasure, 20,000 livres borrowed from the French king and 400 of his subjects. With Edward approaching Durham and their welcome in Scotland rapidly cooling, the Lancastrian cause had been dealt a bitter blow. At least they were safe and all together in one place.

Queen Margaret had overcome difficulties before. While her son still lived, there was always hope.[4]

When King Edward came north with his army, it was 'with the intent to enter Scotland for the subduing of [his] adversaries there'. He had received sound advice from Warwick before setting out, to ensure he had 'sufficient victuals by the sea to serve your people during the time of your abode in the said Scotland'. Artillery was required: 'great guns for the beating of places and other guns for the field'. Powder, stones, 'great quantities' of bows, arrows, strings, spears 'and all other habiliments of war'.[5]

If Edward was not sufficiently supplied, Warwick wrote:

> in no wise should you come but rather defer your most noble purpose to such time as you may be sure of the said provisions, and if your said highness be purveyed as is abovesaid that it may like the same then to come, and I trust in our lord you shall have as worshipful a journey as had any of your noble progenitors.[6]

Warwick would be ready to ride with Edward, and would 'warn all your subjects in these parts to do the same'. An invasion of Scotland on the scale planned would force their hand. If Mary of Guelders had any sense, she would cut her ties with Henry and Margaret and come to terms with the Yorkist government. In Durham, Edward fell ill with measles and plans had to be changed. With Edward had come most of the available Yorkist lords. Rather than war with the Scots they were now to lay siege to the northern castles, under Warwick's overall direction. Fauconberg, Scales and Worcester oversaw the siege of Alnwick; Montagu, with lords Strange and Say, Robert, now lord Ogle, and Sir Ralph Grey took charge at Bamburgh; while Scrope, Greystoke and Powys held joint command at Dunstanburgh. This was a monumental undertaking and the young duke of Norfolk in Newcastle oversaw the daily arrival of supplies.[7]

The younger John Paston had come north with Norfolk and sent a long letter to his brother on 11 December.

> My lord of Warwick lies at the castle of Warkworth but three miles out of Alnwick, and he rides daily to all these castles for to oversee the sieges; and if they want victuals, or any other thing, he is ready to purvey it for them to his power. The king commanded my lord of Norfolk for to send victuals and ordinance out of Newcastle to Warkworth castle, to my lord of Warwick; and so my lord of Norfolk commanded sir John Howard, sir William Peche, sir Robert Chamberlain, Rafe Ascheton and me, Calthorp and Gorge, and others, for to go forth with the victuals and ordinance on to my lord of Warwick; and so we were with my lord of Warwick with the ordinance and victuals yesterday.[8]

It was a 60-mile round trip from Warkworth to Dunstanburgh, the most northerly of the castles. Each evening, Warwick brought back lists of what was required at each of the sieges and these lists would be taken the 30 miles south to Newcastle. Norfolk took receipt of the goods arriving by ship and loaded them onto carts. When the carts and wagons arrived at Warkworth, they were sorted and repacked to speed delivery and unloading at each of the castles. Warwick rode ahead. Had he remained with the carts for the entire 30 miles to Dunstanburgh, they would have slowed him down. As it was, he likely began and ended each day by torchlight.

The sieges lasted two long winter months. With success depending so much on the shipment of supplies, bad weather, bogged, broken or over-turned carts would have been more than minor hiccups. It is likely there were teams of men whose job it was to keep the way north as clear as possible and the road in good repair.

Some time during these difficult months, Warwick and Montagu received sad news from London. Their mother had died. The exact date and cause of her death are no longer known but on 9 December 1462, Warwick was styled 'earl of Warwick and Salisbury'. He was also granted licence to 'enter freely into all castles, lordships, manors, lands and other possessions descending to him on the death of the king's kinswoman, Alice countess of Salisbury'.[9]

Alice's death came hard on the heels of the death of their oldest sister Joan, whose passing so grieved her husband that he withdrew more and more from public life. Joan's effigy, lovingly commissioned by the widowed earl of Arundel, shows a woman of great beauty, even if idealised by fond memory. The effigy has a long narrow face, a fashionably plucked forehead and wears a richly jewelled headdress and collar. Joan was not quite 40 when she died and left behind her five children, the youngest still in the nursery.

Alice Montagu was 55 at the time of her death. Her youngest child, Margaret, was little more than 16. Like many women, medieval or otherwise, Alice was the backbone of her family. She had enjoyed great wealth and status and endured great hardship and grief. She brought ten healthy children into the world and saw them all to adulthood. For her husband's sake, she had committed treason and suffered the penalty of attainder that forced her to leave her home and travel to Ireland. She returned to England just months before the deaths of her husband and second-born son at Wakefield. While her sorrow at the death of her daughter Cecily in 1450 would have diminished in the years since, Joan's death would have been a severe blow. Yet still she was not defeated. At the time of her death, she was engaged in a wrongful death suit against the men she held responsible for the murder of her husband.[10]

Neither Warwick nor Montagu could pause in their endeavours, though they must surely have prayed for their mother's soul. Perhaps her death reminded them of the others they had lost and spurred them on to greater effort.

The day after Christmas, the siege at Bamburgh broke and Somerset surrendered to Montagu. There was no love lost between these two young men. They had a history of violence that stretched back seven years to the first battle of St Albans and the death of Somerset's father. Somerset did not just walk out through the gates of Bamburgh into the unknown. Negotiations had preceded the surrender, though Somerset was hardly in a position to make demands. His men were cold, starving and exhausted. His earlier overtures to Warwick to come to terms with the new king stood him in good stead, however, and both he and Sir Ralph Percy, who surrendered Dunstaburgh two days later, were taken by Warwick to Edward in Durham. 'And they came to Durham, and there they were sworn before our king. And the king gave them his livery and great rewards.'[11]

Somerset soon returned with Warwick to assist with the siege of Alnwick. Percy, despite his poor track record and, no doubt, both Warwick and Montagu's objections, was returned to his post as Constable of Dunstanburgh and Bamburgh, according to the terms of his surrender.[12]

The rehabilitation of Somerset and Percy haS been criticised as examples of poor political judgement on Edward's part. While the argument is stronger in Percy's case, as he had already surrendered castles under his command to the Lancastrians once, it is more difficult, without the benefit of hindsight, to lay the same charge against Somerset. His change of allegiance was not only a public relations coup, Somerset's military experience and skill were too valuable to be wasted. If his change of heart was genuine, and there is nothing to suggest it was otherwise at the time, King Henry's cause had lost a vital component. Edward might have difficulty keeping the peace between Somerset and the Nevills but that was better, surely, than Somerset remaining an implacable and elusive enemy.

With the capitulation of Alnwick, the northern castles were once again back in Yorkist hands. Shortly after Christmas, Edward, now fully recovered from his bout of measles, returned to London. Somerset went with him, high in the king's trust and favour.

> And the king made full much of him; in so much that he lodged with the king in his own bed many nights, and sometimes rode a hunting behind the king, the king having about him not passing six horses at the most and yet three were of the duke of Somerset's men.[13]

On 30 January 1463, Edward laid his father and brother to rest at Fotheringhay. Two weeks later, the funeral of the earl and countess of

Salisbury and their son Thomas was held at Bisham Abbey. It was the Nevills' second funeral in two months, Fauconberg having died on 9 January. He was buried at Guisborough Priory in north Yorkshire.[14]

Fauconberg was not only a loss to his nephew Warwick, whom he had served and guided since his appointment as Captain of Calais, but to Edward IV and the Yorkist cause. Fauconberg's military experience had been forged in France, as for many Englishmen his age. He had been wounded and captured in 1449 and remained a prisoner for the next three years. A member of the royal council since early 1453, he did not immediately join his brother Salisbury's alliance with the duke of York. While he gave able assistance to Warwick in Calais, his loyalty to Henry VI was unquestioned. It was only in 1458 that he threw in his lot with his brother and brother-in-law.[15]

Fauconberg's experience and skill had been invaluable to Warwick and Edward at both Northampton and Towton. During their years in Calais, particularly during their months of exile in 1460, a strong bond was forged between Fauconberg and Warwick. In time to come, Warwick would forge a similar bond with his cousin Thomas, Fauconberg's illegitimate son.[16]

Fauconberg and his wife Joan had three surviving daughters, two of whom married close associates of the Nevills. Elizabeth was married to Richard Strangeways, whose father had been elected speaker of the commons at the 1461 Parliament. Alice married Sir John Conyers, steward of Middleham and a core member of Salisbury's and then Warwick's affinities. Fauconberg was the eighth of Warwick and Montagu's close kin, by blood or by marriage, to die within two years.[17]

With both Warwick and Montagu in the south of England, Ralph Percy once again turned his coat and handed the castles under his command to Queen Margaret. More surprisingly, Sir Ralph Grey, who had been made Constable of Alnwick under the command of Captain Sir John Astley, betrayed his captain and surrendered the castle to the Lancastrians.[18]

> And within three or four months after [the taking of Bamburgh and Dunstanburgh] that false knight sir Ralph Grey, by false treason took the said sir John Astley prisoner, and delivered him to queen Margaret, and then delivered the castle to the lord Hungerford and to the Frenchmen accompanied with him; and by this means he put the king our sovereign lord out of possession.[19]

While Percy's motives might be easy to understand, Grey's are more difficult. He had never been a Lancastrian partisan. His disaffection would seem to have sprung from the preferment of Astley as Captain of Alnwick and his own perceived sidelining as Constable. Just three months after the intricate operation overseen by Warwick and involving almost every available nobleman in England, the castles were once again in Lancastrian hands.[20]

While the campaign in the north was crucial militarily, Warwick had other responsibilities. By 1463, his portfolio had grown considerably. Not only was he warden of the marches, Captain of Calais and keeper of the seas, but warden of the Cinque Ports and both Admiral and Great Chamberlain of England, among other lesser posts. Edward's trust in and reliance on him was immense. He could not stay in the north forever, nor could he continue to divide his time as he had over the last two years. To that end, in May, Montagu was appointed warden of the east march, leaving Warwick in charge of the west. This gave Montagu a level of authority he had not previously enjoyed and left Warwick more time to focus on other matters.[21]

Montagu proved to be more than capable of dealing with matters on his own, at least until a large Scots army, headed by Mary of Guelders, Margaret of Anjou and Piers de Breze, crossed the border and laid siege to Norham Castle. Garrisoned by Ogle, Norham was just south of the River Tweed and some 7 miles from Berwick. Montagu, who had seen off a party of Scots intent on raiding Newcastle and prevented a fleet of French ships delivering supplies to Bamburgh, immediately set off to deal with the invasion.[22]

Warwick was already on his way north again, having left London with his brother-in-law Stanley on 5 June. Edward IV soon followed with Somerset and a sizeable army. On 11 July, Warwick was raising troops at Middleham and, by the end of the month, he and Montagu marched on Norham. Queen Mary and Queen Margaret swiftly retreated across the border, along with their armies, young James III and Henry VI.[23]

There remained but one nameless Scot determined to meet the great earl of Warwick face to face.

> And at the departing of sir Piers de Breze and his fellowship was one manly man that purposed to meet with my lord of Warwick, that was a taborette, for he stood upon a hill with his tabor and his pipes, taboring and piping so merrily as any man might, standing by himself, till my lord came to him he would not lose his ground; and there he became my lord's man; and yet he is with him full good and to his lord.[24]

Lone pipers notwithstanding, the sudden departure of the Scots army from Norham left enough of the border unprotected for Warwick to cross with his army. There followed a brutal raid deep into the Lowlands.[25]

Edward made it no further than Northampton. There, perhaps because of a long-standing grudge or disapproval of his newfound friendship with the king, an angry mob rioted in protest at Somerset's presence. It was only Edward's personal protection that saved him from being lynched. Somerset either slipped away with his men or was sent by Edward to north Wales for his own safety. Either way, it was a final parting for the two men and, as would soon be clear, a parting between Somerset and King Edward's cause. On hearing of Warwick's success at Norham, Edward saw no need to proceed and returned to London.[26]

There was still the ongoing matter of the northern castles to resolve, and while Scotland gave aid and shelter to Henry VI and his queen, it was not one that would be resolved quickly. With Warwick's recent depredations in the Lowlands firm in her memory, and enough internal strife to be dealing with, Mary of Guelders grew less enthusiastic about supporting the deposed Lancastrian royal family and more open to the idea of peace talks with England. Leaving Montagu in Northumberland, Warwick once again went south, planning to join their brother chancellor Nevill in France for peace talks. A year-long truce negotiated with Louis XI and promises not to give aid to each other's enemies cut off one source of revenue, ships, men and supplies to the Lancastrians. After talks with the Scots in York in December, where Edward and Warwick negotiated a temporary peace, all external support for Henry VI evaporated. Further talks were scheduled for the following March, with a view to establishing a longer and more binding treaty. Henry VI retreated to Bamburgh Castle while Queen Margaret made a futile bid to overturn the treaty with England and regain the support of the French king, sailing to France with Prince Edward.[27]

In Wales, Somerset rediscovered his commitment to Henry VI and the Lancastrian dynasty. Just a year earlier, he had been feted by King Edward, enjoying the significant honour of sharing his bed and hunting with him. In London, a joust had been held in his honour.

> And with great insistence the king made him to take harness upon him, and ride in that place, but he would never meet with no man and no man might meet with him till the king prayed him to be merry and sent him a token, and then he ran full justly and merrily, and his helmet was a sorry hat of straw.[28]

Somerset's attainder had been overturned in June and he was fully restored to his honour and estates. Away from Edward's glittering presence, however, he had time to think. His life was no longer in immediate danger, as it had been at Bamburgh, and he may have been receiving secret messages from Jasper Tudor, urging him to return to the fold.[29]

Despite the hindsight of the writer of *Gregory's Chronicle* ('but the duke thought treason under fair cheer and words'), perhaps Somerset had been won over for a time by the hearty good nature of King Edward, and it was only in the cold light of day – and the isolation of Wales – that doubts set in. These doubts were swiftly followed by a plan, and the plan by action.[30]

Though the northern castles were once more, from Somerset's point of view, back in friendly hands, they provided only an intermittent base of operations. What the Lancastrians needed was a sizeable town, preferably with a port. Newcastle was the obvious choice. Newcastle was also where Somerset's men had been sent after the near disaster in Northampton. If he could only get there without being seen and reunite with his 200 retainers, they could take over the town and hand it to King Henry and Queen Margaret. Avoiding detection proved to be an impossibility.[31]

> And on the way thitherward he was espied, and like to have been taken beside Durham in his bed. Notwithstanding he escaped away in his shirt and barefoot, and two of his men were taken. And they took with them that false duke's casket and his harness. And when his men knew that he was escaped, and his false treason espied, his men stole from Newcastle as very false traitors, and some of them were taken and lost their heads for their labour, &c.[32]

Once Edward IV was aware Somerset was once again his enemy and very much at large, he ordered lord Scrope of Bolton to hold Newcastle for the Yorkists. Somerset had no choice but to make his way to Bamburgh.[33]

The plan to take Newcastle was likely deferred rather than abandoned. The town's value as a supply port had been proven during the sieges of late 1462. During those last few days before Alnwick fell, Somerset would have seen at first hand how the operation was run. The crucial role of secure bases in Calais and Ireland in the Yorkist invasion of 1460 would also have been fresh in his memory. Where to source the arms, men, ships and money needed was a question that could be answered another time. There was no point in looking that far ahead until the Lancastrians had a firmer foothold than the three castles on the coast.

Not that the castles were dispensable. Their role in defending the coast of a Lancastrian enclave carved out of eastern Northumberland would be crucial. With a narrow strip of land stretching from Norham on the Scottish border to Newcastle, bounded on one side by the castles and the sea and on the other by the hills and dales of the North Tyne Valley, the house of Lancaster may yet have its much-needed secure foothold on English soil. In the heart of Percy country, any Nevill who ventured near would receive neither welcome nor support. While he could not yet hope to take Newcastle, Somerset did take control of several towns close to the port, including Hexham.[34]

Montagu was still in the north, making ready to travel to the border to meet the Scots delegates for the upcoming peace talks. Though the talks had been postponed from March to April, and were now to be held in York rather than Newcastle, an escort had to be sent to bring the Scots embassy south.

Warwick, Edward and chancellor Nevill were to be the chief negotiators of a peace treaty, 'with many others for the English party, to bring it to a conclusion'. The Lancastrians' seizure of the towns of Prudhoe, Bywell, Hexham and Langley – stretching in a line nearly 30 miles to the west of Newcastle – prompted Montagu to send word to his brother and the king. Their help was needed once again in the north.[35]

Montagu's journey to the border could not be put off, whatever new danger Somerset posed. On his way to Newcastle, he nearly fell into an ambush.

> [B]y the way was full falsely purveyed that false duke Harry of Somerset and Percy, with their fellowship associate with them, a little from Newcastle, in a wood, that false traitor sir Humphrey Nevill, with three score spears, and the bows there too. And there should have fallen on the lord Montagu suddenly, and slain him suddenly, but, God be praised, their false treason was espied and known.[36]

By the time Montagu reached Newcastle, he had gathered some 5,000 men and was soon ready to venture into hostile country. Though he did not stay in Newcastle long, Somerset had enough time to regroup and redeploy his army, this time in open formation just outside Alnwick.[37]

Again, Montagu was forewarned by his scouts and, this time, he took no evasive action but marched on, to meet the enemy face to face. The two forces met on Hedgeley Moor and stood barely 1,500 yards apart prior to the opening of hostilities. The exact disposition of both armies is not known, but it is likely that Somerset and Edmund, lord Grey commanded the Lancastrian centre, with Percy on the right and Hungerford and Roos on the left. The nerve of Hungerford and Roos's men barely survived the opening arrow exchange and broke entirely once Montagu's army began its charge. If either of the Lancastrian commanders attempted to rally and reorganise his men, he failed and neither stayed in the field long enough to witness the outcome of the battle. With so few men and resources at their disposal, and the shelter of Alnwick so close, flight was by far the most prudent option.[38]

Now that the Lancastrian force had been reduced by a third, rather than following those who were fleeing, Montagu reorganised his men to concentrate on those who were left. Somerset's centre was the next to break, and he and lord Grey also fled for their lives, leaving Percy alone on the field. The sole survivor on the Percy side of the feud that had raged through the 1450s, the last of Montagu's warrior cousins, Sir Ralph stood his ground. It must soon have become clear to him that he could not win and was unlikely to survive. He was grossly outnumbered and faced an enemy not only opposed to him ideologically but personally. Perhaps he fought on because there was no way to escape; perhaps he fought on because he would not let a Nevill witness his weakness. Either way, Sir Ralph Percy was slain, as were most of his men, and the way was clear for Montagu to continue his journey to Norham.[39]

On the return journey, with the Scots delegates under his protection, Montagu encountered no trouble. He escorted the delegates to York for the peace talks but did not remain there long himself. Though the Lancastrians had been bloodied at Hedgeley Moor, they were not yet beaten. While they held the northern strongholds and the castles at Bywell and Prudhoe, Montagu still had work to do.

At Alnwick, Somerset was soon aware that a growing army was on its way. To emphasise the importance of the undertaking, and the seriousness of his intention to deal with the Lancastrian resistance once and for all, Edward ordered England's great cannons shipped north. Travelling by land, his army was approaching Leicester when Somerset made his move. King Henry himself was to lead the army. It was hoped this would not only raise the morale of the men who marched behind him but inspire others to join the cause. Somerset was not so foolish as to think he could lead his army south, collecting sufficient followers along the way, to meet Edward's army on anything close to equal terms. Rather, he was banking on a quick victory in Northumberland, enough to give heart and confidence to his men and to any who might otherwise have hesitated to join them.[40]

Having delivered his charges, Montagu immediately returned to Northumberland. Both Warwick and the chancellor were now in York, and he could leave the preliminary talks with the Scots in their hands.

In the early hours of 14 May, Montagu found Somerset's army camped near Hexham, King Henry accommodated in more comfort at the nearby castle of Bywell. The Lancastrian army was just beginning to stir when frantic scouts announced Montagu's imminent arrival. As his men scrambled for their weapons and armour, Somerset had no time to choose his ground. He formed his three divisions along the edge of Devil's Water, taking control of the centre himself, with Hungerford and Roos on the right and Grey and Humphrey Nevill on the left. Montagu deployed his men at the top of a slight rise, Greystoke commanding his left flank and Willoughby his right.[41]

Montagu wasted no time at Hexham. The Lancastrian army arrayed before him was a pale shadow of the great host that had come together at Towton. Montagu had not been at that battle, which might have been a matter of some lasting regret. If he could neutralise Somerset, Hungerford and Roos, he would bring King Henry's cause to its knees. That would leave only Exeter, Richmond and Pembroke to lead what was left of the Lancastrian resistance. He could not allow the weight of this to settle too heavily. This was the best chance he was going to get. This was his moment.[42]

Montagu led his men in a fast downhill charge to immediate and devastating effect. With the river to their backs, the Lancastrians had no room to move. They could not give ground and rally, they could only give ground and drown. Once again, Hungerford's and Roos's men panicked and fled. Lords Nevill and Grey soon followed. Somerset found himself alone on the field with a broken force. He could have fought to the last like Sir Ralph Percy, but he did not; nor did he flee. In his final act as commander of the Lancastrian forces, the duke of Somerset surrendered to Montagu, the bitter enemy of his youth.[43]

Henry VI did not remain long in the relative comfort and safety of Bywell Castle. When Montagu's men arrived, he was nowhere to be seen. They did find a symbol of Henry's kingship, left behind in the scramble to depart, his elaborately decorated 'high cap of estate'. 'Also king Henry's bicocket, richly garnished with two crowns, and his followers trapped with blue velvet … And anon upon this the lord Montagu presented the king at Pontefract with king Henry's bicocket, and his three followers; but where king Henry was become could not be known'.[44]

Before he could present his gift to King Edward, Montagu had other more pressing matters to attend to. In the days following Hexham, he ordered and oversaw the execution of more than thirty men, starting with Somerset, whose head was struck off the day after the battle in Hexham marketplace, along with four others. There followed two days later in Newcastle the executions of Hungerford, Roos and three other men. Six men were beheaded at Middleham the day after that and, finally, on 27 May in York, thirteen men lost their heads, including 'Robert Watts, porter to king Harry'. Lord Humphrey Nevill had not been taken prisoner, nor had Sir Ralph Grey, who still held out in Bamburgh Castle.[45]

With the possible exception of Somerset, whose attainder had been overturned, these executions were, strictly speaking, entirely legal. Had Edward IV been on the scene rather than Montagu, some of the men may have been spared and pardoned but Montagu, like his brother Warwick, was of the view that dead men could not betray their kings and masters a second time, nor could they raise armies. Montagu's actions at Hexham and after broke the Lancastrian cause. It was true that King Henry still had his freedom, but his wife and son were in France, isolated and friendless. There was still a pocket of resistance in Wales, led by the Tudors and Exeter, and the northern castles were still in enemy hands. Humphrey Nevill and Edmund Beaufort, released from captivity during his brother Somerset's brief reconciliation, were also unaccounted for.[46]

Montagu was rewarded for his success in Northumberland on 27 May. In the Archbishop of York's palace, he was elevated to earl of Northumberland and received a substantial grant of forfeited Percy lands.

The Nevill–Percy feud was over at last: the Nevills had won a devastating and resounding victory.[47]

On 1 June, a fifteen-year peace treaty was signed by Edward IV and the Scottish delegation. Wherever he was now, King Henry no longer had the option of seeking support and sanctuary north of the border. Through a combination of military and diplomatic means, the Nevills had plugged the gaps and ended any hopes those loyal to Henry may have harboured for a quick restoration to power.[48]

Edward's army, still on its way but no longer needed, was disbanded, though the great guns he had ordered to be readied and transported by sea – Dijon, London, Newcastle, Richard Bombartell and Edward – continued north. They would be put to good use in the final act of the northern war, which was set in motion on 11 June. Edward, though surely stung by the inconstancy of Somerset, was still prepared to be conciliatory to those willing to submit to him.[49]

> Commission to the king's kinsmen Richard earl of Warwick and Salisbury, great chamberlain of England and warden of the west march of Scotland, and John earl of Northumberland, warden of the east march of Scotland, to receive into grace certain rebels, Ralph Grey and Humphrey Nevill, knights, excepted, and to promise them their land, and to promise rewards to the king's subjects who have endangered their persons in the capture of certain castles in the county of Northumberland.[50]

On 23 June, Alnwick surrendered and the new earl of Northumberland took possession. The following day, Dunstaburgh also surrendered. Bamburgh, stubbornly held by Sir Ralph Grey, held out. The guns in place, Warwick and Montagu blockaded the castle and announced that they were prepared for a long siege.[51]

Negotiations were carried out by Chester and Warwick Heralds. Their message was blunt and uncompromising:

> Item, my said lord lieutenant and my lord warden have given us further commandment to say unto you, if you deliver not this jewel, the which the king our most dread sovereign lord, has so greatly in favour, seeing it marches so nigh his ancient enemies of Scotland, he especially desires to have it whole unbroken with ordinance, if ye suffer any great gun laid unto the wall and be shot, and prejudice the wall, it shall cost you the chieftain's head, and so proceeding for every gun shot to the least head of any person within the said place.[52]

Still Grey refused to surrender, 'clearly determining within himself to live or to die within the said place'. Warwick ordered his gunners to open fire.

'Dijon, a great brass gun of the king's smote through sir Ralph Grey's chamber oftentimes', injuring him and prompting those within to surrender without further reference to their commander. He was handed over and taken to Doncaster to be tried before Worcester, Constable of England.[53]

The sentence was one of degradation and death. He had 'betrayed sir John Astley, knight and brother of the garter' and would have his spurs struck off 'by the hand of the master cook, the which is here ready to do'.[54]

At trial's end, Worcester pronounced the sentence.

> Then sir Ralph Grey this shall be your penance – you shall go on your feet into the town's end, and there you shall be laid down and drawn to a scaffold, made for you, and that you shall have your head smitten off your body, to be buried in the friars, your head where it please the king.[55]

With that, the long drawn out series of sieges was at an end. Montagu brought his wife and children to live in Alnwick, the jewel of his new estate. Warwick travelled first to Middleham then to London, to ready himself and his fleet for an embassy to Burgundy. The previous March, a French embassy had been welcomed to London and the possibility of a marriage between Edward and Bona of Savoy was raised. Nothing was finalised, though Edward was reported to have been happy to give the idea further consideration. Now that Lancastrian resistance in Northumberland had been wiped out, Warwick could give the matter of the king's marriage the time and attention it required.[56]

The king, however, harboured a great secret which, when it was revealed, would change everything.

# 28

# MORE TROUBLES FOR LADY WILLOUGHBY

In the first weeks of February 1463, a chariot pulled by six horses, one draped in the arms of St George, the others in black, made its slow way from Pontefract to Bisham Abbey. Riders in front and behind held banners of St George, the arms of the earl of Salisbury and his personal badge, a golden gryphon segreant, its wings outstretched, clawing at the air. On the chariot were two coffins containing the remains of Salisbury and his second son, Thomas.[1]

The cortège was joined for the last leg of the journey by Salisbury's three most senior heirs. Warwick rode behind his father's banners, with Montagu walking on his right and Latimer's son Henry on his left. Sixteen 'noble knights and squires' followed on foot.[2]

A mile out of Bisham, they were met by a party of kings of arms, heralds and pursuivants, all wearing Salisbury's arms. It must have been a most splendid sight. No bypasser or curious onlooker could mistake who was to be buried. Farmers in their fields would have stopped work and watched as the cortege made its slow way along the road. Salisbury was their good lord, the countess their good lady. Generations of Montagus had been buried at Bisham. Now, for the first time, they were to be joined by Nevills.[3]

The countess of Salisbury's body was carried into the church half an hour before the cortège arrived. Her coffin was laid upon a hearse draped in black cloth. The parclose screen above her was draped in white. Her daughters and daughter-in-law Isobel, now countess of Northumberland, knelt before the hearse in silent prayer. Missing were the countess of Warwick and lady Willoughby, Thomas Nevill's widow. Distance was unlikely to have been the reason for the absence of Warwick's countess. Perhaps she or one of her daughters was unwell. Lady Willoughby's absence may have had more sinister reasons.[4]

At the church door, the cortège was met by high-ranking members of Salisbury's family and several churchmen.

> The body and the bones so coffined, the bishop of Exeter, chancellor of England, the bishop of Salisbury, the bishop of St Asaph, and two abbots, all mitred, with a solemn procession, accompanied with the lord Hastings, the king's chamberlain, the lord Fitzhugh and many other knights and noble squires in great number conveying this corpse, the son before the father, into the choir.[5]

Salisbury's sons had likely been planning and preparing for this funeral since the deaths at Wakefield but it was the passing of their mother that sparked them into action. Even as they were laying siege to the northern castles, letters would have been crossing the country, from Warwick to chancellor Nevill, to their scattered sisters and to the family's agents in Berkshire. Salisbury had left specific instructions for his funeral in his will. His sons, pressed for time as they were, would do their best to comply.

King Edward had recently removed the remains of his father and brother from their temporary graves at Pontefract and reburied them at Fotheringhay. Their funeral was as elaborate as the young king could afford. Over the centuries since, Warwick has been accused of striving to outdo Edward in the lavishness of this family funeral. Warwick was certainly keen to acquire and accumulate income streams, but money was not to be hoarded: it was to be spent. Warwick's wealth was beyond the imagination of most people and since the death of his father he was wealthier still. His generosity was legendary.

> [W]hen he came to London he held such a house that six oxen were eaten at a breakfast, and every tavern was full of his meat, for who had any acquaintance in that house, he should have as much boiled and roast meat as he might carry upon a long dagger.[6]

Largesse was not a matter of choice for the fifteenth-century English nobility, it was a deeply ingrained part of life. Travellers were offered food and a place to sleep in the houses of the great and the good. Leftovers from meals were collected into large receptacles for distribution among the poor. If Warwick's largesse was noteworthy, it was for its scale.[7]

Warwick may have outdone the king when it came to the funerals of their fathers and brothers but Edward IV simply had less money to spend. The funerals at Fotheringhay were as elaborate and lavish as he could afford to make them.

Salisbury had been a soldier all his adult life and he was buried as a soldier.

> [A]t the corner of the hearse, the banner; Garter king of arms in a coat of the said earl's arms; on the left side the standard; Clarence king of arms was

before; at the corners of the feet of the said heirs, two heralds, Windsor and Chester, in coats of the same arms; with many other heralds and pursuivants.[8]

Though the two kings of arms and named heralds had by far the largest roles to play in the proceedings, Salisbury Herald was also in attendance. The 'other heralds and pursuivants' are not identified.

Once the family's dead were reunited in the choir of the church, the long night was spent in silent vigil. While praying for the souls of their loved ones was the purpose of the long night's watch, unbidden memories may have prompted quiet tears and stifled sobs. This was a family bereft of a father they all looked up to, a mother who was brave and resilient, a brother they could ill afford to lose. When the sun rose, the mourners refreshed themselves, possibly with breakfast in Bisham's great hall. They had long hours of ceremony ahead of them. During the course of the day, while the women sat or knelt before the countess's hearse, an elaborate ritual unfolded.

First, they heard mass, then

the said king of arms heralds brought out of the vestry honourably every of them, &c; then Garter of the coat of arms, Clarence the shield, Windsor the sword, Chester the helm and crest, and carried them to the body of the said earl's hearse, holding the coat of arms and the sword on the right side, the shield on the left side, the helm and crest at the head in the middle without the pale and parclose.[9]

If this was not theatre enough, after the reading of the gospel, a mounted knight appeared at the west door of the church, carrying an axe. The horse, one of Salisbury's own, was dressed as for war in his master's colours. He was to be an offering, as were the weapons and harness of the knight. In earlier times, both horse and rider might have been sacrificed so they could serve their lord in death, but such things did not happen inside a Christian church.[10]

Warwick laid the mass-penny on the altar, almost certainly a coin of much greater value than a single penny. Then, in a carefully choreographed ritual, the other offerings were made, each carried to Warwick in a symbolic transfer of power and authority from the earl of Salisbury to his heir.[11]

First, the coat of arms was taken to Worcester,

the earl offering that coat, and after the bishop [of Exeter] delivered the said coat to the earl of Warwick as heir in tokening that the said coat belonging in right to him; after which deliverance, the said earl of Warwick delivered the said coat to the said king of arms, as it appeared unto his office to do.[12]

Next came Montagu with Salisbury's shield, Hastings with his sword and Fitzhugh with his helm and crest. Last came the knight, who 'offered his harness and horse to the church'. Then each of the lords, the dukes first, made their own offerings to the church, followed by the 'ladies and gentle-women with other knights and squires and gentlemen'.[13]

After this, the lords, earls and dukes, in order of seniority beginning again with Clarence, laid lengths of cloth of gold and bawdekin – silk shot with gold – on the coffins. The offerings were then taken to the tomb where Salisbury was to be buried, where was set 'over the tomb, in the middle, the coat of arms; at the head above, the helm and crest; the shield underneath; the sword hanging by the banner on the right side of the head; the standard on the same side at the foot'.[14]

The kings of arms and heralds then 'did off their coats'. Alone, Salisbury Herald, 'reliveried by the heir, the said earl his herald in the said coat revested, stood before the hearse before the presentation of his said lord during the remainder of the mass until the burying of the corpse'.[15]

The anonymous account of the funeral at Bisham ends abruptly, but no doubt there was a feast, with tears and laughter and remembering. At last, Salisbury's surviving daughters, should they have a mind to, could find comfort in each other's company. Since Joan's death the previous year, Alice Fitzhugh was now the oldest. Margaret, as yet unmarried but probably already betrothed to the young earl of Oxford, was the youngest. Between them came Alianor and Katherine. Fatherless for two years, they were now motherless as well. They would surely remember the lessons she had taught them and look to the example she had set. From time to time, one of them might catch herself and think, *I sound more like Mother every day!* There were children yet to be born, and Alice Montagu would not be there to share her daughters' suffering, nor their joy.

Alice had been a covert countess throughout her marriage, all her privilege, authority and status transferred to her husband and wielded by him. Though the flow of inheritance had come in the form of masculine things, the stuff of war, it was from his mother that Warwick inherited the Salisbury title. He would style himself Richard, earl of Warwick and Salisbury from this point on, not simply to honour his mother's family and pedigree but to link himself to the fame and admiration that had been his father's.

The shades of three great men twined around themselves in Warwick, three great soldiers and administrators, diplomats and politicians. It was a lot to live up to. While he carried the blood of Richard Nevill and Thomas Montagu, it was his children who carried Richard Beauchamp's, and his grandchildren to come. Warwick would make himself great, too, if he could, and he would pass this greatness on not to the sons he could not have and longed for, but to his daughters.

Neither Isobel nor Anne attended the funeral. They were likely considered too young. While perhaps surprising, the absence of their mother could be explained by illness or a reluctance to leave an ailing child. It is the absence of Maud Stanhope, lady Willoughby that is harder to understand.

Over the years, Maud had grown used to fighting for what was hers. Deprived of her dower by her stepdaughter, she had turned to her uncle Cromwell for support and it was he who brokered her marriage to Sir Thomas Nevill. Three years later, when Cromwell died, the changed terms of his will set Maud another challenge. Together with her sister and their husbands, she fought to overturn the will, in which he left them far less than he had always promised. Thomas and Jane's husband, Sir Humphrey Bourchier, then took matters into their own hands, seizing property and taking possession of manors worth thousands of pounds. While Thomas was imprisoned in Chester Castle after the battle of Blore Heath, Maud's personal property was illegally seized in the name of King Henry and she was, once again, turned out of her home at Eresby.

We do not know what Maud was doing, or where she was living, during those few months in 1460 between Thomas's release and his death. By all accounts, he spent much of that time in London and the two may have been reunited. Almost certainly, the wrongs done her in King Henry's name were righted. She continued to live at Eresby and enjoy the income from her several estates. In 1463, Maud would be arrested, along with Sir Gervase Clifton, and imprisoned for a period of five weeks. She was confined in the home of lord Scales; Clifton in the Tower.[16]

After Thomas's death, Maud was a royal widow. Some of the property held by her first husband, and subsequently by Maud as her dower, was in the gift of the crown. To safeguard such property from adventurers and mismanagement, widows in Maud's position were required to obtain a licence before marrying. One had been granted to Maud and Thomas in 1452. Some time on or around 10 August 1461, Maud married again, this time without royal licence.

Such marriages were usually forgiven, after investigation as to their legality and the payment of a fine. Joan Fauconberg, widow of William Nevill, earl of Kent, was the subject of one such investigation at the time of his death. Though the nature of her condition is not known, there were questions as to Joan's competence. Concerns were raised, most likely by her daughters and sons-in-law, that Joan had done, was about to do or some time in the future may well do something that jeopardised their inheritance. On 12 March 1463, an investigation was launched.

Commission to James Strangeways, knight, Thomas Witham, chancellor of the exchequer, Thomas Mountford, esquire, John Leyton, esquire, and Ralph

Assheton, esquire, to enquire by oath of good men of the county of York whether Joan Fauconberg, late countess of Kent, is an idiot and incapable of the governance of herself and her possessions, whether she has alienated any of her lands, and who is her next heir.[17]

The wolves may have been circling and, as a royal widow, Joan's interests needed to be looked after. Joan, or those close to her, remedied the matter on their own, without reference to the king.

Two days after Strangeways and company were commissioned to investigate her competency, Joan's name appears once again in the *Calendar of Patent Rolls*: 'Pardon to John Berwyke, esquire, and Joan, countess of Kent, late the wife of the king's uncle William, earl of Kent, tenant in chief, for their trespass in intermarrying without licence.' Little is known about John Berwyke. He was likely a trusted household servant of the widowed countess rather than an opportunist. The marriage, now forgiven, pardoned and recognised as legal, may have outraged Joan's daughters and caused her sons-in-law concern, but it served to protect her interests from any designs they may have had on her wealth. The same cannot be said for Maud Stanhope's third marriage, which began in secrecy. '1461, August 10. Licence for sir Gervase Clifton, knt, and [Maud], widow of sir Thomas Nevill, knt, to be married in the church, or chapel in the manor-house, of Clifton. Banns once.'[18]

Clifton had been named in the late countess of Salisbury's civil suit against those who caused the death of her husband. He was on Edward IV's list of those never to be pardoned, yet he received a pardon in March 1461. This was at least partly due to the intervention of Clifton's stepson, Sir John Scott. In 1460, Scott had been one of the men tasked with resisting the exiled Calais earls in Canterbury. Instead, he quickly joined them and soon became a trusted member of March's inner circle. When March was proclaimed king in 1461, he appointed Scott controller of his household, a position he was to hold for the next ten years. Scott maintained a close relationship with his stepfather and often worked alongside his brother-in-law, John Jernegan.[19]

Scott's commitment to Edward IV was unequivocal and lifelong. If he could persuade Clifton to see what he saw in the young king, and if he could convince the king that Clifton made his submission in good faith, then he could serve the two men who mattered most in his life. The countess of Salisbury would not have been consulted on the matter but perhaps Warwick was.

Clifton had worked for Warwick for five years as treasurer of Calais and his perceived betrayal of Warwick at Ludford hurt him deeply, but Warwick also knew his value. Maud Stanhope was an old friend of Clifton's, a friendship that was renewed when Clifton acted as executor of her uncle Cromwell's will. If Maud was also appealing to Warwick on Clifton's behalf, it may have helped sway his opinion.

After the countess of Salisbury, Maud had perhaps the most compelling reason to feel personal animosity towards Clifton. He had fought at Wakefield, where Thomas Nevill lost his life. Perhaps Clifton was able to convince her he had played no part in her husband's death, that he regretted it and sought reconciliation with the new regime. Maud had distant family connections to the Cliftons of Clifton Hall and, though illegitimate, Gervase had been acknowledged by his father and was a recognised member of the family. If he sought shelter there after Towton, it would not have been difficult to make contact with Maud and ask for her help.

Maud's reasons for marrying Clifton cannot be anything other than a matter for speculation. She may have married for love or because she thought such a marriage would help his case. She must have thought the king would not grant her a licence or she surely would have sought one. It may be that Warwick thought marriage to the widow of a Yorkist stalwart would cement Clifton's loyalty to Edward IV. Such marriages were not uncommon, the marriage between Warwick's sister Margaret and Oxford was arranged for that very reason. If this was the case, it is difficult to explain why Warwick would condone Maud marrying without a licence. She may have been forced into the marriage against her will, but there is nothing solid to support or dismiss any of this. All we know is that they married.[20]

Whatever reason Maud had for standing with Sir Gervase in the church or chapel at Clifton Hall on her wedding day, it was a decision she soon came to regret. While it may have been the disapproval and anger of the Nevills that prevented her from attending the funeral at Bisham, it may also have been the controlling nature of her third husband. He may have forbidden, or even physically prevented her from attending.

Within two years of the wedding, Maud left Clifton, citing economic abuse and mismanagement. Many years later, she claimed her net worth had decreased drastically due to Clifton's negligence and that he refused to give her enough money to live on. In desperation, she turned to her brother-in-law Montagu for help. His willingness to provide that help suggests Maud had not irrevocably burned her bridges with the Nevills.[21]

In 1463, when both he and Maud were arrested and fined £1,000 for their unlicensed marriage, Clifton turned to his stepson and son-in-law for help. Sir John Scott and John Jernegan stood surety for the amount, and payments were to be made from the income of several of Maud's properties. In a suit brought against her by Scott and Jernegan after Clifton's death in 1471, Maud was accused of actively preventing them from collecting revenues from her estates in payment of this debt. They claimed she had changed the officers in charge of several manors and instructed them to give nothing to either Scott or Jernegan. They said Maud had left her husband and refused to comply with the terms of their agreement. For her part, Maud held to the view the £1,000 loan had nothing to do with her. As far as she was aware, Clifton had paid it in full. She had not, she said, left her husband in order to avoid payment of the debt but because of his actions and his mismanagement of her wealth. Maud was not preventing Scott and Jernagan from collecting the money: the king himself had placed control of her lands in Montagu's hands. A measure of Maud's strength of character can be found in her subsequent demand for payment for vexation.[22]

Personal difficulties were not the only reason the marriage broke down. Within three years, Clifton had rejoined the Lancastrian cause and fought alongside Somerset at Hexham. In 1465, he once again sought and received a pardon, this time at a terrible cost to his estranged wife. This time, it was lord Scales who stood surety for Clifton.[23]

> Gervase Clifton knight and Maud his wife, late the wife of Robert lord Willoughby, to Anthony Wydeville lord Scales and lord of Newsels and his assigns. Gift with warranty during the life of the said Maud of the manors of Candlesby, Halom, Lamley, Snawdon, Boston, Bleasby, Gyppersmore, Gourton, Drainsfield, Baseford, Quinton, Rasin, Lutton, Bolcheford and Tuxford with Deyncourts rent there etc, counties Lincolnshire, Notting, Derby and Warwick, and the manner of Tumby county Lincolnshire except a great wood called 'Tumby woods' otherwise 'Tumby chase', all late of Ralph lord Cromwell or of another to his use at his death … and request that all feoffees shall make the said Anthony an estate thereof during the life of the said Maud, with the exception aforesaid.[24]

Had Maud not signed these properties over to Scales, Clifton would most likely have been executed for treason. Whatever her personal feelings for him, it seems she could not allow this. The gross injustice of this 'gift' was that Scales would benefit from the income of these properties for the rest of Maud's life, not Clifton's – she was not the one accused of treason. As it was, Clifton once again returned to the Lancastrian cause in 1468. He was executed in 1471 after the battle of Tewkesbury.[25]

Maud's worth before her marriage to Clifton had been some 1,000 marks per annum. After Clifton's depredations, his 1465 pardon and the grant to Scales, this was reduced to around 300 marks. Her marriage to Clifton cost her more than money. Of illegitimate birth and low rank, he was never going to be considered a suitable holder of the Cromwell title. In 1461, Jane's husband, Sir Humphrey Bourchier, was summoned to Parliament as lord Cromwell.[26]

Maud went to live at Tattershall Castle, which she owned jointly with Jane. It was to be her home for the rest of her life, the last few years spent living in a house she had built for herself in the castle grounds.[27]

# 29

# SECRETS AND CELEBRATIONS

t the council meeting at Reading in September 1464, Warwick had business of some urgency to raise with the king. Instructions were needed on the matter of Edward IV's proposed marriage to Bona of Savoy. Warwick and lord Wenlock were to meet with Louis XI later that month, if not to finalise a treaty between England and France then at least to bring one closer to fruition. Edward's thoughts about the marriage were bound to be brought up. The question could be put off no longer; a decision had to be made.[1]

Edward's marriage had been a matter of concern and discussion since his childhood. Royal and noble marriages had always featured prominently in diplomatic discussions. Princesses of both France and Burgundy had been suggested or sought as brides for Edward long before there was even the slightest prospect he would one day be King of England. Now he was 22 years old, his hold on the throne was firm and the matter could be pursued with some vigour.

In the three years since Edward took the throne, the question had come up three times. First, in October 1461, Wenlock led a peace delegation to France and suggested a marriage between Edward and a sister of the wife of Charles of Charolais, later duke of Burgundy. In 1462, treaty talks with the Scots had included the possibility of a match between Edward and Mary of Guelders, though this was probably more of a kite-flying exercise than a serious proposal. Henry of Castile suggested his sister Isabella as a suitable queen for Edward but this was declined by the English.[2]

In 1461, neither Philip the Bold of Burgundy nor his son had been prepared to risk the safety and future prosperity of Charolais's sister-in-law by giving her in marriage to a king whose hold on his throne was both recent and insecure. Now things had changed and the King of France offered his wife's sister, 21-year-old Bona of Savoy. All that needed to be done was finalise the terms of the treaty and Edward would have a wife, England would have a queen.[3]

Bona was of good noble family. She was one of nineteen children and could provide, through her siblings, connections to France, Luxembourg and Savoy. On paper, it was an excellent proposal and one Edward IV was keen to pursue, at least until May 1464.

When the question was asked, perhaps bluntly – 'What answer do I give King Louis with regard to Bona of Savoy?' – Warwick could not possibly have anticipated the answer. There would be no marriage, to Bona or any other foreign princess. Edward had taken the decision into his own hands and was already married. Though the date of the wedding is a matter of some discussion and dispute, it had taken place not days or even weeks, but some months before the council meeting in Reading. The bride, Isabella of Castile's 'widow of England', was Elizabeth Wydeville, whose first husband, Sir John Grey of Groby, had lost his life at the second battle of St Albans.[4]

Council's reaction was immediate and, as Edward might have anticipated, entirely negative:

> they answered that she was not his match, however good and however fair she might be, and he must know well she was no wife for a prince such as himself; for she was not the daughter of a duke or earl, but her mother, the duchess of Bedford, had married a simple knight, so that though she was the child of a duchess and the niece of the count of St Pol, still she was no wife for him.[5]

Elizabeth Wydeville was herself the product of a marriage conducted in secret and without licence between two parties of unequal rank. Her father, Sir Richard Wydeville, now lord Rivers, had been a member of the duke of Bedford's household at the time of his death and married his widow Jacquetta of Luxembourg some time before March 1437. Rivers may have been of relatively low birth but, since his submission following the battle of Towton, he and his son lord Scales had been of great service to the king. Scales, in particular, had proved himself alongside Warwick and Montagu during the protracted and intermittent sieges of the northern castles.[6]

Council's shock at Edward's revelation was profound. Quite apart from the unsuitability of the match, tradition and long practice dictated that kings consult before taking such momentous decisions. He had put personal preference, perhaps even fleeting passion, before the good of his realm and his people. The woman he married would not just be his wife, she would be queen. Elizabeth Wydeville, they argued, was not the right person for the job. Urgent discussions were had to see if some way might be found to question the legality of the marriage and serve as grounds for annulment. No such impediment was found.[7]

The first thing Warwick had to do, to buy himself some time, was postpone the peace talks with France to the following month. As the days since

Edward's revelation passed and no means was found to extricate the king from this most unsuitable marriage, it became clear the best course of action was to accept it and make the best of it. A chance for the fledgling Yorkist dynasty to gain a foothold, and valuable allies, in Europe had been missed. Edward's council came to terms with the *fait accompli* and the new queen was sent for. On 29 September, Warwick and Edward's brother George, duke of Clarence escorted her into Reading Abbey, her first public appearance as Edward's queen.[8]

By any reckoning, Edward's choice of bride, and his manner of marrying, were extraordinary. While not quite the impoverished low-born commoner she is often perceived to be, Elizabeth Wydeville brought no advantage to Edward the king. Edward the man may have been in love with her, and continued to love her for the rest of his life, but kings were not entitled to marry for love alone. In the more romantic tales of her wooing, Elizabeth is cast as the virtuous widow who refuses to join the king in his bed. Even with a knife at her throat, she refuses to give in. Some versions of the story put the knife in Edward's hands, some say Elizabeth held the knife herself, declaring she would rather die than become his lover. The truth is no doubt far less dramatic. Edward smitten with Elizabeth's beauty and chastity is a common theme across the various accounts.[9]

She was:

> of excellent beauty, but yet of such beauty and favour that with her sober demeanour, lovely looking, and feminine smiling (neither too wanton nor too humble) besides her tongue so eloquent, and her wit so pregnant, she was able to ravish the mind of a mean person, when she allured and made subject to her the heart of so great a king.[10]

Despite, or perhaps because of, his own sexual reputation – for he was so well known that men 'feared that he had not been chaste of his living' and spoke of his attempts on 'the stability and constant modesty of divers ladies and gentlewomen' – Edward had perhaps despaired of meeting any 'of such constant womanhood, wisdom and beauty as dame Elizabeth'.[11]

The secrecy of the wedding – so secret not even his chamberlain and closest friend Hastings knew about it – and the long interval before it was made public might suggest Edward intended to deny it once he got what he wanted from Elizabeth and was ready to move on. The assembling of witnesses, 'the duchess of Bedford her mother, the priest, two gentlewomen and a young man to help the priest sing', would suggest otherwise. Perhaps this could be read as Elizabeth's insurance policy over any future attempt by Edward to back out of his promise, but if she feared this, the question must be asked: why did she consent to marrying him at all? Witnesses or not,

Elizabeth must have been sure enough of Edward, and Edward of himself, to take such a drastic step. There is no evidence Edward had used such a ruse before. Later claims that he had previously secretly married Eleanor Butler were made without any solid evidence. He married Elizabeth because he wanted her to be his wife. Had he still been Edward, earl of March, his choice would have been scandalous enough. As it was, the consequences of his hasty and self-centred choice were to prove dire and damaging to both his kingship and England.[12]

If he had no plans to deny his marriage to Elizabeth, why then did he wait so long to make it known? He must have known the proposed marriage to Bona of Savoy would be brought up sooner or later. The longer he put off telling Warwick, the more difficult Warwick's position would be when it came to talking with King Louis. Even if the traditional date of the wedding, 1 May, is nothing more than a convenient romantic peg on which to hang this tale of impetuous love, the marriage clearly took place some time before the council meeting in Reading.

Edward may simply have been afraid to tell his council what he had done and put it off until it could be put off no longer. Though his intention was always to acknowledge the marriage and stand by his wife, he had good reason to be fearful of the reception his eventual revelation would have. First, he must have anticipated almost exactly the response his council gave. He had not only risked putting the peace talks with France in jeopardy but breached a long-standing understanding between a king and his lords – their right to be consulted on such matters as his marriage. He must have been particularly concerned about Warwick's reaction. He had done so much to put Edward on the throne. Though the term 'kingmaker' comes from a later time, and is something of an overstatement, it was Warwick and the Nevill faction that propelled Edward in 1460 and 1461 and had backed him with arms in the years since.[13]

It was Warwick who took a load of responsibilities off the young king's shoulders. In the first few years of Edward's reign, Warwick was his Minister for Everything. Edward's dependence on him may have been exaggerated in foreign courts – 'They have two rulers in England, M de Warwick and another whose name I have forgotten' – but it was real enough. For three years, the Nevill brothers had been indispensable to Edward, militarily, administratively and diplomatically.[14]

Now he had broken free, at least to some degree. He had made one of the most important decisions of his life on his own, not only in the face of Warwick's certain disapproval but in the knowledge that Warwick was engaged in negotiating a different and far more suitable match. While it did not signal a breakdown in the relationship between the king and his most important subject, nor even the beginning of a breakdown, the cracks would soon start to show. Edward's decision may have been right romantically and in terms of his personal satisfaction and happiness, but politically it was a serious mistake. Rumours swirled through diplomatic circles and ambassadors reached for pen and ink to write to their masters.[15]

By 5 October, rumours of the wedding had reached the ears of Louis XI.

> They also say that the marriage of king Edward will be celebrated shortly, but without stating where. It seems that the espousals and benediction are already over, and thus he has determined to take the daughter of my lord Rivers, a widow with two children, having loved her, it appears.[16]

> It is asserted that king Edward has married a widow of England, daughter of the sister of the count of St Pol. The lady is said to have two children by her first husband, the elder of whom is three years of age. This has greatly offended the people of England.[17]

On 10 October, the rumours were confirmed.

> It is publicly announced here that the king of England has taken to wife an English lady they say out of love. The king here and all the rest of us hoped and expected that he would be sending at this time to marry one of the sisters of the queen here as he had frequently caused his representatives to see them.[18]

Louis was already in Picardy, on his way to St-Omer for the postponed peace and marriage talks. The English delegation did not show up. Instead, Wenlock, who had treated with the French before, urged them to accept Edward's marriage and continue with the peace talks at another time.[19]

Warwick did not, as is often claimed, have a problem at this time with the Wydevilles. He had a problem with one specific Wydeville – lord Rivers. Any detailed history of personal animosity between the two has been lost to history, but Rivers was one of only a handful of men replaced when Warwick took possession of Calais in 1457. His derision of Rivers in 1460, in which the young earl of March enthusiastically joined him, was more than just scorn for the son of a squire. Warwick made no such remarks about Hastings when he brokered the marriage with his sister Katherine.

In the following years, two of Warwick's family, his sister Joan's son lord Maltravers and his elderly aunt, married members of the queen's new family. The latter marriage, of the 65-year-old thrice-widowed Katherine Nevill to the young John Wydeville, most likely did cause Warwick anger and upset. It was universally greeted with scorn, derision and shock. On the other hand, his nephew's marriage to the queen's sister, however low her birth, forged a valuable link to the king.[20]

Another matter discussed at Reading was far more pleasing to the Nevills. On 12 September, the Archbishop of York William Bothe died. Edward immediately set in train the process by which a successor was appointed. On the same day, the temporalities of the diocese of York were granted to chancellor Nevill. Though surely not delighting in the death of Bothe, perhaps it brought Edward some relief from the universal disapproval that greeted the announcement of his marriage. Mollifying the Nevills was surely not Edward's primary reason for recommending George to the pope – he had been chancellor of England for four years and a multiple-term chancellor of the University of Oxford before that – but the opportunity to mend fences was too good to pass up. Letters were written to the pope and on 15 March 1465, Paul II formerly approved George's elevation to archbishop. At just 33, George was the second highest ranking churchman in England. If he had further ambitions, they must lead him to Canterbury or to Rome.[21]

It was not until 21 September that year that George was formally enthroned as archbishop in an elaborate ceremony in York. Two weeks prior, in a small ceremony at Cawood Castle just outside the city, George was presented with his pallium, an important badge of office that was a gift from the pope.[22]

George's first official duty as archbishop was the ordination of more than eighty clergymen of varying degrees at Bishopthorpe Palace in York. The following day, along with the Bishops of Durham and Carlisle, he waited outside the city gates. Dressed in pontifical vestments, sprinkled with holy water and censed, he then walked barefoot in procession from the city gates to the minster. It was a grand procession, led by the Dean of York carrying George's pallium, and the precentor of the choir and the Bishops of Durham, Carlisle and Dromore. Behind the new archbishop came his brothers, the earls of Worcester and Oxford and prominent members of the Nevill affinity, abbots from all over the archdiocese and the Bishops of Ely, Lincoln, Exeter, Coventry and Lichfield.[23]

Once in the cathedral, George knelt in prayer and took his oath to uphold the Church. He was then dressed in his cope and mitre and presented with his crozier. Finally, at the high altar, the Bishop of Lincoln and the Dean of York placed the pallium about George's shoulders. He was then led to his throne, where he received the homage of his suffragan bishops and abbots.[24]

This was a moment for the Nevills to treasure. They had worked hard, fought hard and given so much to the house of York. They had been rewarded with lucrative posts, titles and grants of land. They were collectively Edward IV's right hand. They had won his crown for him and held it in the face of years of resistance and opposition. They deserved this. George deserved this.

Warwick and Montagu were passive participants in their brother's enthronement ceremony. In the cathedral, George belonged to the Church and it was the Church that feted him. At the great feast that traditionally followed such an event, they took control. Warwick bankrolled the occasion and Montagu acted as treasurer. Cooks had gathered in the kitchens of Cawood Castle days before the feast itself, taking receipt of endless cartloads of supplies. Two thousand people would be catered for over three days of feasting, with two major meals served each day. The list of proteins is staggering, as is the menu for the three courses of each meal.[25]

There was enough alcohol for each guest to drink 19 litres of ale, 6.3 litres of wine and just over half a litre of hippocras over the three days, though it is likely a good part of that supply was to be used for cooking, such as in 'brawn and mustard ... served with malmsey'. Each guest was allowed a little less than a quarter each of a swan, a plover, a peacock, a heronshaw and a woodcock; a tenth each of crane, kid, bittern and pheasant; a quarter of a partridge; half a capon; half a sheep; half an egret; one chicken; one piglet; two pigeons, two ducks and two rabbits; a third of a fish; three-quarters of a hot venison pasty and two cold; half a dish of 'parted' jelly and one and a half dishes of plain; two cold baked tarts; one and a half cold baked custards and one hot. Other meats – oxen, veal, mutton, pork and venison – are more difficult to calculate. Some of them, for example, wild bulls, porpoises and seals, are listed in relatively small quantities that suggest they were reserved for the most honoured guests.[26]

Of the 2,000 people in attendance, only fifty are named or otherwise identified. The rest were variously ladies, gentlemen, gentlewomen, squires, judges, servants, franklins, abbots, knights, priors, learned men of law, barons of the chancery, worshipful men of York, the brethren of York Minster, barons, baronesses, head yeomen and 'worshipful esquires wearing the king's livery'. This was Warwick's legendary largesse on a grand scale.[27]

A lot of the dishes served over the three days were relatively plain fare, roast meat and fowl of varying kinds. Others were more elaborate: 'peacock in his jacket', 'bream in sauce ponnyvert', 'pike in marblet', 'tench in jelly' and 'frumenty royal'. Each course was finished off with a subtlety, an extravagant construction, often pastry or a great custard. Three of particular note were 'a dragon', 'a dolphin in foil' and 'a subtlety of St William, with his coat armour between his hands'.[28]

After each meal, leftovers were collected into alms pots for distribution but there was no doubt plenty set aside each morning for those with the stamina and fortitude to attempt breakfast.

With the exception of Montagu, the 'great officers' of the feast do not feature in the lists of who sat where. As treasurer, Montagu's work was largely done and he took his place at the second table in the great chamber along with his cousin Westmorland and his brothers-in-law Fitzhugh and Stanley. After the first meal of each day, he would have attended a meeting over 'bread, wine and ale' with 'the steward … the comptroller, the marshall, the usher, pantlers, butlers, cooks, lardners, caterers and such other officers' to discuss that day's supper and the following day's dinner.[29]

The other great officers held roles that were both ceremonial and supervisory, which kept them busy throughout the three days of the feast. Behind the scenes was the comptroller Hastings, overseeing each day's deliveries of fresh meat, fruit, vegetables and ale. In the days and weeks leading up to the feast, he and his deputies worked closely with Montagu and his deputies on costings and budgets. It was Hastings's job to source supplies and order them. Much, of course, would have come from Warwick's own estates but, even then, the accounts had to be kept straight.[30]

Working under Hastings was the clerk of the kitchens, who kept clean copies of the recipes used by the cooks and a tally of items used for each dish. He was also responsible for expediting service. Forty-two cooks were hard at work in the kitchens. Some were permanent members of the Cawood Castle staff; others were recruited locally. Not everything came from the kitchens, however. Meat, either on the hoof or butchered, was the responsibility of the acatery, which worked closely with the butchery. Fowl, either wild or domesticated, was the responsibility of the poultry. In larger households there were separate kitchens for cooking sauces, wafers and confectionary, as well as a bakehouse that produced bread and trenchers. Fish were kept fresh in cisterns and ponds, replenished from nearby rivers. Seafood was shipped in from the coast as swiftly as possible after it was caught. By far the most expensive items used in medieval cooking were imported spices and these were kept under lock and key and accounted for most stringently.[31]

Though the king himself was not in attendance, he was well represented at the feast. His brother Gloucester, his sister, brother-in-law of Suffolk and a group of squires dressed in his livery were there, as well as the sergeant of his ewery who served as ewerer. It was his job to oversee the covering of tables with cloth of varying degrees of luxury and fineness, as well as the provision and serving of 'damask water to wash in after dinner'.[32]

Warwick was steward and had general oversight of the whole operation and worked closely with the marshall, Sir Walter Morley, and the sewer, Sir Richard Strangeways. Prior to the arrival of 'the estates sitting at the high table in the hall', that is the archbishop, the Bishops of London, Durham and Ely, the duke of Suffolk and the earls of Oxford and Worcester,

> the sewer goes to the dresser and there takes assay of every dish and gives it to the steward and the cook to eat of all porridges, mustard and other sauces. He takes the assay with cornets of trencher bread of his own cutting, and that is

thus: he takes a cornet of bread in his hand and touches three parts of the dish and makes a flourish over it and gives it to the aforenamed persons to eat, and of every stewed meat, roasted, boiled or broiled, being fish or flesh, he cuts a little thereof etc. And if it be baked meat covered, uncover it and take assay thereof as you do of sauces, and that is with cornets of bread, and so with all other meats, as custards, tarts and jelly, with other such like.[33]

The pantler for this feast was Sir John Malyberry, who is difficult to identify further. It was his duty to 'bring forth salt, bread and trenchers, with one broad and one narrow knife and one spoon, and set the salt right under the middle of the cloth of estate, the trenchers before the salt and the bread before the trenchers … properly wrapped in a napkin'. He set the knives and spoon in their proper places, 'all to be covered with a coverpane of cloth of fine silk'. He then oversaw the setting of the various tables of estate with 'salt, bread, trenchers, napkins, spoons and one broad knife'.[34]

The sewer was in charge of table service and communication with the kitchens. Once he had ascertained that the cooks were ready, he informed the marshall and an elaborate ritual began, with the uncovering of salt, assaying of bread, the carving of meat and, finally, the serving of food and wine to the archbishop.[35]

The same ritual was conducted in the other chambers, each with their own table of estate. In the 'chief chamber', the young duke of Gloucester sat with his sister the duchess of Suffolk, the countesses of Westmorland and Northumberland and Warwick's daughters Isobel and Anne. In the second chamber the dowager duchess of Suffolk sat at the high table, with the countess of Warwick and George's sisters, the countess of Oxford, lady Hastings and lady Fitzhugh. In the great chamber, the place of honour was given to the Bishops of Lincoln, Chester, Exeter and Carlisle. Four hundred 'gentlemen, franklins and head yeomen' and 400 servants ate in the low hall and the gallery, each in two sittings. They enjoyed service without the flourishes and the rituals. While they shared in a richer feast by far than was their usual lot, the fancier dishes, the subtleties and the best wine did not find their way to those crowded tables.[36]

With the exception of one table in the second chamber, and the lone male presence of Gloucester among the women in the chief chamber, men and women were quite separated at this feast. This was not unheard of, particularly when the focus of a feast was a churchman, but it was not the usual practice. Getting the seating right was quite a task in itself. With four chambers, and four tables of high estate, it had to be done carefully to ensure no breach of protocol or insult. It was better, for example, to seat the king's brother and sister at a table of honour in a secondary chamber than at a secondary table in the great hall with the archbishop. The place given to Alice Chaucer, dowager duchess of Suffolk, not only reflected her rank but the affection and respect she was held in by the grandchildren of her second husband.[37]

Attitudes towards this feast have varied over the centuries since. While there is no doubt the driving force behind it was Warwick and Montagu's pride in their younger brother's elevation to archbishop, it has been seen by some commentators as a deliberate attempt to outdo, and outspend, the king. Edward's marriage to Elizabeth Wydeville went some way towards changing his relationship with Warwick, though in 1465 there were no signs of the trouble to come. Warwick did not attend the queen's coronation in May, nor was he as comfortable as he had once been in the changing atmosphere of the royal court.[38]

Like many revolutionaries and rebels, before and since, Warwick may have struggled with the transition from taking the throne and holding it in the teeth of determined opposition to a peaceful and stable reign. He was a man of action and great energy. While Montagu was content to serve Edward in the north and, more particularly, in the marches towards Scotland, Warwick needed more. His advice and service to the king had, for more than four years, been received with great appreciation and thanks. Now, with peace at home, both of them could turn their attention to matters of foreign policy. It was this arena, rather than the king's marriage or George Nevill's extravagant feast, that would test their relationship to breaking point.

# PART 5

# THE NEVILLS IN REBELLION

# 30

# RUMBLINGS OF DISCONTENT

rchbishop Nevill was ill in bed in his London house in June 1467 when the king came to call. It was not a social visit; Edward had not come to enquire after his chancellor's health. He came to remove him from his post. Saying he would wait until they were brought to him, Edward demanded the return of the great seals. If George was well enough to rise from his bed and protest, to offer the king wine and refreshments and try to make sense of this turn of events, he met with failure. The seals were removed from his house and King Edward rode away. Almost immediately, the seals were delivered to the Bishop of Bath and Wells, Robert Stillington.[1]

Edward did not set down his reasons for dismissing the chancellor in any form that has survived. It was surely not incompetence, as George had held the position for seven years without his abilities being questioned. He was an able administrator and had demonstrated that over his years as chancellor of the University of Oxford and, since 1465, Archbishop of York. It was true he had ambitions yet to be fulfilled. Like his great uncle Henry Beauchamp, and his predecessor John Kemp, George Nevill saw himself in a cardinal's hat. It was not an unreasonable ambition for someone of his class and ability but his intrigues with Rome, and his determination to step into his brother's shoes whenever Warwick was absent from England, may have tried Edward's patience.[2]

Historically, George has often been viewed as little more than Warwick's creature. While that may hold true to some extent, particularly politically, there were two significant areas of George's life in which Warwick had little, if any, influence – religion and scholarship. George's piety was both conventional and conservative. Early in his tenure as Archbishop of York, he addressed growing concerns about heresy at a grassroots level. He instructed parish priests to 'declare four times a year … the fourteen articles of faith, the ten commandments, the two gospel precepts concerning charity, the seven works of mercy, the seven mortal sins, seven virtues and seven sacraments'. His experience in administration and record-keeping drew his attention to deficiencies in the archdiocesan records. At his first provincial council meeting, he put measures in place to remedy the shortcomings and, as far as was possible, fill in the gaps.[3]

George was also an able arbitrator. A dispute between the Abbey of St Marys and the congregation of the church of St Olave in York had dragged on so long that the church had fallen into disrepair and disuse. The abbot was of the view that repairs and maintenance should be paid for by parishioners who, in turn, saw the church as part of the abbey and, therefore, the abbey's responsibility. This latter view had been upheld by previous archbishops but the abbey had done nothing to provide for the upkeep of the church. When the case was turned over to George, he found that St Olave's was, indeed, a parish church but put forward a solution that was acceptable to both parties. The parishioners were to make repairs over the next two years, and the abbey would contribute the wood of twenty oak trees and £10 towards costs. The abbey was also to provide holy vestments and vessels, a font and a cemetery, and reconsecrate the church once the building works were completed.[4]

George did not take up full-time residence in his archdiocese, though he did visit once a year for an extended period. When in York, he stayed either at Bishopthorpe Palace or Cawood Castle. He also had an official residence in London, York Place, and a private house in Herefordshire where he stayed when he had business in Oxford. George's favourite house was the Moor in Rickmansworth just outside London. The Moor was his most private residence. Here he could hunt in the 600 acres of park and woodland; here he could entertain visiting scholars; here he could be, for a time, neither chancellor nor archbishop. Just how the manor came to be in George's possession is not easy to tease out. Once the property of the Abbey of St Albans, it passed into private hands through a series of leases. By 1462, George 'had purchased and built it right commodiously and pleasantly'.[5]

George's piety may have been conservative, but his interest in scholarship was anything but. Along with Bishop Waynflete, George was one of the first and most important patrons of Greek studies in England. From some time in the 1460s to 1472, he employed a refugee from Byzantium, Emmanuel of Constantinople, as a scribe. Emmanuel taught Greek to both George and his secretary, later Bishop of Durham John Shirwood, dedicating a volume of orations by Demosthenes to his patron and friend in 1468.[6]

The last three years had been a time of consolidation for the fledgling Yorkist dynasty and the Nevill family alike. The shock of the king's marriage died down. On 23 June 1464, Warwick's illegitimate daughter Margaret married Richard Huddlestone, son of a Nevill retainer of long standing. In 1465, George Nevill took up his new role as Archbishop of York with energy and commitment. Montagu, now earl of Northumberland, settled his family into Alnwick Castle, their magnificent new home. He had a son now, as well as several daughters. Young George was born on 22 February 1465 and was still an infant when he was betrothed to the king's niece Anne Holland.[7]

In July, Henry VI's years of wandering finally came to an end.

> Also the same year, king Harry was taken beside a house of religion in Lancashire, by the means of a black monk of Abingdon, in a wood called Clitherwood beside Bungerley Hippingstone by Thomas Talbot ... and John Talbot his cousin of Colebury, with others more; and carried to London on horseback, and his legs bound to the stirrups, and so brought through London to the Tower, where he was kept long time by two squires and two yeomen of the crown and their men.[8]

Also in 1465, the king entrusted his youngest brother Richard, duke of Gloucester into Warwick's care and custody. Gloucester came to live at Middleham, where he soon met Warwick's ward Francis Lovell, and the two quickly developed a lifelong friendship. Gloucester was given a place of honour at George Nevill's enthronement feast, where he sat with his sister of Suffolk and Warwick's daughters Isobel and Anne.[9]

In Calais, Warwick introduced strict new ordinances for the garrison. Concerned at the number of irregular relationships between the women of Calais and soldiers under his command, Warwick ordered his men to either marry their lovers or end their relationships. Men who refused to obey were to be dismissed, the women expelled from Calais.[10]

On 11 February 1466, Edward and his queen welcomed their first child, Elizabeth. Warwick was not only the new princess's godfather but presided over the queen's churching. Fitzhugh's loyalty was finally recognised and rewarded: during a three-month stay at Middleham from July, Warwick appointed his brother-in-law his deputy in the west march. That same year, there was something of a setback with the breaking of the betrothal between Montagu's son George and Anne Holland. Queen Elizabeth paid the duchess of Exeter 4,000 marks to secure the marriage for her older son Thomas. This may have annoyed or even angered the Nevills, but the breaking of betrothals between children was not unusual. Marriage was as much a business matter as anything else, and the queen outbid Montagu for Anne Holland's hand. Anne and Thomas were married in October of that year.[11]

Although he was also busy with his domestic concerns and responsibilities, much of Warwick's time during these three years was taken up with diplomacy. In the first few years of Edward's reign, foreign rulers, particularly on the continent, were reluctant to enter into long-term agreements with the English. Strife between France, Burgundy and Brittany added an extra dimension of difficulty. By 1465, Edward IV's hold on the throne was firm and the three continental powers were all keen to do a deal.

For the first few years of Edward's reign, he and Warwick had been of one mind when it came to foreign policy. Their first priority had been to secure the throne and they worked to cut off as many avenues of support and refuge for the Lancastrian remnant as they could. Their success with the Scots in this regard took a good deal of the pressure off and now they could turn their thoughts to more normalised foreign relations. Edward would have preferred peace and friendship with as many nations as possible, but Warwick was more pragmatic and understood a choice needed to be made between Burgundy and France.[12]

Burgundy's ongoing policy of giving shelter to several Lancastrian exiles, such as Somerset and Exeter, was a huge stumbling block in Warwick's mind. Alliance with France was a better, if less popular, option. England, and Edward, would need to give up any hope of making good the historical claim to the throne of France and this was not an easy policy to sell.[13]

In the summer of 1465, both Burgundy and Brittany had rebelled against King Louis. England had a choice between siding with France or joining the rebellious dukes in a triple alliance, a far more appealing prospect for the general population. The major obstacle to this was Burgundy. Edward had passed trade laws that impacted negatively on Burgundy, and a trade ban was put in place. In his attempts to placate English cloth manufacturers and merchants, Edward lost a valuable market for their goods and made it more difficult for his diplomats to treat with Burgundy. Embassies to both Burgundy and France were scheduled for May 1465 but were postponed due to the conflict.[14]

In spring the following year, Warwick and Wenlock were sent across the Channel for talks with representatives of Burgundy and France. There was no anticipation they would return from either conference with a draft treaty in their hands. This was a fishing expedition.[15]

In Burgundy, the priority was finding a way to end the trade war. Duke Philip of Burgundy was represented by his son, the recently widowed Charles of Charolais, and he proposed a marriage for himself with Edward IV's sister Margaret. Warwick's lack of enthusiasm for an alliance with Burgundy may initially have been based on Burgundy's ongoing support for the exiles but it was exacerbated by an almost instant dislike between the two men. As the writer of the *Croyland Chronicle* commented, 'if great princes have a desire to continue [as] friends … they ought never to meet'.[16]

[T]he earl of Warwick came to visit the duke of Burgundy [*sic*], and ever afterward a mortal hatred continued between them.[17]

[I]t being much against [Warwick's] wishes that the views of Charles, now duke of Burgundy [*sic*], be in any way promoted by means of an alliance with England. The fact is that he pursued that man with a most deadly hatred.[18]

No clues have been left as to the reason for this mutual antipathy. Ideological differences and Burgundy's support of the exiles might account for a tension or a coolness between the two men, but 'hatred' is too strong an emotion to be explained by political differences alone. By the same token, personal animosity is too glib an explanation for Warwick's ongoing resistance to an alliance with Burgundy. Warwick was, in many ways, driven by emotion but Wenlock was not.

In 1466, John Wenlock was around 60 years old. As a young man, he had fought in France under Henry V. His diplomatic career began in the 1440s and he was closely associated with the then duke of Suffolk, and was part of the team that brokered the marriage between Henry VI and Margaret of Anjou. For a time, he was Queen Margaret's chamberlain and in 1447 he was knighted. During the 1450s, particularly after the murder of Suffolk, Wenlock had been sliding towards the cause of Richard, duke of York. This brought his loyalty to Henry VI into question and he was suspended from his post and encouraged to leave England to go on pilgrimage. At the first battle of St Albans, he fought by his king's side and was seriously wounded.[19]

The turning point for Wenlock came in 1458, when he joined Viscount Bourchier and the earls of Salisbury and Warwick on an embassy to France. After decades of loyal service to the Lancastrian kings, Wenlock returned from that journey a staunch Nevill partisan. He joined the rebels at Ludlow in 1459 and, after their overnight departure, followed Warwick and Salisbury to Calais. He fought with distinction at Towton and Edward IV quickly came to see his value as both a soldier and a diplomat. In 1462, Wenlock was admitted to the Order of the Garter and elevated to the peerage. He and Warwick developed a strong working relationship and were a formidable team.[20]

Both men found dealing with France more to their liking than dealing with Burgundy and they soon developed a strong rapport with Louis XI. The French king spared little expense in feting Warwick's embassies, showering them with expensive gifts of gold and silver, silk and velvet. Louis also offered favourable trade terms and a princess of Savoy as a wife for the young duke of Gloucester. His aim was to flatter and dazzle, but Warwick's reasons for preferring and promoting a French alliance went beyond personal considerations and hopes of material gain.[21]

Edward turned over responsibility for treating with Burgundy to his father-in-law Rivers. While a non-aggression pact was agreed and the proposed marriage with the king's sister was further discussed, Burgundy refused to shift on the trade ban on English cloth. It was partly to nudge Burgundy in the right direction that Warwick and Wenlock were sent to France in June 1467. While they were away, a great tournament was held at Smithfield between Anthony Wydeville and the Bastard of Burgundy. Behind the scenes, more serious negotiations took place. Nothing was finalised, however, as duke Philip died on 15 June and the Burgundy delegation returned home.[22]

Warwick arrived back in England to find that his brother had been dismissed as chancellor. Angered by this, and by the knowledge that his most recent trip to France had been nothing more than a smokescreen, in September he was left to engage and entertain a party of French ambassadors kept waiting by the king for six weeks. With the interrupted talks with Burgundy resumed, the trade ban lifted and the marriage between duke Charles and Margaret of York settled, Warwick could take no more. Soon after the departure of the French, he left court and went north to Middleham. On 30 September 1467, Margaret of York formally agreed to the marriage with Charles of Burgundy.[23]

The first murmurs of suspicion that Warwick was rethinking his loyalty to Edward IV came that autumn. A captured messenger sent by Margaret of Anjou to her small band of supporters holed up in Harlech Castle in Wales repeated gossip current in France implicating Warwick.[24]

> There is a fresh report that M Charolais has again opened secret negotiations to take king Edward's sister to wife, confirming once more the old league with the English. If this takes place, they have talked of treating with the earl of Warwick to restore king Henry in England, and the ambassador of the old queen is already here.[25]

While this is likely to have been an attempt by King Louis to unsettle both England and Burgundy, and at least postpone the wedding, Edward took it seriously enough to summon Warwick to London to answer the charges. Warwick refused, demanding his accuser be sent to him in Yorkshire. Warwick was easily able to refute the charges and Edward accepted his denials with good grace.[26]

There was another reason for Edward to be concerned about Warwick's intentions. He had for some time been seeking, in secret, a papal dispensation for his daughter Isobel to marry the king's brother George, duke of Clarence. When Edward discovered this, he put a stop to the plan, declaring that neither of his brothers was to marry without his consent, whatever their private wishes might be.[27]

Even without Warwick, and even with the treaty with Burgundy, diplomatic missions to France continued. In August, Warwick's secretary Robert

Nevill travelled to France 'to negotiate a truce with his Majesty and say that they are content to have an understanding and friendship together, and also to treat about the marriage of that sovereign's second daughter, although they say she is somewhat deformed in person, chiefly in one shoulder, to king Edward's brother'.[28]

In October, Edward risked the shaky goodwill of both Warwick and the Archbishop of York. George had been working for a cardinal's hat for some time and Edward himself had asked the pope to appoint an English cardinal. When the decision came, it was the Archbishop of Canterbury, Thomas Bourchier who was chosen. It is difficult to understand why Edward chose to send the letter confirming Bourchier's appointment to George Nevill's house. If it was a joke, it was particularly pointed – George should be content with what he had and understand just how terminal the loss of his king's confidence was. It was a bitter blow for the ambitious archbishop.[29]

Warwick's ill mood lasted for the rest of 1467. Italian historian Polydor Vergil imagines a conversation had between him and his brothers during the dark winter days. It would seem likely that Warwick, George and Montagu did gather at Middleham at some point. There was a lot to discuss and they were, after all, brothers. Vergil's version of events is out of time, but it might stand as a fair representation of the dynamic between the three men, not over the course of a single conversation but several years: '[Warwick] found a suitable occasion to complain about the king and share his plan' to depose Edward IV and restore Henry.[30]

Henry, Vergil has Warwick declare, was 'a most pious man, very friendly to his followers and he remembered favours done him'. He had a son 'born to praise, grace and liberality, from whom every man can expect yet more and who will support his father in his calamity'. Edward IV, on the other hand, 'is insulting, ungrateful, given over to pleasure and shuns labour. He has decided to put upstarts in places of honour in lieu of gentlemen of ancient breeding'. From the very start, he 'begrudged our house of its honour'.[31]

> [Warwick] easily induced the archbishop to his side with him, but not so [Montagu], since originally he could not be led to approve of making any kind of attempt against Edward. But in the end, when Warwick promised that many nobles would contribute their help and their wealth, he was drawn into the alliance.[32]

If these were Warwick's sentiments, the winter of 1467–68 was too early for them to be given voice. It was certainly too early for Montagu to join the conspiracy. He was content with his lot and, unlike Warwick and George, had not felt the sting of Edward's perceived ingratitude and growing distrust. Rather than Warwick persuading his brothers to come round to his way of thinking, to buy into his disaffection, it is more likely that between them they managed to keep Warwick from taking the kind of action they would all come to regret.[33]

Summoned to council in January 1468, Warwick refused to attend while the king kept about him such men as the Herberts, the Wydevilles and lord Audley. It was George who soothed the troubled waters on this occasion, persuading his brother to make the journey to Coventry and brokering a reconciliation of sorts. Warwick was prepared to come to terms with the Herbert brothers, but he flatly refused to countenance any such rapprochement with Rivers and his son: 'many murmurous tales ran in the city between the earl of Warwick and the queen's blood.'[34]

However much Warwick and Edward wished to be reconciled, their foreign policy differences lay between them, an unbridgeable chasm. Edward wanted Warwick's support for a triple alliance between England, Burgundy and Brittany. Warwick was against it, both seeing the dangers should either Brittany or Burgundy crumple under the weight of France, and the advantages that long-term peace with France would bring.[35]

Edward needed guarantors to cover the down payment of Margaret of York's dowry. Though it would have cost him little in financial terms, Warwick refused to help. He would not back down when it came to treating with Burgundy and he would not give Edward his approval for the marriage.[36]

Louis XI was not happy with the idea of the new duke of Burgundy marrying the King of England's sister and did all he could to stir up trouble. As is frequently the case, the moral reputation of a woman was used as ammunition. The wedding had already been postponed several times due to Edward's insolvency and duke Charles was anxious for it to go ahead. Perhaps influenced by Louis XI's unique spin, the Milanese ambassador reported a rather more sinister reason for Charles's impatience.[37]

> [B]ecause he is informed of what more and more people know, to wit that his future consort in the past has been somewhat devoted to love affairs, indeed in the opinion of many she even has a son, he has issued a public edict and ordinance that no one in his country, in the presence of his lordship or elsewhere in private or public, shall be so bold as to make mention or speak of such a thing, under pain of being thrown into the river forthwith, when he is found in such error.[38]

In June, recognising he could do nothing now to prevent her marriage, Warwick escorted Margaret of York on the first leg of her journey. Margaret rode pillion behind her cousin when they left London in procession. He took her as far as Margate, where she was to take ship, but he did not cross the Channel to attend the wedding. Nor did Edward IV. There were plenty who did, and they reported a most splendid celebration lasting several days.[39]

The presence of the Lancastrian exiles in Bruges, and the support they received from duke Charles and his father Philip before him, had been of concern to Edward IV, and more particularly to Warwick, for some time. If nothing else, the wedding served to change that.

> Other tidings have we none here, but that the duke of Somerset, and all his bands departed well seen out of Bruges a day before that my lady the duchess came there, and they say here that he is to queen Margaret that was, and shall no more come here again, nor be helped by the duke.[40]

If Warwick expected his return to court and council to mark the end of his troubles, he was mistaken. When France invaded Brittany, the terms of the tripartite agreement were invoked and Edward was called on to provide military support. Edward hoped Warwick would release his brother Montagu to lead the expedition to Brittany, but Montagu was still needed in the north. Instead, Edward sent Scales with a force to cross the Channel. They did little more than retake Jersey but Scales was rewarded with the governorship of the Channel Isles, a prize that had long eluded Warwick.[41]

In October, fearing his duchy would suffer the same fate as Brittany, Charles of Burgundy signed a treaty with France. England was now isolated, Edward IV's tripartite alliance in tatters. Scales's expeditionary force sailed for home. Warwick may have been proved right but it came at a cost – the breaking of the partnership that had brought the young earl of March from exile in Calais to the throne. Despite the rumours in France, which may have been made up from whole cloth and deliberately spread by Louis XI, Warwick was not at this stage even close to contemplating the restoration of Henry VI. Not that the exiled Lancastrians would have welcomed his help if he had been thinking along these lines. 'There was nobody more difficult for Lancaster to reconcile with than their destroyer, the most ruthless and merciless of their opponents.'[42]

Not long after this, another Lancastrian conspiracy was uncovered, implicating both the Mayor of London and a servant of Wenlock. Oxford, also implicated in the plot, turned king's evidence, thus securing his own life and safety. Henry Courtenay, son of the executed earl of Devon, and Hungerford's heir Thomas were executed for their part in the conspiracy and suspicion edged dangerously close to Warwick's most trusted friends. He cannot have been unaware of Oxford's continuing contact with the Lancastrian exiles though there was nothing to suggest he himself was involved in any way. Perhaps erring on the side of caution, or because he had real concerns about Warwick's loyalty, Edward recalled his brother Gloucester to court, removing him from Warwick's care and tutelage.[43]

Whatever reservations, doubts or suspicions may have hung over the two men, there was, on one occasion, something of a return of the old intimacy between Warwick and Edward. It was in the king's chambers that Warwick and his brother George had 'language' with Norfolk. Warwick also felt confident and comfortable enough to continue to argue the case for alliance with France but Edward would not be moved. While Warwick still saw himself as Edward's natural chief councillor and advisor, Edward did not. It was important to the king that he retain his cousin's goodwill and friendship, but he would not forego his right to choose his own counsel. Edward was coming to rely more and more on his father-in-law Rivers.[44]

Warwick was not alone in his response to the rise of the Wydevilles. Earl Rivers's estates in Kent were plundered during riots and even King Edward's jester, 'wearing high boots and clutching a staff', made him the butt of a joke that quickly, in fifteenth-century terms, went viral. 'I have passed through many countries of your realm, and in places that I have passed the rivers have been so high that I could hardly escape through them, but was fain to search the depth with this long staff.'[45]

Warwick was in Calais in April 1469, where he engaged in talks with Charles of Burgundy and representatives of the Holy Roman Emperor. In June, while Edward IV was on pilgrimage to Our Lady of Walsingham, Warwick was in Sandwich for the relaunch of his flagship *Trinity*. He did not go alone.[46]

On the Monday following [12 June], the ... archbishop [of York] with great solemnity blessed the great ship called *The Trinity*, which Richard Nevill earl of Warwick had recently had built. Present at that solemn service were George duke of Clarence, Richard earl of Warwick, the archbishop of York, the bishop of London and one Oxney prior of Christ Church Canterbury. These three put on their vestments in the town of Sandwich and crossed over by boat to the ship where the archbishop celebrated high mass. Singers of this church present at mass, three monks together with all the boys. And in the second hour they went to dinner, and it was past the fifth hour before they had finished eating.[47]

Two days later, the duchess of York arrived in Canterbury: 'the next day she left for Sandwich where she joined her son the duke of Clarence.' She did not stay long. Something was going on that the duchess of York may have been hoping, at the last minute, to put a stop to. Like his brother the king, Clarence had taken the decision of who to marry into his own hands: 'The following day at Calais, the said archbishop [George Nevill] solemnised the marriage between George duke of Clarence and the lady [Isobel], daughter of Richard Nevill earl of Warwick.'[48]

The wedding itself was no hole-in-the-corner secret ceremony but a most splendid affair, befitting the brother of a king and the daughter of the most powerful man in the kingdom. Among the guests were earl of Oxford and 'five other knights of the garter, and many other lords and ladies, and worshipful knights, well accompanied with wise and discreet esquires, in right great number'.[49]

The next day, a manifesto was issued, under the joint names of Clarence, Warwick and the Archbishop of York. They would be in Canterbury in four days, they declared, and they called the lords and commons of England to join them and 'to dispose and array yourselves to accompany us thither, with as many persons defensibly arrayed as you can make'.[50]

There was no danger of a swift response from Edward IV, as Warwick knew. He was on his way north, to deal with a sudden rebellion that had risen in Yorkshire under the banner of one Robin of Redesdale. A rebellion led by prominent members of the Nevill affinity, organised, equipped and financed entirely by the earl of Warwick.

# 31

# ROBIN OF REDESDALE AND THE CAPTURE OF THE KING

he manifesto of 12 July 1469 followed the pattern laid down by previous Yorkist manifestos in the late 1450s and early 1460s. The king, and England, were beset by the 'deceivable and covetous rule and guiding of certain seditious persons'. The realm had been driven to poverty and the rule of law disturbed, the king's 'true subjects, with piteous lamentations, calling upon us and other lords to be means to our said sovereign lord for a remedy and reformation'.[1]

The manifesto named Rivers, the king's father-in-law and treasurer of England, his sons and his wife; William Herbert, earl of Pembroke; Humphrey Stafford, earl of Devon; lord Audley; John Fogge 'and others of mischievous rule opinion and assent'. William Herbert was one of Edward IV's new-made men. He and his father had both served the cause of York since 1455. In 1453, Herbert senior had been appointed Sheriff of Glamorgan and, at that time, worked closely with Warwick. After the battle of Northampton in 1460, Herbert had been commissioned to keep order in Wales. He enjoyed great success in this, negotiating the surrender of Pembroke Castle in 1461 and taking custody of the fatherless Henry Tudor. He represented Herefordshire in the Commons before being elevated to the earldom of Pembroke in February 1462. Herbert soon became a part of Edward IV's intimate circle, his oldest son marrying the queen's sister Mary in 1467. He was rewarded with lands and positions of authority in Wales and, by 1468, was in a position to take the last remaining Lancastrian stronghold, Harlech Castle. Herbert's subsequent domination of Wales was unprecedented.[2]

William Herbert's life and career are most often viewed through the filter of a specifically English conflict but his importance in Wales, and to the Welsh, should not be forgotten. He was the close friend of an English king but his home in Wales was a centre of Welsh culture. Herbert's patronage of itinerant poets, a far more organised and professional career in Wales than in England, points to a strong and enduring sense of his own nationality and heritage.[3]

Herbert's advancement in Wales no doubt impacted on Warwick's own ambitions in the principality. Edward IV, however, can hardly be faulted for his prudent use of the resources he had available to him – the Nevills in the north of England and the Herberts in Wales. Warwick is often accused of unreconstructed snobbery – characterised by his dislike of 'upstarts' and the raising of men of low birth to stations they did not deserve. This is, perhaps, a rather more simplistic view of Warwick than he deserves. He certainly had no problem brokering a marriage between his sister Katherine and the newly created lord Hastings. Nor did he object to his brother John's elevation, first to the barony and later to the ranks of England's earls. Robert Ogle, a long-standing member of the Nevill affinity, was also made a lord in the 1460s. Warwick had little problem with the concept of the creation of new nobles, so long as they were not men he disliked personally or who he felt threatened his own position. Both of these concerns applied in the case of William Herbert.

When it came to earl Rivers, Warwick's long-standing antipathy was no secret. William Herbert could at least point to his demonstrated abilities when defending his dizzying rise to both an earldom and intimacy with the king. Questions about Rivers's abilities had been raised as far back as his service in Calais under Richard Beauchamp's captaincy. After Warwick's appointment to the position, Rivers was dismissed from his post. In the early months of 1460, when Somerset was forced to seek shelter in Guines Castle, he held Rivers largely responsible for his unpreparedness to take Calais. Later that year, commissioned to hold the town of Sandwich and guard Henry VI's fleet, Rivers had not only allowed the king's ships to be captured but had been taken prisoner himself, along with his son. Now he was treasurer of England and father of the queen. If Warwick saw him as a man who had risen above his natural abilities on the back of, first, his own marriage and, second, the marriage of his daughter, he may not have been so far from the mark as has been suggested.[4]

It should not be forgotten, however, that Warwick was not above acting out of personal vengeance and vindictiveness. His treatment of members of the Calais garrison he deemed disloyal, the beheading of Osbert Mountfort and the executions after the battle of Hexham give sufficient evidence of this. On the other hand, his protestations about the government of England should not be dismissed too quickly. As in 1455 and 1459, there were real concerns in 1469 and, as subsequent events would show, Edward IV's popularity was waning quite dangerously.

Warwick and Edward had both lost a father and a brother in the struggle to reform Henry VI's government. Now, with unpopular and even undeserving councillors close to Edward's ear and his old associates and blood kin pushed aside, the promises of reform and good government rang hollow. The named culprits had 'advised and caused our said sovereign lord to give … livelihoods and possessions to them above their deserts and degrees, so that he may not live honourably and maintain his estates and charges ordinary within this land'. A set of articles issued by the leaders of the Yorkshire rebellion, but surely written by Warwick himself, likened the current state of affairs in England to the reigns of Edward II, Richard II and Henry VI. Drawing parallels between Edward IV and these three failed and deposed kings was a stark and frightening warning.[5]

The three lords were well received in Canterbury when they arrived on 16 July, and many men flocked to their side. Two days later, they were in London, where they were also well received, though with perhaps a little less enthusiasm. The city offered them a £1,000 loan to aid their cause or, perhaps, speed their departure. London's mayor and council could not, of course, show any sign of disloyalty to the king, but they also 'had to reckon with Warwick's popularity among the commons and the danger of pillage and bloodshed if they resisted him'. Warwick and his party left for Coventry the following day, to join up with the rebels marching under the name of Robin of Redesdale.[6]

Edward IV was already in Newark, no doubt hoping for a swift victory over a band of unorganised rebels. An earlier rising, led by one Robin of Holderness, had already been put down by Montagu at the gates of York and the captain executed. Robin of Holderness's concerns had been unfair taxation and a bid to have Henry Percy restored to his family title and lands. It was thus very much in Montagu's interests to suppress it as quickly and as finally as he could. When news reached London of yet another northern revolt, Edward IV had ridden out with an alarmingly small army. He had just his brother Gloucester, Hastings, Rivers and Scales with him.[7]

Unlike the decisive action he had taken against the earlier rebels, Montagu did little to prevent the movements of Robin of Redesdale's army. He was not yet committed to his brothers' cause, but nor was he prepared to take up arms against the prominent members of his family's affinity who led the rising. These included John and William Conyers, and Robert, lord Ogle, all of whom have been identified as the 'real' Robin of Redesdale, but there are as many arguments against each as there are in favour. It may well be that Robin of Redesdale will never be definitively identified, though it is likely John Conyers was the overall leader of the enterprise.[8]

As the rebels moved further south, Edward IV finally realised the seriousness of the situation. As the Wydevilles featured prominently in both the manifesto and the rebel articles, Edward sent them away for their own safety,

Rivers and John Wydeville to Wales and Scales to Norfolk. In Nottingham, Edward set about recruiting men to his banner, but met with little success. Though Herbert and Stafford were on their way, Edward had few others he could count on.[9]

The one thing historians agree on about the battle of Edgecote Moor is that it was poorly recorded and understood. Even the date is in dispute, with most chroniclers citing 26 July. It is more likely to have taken place two days earlier, on 24 July, as given in accounts written closest to the time itself. These consist of various Welsh poems, all written within a year of the battle. The very existence of these poems points to the importance of the battle in Welsh history. Far from a minor, half-remembered skirmish set within the larger picture of the Wars of the Roses, it is, from a Welsh perspective, a momentous event. The poems commemorate the deaths of many thousands of Welshmen and the destruction of the Herberts, a political disaster for Edward IV but both a personal and national tragedy in Wales.[10]

Robin of Redesdale's army bypassed the king in Nottingham. In doing so, he hoped simultaneously to cut Edward off from his fast-approaching reinforcements and join up with Warwick in Coventry. Still in Nottingham, Edward IV had not yet made the connection between his brother and cousins and the northern rebels. There had clearly been rumours for, on 9 July, Edward wrote three letters, calling on the three lords to join him. '[W]e trust not that you should be of any such disposition towards us as the rumour here runs, considering the trust and affection we bear in you.'[11]

Despite the trouble there had been between him and Warwick, despite his difficulties with the archbishop, despite Clarence's rank disobedience in the matter of his marriage, Edward could not countenance the idea they had come from Calais, Canterbury and London to do anything but support him. Clarence's marriage could, and would, be forgiven. With the Wydevilles gone from his company, Warwick would surely join his men with the approaching armies of Herbert and Stafford. The northern rebels would be dealt with and all would once again be well.

Perhaps this is why Edward failed to make a move. He was under-strength, that is certain, and had failed to rally the men of Nottingham behind him. He was content, as he had been since the great victory at Towton, to let other generals do the fighting. Not that he was a coward, as the next three years would show, but he was the king and close by were men who had more than proved themselves dependable. Edward did not understand the seriousness of the situation until it was too late.

On 10 July, Edward wrote to the Mayor of Coventry, requesting '100 archers well and defensibly arrayed'. Two days later, a letter written by Warwick late in June to 'his servants and wellwillers within the city' was received and read.

Forasmuch as it has pleased the king's good grace to send at this time for his lords and other his subjects to stand upon his highness northward, and that both the right high and mighty prince, my lord the duke of Clarence, and I be fully purposed, after the solemnisation of the marriage by God's grace in short time to be had between my lord and my daughter, to await on the same and to draw to our said sovereign lord highness, I therefore desire and pray you that you will in the meantime give knowledge to all such fellowship as you can make to ready them in the best wise you can, and that both you and they defensibly arrayed be ready upon a day's warning to accompany my said lord and me towards the said highness, as my especial trust is in you.[12]

On the face of it, these were the words of a loyal lord calling up his affinity in the service of their king. The words 'giving credence to the bearer of this letter in that he shall open to you on my behalf' would seem to indicate some rather more secret and sinister orders were to be given at the same time, by word of mouth.[13]

That same day, the mayor of Coventry received a second, more desperate, letter from Edward, asking that he 'send to us such men in defensible array as we late wrote to you for, with more if you goodly may, without fail'. This request was apparently granted, as the mayor received a further letter from the king on 29 July, thanking him for his faithful service.[14]

As Edward and Redesdale's armies marched blindly towards one another, an unexpected, and ultimately disastrous variable of human frailty came into play. Herbert and Stafford quarrelled and their armies split. At Banbury 'their harbingers fell at variance for lodgings, in so much that the said lord Stafford ... withdrew himself back ten or twelve miles.' Stafford had the bulk of the archers with him and he was not only far from Herbert's force but separated from it by the River Cherwell. When Robin of Redesdale's army set up camp nearby, it was too late in the night to fight but also too late for Stafford to rejoin Herbert.[15]

The details of the battle are difficult to piece together but it seems Herbert's men came under attack twice. He was forced to retreat after the first assault, the lack of archers hampering both his defence and attack. The northern army followed and attacked again. Around one in the afternoon, the vanguard of Stafford's army arrived, as did a group of men wearing Warwick's livery, which was taken to be the vanguard of a larger Nevill-led force. This both gave heart to the rebels and broke the resolve of Herbert's army, which turned and fled.[16]

Two thousand Welshmen were killed in the battle. William Herbert and his brother Richard were taken alive. On the rebel side, William Conyers and lord Latimer's son Henry lost their lives. Stafford, who was unlikely to have actually reached the battle itself by this time, took to his heels, though this did not save him.[17]

The lord of Devonshire, his service was worthless,
Fled – he didn't have a long life.[18]
and the lord Stafford, the which came too late to the field, returned into his
country, and was taken by the commons and beheaded at Bridgewater.[19]

Once again, with his enemies in his hands, Warwick demonstrated his ruthlessness and thirst for payback. With no legal justification whatsoever, after
the briefest of show trials, William and Richard Herbert were beheaded in
Coventry. Both Warwick and Montagu had, after previous battles, supervised the drumhead trials and executions of captured enemy combatants,
as had Edward IV himself after the battle of Towton. The Herberts may
have been 'enemy combatants' from Warwick's point of view but they were
demonstrably not enemies of the king and their deaths could not be justified
from any but the most partisan perspective.[20]

Edward IV did not learn of the defeat and deaths of the Herbert brothers
until he was on his way from Nottingham to Northampton in the last days
of July. When the news arrived, the king was abandoned wholesale by his
remaining supporters. Only his brother Gloucester and William Hastings
were willing to stand by him to the last. Confronted by Archbishop Nevill,
who had been sent to escort him to Coventry, Edward finally had to face
the fact of his brother's and cousins' disloyalty. The 16-year-old duke of
Gloucester was dismissed, free to go without hindrance. Perhaps Warwick
still held out hopes he could broker a marriage between the young man and
his daughter Anne. Hastings was also sent away, perhaps to be worked on at
a later date and brought around to Clarence and Warwick's side. Edward
had no choice but to let the archbishop take him to Coventry. From there, he
was escorted to Warwick Castle, Warwick's captive but not, as would soon
prove, his puppet. Just as York's ambitions, until 1460, began and ended
with the firm view he was by right of birth, ability and experience uniquely
qualified to act as Henry VI's chief councillor, so it was with Warwick and
Edward IV. In 1469, Warwick had no plans to depose Edward. He and the
archbishop both assured Edward of their continued loyalty.[21]

On their first arrival, in consequence of the extreme indignation which
[Edward IV] felt, he presented a lowering countenance; but after they had
fairly stated to him their intentions to remain firm in their allegiance, and had
resolutely exposed the treachery of those who had adhered to him, he became
more calm, and received them more freely into his favour and good will.[22]

Early in August, Rivers and his son John were captured and taken to
Coventry. Again, motivated by personal animosity and terminal ill will,
Warwick ordered both to be summarily beheaded. He must have thought

himself unassailable to take the lives of the queen's father and brother without authority or justification. Edward was fond of his father-in-law and it must have been hard to be away from Queen Elizabeth's side during this time. He could not, however, give in to grief or anger.[23]

Rumours swirled around the courts of Europe. The renewed instability of the English government was good news to some foreign rulers, such as King Louis of France, but others were very concerned. The duke of Milan received regular reports from both his envoy in England and his ambassador to France. On 16 August, the Milanese envoy had no hesitation in holding the queen and her family responsible for the current situation.

> She had five brothers and as many sisters, and had brought things to such a pass that they had the entire government of this realm, to such an extent that the rest of the lords about the government were one, the earl of Warwick, who has always been great and deservedly so. He made a plan rendering himself the chief man in the government.[24]

The same letter also reported the capture of King Edward. 'The earl of Warwick, as astute a man as ever was Ulysses, is at the king's side, and from what they say the king is not at liberty to go where he wishes.'[25]

Information was scant and uncertain. King Louis was reported to be waiting 'for more precise and better advice'. He was 'as puzzled as well as everyone else'. By November, Edward was reported to be with Warwick in the north of England, 'going freely to amuse himself by hunting wherever he chose'. On 8 December, the Milanese ambassador to France wrote that 'the king of England has recovered himself to a great extent'. On 29 December, there was still 'nothing clear from England but we hear that the king there is strongly reinforced and that he prospers constantly'. The realm, however, was 'plunged in war and the most serious troubles'. This was seen as good news for foreign rulers, as 'the English have enough to think about at home at present without making things unpleasant for others'.[26]

Despite their hesitancy, Milan's envoy and ambassador both had clearer information from and about England than they imagined. By the end of October 1469, Edward IV was once again at liberty and in control of the government. Warwick and Clarence had had great difficulty ruling in the name of a captive king. Warwick had no authority in his own right and could exercise little in Edward's name. With the king in custody, old feuds resurfaced in Gloucestershire, Lancashire and Yorkshire. The duke of Norfolk took the opportunity to lay siege to Caister Castle in Norfolk, to the great distress of the Paston family. London saw riots and lawlessness. Warwick summoned Parliament to York but quickly rescinded the command when events overtook him. Just what he and Clarence had been planning is not known for certain, but it may have been a joint protectorship at the very least, and the deposition of Edward and the election of Clarence as king at worst. It took another Nevill – a distant cousin, Humphrey of Brancepeth – to bring things to a head.[27]

Humphrey Nevill and his brother Charles rose in the north of England, their aim to rescue Henry VI from the Tower and reinstate him as king. Warwick intended to lead an army to oppose them but no one was prepared to raise troops on his behalf while the king remained a prisoner. Warwick's hand was forced.[28]

> Lest it should come to pass that the faithful subjects of the said king, in the southern parts of the kingdom, should attempt to avenge the commission of so great an injury, and liberate him from his captivity in [Warwick] castle, they now transferred him to Middleham castle, in the north, from which place, however, in a manner most miraculous, and beyond all expectation, he did not so much make his escape, as find himself released by the express consent of the earl of Warwick.[29]

Early in September, Edward was in York, demonstrably at liberty. It was only then that Warwick was able to raise the required troops and, without much difficulty, put down the revolt. Both Humphrey and Charles Nevill were brought to York and executed in the presence of the king. Neither Warwick nor the Archbishop of York could hope any longer to maintain custody and control of the king. '[A]nd there by fair speech and promise, the king escaped out of the bishop's hands and came to London, and did what him liked.'[30]

There could no longer be any pretence that the king was under Warwick's control. From York, Edward summoned his lords, the dukes of Gloucester and Suffolk, and Warwick's brother Montagu and brothers-in-law Hastings and Arundel. Warwick and Clarence's coup had collapsed.[31]

Any other of Edward's subjects might have expected swift retribution for their treasonous actions. Edward was, however, loath to punish his brother and the cousin he had shared so much with and relied on to win his crown. This should have served to dampen the rebellious spirits of both Warwick and Clarence, but neither, no matter how much Edward professed a desire for both peace and their counsel, was prepared to let things lie. Edward's customary practice of reconciliation and rehabilitation was to be sorely tested in the months to come.

# 32

# THE LINCOLNSHIRE REBELLION

> The king is come to London, and there came with him, and rode with him, the duke of Gloucester, the duke of Suffolk, the earl of Arundel, the earl of Northumberland, the earl of Essex, the lords Harry and John of Buckingham, the lord Dacres, the lord chamberlain [Hastings], the lord Mountjoy and many other knights and squires.[1]

His authority firmly re-established, Edward entered his capital in style and force. He had with him the brothers of the lords who had recently held him captive, as well as two of Warwick's brothers-in-law, Hastings and Arundel. The Archbishop of York and earl of Oxford were at the Moor, the archbishop's favourite home. When they attempted to join Edward, he sent them a message that they were not needed, 'that they should come when that he sent for them'.[2]

When Warwick returned to London some time before Christmas, he was made welcome by the king. As reported by John Paston, 'the king himself has good language of the lords of Clarence, of Warwick and my lords of York and Oxford, saying they be his best friends, but his household men have other language.' On the face of it, Warwick's crimes and Clarence's treachery against his brother are impossible to forgive, yet forgiveness was offered. That there were those around the king who looked askance at this and spoke of the recent rebels in less conciliatory tones should not be surprising. Warwick might have proved his worth in times past, but he had been most amply rewarded and his ingratitude must have grated on men less convinced of their own worth and more sure of their own loyalty.[3]

Queen Elizabeth was faced with the difficulty of reconciling herself with the man responsible for the deaths of her father and brother. If the queen must be an obedient and compliant wife and understand the political necessity for it, her mother need not. As soon as the opportunity arose, the widowed dowager duchess of Bedford brought a suit of wrongful death against Warwick and others she held responsible for her husband's execution.[4]

The establishment of peace between Edward, Warwick and Clarence was no easy undertaking.

> [T]here were repeated messages and embassies to and fro between the king and the dissatisfied nobles. In the end, a grand council of all the peers of the kingdom was summoned, and on a certain day which had been previously named, there appeared in the great chamber of parliament the duke of Clarence, the earl of Warwick, and the rest of their confederates; upon which, peace and entire oblivion of the grievances on both sides were agreed to.[5]

While this may have been good news for England, it was not received so well in France. On 10 January 1470, the Milanese ambassador to France wrote to his master: 'From England we hear that the king and the earl of Warwick are thoroughly agreed together. We also hear that they are preparing a fleet to descend upon France, but this seems unlikely.' It was more than just 'unlikely'. Whatever else they agreed about, foreign policy differences still divided Edward IV and Warwick.

At this time, Edward was giving serious consideration to the restoration of Henry Percy to his family estates and title. This would, of course, impact heavily on John Nevill. If Percy were to be reinstated as earl of Northumberland, then Montagu must give the title up. Edward had been given no cause to question Montagu's loyalty. He may have let the leaders of Robin of Redesdale's army slip past him, but he was not implicated in his brothers' attempted coup. He had, after all, been by Edward's side when he triumphantly entered his capital in October. While Edward may have wished to break the Nevill hegemony in the north, or at least temper it, it is unlikely his decision was designed to test Montagu's loyalty. What is more likely is that his loyalty was taken for granted. Edward felt he could take back the rewards he had only recently bestowed on Montagu with fair compensation. Montagu lost an earldom but he was to be elevated: from now on he would be Marquis Montagu. He was given forfeited Courtenay properties in Devon, far from his family's heartland. His son George was to be duke of Bedford and betrothed to Edward's daughter Elizabeth, cementing the Nevill connection to the royal family.[6]

This betrothal was designed to make continued loyalty to Edward more attractive to Montagu than taking his brothers' side in any future quarrel with the king. If Warwick and the Archbishop of York came to identify the family's future prosperity and position with their new connection to Edward, and distanced themselves from Clarence, all the better.[7]

Montagu's son and Edward's daughter were still children, it should be remembered, and many things could happen before they reached adulthood. The betrothal could be broken, as many had in the past and would be in the future. Either party might die. Edward and his queen may yet have a son. Edward IV himself was not yet 30 years old. He was hale and hearty. His queen, though older, had already proved herself fertile, giving birth to three daughters in three years. But gambling present disaffection against potential benefits long into the future, with no guarantees the same conditions would apply, was not Warwick's style.[8]

From Clarence's point of view, the betrothal served only to further isolate him from the centre of power. The settlement of the succession on Elizabeth of York removed Clarence as his brother's heir presumptive. Clarence had come out of the 1469 campaign with nothing more than a pardon, which was more than most men could have hoped for under the circumstances, and a public display of reconciliation with his brother the king. His personal circumstances had changed very much for the better. He had a young wife who stood to inherit a considerable fortune. Though the couple had spent little time together, they had used that time well. By Christmas 1469, Isobel was expecting their first child.[9]

Warwick had achieved little beyond the elimination of the Herberts and two of the queen's kinsmen. He was not reinstated as Edward's chief councillor and his foreign policy preferences were not given precedence over the king's. His disaffection with the brokered peace was swift and uncompromising. Before council broke for Lent in February, a new opportunity arose to finish what had been begun the previous year. This time there were to be no manifestos, no appeal to the commons, no pretence at anything other than regime change. This time, the duke of Clarence was the driving force.[10]

In early February 1470, Clarence approached Richard Welles, who held the lordships of Welles and Willoughby and was a leading figure in Lincolnshire. Welles had a fairly long-standing connection to the Nevills. He had fought alongside Montagu at Hexham. He had attended George Nevill's enthronement feast in 1465. His wife was the daughter of the late Robert, lord Willoughby, who had once been married to Warwick's sister-in-law, Maud Stanhope. Richard Welles's association with the Nevills may have begun while Thomas Nevill, Maud's second husband, was prominent in Lincolnshire in the late 1450s.[11]

Clarence was keen to exploit discordant rumblings in Lincolnshire. According to the later confession of Welles's son Robert:

> About Candlemass last, a chaplain of my lord of Clarence, called Master John Barnaby, and with him sir John Clare, priest, came to my lord my father and me to Hellow, with letters of credence given to the said John, which he opened in this wise; that my lord of Warwick was at London with the king, whereupon for their both sureties he prayed us in both their names to be ready with all the fellowship we could or might make and assemble of the commons, what time so ever my said lord of Clarence should send us word.[12]

314

The promotion of a body servant of the king, one Thomas Burgh, put several prominent Lincolnshire noses out of joint. Richard Welles and his brother-in-law, Sir Thomas Dymmock, stirred their supporters to sack Burgh's house and chase him from the county. Richard Welles was summoned to London to answer for his actions.[13]

Presumably concerned for his father's safety, Sir Robert took immediate action, issuing the proclamation 'in the king's name, the duke, earl and his own name, every man to come to Ranbyhawe upon the Tuesday the 6th day of March, upon pain of death, to resist the king in his coming down into the said shire, saying that his coming there was to destroy the commons of the same shire'. The king, Robert Welles understood, 'was coming down ... with great power into Lincolnshire, where the king's judges should sit, and hang and draw a great number of the commons'.[14]

Clarence returned to London, meeting Edward at Baynard's Castle, on 4 March, the day after a pardon was finally issued to Richard Welles. He 'dissimulated right untruly with the king, for as soon as the lord Welles was come to London to the king he came also there, under pretence that he would have taken his leave to have gone westward, where he had sent his wife'.[15]

Clarence may have been concerned about the life and safety of Richard Welles, but his principal intention was 'to have delayed the king's coming'. The plan was to wait until Edward was north of Leicester before making a move. His access to reinforcements in the south was to be cut off. An army led by John Conyers and Scrope of Bolton was on its way from Yorkshire, and Edward and his men were to be caught between the two forces. Clarence only delayed Edward's departure by two days, but that was long enough.[16]

Edward left London on 6 March, arriving in Royston two days later. Here, he received a letter from his brother. Clarence had not gone west as he had told the king, but 'for to do him service in this his journey, he would array himself and come towards his highness at such time and place appointed, as the earl of Warwick should also come, as he had promised the king at London'. Edward wrote to his brother 'of his own hand', thanking him. He also sent commissions of array for Warwick and Clarence to raise troops on his behalf. He continued his journey north, reaching Huntingdon the following day.[17]

Neither Clarence nor Warwick had any intention of joining the king. They rode towards Leicester, where they were to meet Robert Welles and his army. Along the way, they kept their secretaries and scribes busy writing letters, both to the rebels and the king. The first they urged to 'be of good cheer and comfort and hold forth their way towards Leicester'. To the king they sent reassurances they were on their way and would be with him soon.[18]

Robert Welles, however, did not reach Leicester and the planned coup quickly fell apart. Near Stamford, he received a letter written by his father on the king's instructions, 'commanding him to leave his fellowship, and humbly submit himself, or else they for their said treasons should have death, as they deserved'.[19]

Concern for his father overriding everything else, Robert Welles turned aside near Stamford, determined to rescue his father from the king's clutches. The rebel force was now divided. Warwick or Clarence were some 30 miles away in Leicester, and there was nothing they could do. When Edward arrived in Stamford, he found Robert Welles waiting, 'with banners displayed against him, disposed to fight'.[20]

By this time, Edward must have suspected Warwick and Clarence's involvement in the rebellion. Despite assurances they were on their way to join him, they had not left Leicester, and Leicester was where Robert Welles was heading before he stopped his journey. With Conyers and Scrope of Bolton moving south and Welles's rebel army facing him, Edward had to take decisive action. Richard Welles was brought before his son's army and beheaded. He and his son had gambled everything to topple Edward and set Clarence in his place and now everything was lost.[21]

The battle of Empingham was swift, brutal and decisive. Though outnumbered, Edward's army was better trained, better equipped and better disciplined. It was led by a man who was determined to hold on to his throne. The army from Yorkshire, which had struggled to recruit men without a commission of array or authority from the king, would not arrive in time. Robert Welles had just witnessed the death of his father and his men faced the army of an anointed king. The cries of 'A Warwick!' and 'A Clarence!' from rebel throats left Edward in no doubt as to the depths of their treason. The battle quickly turned into a rout, livery jackets handed out on behalf of Warwick and Clarence, and proudly worn, were now torn off in the panic and left behind to be trampled by the king's victorious army. As if this was not enough to cement their guilt, letters from both Warwick and Clarence 'containing matters of great sedition … and the most abominable treason' were found on the body of a slain messenger. After his resounding victory, Edward IV sat down in nearby Stamford and wrote to his rebellious kinsmen and to the one Nevill he still felt he could count on. Montagu was sent a commission of array to deal with the nearby army from Yorkshire.[22]

In Leicester, the failure of the rebellion was starkly clear. Warwick and Clarence were summoned to the king's presence by 'two letters of his own hand, signifying to them the victory that God had sent him, and [that Edward] desired them to come toward him with convenient number for their estate'.

In Grantham on 14 March, Robert Welles made a stunning confession. He not only implicated Warwick and Clarence but lay the seeds of the rebellion at their door. They were 'partners and chief provokers of all their treasons'. Their purpose had been 'to destroy the king' and replace him with Clarence. Edward moved north to Doncaster, where Robert Welles was tried and executed, and then to York. Here, on 22 March, the leaders of the Yorkshire contingent, John Conyers, William Parr and Scrope of Bolton, submitted to the king and were granted pardons.[23]

With the collapse of their enterprise, and the deaths of their co-conspirators, Warwick and Clarence could not hope to achieve their goal. Edward's letter to Clarence left them in no doubt that their part in it was now known. They were to come to him in York, leaving their fellowship behind, in all haste: 'if you so do not, but continue this unlawful assembly of our people in perturbation and contempt of our peace and commandment, we must proceed to that we were loath to do, to the punishment of you, to the grievous example of all others our subjects.'[24]

They wrote back, promising they would join the king soon. They needed assurances, however, that they would be well received and pardoned. Edward's response fell short. He had already pardoned them, he pointed out, and look how they rewarded him! He would treat them as a king ought to treat his subjects. Their defence, as reported in Edward IV's official account of the rebellion, had not yet been heard. Once it was, it might not serve to clear their names. 'If he should be too liberal of his pardon, considering the heinous accusations … it should be too perilous and evil example to all other his subjects in like case, and too great an usurety to his person and common weal of his realm.'[25]

The letter was chilling in its tone. If Warwick and Clarence could establish their innocence, the king would gladly take them in his grace and favour. He remembered the 'nighness of their blood' and 'the old love and affection which of long time he had borne to them'. They would be treated with 'favour and pity'. It would please him greatly if they came to him in York. If they did not, 'he would repute, take and declare them, as reason would, after as their deserts, obstinacy and unnatural demeaning required'.[26]

Neither Warwick nor Clarence had any intention of submitting to Edward. Warwick had pulled triumph from the ashes of disaster before and would attempt to do so now. While the king's messenger was still in Leicester, they readied their men to leave. They did not head towards York, however, but to Burton-upon-Trent. When it was pointed out to them they were going the wrong way, Warwick assured the messenger he just needed to speak to some footmen who were up that way. Then they would turn their feet towards the king. They went first to Derby then to Manchester, where Warwick appealed for help to his brother-in-law Stanley. When Stanley refused, Warwick found that he had played his last card. There was nothing for it but to remove themselves from England, regroup and reassess the situation.[27]

They had to move quickly and they were determined that their families would not be left behind to fall into Edward's hands as hostages. Warwick collected his countess and younger daughter from Warwick Castle. With just 5,000 men-at-arms, they rode swiftly to Bristol. Leaving their artillery behind, they moved to Exeter, where the pregnant duchess of Clarence awaited them. They stayed there for five days, but their scattered forces could not be consolidated before the king arrived. At Dartmouth, they took ship, sailing first to Southampton, where Warwick hoped to take possession of his great flagship, *Trinity*. Anthony Wydeville, now earl Rivers following his father's death, did not let the ship fall into Warwick's hands and he was forced to sail on without it.[28]

Calais had been a safe haven for Warwick since 1457. He had been welcomed before in dark times and would surely be welcomed again. From Calais, he could gather his thoughts and his men. He and Clarence would formulate a new plan and launch a new invasion. In refusing Edward's summons and leaving England, they had burned their bridges. Warwick would not allow himself to accept failure, the consequences were too dire to contemplate.

Outside Calais harbour, Warwick received a message from Wenlock that threw even these tentative plans into turmoil. He would not be allowed to land. Wenlock would hold Calais firm for Edward IV, whatever sympathies and personal loyalty he felt towards Warwick. As if this were not enough to deal with, 18-year-old Isobel, not yet a year married, went into labour, possibly before her time.

# 33

# Strange Bedfellows

dward IV arrived in Dartmouth too late. Clarence and Warwick had already left. The Archbishop of York was immediately arrested and sent to the Tower. A proclamation was published, giving the rebel lords until 28 March to 'appear before his highness, wheresoever he then shall be, to answer unto the said accusations'. They had rebelled against him, stirred his subjects against him. They had planned to make the duke of Clarence king 'against God's law, man's law, and all reason and conscience'. If they refused to obey this summons, they would be declared rebels and traitors, and rewards offered to any who could take them and bring them to the king to answer these gravest of charges.[1]

Rivers was sent to Southampton to guard the fleet. Warwick's great flagship *Trinity* was docked there and he would surely do all he could to secure it. Others put to sea in an attempt to chase down the fugitives. Word was sent to Calais. Warwick was not to be welcomed there. Edward knew well how important Calais had been in 1460 and would not allow Warwick to make it his base of operations now.

Geoffrey Gate, a firm supporter of Warwick and once Governor of the Isle of Wight, was captured in Warwick's attempt to liberate *Trinity*, along with about twenty others. They were tried for treason by John Tiptoft, earl of Worcester and Constable of England. Gate was pardoned but many others were executed. Their bodies were treated in a way that caused great outrage and forever earned Worcester the nickname 'Butcher of England'. '[A]fter that they hanged up by the legs, and a stake made sharp at both ends, whereof one end was put in at the buttocks and the other end their head was put upon; for the which the people of the land were greatly displeased'. Warwick considered this not only an outrage against his men but a personal betrayal by a man who had once been a brother-in-law and close friend.[2]

Both Warwick and Clarence had left instructions with their supporters before they took ship at Dartmouth. None was to make a move before receiving further word, but Warwick, at least, knew who he could count on.

On the face of it, his brother Montagu was not one of them. He had not supported the previous attempted coups nor acted in any capacity that would attract suspicion. So far as Edward IV was concerned, Montagu was as loyal as he had ever been. Though none of it survives, there must have been correspondence between the brothers. Was Montagu simply keeping a low profile at this time, waiting for the signal to act? Or was there a genuine rift between him, on the one hand, and Warwick and the archbishop on the other? Whatever the truth of it, Edward IV gave no indication he doubted Montagu's loyalty.[3]

Warwick fully expected to sail into Calais harbour and take possession of the outpost. He had worked hard to win the support of both garrison and townspeople. In Calais, he could regroup, gather his men, collect supplies and arms. The castle would provide safety for the countess and their daughters. Isobel could give birth in comfort. Warwick and Clarence could plan their return, well supplied, well armed and safe from any attempt Edward IV might make to dislodge them. It should have been easy, but they found no welcome in Calais this time. Instead, Wenlock 'fired his great guns upon [them]'.[4]

Wenlock was in a difficult position. The marshall of Calais, lord Duras, was less than cooperative. Once a refugee from Gascony, Duras had acted as Warwick's admiral back in 1460, when he sailed his fleet to Ireland for talks with the duke of York. Then, he had agreed to help Warwick so long as the person of Henry VI was not threatened. Now, conscious perhaps of the favour shown to him by Edward IV, he again refused to participate in the overthrow of an anointed king. Wenlock publicly professed to share his views. As a reward, Edward made him Governor of Calais and the duke of Burgundy promised him a pension of 1,000 crowns. Philippe de Commines, a Burgundian diplomat, took Wenlock's assurances at face value. 'I found him fixed and resolved to be so and in the Hotel de l'Etaple in that town, he swore solemnly to me, that he would serve the king of England against all opposers whatsoever; and when he had done, all the garrison and townsmen took the same oath.'[5]

But Wenlock was playing a double game. He sent secret word to Warwick that 'if he entered, he was a lost man', and that lord Duras could not be won over. It was during these fruitless negotiations that Isobel Nevill 'was brought to bed of a son'. It is possible the birth was premature and the labour brought on early by stress, or he succumbed to the same difficulties many other infants did in the fifteenth century, for he did not survive. Richard Rous later commented on the countess of Warwick's skill 'with women that travailed of child', but it cannot have been easy, either giving birth or assisting, in the cramped quarters of a ship. While a raging storm and a traumatic ordeal are favourites of novelists, we have been left with no details of the birth itself. The baby, whose name is unrecorded, was buried at sea. All his grandfather could do was send to Calais for wine, in the hope it would give his grieving, exhausted daughter strength.[6]

This must have been the family's darkest hour. The birth of Isobel's first child should have been a time of great solemnity and joy. When she went to Exeter to prepare herself for the birth, the last thing Isobel would have expected was to be hurried aboard ship and taken into exile. She had her husband and father nearby, her mother and sister to help and comfort her. Perhaps her first glimpse of her son was also her last, before he was wrapped up, weighed down with stones and committed to the deep. Perhaps she did not even get that, if the boy was stillborn.

Warwick, however much he grieved, could not give up. Calais was closed to him, but there was always France. King Louis was his friend, as Charles of Burgundy was not. He would turn this friendship to his advantage.

Charles of Burgundy declared early and openly for Edward IV. Warwick was not well loved in Burgundy and his attempts to drive a wedge between Burgundy and France did nothing to change that. His best chance of winning French backing was to reignite the war. To this effect, and to replenish his fleet and his treasury, he took to piracy. Joined by his cousin Thomas, Bastard of Fauconberg, joint commander of Edward IV's fleet, his success was spectacular. On 20 April, he took forty merchantmen from Burgundy and Brittany. Most of these were small and poorly equipped defensively, but their cargoes could be sold and Warwick's men rewarded for their service.[7]

Still, Warwick had no base and without that he was powerless. He also had his countess and daughters to consider. They had already suffered greatly, and a sea battle towards the end of April against Edward's fleet must have brought home to Warwick and Clarence the danger they were in. The women had to be found a refuge. As spirited and determined to support her husband as the countess of Warwick may have been, she was no mariner, no soldier and certainly no pirate. It would seem Isobel recovered quickly from the birth and death of her son, but she could get no proper rest aboard ship in cramped quarters. Finally, on 1 May, the fleet, numbering some eighty ships, sailed into Honfleur and Harfleur harbours in the Seine estuary. The Bastard of Fauconberg remained at sea, taking a further fifteen or so Dutch ships on 27 May.[8]

King Louis was not convinced that Warwick's presence in France would be to his benefit. While he appreciated the damage done to Burgundian shipping, and the possibility of continued strife in England, he was reluctant to commit to anything more than secret meetings with Warwick and Clarence. Louis offered them ships and money, in the hopes it would lead to their swift departure, but Warwick needed more than that. He needed time and he needed a plan.[9]

King Louis suggested that the Channel Islands might make a suitable base of operations but Warwick knew they were too vulnerable to be safe for long. Little by little, he chipped away at Louis's determination. The countess of Warwick, Isobel and Anne were given lodgings in Valognes in Lower Normandy. Louis instructed a trusted agent to offer Warwick and Clarence anything they required in order to speed their departure. Costs blew out, and this concerned him – he could not afford to back a failed enterprise and failure was what he feared.[10]

Warwick knew he was dependent on Louis's aid and was determined to secure it on his own terms. He would not suffer the uncertain generosity grudgingly given to exiles who lived in despairing hope of return. He would not be used as bait for future peace treaties, to be handed over to Edward to be punished. He wanted to return to England in strength and he wanted to put an end to Edward IV's kingship.[11]

> [Warwick and Clarence] compelled Louis to accept their presence in France, then in ports where he did not want them, to receive them publicly, to give them more money than he wished and to await their convenience on the date of departure.[12]

Warwick and Clarence insisted on being publicly received and welcomed by Louis and, on 8 June, they finally were. With the countess of Warwick and her daughters safe in Valognes, Warwick and Clarence travelled south to Amboise to meet with the King of France.

> The duke of Clarence and the earl of Warwick arrived in this place on the 8th inst and were received by the Most Christian King in the most honourable and distinguished manner imaginable. His Majesty, all the principal lords who happened to be at the court, [rode] three of four leagues to meet them, and he himself went some distance out from the castle on foot to receive them, embracing them in a most friendly way. He also made her Majesty the queen come to the door of the castle to receive them and to be kissed, according to the custom here. His Majesty then took them to their chambers in the castle and remained with their lordships two long hours most privately and with great familiarity. And so every day his Majesty has gone to visit them in their rooms and has remained with them in long discussions, while he honours and feasts them, giving them tournaments and dancing and everything else of distinction.[13]

It was at this point that Warwick made the most startling of decisions. He would seek an alliance with the exiled Margaret of Anjou and restore Henry VI to his throne. This had not been part of his plans when he sought shelter in France. An open letter to the commons of England was sent from France to their various supporters some time in May or June.[14]

Copies of this letter were 'set upon the standard at Chepe, upon the stulpes of London bridge and upon divers church doors in London and in other parts of England'. In language reminiscent of earlier manifestos, the letter referred to 'covetous seditious persons' who cared only for 'their own singular and insatiable covetous to the magnifying of their friends and adherents'. These unspecified people cared nothing for the king, nor his people, 'to the great hurt, impoverishing and the utter destruction' of the commons. Warwick and Clarence cared, they declared; they cared deeply, they always had and they always would, 'greatly sorrowing and abhorrent of the cruel and detestable tyranny, the vengeable murder and manslaughter reigning among you'. There were calls to almighty God, his 'blessed mother and glorious virgin', to St George and to 'every true Englishman', but there was no mention of Henry VI. At the time this letter was written, he did not figure in Warwick's plans.[15]

At some point, Warwick was joined by his brother-in-law Oxford who, 'hearing of the duke of Clarence and the earl of Warwick being in France, went over to them'. Oxford, who had always been a closet supporter of the house of Lancaster, may well have planted the seed in Warwick's mind. Certainly Sir John Fortescue, Margaret of Anjou's chancellor-in-exile, saw an alliance with Warwick as their best chance to restore Henry VI to the throne and his son to the succession.[16]

As with most of Warwick's activities at the time, detailed reports were sent from various ambassadors to their royal masters, particularly in France, Burgundy and Milan. Louis made immediate overtures to Margaret, inviting her to Amboise to meet with him. Warwick would not be there. He would give Louis time to discuss the idea with the exiled queen. 'That done, Warwick will return here to give the finishing touches to everything, and immediately afterwards, according to all accounts, he will return to England with a great fleet, taking with him the … prince, in order to raise up the party of King Henry.'[17]

Warwick made the long journey north to Valognes to give Louis time and space to work on Queen Margaret. It was now that Warwick most likely told his wife and then his daughter Anne of the part she was to play. If all went according to plan, Anne would be married to the Prince of Wales. In time, she would be Queen of England. It was not long ago that Isobel had been promised the same future. For Clarence, this was a disaster. His position was now impossible. He had turned against his brother for nothing. He could not return to England and there was no good reason for him to remain in France. Whatever promises Warwick could make, whatever lands, positions and titles he might be given, and the dukedom of York was certainly among these, it could not make up for the lost glory of being king. If Clarence and his duchess grew susceptible to offers of pardon and reconciliation from Edward IV, it is hardly to be wondered at.[18]

The marriage between Warwick's daughter and Margaret of Anjou's son was crucial to his plan. It would forge a connection between them that could not easily be broken and it would demonstrably give both sides a vested interest in the success of the venture. Edward IV must have known by now the depths of Warwick's betrayal. If he was careful, there might be a chance to prise Clarence away from Warwick's side. When it came, secret contact was first made with the duchess. Isobel, like all noblewomen, had to look to her husband now for support, both material and emotional. Though she might love her father, though she might be loath to see him fail, she must look after her own interests and those of her husband. Letters were written by Edward, the duchess of York and her daughters. They were entrusted to a woman of Isobel's household who had to make her way first to Calais then to France.[19]

If Warwick's decision to restore Henry VI to his throne was made on the run, Margaret of Anjou's agreement was not. The most coherent account we have of their meeting, the negotiations and the final agreement, Warwick's *The Maner and Guyding*, was written to show both parties in the best possible light. Warwick had to be seen to be contrite and sincere and Margaret not too eager to forgive the man who had brought her and her family so much harm. The tract covers the period 15 July to 4 August, from Margaret's initial reluctance to accept King Louis's promises of money and men to aid the quest.[20]

Just how reluctant Margaret was at this point is open to question. If initial discussions had taken place between Oxford and Margaret's chancellor Fortescue, there was time to get agreement from both Warwick and Margaret well before their carefully stage-managed meeting took place. There was certainly an element of theatre in the meeting between the exiled queen and the earl who had done so much to bring about her current state. Though she likely saw the sense in allying herself with Warwick from the start, she could not easily forget his past trespasses, nor could she be seen to forgive them easily. If he was to be pardoned, he must earn it. He arrived back in Amboise on the same day as the queen and, that evening, 'went on his knee and asked her pardon for the injuries and wrongs done to her in the past'.[21]

If the exiled queen was reluctant to offer Warwick pardon, it was hardly to be wondered at. He had been 'the greatest causer of the fall of king Henry, of her and of her son'. They had friends currently in exile, and such pardon and alliance 'greatly might grieve them', bringing more harm than Warwick could offer good. For his part, Warwick explained that he had

had no choice but to act as he did, for 'king Henry and she by their false counterfeit had enterprised the destruction of his friends in body and in goods', which he had never deserved. 'And him seemed that for such causes and the great evil will that they have showed him he had a righteous cause to labour their undoing and destruction and that therein he had done but that a nobleman outraged and impaired ought to have done.'[22]

King Louis would stand surety for his good word, Warwick declared. Louis urged the queen to 'pardon the said earl', for he was 'bound and beholden to the said earl more than any other man'. Servants of Margaret's father, René of Anjou, added their voices in Warwick's favour. Finally, 'after many treaties and meetings', Warwick was pardoned by Margaret and her son, as was Oxford. 'And after that they pardoned the earl of Oxford being with the earl of Warwick, to whom the queen said that his pardon was easy to purchase, for she knew well that he and his friends had suffered much thing for king Henry's quarrels.'[23]

The proposed marriage between Prince Edward and Anne Nevill was also agreed, again after a show of reluctance from Margaret. She might find him a better wife, she said. King Edward himself had written to her, offering her son Princess Elizabeth's hand, 'and so the queen persevered fifteen days before she would any thing intend to the said treaty of marriage'. All parties involved 'swore upon the very cross in St Mary's church of Angers'. Margaret swore she would treat Warwick as a true liegemen of King Henry, herself and their son, '[a]nd for the deeds passed never hereafter to make him reproach'. Clarence was not forgotten, though his role and position would be much diminished. He was to have all the land he had held before he left England, as well as his late father's title.[24]

The marriage was to proceed and Anne to 'remain in the hands and keeping of queen Margaret' until England was secure. If Louis could supply him with 'a few folks, ships and money', Warwick would set sail without delay. The prince was not to go with him. His mother refused to send him into uncertainty and danger. He was not just her only child but the last hope of the Lancastrians. Without him, everything was pointless. Once Warwick and Clarence had England firmly in their grip, once Henry VI was released from the Tower and Edward IV dealt with, Margaret of Anjou and Edward Prince of Wales would cross the Channel and enter their realm in triumph.[25]

A ceremony of betrothal between Anne Nevill and the prince took place at Angers Cathedral on 25 July. Dispensations were needed from Rome before the wedding itself could take place. Warwick could not afford to wait in France any longer. His daughter would have to get married without him. The personal feelings of the young couple are not known, their voices are silent. Assumptions that both Margaret and her son were cruel and bitter, and visited this on Anne in the months leading up to the wedding, are without basis. Assessments of Prince Edward's character often rest on two things. The first is his involvement in the trial of lord Bonville and Thomas Kyriell after the second battle of St Albans, where he was given the task of pronouncing sentence. The image is sinister but it is highly unlikely a 7-year-old boy could order the executions of two men without being coached. This act was formal and symbolic, a demonstration both to the prince and others of his future role as king.[26]

The second is a quote, often truncated, from a 1467 dispatch to Milan: 'This boy, though only thirteen years of age, already talks of nothing but of cutting off heads or making war, as if he had everything in his hands or was the god of battle or the peaceful occupant of that throne.' 'This boy' was a Prince of Wales in exile, the son of an imprisoned king and a deposed queen. He was brought up fully aware of who he was and who he should be. If he dreamed of taking back his birthright and punishing those who had wrested it from him, it should hardly be surprising.[27]

None of this suggests Prince Edward was of a cruel or sadistic nature. It was not in his interests, nor his mother's, to be deliberately unkind to his bride. Too much was riding on Warwick's continued goodwill and support to risk his anger at ill treatment of his daughter. The young couple may have delighted in each other's company; they may have disliked each other from the start. Without their voices, this is something that cannot be known.

It was around this time that a mysterious woman arrived in France to intervene with the duke and duchess of Clarence on King Edward's behalf. '[She] managed the affair that was committed to her charge with so much cunning and dexterity that she prevailed with the duke of Clarence to come over to the king's party as soon as he was in England.' The events of the next few months give no indication Clarence was regretting his decision to follow his father-in-law's programme. He did not abandon Warwick on their arrival in England. Given that the woman in question was a member of the duchess's household, Isobel may have been the recipient of the letters from England. If she showed them to her husband, they did not, at this point, achieve their aim.[28]

The intention was for Warwick, Clarence and Oxford, accompanied by Henry VI's half-brother Jasper Tudor, to set sail for England immediately after the betrothal, while the bride and groom waited for dispensations from Rome. Warwick had already primed his supporters in Yorkshire. Under the command of Fitzhugh, they were to rise, drawing Edward IV away from London just as Warwick and Clarence's fleet landed. This strategy had been tried twice before. On the first occasion, in July 1469, it had been a success. Edward had been cut off from reinforcements and deserted by his followers, and captured. The second time, in March 1470, the plan's reliance on

Richard and Robert Welles had caused its failure. This time, with Warwick's affinity in Yorkshire under the command of his brother-in-law Fitzhugh, there was a good chance it would succeed. Edward IV would go north to deal with the rising; Warwick, Clarence and their new Lancastrian allies would land in the south and Edward would be trapped.

There were two potential difficulties with this plan: Warwick's brother Montagu and the newly reinstated earl of Northumberland. While Warwick had no hope, nor any desire, to recruit the latter to his cause, Montagu's support was crucial. He had thus far remained loyal to Edward IV and, given their respective track records, Warwick must have known he would be hard pressed to win a pitched battle against his brother. Warwick had to know he had Montagu on his side before he set sail. He had to know Montagu would not raise a hand to quell Fitzhugh's rising. It would be up to Montagu to find the means to keep himself out of the way without raising suspicion. If he showed his hand too early, the entire plan would fail.

With so much resting on others, Warwick, Clarence, Oxford and Jasper Tudor left Angers for the coast, with the immediate intention of setting sail. Poor weather, and the nearby presence of a Burgundian fleet, kept them in harbour for weeks. When a storm blew up and scattered the Burgundians, 'some into Scotland, some into Holland, and all of them dispersed', they took their chance and left the harbour.[29]

Finally, on 9 September, the fleet sailed. Landing at Portsmouth and Plymouth, the invading army was substantial. A new proclamation was issued in the names of Clarence, Tudor, Warwick and Oxford. Henry VI was the 'very true and undoubted king of England'. Edward IV was a 'usurper, oppressor and destroyer of our said sovereign lord', of the nobility and the commons. They had come to England to 'deliver our said sovereign lord out of his captivity and danger out of the hands of his enemies unto his liberty',

> to reform, redress and amend all the great mischiefs, oppressions and all other inordinate abuses now reigning in the said realm, to the perpetual peace and prosperity and common weal of all this realm.[30]

Everyone was to be pardoned for anything they had done 'contrary to their allegiance' to Henry VI. All men between 16 and 60, except the sick and the weak, must ready themselves 'in their best array defensible to await and attend upon the said dukes and earls to assist them in their journey'. The law must be upheld: this was not the time to take advantage of a fluid situation. There was to be no stealing from the Church or each other; no 'defouling or ravishing' of widows, wives, daughters or servants; no 'affray or debate' among those who joined the cause.[31]

Thousands flocked to the Lancastrian banners, drawn by their love for Warwick and residual feelings of allegiance to Henry VI. Edward, who had tarried in the north after the collapse of Fitzhugh's rising, sent a commission of array to Montagu. Now was the moment for Montagu to declare his hand.[32]

# 34

# ENDGAME

As for tidings, my lord archbishop is at the Moor, but there is left with him divers of the king's servants, and as I understand he has licence to tarry there till he be sent for. There be many folks up in the north, so that Percy is not able to resist them; and so the king has sent for his feed men to come to him, for he will go to put them down … Item, that the lords Clarence and Warwick will assay to land in England every day, as folks fear.[1]

This was the report Sir John Paston sent to his brother on 5 August 1470. The 'many folks' up in the north were members of the Nevill affinity, called out by Fitzhugh on Warwick's instructions. The rising was supposed to coincide with the landing of the fleet in the West Country. Held up by storms, and the Burgundian blockade, there was no way Warwick could send reliable news of a revised timetable. Fitzhugh did not bring his force to battle, but there was no need to. The rebel army dispersed as Edward IV approached. Fitzhugh fled into Scotland. Others submitted to Edward and received pardon, including Alice Fitzhugh, their children and son-in-law Francis Lovell. Without word from Warwick, there was nothing they could reasonably do but disband, disperse and make their peace with the king.[2]

Warwick had urged his followers before to seek pardon if things did not go according to plan. His affinity was more use to him intact and at liberty than in prison, beheaded or on the run. In this case, their job was done without the need to come to blows with the king's forces. They had lured him north and kept him there until Warwick was safely on English soil.

In Bristol, Warwick's party was met by Shrewsbury and Stanley, who had both deserted him after the Lincolnshire rebellion. Warwick collected his artillery in Exeter and marched to Coventry. On his way south, Edward IV was followed by Montagu and his army. Still confident of his loyalty, Edward expected Montagu to join him, but

Montagu hated the king, and purposed to have taken him; and when he was within a mile of king Edward, he declared to the people that were gathered with him, how king Edward had first given to him the earldom of Northumberland and how he took it from him and gave it to Henry Percy … and how, of late time, he had made him marquis Montagu and give him a [mag]pie's nest to maintain his estate with; whereof he gave knowledge to his people that he would hold with the earl of Warwick, his brother, and take king Edward if he might, and all those that would hold with him.[3]

When news of this reached Edward, he understood the deep peril of his situation, 'for he knew he was not strong enough to give battle to the marquis Montagu'. Again, he was left with just a few of his most loyal supporters and friends: his brother Gloucester, Hastings and Rivers. They rode to the coast and, at Bishop's Lynn, took to the sea and sailed to Holland.[4]

Henry VI had not been treated kindly during his years in the Tower. When he was released at the beginning of October, he was 'not worshipfully arrayed as a prince, and not so cleanly kept, as should seem a prince'. He was washed and dressed in finer clothes than he had long been used to and brought to Westminster, King of England once more. When Warwick entered London on 6 October, he knelt before King Henry as he had knelt before Queen Margaret.[5]

Edward's queen, heavily pregnant and surrounded by her daughters, had already taken to sanctuary, as had many others. A proclamation ensuring the inviolability of both Westminster and St Martin's sanctuaries in London was probably designed to give those within time to come to terms with the new regime. In the end, however, it served only to ensure that those lords who might hope for Edward IV's speedy return were gathered together in one place.[6]

On 2 November, Elizabeth Wydeville gave birth to a son. This news, when it reached Edward, would have given him heart. Now he not only had his own kingdom to regain but the birthright of his son.

Warwick was reinstated as Great Chamberlain of England and Admiral. His captaincy of Calais was confirmed. In his capacity as Henry VI's lieutenant, he summoned Parliament for 26 November. George Nevill was once again chancellor and John Langstrother treasurer. Both Oxford and Jasper Tudor, earl of Pembroke, were restored to their lands and titles. Montagu, who had relinquished wardenship of the east march to Northumberland, was reinstated.[7]

The rolls of Henry VI's readeption Parliament have not survived. They were likely deliberately destroyed. Its main purpose was to attaint Edward IV and his brother Richard, duke of Gloucester, and bestow the dukedom of York on Clarence. There were no wholesale attainders, no mass trials or executions. Those lords who would not submit were allowed to remain in sanctuary or on their estates, with one notable exception.[8]

Worcester could not be forgiven his inhumane treatment of those executed at Southampton. He was arrested and tried by Oxford in his temporary capacity as Constable. Some nine years earlier, Worcester had tried Oxford's father and brother and sentenced them to death. Now, Oxford had the opportunity to extract his revenge: 'the earl of Worcester was judged by such law as he did to other men.' On his own request, Worcester was beheaded with three strokes of the axe, signifying the Holy Trinity.[9]

Oxford was one of the more intriguing characters of his age. He could certainly bear a grudge, as he did against both Worcester and Edward IV. He remained on the edge of treason for years. Arrested and committed to the Tower on several occasions, 'kept in irons' on one at least, he managed to secure his release and a pardon every time. Almost certainly in secret communication with Margaret of Anjou – her words to him in Amboise are suggestive of that – he kept this so secret that nothing could be pinned on him. Now he had achieved a long-cherished hope. Henry VI was restored. The man who had deposed him, and was responsible for the arrest and trial of Oxford's father and brother, had fled the country. Oxford had made no real enemies, either among Yorkists or Lancastrians, and was the only prominent member of the readeption government acceptable to both sides.[10]

Oxford was visibly rewarded for his commitment to the Lancastrian cause during the ceremony to recrown Henry VI, where he carried the sword of state. In the absence of Suffolk, the staunchly Yorkist Norfolk and the earl of Essex, Oxford stepped into a newly created power vacuum in East Anglia, where he was commissioned to keep order. Involved in a long-running dispute with Norfolk over Caister Castle, a dispute that had descended into siege, the Pastons were certainly pleased by Oxford's new ascendancy and influence. Soon after the departure of Edward IV, Sir John Paston wrote to his brother about Oxford's good lordship: 'as for my lord of Oxford, he is better lord to me, by my truth, than I can wish him in many matters.' When Oxford started recruiting in Norfolk, both Paston brothers joined his side.[11]

If Oxford prospered under the readeption, Clarence did not. Though he was confirmed by Parliament as duke of York, and all that went with that title, other lands he had been awarded had been held by Queen Elizabeth. When Margaret of Anjou arrived in England, queen once more, they would have to be surrendered to her. Rather than emerging from Edward IV's shadow, he now found himself in a worse position than ever. He was no longer brother to the King of England. His wife was to have been queen, but now that role would be played by her younger sister.

The readeption sorely disadvantaged Clarence's sisters Elizabeth and Anne. Anne, in particular, was put in a most uncomfortable position.

The return of her estranged husband Exeter forced her from her home at Coldharbour, where she had been living with her lover Thomas St Leger. With Edward and Richard in exile, Clarence was bereft of both his brothers. Margaret of Burgundy, often described as Clarence's favourite sister, stood to lose all she had if France and England went to war against her husband. It is little wonder he was ready to listen to those family members – mother, sisters and Bourchier cousins – who urged him to reconcile with Edward. In Burgundy, Margaret was able to put the brothers into direct communication. It is highly likely, though he did nothing to jeopardise his life and safety while Edward was still in exile, that Clarence had already come to an understanding with him before his return to England.[12]

War with Burgundy was not just a remote possibility. It had been an important part of the agreement between Warwick and Louis XI, and a key clause in the treaty ratified by Louis and Henry VI. Burgundy was to be crushed, dismembered. Warwick stood to gain not only politically but personally. Holland and Zeeland were to be granted to him once the war was won.[13]

France, Burgundy and England were caught in an endless dance. Each ruler feared an alliance between the other two. Louis had been concerned about a possible Anglo-Burgundian alliance since the marriage of Edward's sister to Charles the Bold. Warwick needed Louis's support if he wanted to hold on to power. Charles of Burgundy was caught between his long-held preference for a Lancastrian government in England and fear of what would become of his duchy if France and England joined forces against him. In the end, England's declaration of war forced Charles's hand. Despite protestations from the Lancastrian exiles he had been sheltering for years, he threw his support behind Edward IV. The one thing that guaranteed France's support for Warwick's return to England and power – war with Burgundy – was the single most important cause of his eventual downfall. As Warwick had needed Louis's support when he left England in April, so Edward now needed Burgundy's. The spectre of crushing defeat by an Anglo-French army secured that for him.[14]

On 12 December, a French embassy was able to report to King Louis and Queen Margaret that Warwick had established control in England. The following day, Anne Nevill and Prince Edward were married at Amboise.

Warwick spent much of his time in the first two months of 1471 in preparation for war against Burgundy. He resumed his post as Warden of the Cinq Ports, lost the previous July to his brother-in-law Arundel. He also resumed the captaincy of Calais and, once again, took charge of the English fleet. In February, war was declared against Burgundy.[15]

Warwick that very day [6 February] was sending orders to Calais to begin the war ... orders had already gone forth for the assembling of a large army – and of this army he himself would take command and would convey it across the sea within the time Louis named.[16]

They were ready for him in Calais. Wenlock was once again openly supporting Warwick. Charles the Bold's agent, Philippe de Commines, dined with him and found that all the guests wore Warwick's badge, the ragged staff. Wenlock's was gold, others made from cloth. The change in allegiance since his previous visit startled Commines by both its completeness and suddenness:

> within a quarter of an hour after the arrival of an express from England with the news, the whole town had got this livery and sudden was the change; and this was the first time that I had ever seen or considered such an instance of the instability of all human affairs.[17]

That month, Exeter and Somerset, among other exiles, returned to England and took possession of their estates for the first time in years. Using 'all their artifice', they had tried, and failed, to dissuade Burgundy from giving aid and support to the fugitive Edward IV. Now they were back in England to await the arrival of Queen Margaret and Prince Edward. Neither of them had much love for the Nevills. There was little trust between these committed Lancastrians and those who had come late to the cause, they believed, out of self-interest alone.[18]

The readeption was weak. Few of England's nobles submitted to King Henry. There was little money, an imminent war few wanted and the threat of yet more instability and strife should Edward IV find a way to return to reclaim his crown. As it had been in the early 1460s, the government was once again dominated by the Nevills. Among the Lancastrians of old were some who feared, and possibly even expected, that Warwick, Montagu and the Archbishop of York would rethink their commitment if Edward returned.[19]

Montagu had been required to explain and excuse himself before Parliament, which might be interpreted as an indication of mistrust. Doubts about Montagu's commitment would continue to be felt and recorded. It is not known whether Edward IV made direct overtures to him but it is possible. He was certainly working on Clarence. The Nevill brothers were close. They had shared a great deal of both sorrow and joy. In the early years of Edward IV's reign, they had worked tirelessly to end Lancastrian resistance in the north-east. Montagu had refused to join Warwick in France but declared himself on his brother's side as soon as he got word he had returned. He was, once again, warden of both the east and west marches, but reinstatement to the earldom of Northumberland had not been among his rewards. He had also had to relinquish the estates in Devonshire which he had been granted by Edward IV as compensation. With the Courtenay earl now back in England, Montagu had no choice. Whether these disappointments were enough to break the bonds between him and his brothers irrevocably has been a matter of much speculation.[20]

Montagu was in the north of England when Edward IV's small fleet landed in March. On 3 October 1470, Edward had been blown onto an island off the north coast of Holland with his small band of friends, family and supporters. Two days later, word reached Gruythuse, Governor of Holland, and he made his way to the coast to meet the English refugees. In the Hague, Edward wrote to the duke of Burgundy, asking for his help. At Aire, he was received by the dowager duchess. In Bruges, his party enjoyed the hospitality of Gruythuse. Gloucester met with their sister Margaret in Lille. Her husband would not publicly support Edward's cause. He had long been a supporter of the exiled Lancastrians. His people lived in fear of Warwick and what would happen to them should a combined Anglo-French force attack. Charles of Burgundy had a difficult decision to make.[21]

Edward kept in touch with his supporters in England, orchestrating the family campaign to persuade Clarence to leave his father-in-law. From Northumberland he learned how little supported the readeption was. News would surely have reached him in November of the birth of his son.[22]

The threat of war did more to shift Charles the Bold from the Lancastrian camp to Edward IV's than anything the exiled king could have said. Eviscerated and carved up between France, England and Warwick himself, his duchy would cease to exist. Charles gave Edward ships, money and men. Rivers hired more ships in Bruges. Edward secured loans from English merchants. By February 1471, a fleet of thirty-six ships and a band of some 1,200 men were ready to leave the continent. Held up for days 'abiding good wind and weather', they finally set sail on 11 March.[23]

Margaret of Anjou was also waiting to make the crossing to England, her son and daughter-in-law with her. The countess of Warwick, too, made ready to sail. The winds that sprang up in March, and so aided Edward's fleet, held both Margaret and the countess back.

On 12 March, Edward attempted a landing at Cromer in Norfolk, 'where the king set on land [two] knights, and others, trusting by them to have some knowledge how the land inward was disposed towards him'. The knights returned, telling Edward that Norfolk was held by Warwick and his supporters, 'in especial, by the earl of Oxford' and that 'it might not be for his weal to land in that country'. The proximity of Oxford's brother Thomas was enough to send Edward's fleet back out to sea.[24]

Oxford was on his way to join Thomas, and wrote to him from Hedingham Castle:

I have disposed me with all the power that I can make in Essex and Suffolk and Cambridgeshire and other places, to be on Monday next coming at Bury, which purpose I intend to observe, with God's grace, towards you into Norfolk, to the assistance of you and that county, in case Edward with his company had arrived there, and yet I shall do the same notwithstanding; for if he arrive northward, like as you know by likelihood he should, I intend to follow and pursue him.[25]

Edward did indeed 'arrive northward' the following day, landing at Ravenspur in Yorkshire. While 'great storms, winds and tempests upon the sea' scattered his fleet, Edward's ship, carrying Hastings and others, made safe landfall. Gloucester's ship came to land not far away and Rivers's some 13 miles distant. After lodging the night in a 'poor village', Edward was reunited with his brother, brother-in-law and the rest of his fellowship.[26]

Few rallied to his cause but none opposed him. Declaring he had only returned to reclaim his title as duke of York, he reached that city without incident. The two great northern magnates, Montagu and Northumberland, could have either opposed or joined him, separately or independently. The seeds sewn during the Nevill–Percy feud in the 1450s, and civil war in the 1460s, had borne bitter fruit, however.[27]

Montagu was at Pontefract, unable to 'have gathered, nor have made, a fellowship of number sufficient to have openly resisted [Edward] in his quarrel'. Not only could Montagu not expect support from a Percy, but

[the] great part of the noblemen and commons in those parts were towards the earl of Northumberland, and would not stir with any lord or nobleman other than with the said earl, or at least by his commandment ... if the marquis would have done his business to have assembled them in any manner quarrel, neither for his love, which they bear him none, nor for any commandment of higher authority, they would not in no cause, nor quarrel, have assisted him.[28]

Montagu 'in no wise troubled [Edward] nor none of his fellowship, but suffered him to pass in peaceable wise, were it with good will, or no, men may judge at their pleasure'. In the end, neither Montagu nor Northumberland made a move and Edward passed peacefully south to Nottingham.[29]

Here, he was joined by Sir William Parr and Sir James Harrington, who brought 600 men with them. Near Retford, the combined forces of Oxford and Exeter failed to confront him. Hastings called up 3,000 men in Leicester, led by Sir William Norreys.[30]

Though it was a slower process than Edward would have liked, his patience paid off. By the time he reached Coventry, he was ready to confront Warwick. Warwick would not give battle, however, until he was at full strength. He was waiting for Oxford and Exeter from the north, and Clarence from the west.

> And when he understood the said earl within the town was closed, and with him great people to the number of six or seven thousand men, the king desired him to come out, with all his people, into the field, to determine his quarrel in plain field, which the same earl refused to do at that time, and so he did three days after ensuing continually.[31]

The longer Warwick delayed, the more men he leaked to Edward IV's army. *The Historie of the Arrivall of King Edward IV*, the official record of events, has Warwick sending messengers to the king to say that he was willing to talk. Edward, 'by the advice of his counsellors', was prepared to offer Warwick surety of his life, but Warwick would not accept his terms.[32]

Edward moved his men the short distance from Coventry to the town of Warwick and took over the castle. Here he played his trump card. Swayed, no doubt, by many things, not least the pleas of 'my lady, their mother; my lady of Exeter, my lady of Suffolk, their sisters; my lord cardinal of Canterbury; my lord of Bath, my lord of Essex and, most specially, my lady of Burgundy', Clarence took the decision to reconcile with his brother.

> The king ... understanding his near approaching, issued out of Warwick, with all his fellowship, by the space of three miles, into a fair field towards Banbury, where he saw the duke, his brother, in fair array, come towards him, with a great fellowship.[33]

Leaving his men behind him 'in array, the banners displayed', Edward, Gloucester, Rivers and Hastings went to meet Clarence.

> And so they met, between the two hosts where there was right kind and loving language between the two, with perfect accord knit together for ever hereafter, with as heartily loving cheer and countenance as might be between two brothers of so great nobility and estate.[34]

Clarence tried to broker a peace between Edward and Warwick, without success. '[B]ut the earl of Oxford, and others being disposed to extreme malice against the king, would not suffer him to accept any manner of appointment, were it reasonable or unreasonable, but caused him to refuse all manner of appointments.'[35]

Warwick was now joined by his brother Montagu and their Lancastrian allies, Oxford and Exeter. Edward, unable to provoke battle and growing

336

uncertain of his chances of success against this now bolstered force, withdrew to London.[36]

He found his city not a fortress held by Henry VI's supporters but welcoming. The Archbishop of York had attempted to rally the citizens behind the Lancastrian king by parading Henry through the streets but this failed to rouse them. On 9 April, the Yorkist prisoners in the Tower overcame their guards and took the Tower for Edward. Two days later, 'understanding the king's coming and approaching near to the city', the archbishop sent him word he was willing to come to terms and let Edward into London.[37]

Somerset and Devon had left London before Edward arrived. They went not to join Warwick in the Midlands but south, to meet Margaret of Anjou's ships, which had finally left France. After accepting the archbishop's submission and arresting Henry VI, Edward 'then went to the queen and comforted her'. He met his now 5-month-old son and heir, Prince Edward, for the first time, 'to his heart's singular comfort and gladness'. Then he took his queen and their children to Baynard's Castle, where they spent their first night together as a family for many months.[38]

Edward had to move quickly. Warwick's army was approaching London. Margaret of Anjou's arrival was imminent. Despite Archbishop Nevill's promises, he might yet be looking for a way to aid his brothers. Edward had spent a pleasant evening with his queen. He had seen his son and daughters. He would waste no more time but leave London at the head of the largest force he could muster and meet Warwick, Montagu and their allies head on.[39]

The two forces met at Barnet, just north of London. Warwick arrived first and chose his ground. It was nightfall before Edward arrived. Both armies were to sleep in their lines, not knowing they were just 500 yards apart. All were ordered to silence, 'without any manner language, or noise, but as little as they well might', and no fires were to be lit. Warwick, who had more guns than Edward, kept up an artillery barrage all night. The cannon stones overshot the king's army, though the noise, no doubt, left neither side much chance of sleep.[40]

The darkness not only masked how close the two armies were but the fact that they were out of alignment. On Warwick's side, his right, commanded by Oxford, overshot Edward's left, under the command of Hastings. Edward's left, under Gloucester, overshot Exeter on Warwick's right. Warwick himself, as was his custom, commanded the reserves. The two centres, also out of alignment, were led by Montagu and King Edward respectively.[41]

The morning brought light but little better visibility, for a great mist hung over the battlefield. Warwick made the opening moves, sending cannon fire and arrow shot into the enemy. Edward could see no better than Warwick, 'yet he admitted his quarrel and cause to almighty God, advanced banners, did blow up trumpets, and set upon them'.[42]

We cannot know what was going through the minds of the Nevill brothers and their cousin, and one-time ally, Edward IV. *The Arrivall* suggests there was some regret on Edward's part that he must face two men who had been so important to him throughout his reign and in the years before. *Warkworth's Chronicle* states that, in the days before the battle, he and Montagu had come to terms and that Montagu was planning to switch sides. That, however, does not fit the picture we have of the Nevills. Archbishop George Nevill had submitted to the king in London, but that may have been more a matter of survival than anything else. He had no men to send to Barnet to fight alongside his brothers. If Warwick took the victory, George would, once again, be his loyal deputy. Montagu knew what it was like to break with Warwick. For months, while Warwick and Clarence were in France, he had remained loyal to Edward. When it came down to it, when it became clear that endgame was near, he had not been able to sustain his estrangement.

Montagu, more than anyone, understood the level of mistrust the Lancastrian returnees felt. He had been responsible for the defeat and execution of Somerset's brother at the battle of Hexham in 1464. He knew there would be no more easy reconciliation there than with the newly restored Percy earl of Northumberland. If they won this battle, the cracks in the shaky readeption government might well open into chasms. That is not to suggest Montagu wished things to go ill. At 40, he had no more desire to die than anyone else. He had a wife he was fond of and children he loved. He was committed to his brother's cause and would live or die with him.

Had Oxford not persuaded Warwick to refuse Edward's offers of terms, had he accepted the guarantee of his life given in Coventry, Montagu would have followed suit. Whether either of them would have been given the chance to join Edward in battle or, like Clarence, kept well out of the fight is impossible to say. It is what many of the Lancastrian lords feared. That Montagu's men feared their allies would turn on them in battle is clear from the panic and the cries of 'Treason!' that rang out when, in the fog and confusion, they were attacked by Oxford's men.[43]

The misalignment of the armies meant that Edward's right, under Hastings, and Warwick's left, under Exeter, came close to collapse. Warwick committed some of his reserve to support Exeter and the fight with Gloucester's men turned into a bitter slog. Hastings's men gave way then broke under Oxford's onslaught. They fled the battle, into Barnet and beyond, some managing to reach London. Oxford followed, rallying those he could find.[44]

Warwick now committed the last of his reserve against Edward's centre and slowly pushed them back. He was close to victory when Oxford returned to the field with the few men he had managed to gather. In the fog, they crashed into Montagu's men. With no time to do more than react, Montagu ordered his archers to bring the rapidly approaching cavalry down. This, in turn, brought cries of 'Treason!' from the throats of Oxford's men, and they quit the field. Panic set in, rippling through the Lancastrian lines. They had been betrayed! By whom they could not know, nor could they know of the fatal mistakes both Montagu and Oxford had made.[45]

Warwick's remaining commanders struggled to hold their lines, but Edward saw his chance and redoubled his efforts, throwing his men into the thick of it. When Montagu fell, the battle was done. Warwick also died, 'somewhat fleeing' according to *The Arrivall* or, according to *Warkworth's Chronicle*, lost in a wood near the battlefield, where he was found by one of Edward's men and killed. A third version of the story has Warwick found alive after the battle was won. Seeking an audience with Edward, he was quietly despatched by his escort before he got to the king's side. If this version is true, it fits well with what we know of Edward IV's character. Always quick to forgive and pardon, he would have found it impossible in Warwick's case in 1471. If he survived the battle, Warwick could not be allowed to live, nor could Edward bring himself to have his cousin tried and executed for treason. Better to die seeking escape, better a quick and painless assassination, than to die on the scaffold.[46]

Many hundreds lay dead on the battlefield. One was Humphrey Bourchier, lord Cromwell, husband of Maud Stanhope's sister. Exeter was so badly wounded that he was presumed dead and left on the field, unrecognised by scavengers and those sent to collect the bodies of the great and the good. He survived and escaped the field. Oxford fled into Scotland. One of the Paston brothers fighting under Oxford's banner was wounded; the other was not. But the dead who mattered most were Richard Nevill, earl of Warwick, and John Nevill, Marquis Montagu. They were stripped of their armour and their bodies taken to the steps of St Paul's, where all could see the great Nevill dynasty had come to an end. The Archbishop of York was later given leave to bury his brothers alongside their parents at Bisham Priory.

# 35

# EMBERS OF RESISTANCE

On 14 April 1471, Anne Nevill arrived at Cerne Abbey with her husband and mother-in-law to the dreadful news of her father's death. Though it had been reported in May that Queen Margaret had written to the King of France saying that Warwick was still alive, having been 'wounded in the fight' and withdrawn 'to a secret and solitary place to get well of his wounds and sickness', previous reports in late April made it clear that both Warwick and Montagu were dead. 'We have not heard this by letters, however, but by word of mouth from three who say that they saw [their bodies] and so we believe it.'[1]

If Anne and the queen held out any hope that Warwick had somehow survived, his widow did not. Landing at Portsmouth on the same day, intending to join her daughter and Queen Margaret, the countess of Warwick quickly changed her plans once she reached Southampton.[2]

> [B]eing there, she had certain knowledge that the king had won the field upon her husband, at Barnet, and there slain him, wherefore she would no further go towards the queen but secretly, got over [Southampton] Water into the New Forest, where she took her to the fraunches of an abbey called Beaulieu.[3]

In their shock and grief, the countess of Warwick and her daughters were separated by both distance and circumstance. Isobel, her husband now back in the Yorkist fold, could do nothing to help either of them. Anne had to stay with her mother-in-law and Prince Edward, wherever that took her. The countess, without the man who had been the one constant in her life since childhood and faced with a journey of 80 miles if she was to link up with Queen Margaret, took the only clear course she could see. It was a decision she would come to regret.

While there were some in Queen Margaret's camp who felt no sorrow at the deaths of Warwick and Montagu, their defeat at Barnet, the capture of Exeter and the flight of Oxford threw their plans into disarray. The news left Margaret feeling 'right heavy and sorry', but she could not afford to falter. Speed was now of the essence. Somerset was given command of the army and had to make a decision. Either they marched north and west towards Wales, in hopes of meeting up with Jasper Tudor, or they must go towards London. The capital was held firm by Edward IV and he would hope to draw the enemy as close as possible before giving battle. It was a risky course of action and, in the end, the potential benefit of a Welsh force led by Tudor proved the more sensible.[4]

The two forces met at Tewkesbury in Gloucestershire on 4 May 1471. Through a series of forced marches, Edward IV arrived in time to prevent Tudor linking up with the Lancastrians. Queen Margaret's army was commanded by Somerset, Wenlock and Devon. There was little cohesion and less trust between them. The death of Warwick brought Wenlock's loyalty into question. He might have been prepared to risk his life for his master the Captain of Calais, but would he do so for Henry VI and his son?[5]

Prince Edward, untried in battle but from all accounts fierce and well trained, took his place in the centre. He was fighting for his future, for the dynasty he hoped to forge with his Nevill queen. His father, whom he had not seen for ten years, was once more a prisoner in London. His mother and wife took refuge in a nearby house of religion, from where they could watch the battle unfold. Anne Nevill left no clue as to her feelings for her husband of just six months. With her father dead, her mother in sanctuary and her sister on the opposing side, all she could see of the future depended on Prince Edward's survival, on his triumph. Though kept close by her warrior father's side since childhood, she had never been this close to the business of war. It was brutal and noisy. For a time, it looked like Somerset might prevail, but his audacious move to outflank Gloucester's men failed. Wenlock's men were expected in support of Somerset, but failed to appear and Somerset's force was routed.[6]

Escaping the slaughter, Somerset sought out Wenlock and struck him down with a single blow of his battle axe. Prince Edward, young and inexperienced as he was, was now in command of the remnants of the Lancastrian army. He was killed in the dying stages of the fight, 'fleeing to the townward'. The hopes of the Lancastrian dynasty were now at an end. Edward IV was finally secure on his throne.[7]

The battle might have been over, but the killings were not. Among those captured, either caught in flight or dragged from the false safety of Tewkesbury Abbey, were Somerset and Gervase Clifton. Tried by Gloucester as Constable of England and Norfolk as Marshall, they were executed on 6 May in the marketplace at Tewkesbury. Anne Nevill and her mother-in-law were taken into custody the following day. Transported to London, Margaret was confined in the Tower and Anne sent into the care of the duke and duchess of Clarence.[9]

The two main threats to Edward's kingship were now gone but it was not quite over. Oxford was at large and on the run. Jasper Tudor was still somewhere in Wales. Warwick's cousin Thomas, Bastard of Fauconberg had raised troops in Kent and now threatened London.

There had been a seismic shift in the capital. Those who had spent the months of Edward's exile in sanctuary were now at liberty. Henry VI was once more a deposed and captive king. Edward's sisters were once again free to return to their London homes. The Archbishop of York was a prisoner, left bereft by the deaths of his brothers and the collapse of the readeption. It is difficult to know just what Fauconberg sought to gain by stirring the men of Kent to revolt. Perhaps he believed, as he had not seen their bodies lying on the steps of St Paul's, that Warwick and Montagu were still alive. If they were, they would need their cousin. Fauconberg was determined to pass through the city with his men.[9]

In a letter to the common council of London, he lamented the attempts to keep him out of the city: 'I am informed how the party of the usurper of our said liege lord's crown has made you to understand that I with the king's people should purpose to despoil the city of London if I came therein.' Fauconberg had no intention of rifling the city, he assured its citizens. He wanted only to 'avenge [Henry VI's] quarrel against the said usurper and his adherents and to seek him in what parts he be within the realm of England to abridge the painful labour and to shorten the way of the king's people heartily set and disposed against the said usurper'.[10]

Fauconberg had demanded a quick response from the council and duly received one. Though couched in terms of respect for Fauconberg's lineage and status, it was firm and uncompromising. Fauconberg was not merely the illegitimate son of the late earl of Kent; during the readeption he had, by the commandment of King Henry, Queen Margaret and the Prince of Wales, 'and by the advice of the earl of Warwick, who you suppose to be alive as we are informed, and other, you be ordained captain of the navy of England and men of war both by sea and by land'.[11]

He was the son of a man still revered in England, 'whose steps we would that you should follow', and himself a man of 'good disposition and virtue', but the gates of London would not be opened to him. Before he left in pursuit of Queen Margaret's army, Edward IV had commanded the mayor and council to suffer no one to enter the city without his authority. Besides, they doubted his ability to control his men: 'it would not be in your power to let your said fellowship from despoilage and robbery'.[12]

It was time Fauconberg was disabused of his illusions that Warwick had survived Barnet.

Right worshipful sir, we marvel greatly that you being a man of so great wisdom and discretion should be deceived by the simple sayings and feigned tales we certify upon our worships and truths that both the said Edward late prince of Wales and the earl of Warwick are slain and dead for we know for certain not only by the reports of men of great credence both of this city and by others which were with the said earl of Warwick in the field when he and his brother marquis Montagu were slain but also by open lying of their bodies in the church of Paul's by the space of two days which many of us did see and understand for certain to be the bodies of the said earl of Warwick and marquis.[13]

The dead from Tewkesbury were also named, giving Fauconberg little doubt as to the utter destruction of the Lancastrian cause. He should give credence to these reports and accept Edward IV as his sovereign lord. 'And you so doing shall cause the king rather to be your good lord and thereby you shall eschew great jeopardies, perils and inconveniences that might ensue of the contrary.' Whatever Fauconberg chose to do, the mayor and aldermen of London ended their reply to his request by 'letting you know for certain that you nor your host shall not come within the said city'.[14]

Fauconberg's timing had been off for some time. When he should have been patrolling the Channel to assist the crossing of Margaret of Anjou's fleet or challenge Edward IV's, he was engaged in piracy against Portuguese shipping. His popularity in Kent was immense. The army he raised was large and well organised. He had with him men from the Calais garrison. Had they arrived in time, Fauconberg's force might have turned the tide at Barnet.[15]

The defence of London was as serious as the assault. A 3-mile stretch of the Thames, from Baynard's Castle to the Tower, was fortified 'with men at arms, bombards and other implements of war'. Fauconberg 'brought a large fleet of ships near the Tower, and the said bank was held by the aldermen and the rest of the citizens in great numbers'. London Bridge was attacked and many houses set on fire, '[t]he citizens, however, sallied out of the gates and made a stout resistance and put them to flight, and nearly 300 men fell in battle and in flight besides those who were drowned in endeavouring to get on board their ships at Blackwall &c'.[16]

Rivers led the defence of London alongside Edward IV's uncle, the earl of Essex. Edward IV's victories at Barnet and Tewkesbury lent heart, courage and determination to those within the city gates. As disciplined and experienced as Fauconberg's men were, and as personally devoted to both him and the memory of Warwick, their cause was lost. They had little to gain from entering the city. They had no allies to rally and it is unlikely Fauconberg planned to march as far as Wales in the hopes of a rendezvous with Jasper Tudor. On 14 May, Fauconberg's men retreated to their ships and he himself moved back to Blackheath. A week later, when Edward entered London, Fauconberg had withdrawn to Canterbury.[17]

He sent word to Edward,

> humbly to sue for his grace and pardon, and them of his fellowship and, by appointment, will there to be delivered to the king's behalf all his ships and became his true liegeman, with as straight promise of true allegiance as could be devised for them to be made which, after … certain great considerations was granted.[18]

Fauconberg submitted himself, his ships and his men to Gloucester on 26 June. He went north with Gloucester, now warden of the west march, towards Scotland, and received a pardon on 16 July. Just three short months later, something changed, though we have no record of what it was. On 15 September, Sir John Paston reported: 'I understand that Bastard Fauconberg is either headed or like to be and his brother both, some men say he would have deserved it, and some say nay.' Just a fortnight later, he further confirmed that 'Thomas Fauconberg his head was yesterday set upon London Bridge, looking into Kentward; and men say that his brother was sore hurt and escaped to sanctuary in Beverly.'[19]

A generation of Nevill men was now gone, all but the Archbishop of York. As a man of the cloth, and the second highest in England, he could not be punished for his treason to the full extent of the law. He was freed from the Tower on 4 June 1471 and returned to his home at the Moor.[20]

In December, Sir John Paston wrote in a letter to his mother that 'I come to my lord archbishop, where I have had as great cheer, and been as welcome as I could devise.' By the following April, however, George Nevill was once again under arrest and committed to the Tower, and Edward seized from him £20,000 of goods, including the Moor itself.[21]

The charges against the archbishop were thin. He had been in discussion with obscure and rebellious Yorkshiremen. But there was something else afoot that might have troubled Edward IV and made him question George's loyalty. The earl of Oxford had emerged from exile in Scotland and was once again making trouble.[22]

# PART 6

# THE LAST OF
# THE NEVILLS

# 36

# THE EARL AND
# THE ARCHBISHOP

When her husband's letter arrived after the turmoil and tragedy of Barnet, Margaret, countess of Oxford must have read it with a mixture of relief and trepidation. He was alive, at least, though in the most desperate straits and 'great heaviness'. He did not write simply to let her know he was relatively safe 'by favour of strange people', but to ask for her help.[1]

> Also you shall send me in all haste all the ready money that you can make, and as many of my men as can come well horsed; and that they come in divers parcels. Also that my horse be sent, with my steel saddles; and bid the yeoman of the horse cover them with leather. Also you shall send to my mother, and let her know of this letter, and pray her of her blessing, and bid her send me my casket, by this token; that she has the key thereof, but it is broken.[2]

After a barrage of instructions, Oxford finished his letter on an uplifting note: 'Also you shall be of good cheer, and take no thought, for I shall bring my purpose about now by the grace of God, whom have you in his keeping.'[3]

This is the only extant letter from Oxford to his countess, written under extraordinary circumstances at an extraordinary time. It signalled the start of a fourteen-year separation. If there was other correspondence between them during Oxford's long exile, it is likely to have contained much that was treasonous. If both the earl and countess destroyed such letters, it is entirely understandable.

Though it is difficult to guess at the relationship between them through this single letter, it does contain one or two clues. First, Oxford was confident his wife would understand the seriousness of his situation and carry out his wishes. Like other fifteenth-century noblewomen, Margaret had acted as her husband's deputy during his absences from home. She had the authority to see his instructions carried out. Second, his closing sentence suggests he was both aware of and concerned about her welfare. In April and May 1471, Margaret was grieving for her two slain brothers, Warwick and Montagu. Oxford needed her to know that he was still alive, still determined to return to her in triumph.

After Tewkesbury, there could be no triumph for the Lancastrian cause. By the end of May, Henry VI was dead, quietly murdered in his cell in the Tower. Whatever purpose Oxford had, it no longer concerned the restoration of the Lancastrian dynasty. Perhaps it never had. Oxford's motives were personal. He held Edward IV responsible for the deaths of his father and brother in 1462. It was the end of Edward's reign – and life – that drove him.

After Barnet and the flight of her husband, Margaret took sanctuary in St Martin's church in London, where she remained for some time. Whether she was able to send the money, men and horses her husband needed is not known. She may have received the letter in sanctuary and been able to do little to help him. If his letter arrived shortly after the battle, she may have had time to act before looking to her own safety. She had no lands of her own, and no dower to fall back on. Her sisters Alianor and Katherine were married to men who remained loyal to Edward IV. Her sister Alice had her own troubles to deal with. Although she was in desperate need of help and support, Margaret could not look to her family for aid.[4]

Oxford fled to Scotland, where he was granted a six-month safe conduct. Nothing is known of his activities or his whereabouts for nearly a year. He next surfaces in France, in April 1472, involved in 'diverse assaults by diverse enemies of the lord king called "Easterlings" and others in the company of John, recently earl of Oxford, landing both on the shore of the port of Calais as well as in divers places within the march'.[5]

Perhaps it was a coincidence that, around this time, the Archbishop of York came under suspicion of treason. Up until then, he had been enjoying something of a rehabilitation. He continued his duties as archbishop, though largely *in absentia*. He had a good team of competent and talented deputies in place, including his old friend and Oxford colleague John Shirwood.

The fractured relationship between George and the king seems to have been mended to the point that George 'was with king Edward at Windsor and hunted and that there right good cheer; and supposed he had stood in great favour with the king, for the king said to the said archbishop that he would come for to hunt and disport with him in his manor at Moor'. But, on 25 April, Edward sent for George, 'and as soon as he came, he was arrested and impeached of high treason, for that he should keep the earl of Oxford, and anon right he was put to ward'. He was first taken to the Tower and from there, in the dead of night, to Hammes Castle in Calais. There is nothing concrete to connect George Nevill to the activities of his brother-in-law Oxford, though he may well have been in correspondence with him. The timing of George's contact with the rebellious Yorkshiremen may have been enough to goad Edward IV into action – it was better to have a potential traitor safely under lock and key while Oxford was at large and causing trouble.[6]

George spent two years in Hammes Castle, sinking lower and lower into despair and depression. His physical health also suffered. He had been shielded and supported by his family all his life. He had enjoyed a privileged childhood crowded with siblings. It might have been his high birth and family wealth that propelled him into the higher offices of the Church but he acquitted himself more than ably once there. Warwick had been his lodestar and now Warwick was dead. George was left to forge his own path through the labyrinths of fifteenth-century politics and, without Warwick to guide him, he was lost.

John Shirwood visited him and was shocked by what he found. In an attempt to keep him occupied, Shirwood taught George to play rithmomachia, an intensely complex board game favoured by mathematicians and men of science. He also promised to write a treatise on the game for his old friend. Unfortunately, the book was not published until long after George's death, though it was dedicated to his memory.[7]

It might have set Edward IV's mind at rest, but George Nevill's imprisonment did nothing to dampen Oxford's enthusiasm for his mission. His presence in France during 1472 was not welcomed by the duke of Burgundy, who feared Oxford had secretly come to terms with Edward IV and was playing a double game. In April 1473, Oxford was once again on the move. Sailing from Dieppe, he 'purposed into Scotland with twelve ships'. Though he was initially welcomed and his safe conduct extended, the Scots were not prepared to shelter Oxford indefinitely, nor support his cause, and he was soon back in France.[8]

In Calais, Sir John Paston was remarkably well informed of Oxford's movements and activities and regularly wrote to his brother to keep him up to date. Once a close associate of the earl – indeed in his letter to his countess, Oxford asks her to send Paston to join him – Sir John was interested in Oxford's activities, but not himself involved. Despite his own doubts, Paston's information was sound. In May, he wrote of a 'great treasure' being sent to Oxford in the custody of a monk. Shortly after that, he reported that Oxford was expected to land in southern England within a few days with 'one hundred gentlemen in Norfolk and Suffolk that have agreed to assist the said earl in his coming there'. A few days later, he confirmed that Oxford had indeed landed in Essex on 28 May, but 'he tarried not long, for if he had, the earl of Essex rode to him wards and the lords Dynham and Duras, and others more, which by likelihood should have distressed him'.[9]

King Louis had thrown his support behind Oxford, always happy to exploit dissension among the English. He saw Oxford as Warwick's successor in opposition and rebellion. Unlike Warwick, however, Oxford issued no manifestos. He had no plan of government reform, no real plans for dynastic change. He wanted his revenge against Edward IV, plain and simple. Always suspicious and always on the watch for double-dealing, Louis did not entirely trust him.[10]

Those watching England, including the Milanese ambassador to France, saw little sign of the trouble reported by Oxford. Edward IV installed his son, also Edward, as Prince of Wales and set him up in his own household at Ludlow Castle. When he immediately followed this with a trip to the northern border, it was seen as evidence his realm was at peace.[11]

Oxford sent king Louis the seals of twenty-four 'cavaliers, lords and one duke who have promised to pledge their Troth to make war on king Edward'. He asked for monetary support but Louis hesitated 'because he feared art and fraud in the earl and that the seals may be counterfeit'. Louis immediately ordered his fleet to patrol the Channel and refused to welcome Oxford's brother Thomas to France.

> I fear that the affairs of England are at peace without war or other internal dissension, and that the earl of Oxford, who reported the exact opposite here, has at length come in and taken his place at the court of king Edward.[12]

Oxford had not come to terms with Edward IV and never would. In September, he took and held St Michael's Mount, a fortress just off the Cornish coast near Penzance. He had with him only a handful of men, including his brothers and Viscount Beaumont. His venture was partially funded by the proceeds of piracy but he needed additional help from King Louis. The first ship sent by the latter, despite his doubts about Oxford, foundered in a storm and the food and weapons were jettisoned to save the crew.[13]

Edward IV ordered the castle besieged and blockaded by ships to prevent the arrival of French relief. The first commander of the siege, who parlayed with Oxford and 'suffered him to be victualled', was soon replaced, in disgrace, and the siege resumed in earnest. Edward sent private promises of pardon and reward to any of Oxford's men who would leave the Mount, 'by the which divers of them were turned to the king against the earl; and so in conclusion the earl had not more than eight or nine men that would hold with him, the which was the undoing of the earl'. Offered terms of his life, Oxford had no choice but to give himself up; 'if he had not done so, his own men would have brought him out'. The siege was raised on 15 February 1472. Oxford's one-man stand against Edward IV was over. His goods and property forfeit to the crown, he was sent to Hammes Castle to spend the rest of his life in prison.[14]

The countess of Oxford left St Martin's sanctuary soon after her husband's arrest, her life and liberty no longer in danger. With no income of her own and little help from her family, Margaret suffered greatly. She had nothing to live on 'but as the people of their charities would give her, or what she might get with her needle or other such cunning as she exercised'. She was eventually granted a pension of £100 a year, but not until 1482. Oxford's mother the dowager countess also suffered, Gloucester forcing her to sign over property to him in exchange for a much-reduced income. Though those looking after the dowager's interests tried, they could do nothing to stop the brother of the king getting his way.[15]

Oxford's imprisonment brought a change of circumstances not only for him and his family but for the Archbishop of York. Now no longer concerned about his potential for treason, and under considerable pressure from the pope, Edward IV ordered George's release in 1474. On 19 December, George Nevill landed at Dover and spent Christmas as a guest of the Archbishop of Canterbury. George Nevill's deputies had repaid his trust in them and his vast diocese had been well run and well administered in his absence. He was immediately able to take up his ecclesiastical duties once more. Even before he left Calais, Pope Sixtus IV was calling on him to resolve an issue that had been brought to his attention. Members of a parish in the diocese of York were unable to attend church during bad weather due to the rising of a nearby river. As archbishop, it was George's responsibility to deal with such issues. As he did not return to England for another five months, this was something he had to leave in his deputies' hands.[16]

George enjoyed his rehabilitation for just two years. Already ill, probably with kidney stones, in May 1476, he set out for York. He was prescribed 'a mixture compounded of barley, water, herbs and honey', but it did him no good. On 9 June, the sole surviving son of the earl and countess of Salisbury died at Blythe in Nottinghamshire. He was buried in York Minster but the location of his grave has been forgotten over the centuries.[17]

In Hammes Castle, Oxford's adventures were not quite over. Contemplating his own bleak future and deeply troubled by the ill treatment of his wife and mother, he was driven to desperate action. In August 1478, Sir John Paston once again sent news of his old patron to his brother. '[A]s I hear say, [Oxford] leapt the walls and went to the dyke, and into the dyke to the chin, to what intent I cannot tell; some say to steal away, and some think he would have drowned himself, and so it is deemed.'[18]

Though the misery of his confinement, the bleakness of his life and his inability to help those he loved may well have driven Oxford to a suicide attempt, everything we know about his life would suggest otherwise. His wife was prevented from visiting him, and his existence was comfortable but lonely. Just what he might have done, or where he might have gone, had his escape attempt succeeded, is a mystery. He may have thought to throw himself once again on the mercy of the King of France. He may still have harboured hopes of unseating Edward IV. He was fished out of the moat, broken bones and all, and returned to captivity.[19]

In 1483, after the unexpected death of Edward IV, Oxford had hopes of being allowed to return to England. Richard III, who deposed his nephews and took the throne himself in June that year, refused to release Oxford. Late in 1484, Oxford befriended his gaoler and together they left Hammes to join Henry Tudor, then in exile in France. When Tudor landed in England in 1485, Oxford was with him. He fought at Bosworth, where Richard III lost his life. Reunited with his wife, Oxford rose to dizzying heights in the government of Henry VII.[20]

# 37

# BITTER HARVEST

solated in Beaulieu Abbey, prevented from leaving by the presence of armed men and the collusion of the abbot, the countess of Warwick had to deal with widowhood and the disintegration of her family alone. She knew her daughters were safe, though Anne's future was far from certain. She was in the custody of the duke of Clarence, closely watched in case she was pregnant. This was not Clarence's only reason for wanting to keep Anne under his control. With their father dead, the sisters stood to inherit a vast fortune. If Warwick left a will, its terms were not honoured and the king's brothers had other plans for his wealth.

Anne Nevill made her escape, most likely with Gloucester's collusion, and entered St Martin's sanctuary in London. A colourful story that has withstood the test of time has her concealed by Clarence 'disguised in the habit of a cookmaid'. She was discovered by Gloucester, who took her to St Martin's to keep her from his brother's clutches.[1]

Gloucester wished to marry Anne and, given her difficult situation and her need for both protection and independence from Clarence, it is highly likely she wished to marry him. The plan was risky though. Even with the stated consent and collusion of the bride, a marriage following an abduction could be challenged and set aside.

That there was some question as to the validity of the marriage, which cannot be dated with any certainty, is clear from the record of the 1472 Parliament. Anne and Richard were certainly married before 1474, when their union was reported by the Milanese ambassador to France. The fact of an abduction seems to have been well known on the continent, though the nuances of Anne's likely collusion were not. The marriage caused conflict between Gloucester and Clarence that, without the intervention of their brother the king, may well have broken out into open war.

the duke of Gloucester, who by force had taken to wife the daughter of the late earl of Warwick, who had been married to the prince of Wales, was constantly preparing for war with the duke of Clarence. The latter, because his brother king Edward had promised him Warwick's country, did not want the former to have it by reason of his marriage with the earl's second daughter.[2]

Such squabbling over the late earl of Warwick's property might be thought premature, given his widow was still alive and 'to whom for the whole of her life the most noble inheritance of the Warwick and the Despencers properly belonged'.[3]

Kept in sanctuary by force, the countess of Warwick wrote desperate letters to anyone she could think of, including one to the 'commons of this present parliament'. She had entered sanctuary on hearing of the death of her husband 'for surety of her person, to dispose for the weal and health of the soul of her said lord and husband, as right and conscience required her so to do'. Within five days, she made over 'her labours, suits and means to the king's highness for her safeguard, to be had as diligently and effectually as her power would extend'. Without the help of a clerk or secretary, she wrote 'with her own hand'. She had, she asserted, committed no offence, despite 'some sinister information' provided to the king. She had, as wives were supposed to do, been obedient to the wishes of her husband. During his life, he held his title by her right; any treasonous actions taken by him could not be ascribed to her. She wished to see the king, 'to make suits to the king's highness in her own person for her livelihood and rightful inheritance' which 'wholly has been restrained from her from the time of the death of her said lord and husband unto this day'.[4]

There were to be no charges of treason laid against the countess of Warwick nor, more surprisingly, her late husband or his brother Montagu. Had they been attainted, their property would have been forfeit to the crown, uninheritable by their children. Edward IV had already made provision for Montagu's widow, Isobel Ingoldisthorpe. He had brokered a second marriage for her with one of his body squires, William Norreys. She was given the wardship of her son George and was free to hold both her own property and that which she had inherited from her late husband.[5]

In 1478, George was degraded from his title duke of Bedford on the grounds he had insufficient income to maintain it. He was the sole male heir of the entailed Nevill properties but these had been put into Gloucester's hands. They were to remain there after George came of age and married, so long as he or his male heirs lived. Though she held his wardship, George's mother did not have the rights to his marriage. On Isobel's death, he became a royal ward but died himself before a suitable bride was found for him.[6]

Isobel enjoyed only four years of marriage to Norreys before she died in 1476. Despite her considerable wealth, she and Norreys managed to get themselves into financial trouble and had to appeal to her mother, Joan Tiptoft, to bail them out. In 1473, they owed £1,000 to a London tailor, William Parker. Joan was required to sign over several properties to the tailor until such time as the debt was paid. Should she die in the meantime, he was to continue to hold her property until he had recovered his money, then it was to be disposed of according to the terms of her will. Joan made her feelings on the matter quite clear. '[B]e it known to all people that [Joan] Ingoldisthorpe has not agreed to the premises for any cause, but only by reason of divers requests by the foresaid William Norreys and marquess [of Montagu] made to her'. Isobel and Norreys had three daughters and a short-lived son. When Isobel died, she was buried with her first husband John Nevill at Bisham Abbey.[7]

Like Isobel, Maud Stanhope did not suffer for her husband's treason in 1471. Gervase Clifton's execution after the battle of Tewkesbury left her a widow for the third time. She had already lost much on his account and she is unlikely to have grieved deeply at his passing. Living at Tattershall with her sister Jane, also widowed since the battle of Barnet, she continued to fight for what was hers until her death. In 1493, John Gigur, warden of the college set up by Ralph, lord Cromwell, complained about her in a letter to William Waynflete.

> [S]he has desired that her meat might be cooked in the college kitchen all this winter and I would not grant it till I had word from my lord and from you; for without my lord might agree with her I would in no wise meddle no more with her for I take great hurt by her. She has written an answer to my lord of her disposition, the which I have sent to my lord and what is in it I am not of counsel.[8]

Maud's finances never recovered. In 1472, she needed to borrow £40 from a London merchant so she could celebrate Christmas. In 1481, when Hastings turned his attention to acquiring the remains of Maud's estate, and that of her sister lady Cromwell, Gigur proved himself to be more of a friend than his letter suggests. He urged Bishop Waynflete to throw his support behind Maud and a satisfactory agreement was reached between all parties. When Maud's sister Jane died in 1481, Maud at last held the title lady Cromwell.[9]

In 1483, Anthony Wydeville, earl Rivers went some way to redressing the harm he had done Maud in 1465. He remembered her in his will, written shortly before his execution on Gloucester's orders.

> Also I will that my lady Willoughby late the wife of sir Gervase Clifton, be commoned with all by mine executors touching such stuff as sir Ewan parson

of Wolverton and other of my servants had away from her place and she to
be dealt with therein and answered according to good right and conscience.[10]

Maud died on 30 August 1492. In her will, she asked for prayers to be said
for all three of her husbands.[11]

In contrast, the countess of Warwick's long years of widowhood left her
neither free nor comfortable. Edward IV's desire to bring peace between
his warring brothers, and to see them well provided for, rendered Anne
Beauchamp a non-person. It was a complex process and began with her
daughter Anne's marriage to the duke of Gloucester.

That there was a possible impediment to the marriage – perhaps involving
the duke's 'abduction' of his bride – is clear from the Rolls of Parliament.
The most likely source of a challenge to the legality of their marriage was
Gloucester's brother Clarence. If the marriage were annulled, he could
conceivably get Anne's inheritance for himself by regaining control of her
person. It was to pre-empt and prevent this that the status of their marriage
was discussed in Parliament.

[I]t is ordained by the said authority, that if the said Richard duke of
Gloucester and Anne be hereafter divorced and after that he do his effectual
diligence and continual endeavour, by all convenient and lawful means, to be
lawfully married to the said Anne ... and during the life of the same Anne
be not wedded nor married to any other woman: that yet the said duke of
Gloucester shall have and enjoy as much of the premises as shall appertain to
the said Anne, during the life of the said duke of Gloucester.[12]

A challenge by Clarence would not wrest Anne's property from Gloucester's
grip. Nor could Gloucester use this act of Parliament to end his marriage
to Anne without severe penalty – his choice then would be to remain
unmarried or forego the benefits of her wealth. Although this act has been
interpreted by some as a threat to Anne, it offered her the best protection
available. It was far more in Gloucester's interests to ensure the regularity
of their marriage than to see it end in annulment or divorce.[13]

In the ordinary course of events, given their father's death, Isobel and
Anne Nevill would have inherited a sizeable portion of his estate, excluding
that held in tail male, which would go to Montagu's son George. Clarence
already held much of that estate, though only for the term of his life, as if
Warwick had been attainted and his property forfeit to the crown. For Isobel
and Anne to inherit anything from their father, he must not be attainted.
Given that the earl of Oxford and both Robert and Richard Welles were
attainted by the 1472 Parliament, the non-attainder of both Warwick and
Montagu must have caused a good deal of wonder. That it was not, as

claimed, due to the intervention of Gloucester and 'other lords', would have been clear. This was an exercise in providing an income for both Clarence and Gloucester. Montagu had, after all, committed 'great and horrible treasons and other offences'.[14]

That was not, however, the worst action of the 1472 Parliament. As Clarence would not agree to share his spoils with his brother, the countess of Warwick's property was to be taken from her and added to the pot. No charges of treason were drawn up against her and, apart from the 'sinister information' alluded to in her letter to the Commons, no justification was offered. The act of Parliament simply states that Clarence and Gloucester were to

> have, possess, inherit and enjoy, as in the right of their said wives, all honours, lordships, castles, towns, manors, lands, tenements, liberties, franchises, possessions and inheritance which were or be belonging to the said Anne, countess of Warwick, or any other person or persons to their use, to have and to hold to the said dukes and their said wives, and to the heirs of their said wives, in like manner and form, as if the said countess were now naturally dead.[15]

Still held confined in sanctuary, there was nothing the countess of Warwick could do to prevent this. Shortly after, she was released from Beaulieu on the orders of her son-in-law Gloucester and taken north to Middleham Castle to live in his custody.

Isobel Nevill died on 22 December 1476, shortly after the birth of her fourth child, who did not long outlive her. Her funeral at Tewkesbury Abbey was splendid and her husband greatly mourned her loss. It was soon after her death that Clarence's life spiralled out of control. Arrested for bringing the laws of England into disrepute, he was further charged with treason, tried before the duke of Buckingham and executed in the Tower on 18 February 1478. He and Isobel had two surviving children, Margaret, countess of Salisbury and Edward, earl of Warwick. Both would be executed on the orders of Tudor kings.[16]

The duke and duchess of Gloucester spent the first ten years of their marriage in the north of England, based at Middleham Castle. It was here their only child Edward was born, most likely in 1472 or 1473.

Warwick had wanted one of his daughters to be queen of England. This finally came to pass some twelve years after his death. When Edward IV unexpectedly died in May 1483, his son and successor was just 12 years old. In the ensuing power struggle, Gloucester deposed his nephew and took the crown. Anne Nevill was crowned queen alongside her husband, Richard III, on 22 June 1483. Their son died the following year, throwing Anne and Richard into the depths of grief and sorrow. Anne herself died after a short but ferocious illness on 16 March 1485. She did not live to see her husband defeated at the battle of Bosworth on 22 August of that year. Rous described her as 'In presence ... seemly, amiable and beauteous. and in conditions, full commendable and right virtuous and, according to the interpretation of her name Anne, full gracious'.[17]

During Anne Nevill's short queenship, she was attended by her aunt Alice Fitzhugh and cousin Elizabeth. Alice's daughter Anne was married to Richard III's close friend and councillor Francis, Viscount Lovell. Alice's son Richard, lord Fitzhugh fought for Richard III at Bosworth but submitted to Henry VII after his victory. He was appointed Henry's lieutenant in the north of England until his death. Alice, then living in her dower property, returned to Ravensworth to take custody of her grandson George, now lord Fitzhugh.[18]

The surviving Nevill sisters were not united in the last decades of their lives. All three were touched by the tumultuous events of 1483–85. Alice Fitzhugh was widowed by 1472, her husband dying soon after his return from exile in Scotland. She had attended the coronation of a queen and attended her at court. Katherine, married to Edward IV's closest friend, spent little time at court. Her husband William, lord Hastings was summarily executed on Gloucester's orders in June 1483. Until her husband's return to England in 1485, Margaret, countess of Oxford lived in penury.

Nothing better illustrates the differences between the sisters than a pair of letters sent to Sir John Paston in February and May 1486. This was shortly after the battle of Stoke, a last-ditch attempt by the sons of Elizabeth, duchess of Suffolk, Viscount Lovell and others to unseat Henry VII. It ended in Henry's victory and John de la Pole's death, and rendered Lovell a fugitive.[19]

The countess of Oxford and the dowager lady Fitzhugh were both concerned about Lovell's whereabouts but for very different reasons. In February, Alice wrote to Sir John Paston from London touching on a business deal. Her other great concern was her son-in-law.

> Also my daughter Lovell makes great suit and labour for my son her husband. Sir Edward Frank has been in the north to enquire for him; he is come again and cannot understand where he is. Wherefore her benevolers will her to continue her suit and labour; and so I cannot depart nor leave her as you know well.[20]

Margaret's concerns about Lovell were not so benign. He was rumoured to be on the Isle of Ely, planning to take ship to Norfolk or find his way to sanctuary.

I therefore heartily desire, pray you and nevertheless, in the king's name, straightly charge you that you in all goodly haste endeavour yourself that such watch or other means be used and had in the ports and creeks and other places where you think necessary by your discretion, to the letting of his said purpose; and that you also use all the ways you can or may by your wisdom to the taking of the same late lord Lovell. And what pleasure you may do to the king's grace in this matter, I am sure, is not to you unknown.[21]

In the end, Lovell was never found. He may have gone to the continent or died in hiding. His wife continued to live with her mother, unable to secure a pardon for her husband or an income for herself.

Alianor Nevill died around 1471. Her widower lord Stanley married Margaret Beaufort the following June. Margaret was the mother of the exiled Henry Tudor. Stanley and his brother William threw in their lot with Tudor at the Battle of Bosworth after Stanley's son George, lord Strange was held hostage by Richard III and threatened with summary execution should his father's loyalty waver.[22]

Alice and Katherine both died in 1503. Alice's daughter Elizabeth married William Parr and was the grandmother of Henry VIII's sixth wife, Catherine Parr. Katherine's daughter Cecily Bonville married Elizabeth Wydeville's son Thomas Grey, Marquis of Dorset. Her son Thomas was the grandfather of lady Jane Grey, briefly Queen of England and executed in February 1554 by Mary I.

Margaret died in late 1506 or early 1507. Two years later, the 64-year-old earl of Oxford remarried. He died in 1531.[23]

The Nevills, both men and women, had extraordinary lives. They dominated English politics for more than thirty years and their fall was as spectacular as their rise. Though the male line died out with the death of Montagu's son George, the descendants of the earl of Salisbury's daughters and grandsons continued to play their parts, both large and small, for generations to come.

# NOTES

## 1. The Beginnings of Greatness

1    Walker 2004a; Walker 2004b.

2    Ibid.

3    Ibid.

4    Ibid.

5    Tuck 2004a.

6    John and Constance also had two children in the early 1370s: Catherine, who later became Queen of Castile, and John, who died in infancy. See Tuck 2004a.

7    The date of the papal pull is disputed. See Tuck 2009; Walker 2004; Walker 2004b.

8    Tuck 2004a.

9    Young 1996.

10   Lower 1851, 123–4.

11   Cokayne 1887b, 494.

12   Hall & Jewitt 1876, 233–5.

13   Phillips 2005.

14   Chambers 1914, 11 (modern spelling by the author).

15   Ibid; Philips 2005. One of the best known examples of a courtesy book was probably written for use in the household of Ralph's grandson, Richard Nevill, 16th earl of Warwick, who was very conscious of his own status and claimed for himself both the mythical ancestry of his Beauchamp wife and his Nevill and FitzMaldred forebears.

16   Chambers 1914; Embleton et al. 1994.

17   Young 1996, 122.

18   Up until the 1450s, the organisation of the marches was fluid. Sometimes there were two – the east march and the west march; sometimes there were three, with a middle march interposed between the two. When they didn't hold wardenship of both, the Nevills were most closely associated with the west march, centred around Carlisle, and the Percies the east, administered from their base at Alnwick. See Reid 1917; Cokayne 1887b, 495, 498–9; Storey 1957.

19   Neville 1994.

20   Tuck 2004b.

21   A colourful account of the battle of Neville's Cross can be found in Swallow 18–29; Tuck 2004b.

22 Tuck 2004b.
23 Ibid.
24 Ibid.
25 As did Swynford's daughter Blanche from her first marriage to Hugh Swynford. The duke and duchess of Lancaster were her godparents.
26 Jambeck 1996; McDonald 2001, 25–6.
27 Thomas Walsingham, *Historia Anglicana*, quoted in McDonald 2001, 26. Not all the women mentioned were admitted at the same time. Joan Beaufort did not receive her robes until 1399, so the idea that these women formed a constant and cohesive group is a false one. However, they do represent, the fluidity of movement between the worlds of men and women during the reign of Richard II and, to a lesser extent, his successors. See Gillespie 1975; McDonald 2001, 25–7.
28 Jambeck 1996.
29 A copy of Troilus and Cressida is said to have been owned by Joan Beaufort or her daughter Anne, duchess of Buckingham. See McDonald 2001; Powell 2003; Staley 1996 (modern spelling by the author).
30 Staley 1996.
31 Ibid; Tuck 2004c.
32 Ralph Nevill did not fight at Agincourt and his relationship with Henry V was not as close as had been his father's. In addition, the husband of Nevill's daughter Alice, Sir Thomas Grey, was beheaded after the Southampton Plot, which also saw the execution of Richard, earl of Cambridge, father of Richard, duke of York.

## 2. Richard II, Bolingbroke and Hotspur

1 Curry 2002, 56–7.
2 Ibid.
3 Though he does mistakenly put Westmorland at Agincourt. Two Robert Nevilles are listed in the Medieval Soldiers muster roll database, both serving under Edward duke of York, who lost his life in the battle. www.medievalsoldier.org/search_musterdb.php.
4 Curry 2002, 60.
5 Tuck 2004b.
6 Ibid.
7 Dobson 2004; Society of Antiquaries 1812, 82–3.
8 Dobson 2004; Whitaker 1823 (Vol. 1), 395.
9 Tuck 2004d.
10 Myers 1927, 20–33.
11 Given-Wilson 2004.
12 Tuck 2004d.
13 Given-Wilson 2004.
14 Tuck 2004d; Given-Wilson 2004.
15 Ibid; Tuck 2004d.
16 Given-Wilson 1995, 54.
17 Tuck 2004e.
18 Tuck 2004e; Tuck 2004d.
19 Given-Wilson 1995, 118, 119.
20 Given-Wilson 1995, 139–52.
21 Given-Wilson 1995, 139.

22  Goodman 2004; Given-Wilson 1995, 135–6.
23  Given-Wilson 1995, 146.
24  Ibid, 146–51.
25  Ibid, 161, 163.
26  Ibid, 164.
27  Ibid, 171. This was the official Lancastrian record of events and heavily biased in favour of Bolingbroke.
28  Ibid, 166.
29  Ibid.
30  Tuck 2004d.
31  Given-Wilson 1995, 225.
32  Ibid, 226.
33  Ibid, 227.
34  Goodman 2004.
35  Unless specified, all earlier Nevills mentioned in this book are from Ralph Nevill's direct ancestral line. See Nevill Family Tree for reference. See also Young 1996, 30–52.
36  Ibid, 85.
37  Tuck 2004e.
38  Barratt 2010, loc 483, 588–674.
39  Ibid, loc 920–1176.
40  Ibid, loc 1180–261.
41  Ibid, loc 1398–403.
42  Ibid, loc 1524.
43  Ibid.
44  Given-Wilson 1995, 194.
45  Barratt 2010, loc. 1645–839.
46  Ibid, loc 1891–5, 1920.
47  Ibid, loc. 2088.
48  Bean 2004.
49  Tuck 2004e.
50  Storey 1957, 603.


## 3. Joan Beaufort's Daughters and the Young Duke of York

1  Pugh 1988, 173.
2  Though there are questions about Cambridge's legitimacy. His mother engaged in a well-documented affair with her husband's half-brother John Holland, and Cambridge was left nothing in his father's will. While this may point to Langley's own doubts, it is not sufficient to establish Cambridge's illegitimacy as fact; Latimer was Ralph Nevill's younger half-brother, who inherited his title from his mother. Maud Clifford divorced him on grounds of impotence and it has been speculated that he was homosexual. See Pugh 1988, 88–117.
3  Pugh 1988, 88–117.
4  Ibid.
5  Ibid.
6  Ibid.
7  Ibid, 88–117, 117–20.
8  Pugh 1988.
9  Johnson 1988, 1.

10 Tuck 2004e.
11 Lander 1963, 121.
12 Crane 2010, 9.
13 Ibid, 6.
14 Ibid, 9.
15 The decidedly businesslike tinge to their marriage did not stop John Paston writing rather giddily to his wife of twenty-five years in September 1465. 'My own dear sovereign lady' is his romantic greeting. He thanks her for her recent visit to him in London and 'the great cheer you made me'. As is customary, the bulk of his letter comprises a set of instructions, which he most uncharacteristically ends with a not particularly good poem ('And wyshe ye had be here stille/For the sey you are a good gille'). Again uncharacteristically, he closes his letter with 'by your true and trusty husband'. In her response, Margaret writes, 'thanking you of your great cheer that you made me, and of the cost that you did on me. You did more cost than my will was that you should do, but that it pleased you to do so, God give me grace to do that may please you.' John and Margaret Paston seem to have achieved what many married couples of their time strove for – a strong business partnership, mutual trust, deep affection, and joy and pleasure in each other's company. See Gairdner 1904b, 188–91.
16 Johnson 1988, 10.
17 Lander 1963, 121.
18 The earl of Albany's son, the earl of Fife, had been a prisoner in England for some time and was to be ransomed by Northumberland for some £10,000 and returned home. Westmorland's son-in-law, Sir Thomas Grey, hatched a plan to intercept Fife and deal directly with Albany. The plan involved Northumberland bringing a Scots army south with him and overthrowing Henry V. Fife was, in fact, seized but was soon recaptured. Northumberland seems to have known nothing about his planned role in the venture. For his part in the plot, Grey was executed along with the earl of Cambridge. Griffiths 2004a.
19 Griffiths, 2004a.
20 Rawcliffe 2004.
21 Archer, 2004b.
22 Archer, 2004a
23 Ibid.
24 Tuck 2004c.
25 Johnson 1988, 28; Watts 2004.
26 In some genealogies, there is reference to a short-lived daughter Joan, born before Anne. This has not been substantiated or confirmed by primary sources. See Johnson 1988, 47.
27 Wolffe 1981, 29–30.
28 Curry 2010.
29 The early earls and dukes of Beaufort followed one another in quick succession and it is worth setting them down briefly to allay any confusion. John Beaufort, earl of Somerset (the son of John of Gaunt and Katherine Swynford) died in 1410 and was succeeded by his son, Henry. Henry died childless in 1418 and the title passed to his brother John, who was elevated from earl to duke of Somerset. When he died in 1444, the title passed to his younger brother, Edmund. When Edmund died in 1455, he was succeeded by his son Henry. Henry died without legitimate issue and the title went into abeyance. See Curry 2010, 44.
30 Harriss 2004a, 2.

31  Johnson 1988, 46.
32  Ibid.
33  Ibid, 48–56.


## 4. Joan Beaufort's Sons and the Family Feud

1   Letter from Henry VI cited in Bentley 1831, 2–3. No provenance is given for this letter nor are the reported incidents mentioned in any of the chronicles of the time. There is an entry in the *Proceedings and Ordinances of the Privy Council, Volume V* (90) which mentions the summons dated February 1438: 'þt łres be send to my lady of Westmł and to þerle of Westmł to be her on þe xv. of Pasq'. As the date mentioned in the letter in *Excerpta Historica* is St Hillary's Day (in January), this may have been an earlier attempt to get the parties to London but since it has no provenance, the letter's authenticity can't be confirmed.
2   Bentley 1831, 2–3.
3   Tuck 2004a.
4   Bentley 1831, 2–3.
5   Nicholas, 1831a, 90.
6   Ward 1992, 85, 87.
7   Ibid.
8   Kingsford 1921, 28.
9   Ibid, 27–31.
10  Pollard 2004a
11  Ibid.
12  Ibid.
13  A prebend is a payment made from the funds of a cathedral or collegiate church, usually attached to administrative functions. See Pollard 2004a.
14  Ibid.
15  Pollard 1990, 248–51.
16  Cokayne 1887c, 25; Pollard 1990, 25–51.
17  Pugh 2004.
18  Ibid.
19  Pollard 2004b.
20  Lander 1963, 121.
21  Pollard 2004f.
22  Though Alice had no legitimate brothers or sisters, her father did acknowledge an illegitimate son: John, Bastard of Salisbury. He is listed in an 'Enumeration of the troops in various garrisons in Normandy in the hands of the English, from Michelmas 1833 to Michelmas 1834' as present in Argentan and, later, serving on a commission to the French king with, among other, John Fastolf, regarding the return of Maine to the French some years later. See Stevenson 1864, 545, 687. As he would have been at least in his forties in 1460, it is difficult to accept Hall's description of 'a valiant young gentleman'. He is also said to have 'fled' after the siege of St Severin in 1434. See *The Chronicles of Guerrand de Montstrelet*, 631. See also Curry 2004a; Anderson 1945, 27–9.
23  Curry 2004a; Anderson 1945, 27–9.
24  Fabyan 1811, 598.
25  Ibid, 3.
26  Pollard 2004c.

## 5. The Road to Dartford

1   Watts 2004.
2   Ibid.
3   Ibid.
4   MacCracken 1911; Anderson 1945.
5   Watts 2004.
6   MacCracken 1911.
7   Watts 2004; Virgoe 1965.
8   Watts 2004.
9   Ibid.
10  Gairdner 1904b, 142 (modern spelling by the author).
11  Virgoe 1965
12  Ibid.
13  Anderson 1945, 38.
14  Ibid, 142–3.
15  Ibid.
16  Virgoe 1965.
17  Nichols 1852, 3 (modern spelling by the author).
18  Mate 1992.
19  Fabyan 1811, 623.
20  Ibid.
21  Ibid.
22  Ibid, 624.
23  Ibid.
24  Ibid, 625; Cardinal Archbishop John Kemp was Chancellor at this time.
25  Ibid.
26  Ibid.
27  Johnson 1988, 78.
28  Storey 1975, 74–5.
29  Gairdner 1853, 95 (modern spelling by the author).
30  Ibid, 95, 97.
31  Griffiths 1975, 196.
32  Ibid, 199.
33  Johnson 1988, 86.
34  Griffiths 1975, 203 (modern spelling by the author).
35  Ibid.
36  Gairdner 1904a, 177–8 (modern spelling by the author); Griffiths 1975, 204.
37  Griffiths 1975, 102; Storey 1999, 79.
38  Johnson 1988, 86, 89.
39  Ibid, 90.
40  Gairdner 1876, 6 (modern spelling by the author); Storey 1975, 80; Flenley 1911, 137.
41  Johnson 1988, 94–5; Gairdner 1876, 1 (modern spelling by the author).
42  Johnson 1988, 99.
43  Storey 1999, 74–5.
44  Johnson 1988, 102.

## 6. The Edge of Rebellion

1   Johnson 1988, 107.
2   Kekewich et al. 1995 (modern spelling by the author).
3   Johnson 1988, 107–8; *Chronicles of the White Rose*, xl-xlii (hereafter, *CWR*) (modern spelling by the author).
4   Anon, 1845, *CWR*, xl-xlii.
5   Ibid; Johnson 1988, 110; Storey 1975, 108–10.
6   Johnson 1988, 110.
7   Storey 1975, 100; Johnson 1988, 110.
8   Kingsford 1913, 297 (modern spelling by the author); Johnson 1988, 110; Gairdner 1904a, 290–2 (modern spelling by the author).
9   Johnson 1988, 115.
10  Flenley 1911, 373 (modern spelling by the author).
11  Kingsford 1913, 298.
12  Gairdner 1893, 69 (modern spelling by the author).
13  Kingsford 1905, 163 (modern spelling by the author).
14  Kekewich et al. 1995, 194 (modern spelling by the author). The full modern English text of York's oath can be found at: www.gutenberg.org/files/43348/43348-h/43348-h.htm#note102_2.
15  Johnson 1988, 115, 116–9.
16  Ibid.
17  Ibid, 117.
18  Ibid, 122–4.

## 7. The Nevills of Middleham and the Percies of Alnwick

1   Pollard 1990, 222.
2   Ibid.
3   This is why we now have the complicated situation of there being several 1st earls of This or 1st dukes of That. Unbroken numbering relates only to those cases where a title has been passed through an unbroken line, from father to son, or in cases where the only heir is a daughter, from father to daughter to son, via the daughter's husband. Every time a title goes into abeyance, where there is no clear heir to inherit, or upon attainder of the holder of the title, the number is reset at its next creation; Warner & Lacey 1996.
4   Ibid.
5   Ibid, 214–7 (modern spelling by the author).
6   Warner & Lacey 1996.
7   Griffiths 2004a.
8   Horrox 2004a.
9   Griffiths 2004b.
10  Keir 1970, 25–6.
11  Ibid, 15.
12  Wood 1876, 7–8.
13  Hicks, 2008.
14  Wood 1876, 598–600.
15  Ibid, 599; Keir 1970, 36–45.
16  Friedrichs 2006.

17　Seaton 1961; Friedrichs 2006.
18　Friedrichs 2006; Booth 2003; Storey 1975, 125.
19　Storey 1975, 125, 126–7.
20　The Battle of Castillon on 17 July 1453 was a humiliating defeat for the English and resulted in the death of John Talbot, earl of Shrewsbury, one of England's most accomplished and experienced commanders in the wars against the French. See Curry 2002, 90.
21　Nicholas 1831b (modern spelling by the author).
22　Ibid.
23　Ibid.
24　Ibid.
25　Ibid.
26　Griffiths 1968, 594.
27　Ibid, 595–6.
28　Hicks 1998.
29　Ibid.
30　Ibid.
31　Griffiths 1968, 602.
32　Hicks 1988.
33　Ibid.

## 8. The Beauchamp Earls of Warwick

1　Gairdner 1874, 106; Sinclair 2003, 27.
2　Gairdner 1874, 106 (modern spelling by the author).
3　Ibid, 107.
4　Ibid; Sinclair 2003, 27.
5　Gairdner 1874, 108.
6　Sinclair 2003, 27; Gillespie 2008, 2.
7　Ibid, 109; Sinclair 2003, 27.
8　Ibid.
9　Ibid, 112.
10　Sinclair 2003, 28.
11　Rous 1980, viii–x, 8–9.
12　Ibid, 5.
13　Ibid, 7.
14　Ibid.
15　Rous, 20–2; Crane 2010, 8–9.
16　Ibid, 30.
17　Sharpe nd, 139; Davis 1980, 599–601.
18　Sharpe nd, 156.
19　Ibid, 145–7.
20　Rous 1980, 31; Cokayne 1887c, 359.
21　Ibid, 369, 371, 372–4.
22　Ibid 375–8; for more on the Lords Appellant and the Battle of Radcot Bridge, see pp. 8–10.
23　Carpenter 2013, 1; Cokayne 1887c, 378; Sinclair 2003, 26–7.
24　Sinclair 2003, 26–7.

25  Ibid, 28.
26  Sinclair 2003, 60 (modern spelling by the author).
27  Ibid, 28; Brindley 2001, 34–5.
28  Sinclair 2003, 28–9, 95, 83–91, 29.
29  Ibid, 76, 79.
30  Ibid, 95, 29–30.
31  Ibid, 31; Grummit 2008, 5, 37, 6
32  Power 1941, 102.
33  Sinclair 2003, 119, 120. For a brief description of the Council of Constance, see www.britannica.com/EBchecked/topic/133699/Council-of-Constance.
34  Sinclair 2003, 32.
35  Ibid, 33–5.
36  Ibid, 36.
37  Ibid.
38  Sinclair 2003, 32; Adams 2010, 206–8.
39  Sinclair 2003, 36.
40  Sinclair 2003, 37; Rous 1951, 89.
41  Sinclair 2003, 37–8.
42  Ibid, 39.
43  For the full text of this ballad, see Brindley 2001, 110–11. Isabel Despenser's first husband was also named Richard Beauchamp, 1st earl of Worcester. He was killed at the siege of Meaux in 1422. See Sinclair 2003, 39.
44  Sinclair 2003, 40.
45  Richard Wydeville was to marry Bedford's widow Jacquetta of Luxembourg in secret. His daughter Elizabeth later married Edward IV, also in secret. Monro 1843, 37 (modern spelling by the author).
46  Sinclair 2003, 40–1.
47  Monro 1843, 40.
48  Monro 1843, 42.
49  Sinclair 2003, 41.
50  Brindley 2001, 112–3.
51  Sinclair 2003, 43.
52  Ibid, 43; Brindley 2001, 123–4, 127
53  Ibid, 129, 131.
54  Ibid, 134–7.
55  Stevenson 1864, xlix.
56  Sinclair 2003, 151.
57  Brindley 2001, 142.
58  Sinclair 2003, 156.
59  Rous 1980, 51; 55.
60  Ibid, 56.

## 9. Death of a Grandchild and the Making of an Earl

1  Carpenter 2008.
2  Ibid.
3  *Calendar of Patent Rolls, Henry VI, 1446–1453 Vol. V*, 1 (hereafter, *CPR HVI V*). Lord Sudeley was distantly related to both young Anne Beauchamp and John Beauchamp of Powick.
4  Hicks 1998, 35–6.

5    Ibid, 41.
6    Hicks 1998, 32.
7    Pollard 2007a, 11.
8    *Calendar of Patent Rolls, Henry VI, 1441–1446 Vol. IV*, (hereafter, *CPR HVI IV*), 437;
     Hicks 1999, 34.
9    Hicks 1999, 33.
10   Ibid; Nicholas 1831b.
11   Hicks 1998, 37.
12   *CPR HVI V*, 236.
13   For a fuller and more detailed account of the Warwick inheritance dispute, see
     Pollard 2007a and Hicks 1998.
14   Pollard 2007a, 17.
15   Ibid, 18, 20–1.
16   Hicks 1998, 46–7.
17   Pollard 2007a, 17.
18   Ibid, 17, 19.
19   Ibid, 22–3.
20   *CPR HVI V*, 451.
21   Hicks 1998, 45.
22   Bloom 1919.
23   Hicks 1998, 45.
24   Ibid, 49–50.

## 10. A Crisis of Government

1    Vale 1969.
2    Wolffe 1981, 270.
3    Vale 1969, 131–2.
4    Ibid, 135.
5    Ibid, 133.
6    Johnson 1988, 269.
7    Flenley 1911, 140 (modern spelling by the author); Wolffe 1981, 270; Storey 1999, 136.
8    Storey 1999, 137; Johnson 1988, 126.
9    Griffiths 1984, 71–2; Baldwin 2009, 54, 58.
10   Johnson 1988, 126–7.
11   Gairdner 1904a, 290–2 (modern spelling by the author).
12   Johnson 1988, 126.
13   Griffiths 1984, 77–8.
14   Johnson 1988, 127. A large part of the business of government involved the signing
     of chancery warrants. One, mentioned in Johnson and housed in the National
     Archives, relates to 'the replacement of the treasury keys lost by the earl of Warwick'.
15   Griffiths 1984, 79.
16   Gairdner 1904a, 297–8.
17   Storey 1999, 138.
18   Ibid, 297. A harbinger was someone sent ahead of a travelling party to secure lodgings
     or, in Somerset's case, lodgings near where a lord was already lodged or imprisoned.
19   Ibid.
20   Ibid, 295–6.
21   Griffiths 1984, 74.

22  Gairdner 1904a, 297.
23  Ibid; Given-Wilson 2005a; Griffiths 1984, 74.
24  Given-Wilson 2005a.
25  Ibid.
26  Ibid (modern spelling by the author).
27  Hicks 1998, 98; Storey 1999, 138.
28  Griffiths 1984, 79, 75.
29  Ibid, 80–1 (modern spelling by the author).
30  Ibid.
31  Ibid.
32  Ibid.
33  Ibid.
34  Ibid.
35  Ibid.
36  Ibid.
37  Ibid.
38  Ibid, 137–8.
39  Gairdner 1904a, 297.

## 11. A Time for Women

1   Laynesmith 2004, 117.
2   Maurer 2003, 44–5.
3   Ibid, 43.
4   Rawcliffe 2007, 237 (modern spelling by the author).
5   Dunn 2004, 1.
6   Ibid
7   Wolffe 1981, 129–31.
8   Griffiths nd; Harriss 2008.
9   Wolffe 1981, 129–31.
10  Ibid, 184–98.
11  Rawcliffe 2007, 237 (modern spelling by the author); Maurer 2003, 42, 44.
12  Maurer 2003, 45.
13  Flenley 1911, 140–1; Maurer 2003, 45.
14  Laynesmith 2004, 117.
15  A full list of women in attendance at Margaret of Anjou's churching: Jacquetta, duchess of Bedford; Alice Chaucer, duchess of Suffolk; Cecily Nevill, duchess of York; Eleanor Bourchier, duchess of Norfolk; Anne Nevill, duchess of Buckingham; Eleanor Beauchamp, duchess of Somerset; Anne of York, duchess of Exeter; Joan Nevill, countess of Arundel; Anne Beauchamp, countess of Warwick; Eleanor Nevill, countess of Northumberland; Alice Montagu, countess of Salisbury; Eleanor Beaufort, countess of Wiltshire; Elizabeth Butler, countess of Shrewsbury; Katherine Percy, lady Grey of Ruthyn; Philippa Tiptoft, lady Roos; Joan Beaumont, lady Lovell; Margaret, lady Cromwell; Margaret, lady Botreaux; Margery, lady Berners; Elizabeth Grey, lady Ferrers of Groby; Alice Camoy, lady Hastings; Elizabeth St John, lady Zouche; Elizabeth, lady Fitzwalter; Thomasina Hankeford, lady Fitzwarren; Maud Stanhope, lady Willoughby; Catherine Howard, lady Bergavenny; and Elizabeth Beauchamp, lady Latimer.
16  Laynesmith 2004.

## 12. A Reckoning in the North

1   Hicks 2004b.
2   Ibid; Johnson 1988, 68.
3   Hicks 2004b; Stansfield 1987, 236–42.
4   Griffiths 1968, 611.
5   Nicholas 1831b, 193.
6   Ibid, 191–7.
7   Rawcliffe 1987, 238 (modern spelling by the author).
8   Ibid, 239.
9   Reeves 2004a; Friedrichs 1998, 214–6.
10  Friedrichs 2000, 216.
11  Friedrichs 1998, 221.
12  Ibid, 222; Virgoe 1973, 469.
13  Friedrichs 2000, 222–3.
14  Griffiths 1968, 612.
15  Ibid, 611–3.
16  Ibid.
17  Ibid, 616.
18  Stansfield 1987, 241–2; Griffiths 1968, 618.
19  Ralph, lord Greystoke was the son of Elizabeth Ferrers, Joan Beaufort's daughter from her first marriage. He married Elizabeth Fitzhugh, Henry Fitzhugh's sister, husband of the earl of Salisbury's daughter Alice. See Griffiths 1968, 618–20.
20  Gairdner 1904a, 321 (modern spelling by the author); Johnson 1988, 142.
21  Pollard 1990, 260; Fisher 1954, 35–6; Storey 1999, 148.
22  Flenley 1911, 158 (modern spelling by the author); Pollard 1990, 260; Brie 1905, 523–4 (modern spelling by the author).
23  Brie 1905, 523–4.
24  Bennett 2008; Baldwin 2002, 67–8.
25  Johnson 1988, 152–3.

## 13. 'Loyal Liegemen'

1   Gairdner 1904b, 13 (modern spelling by the author).
2   Ibid, 31.
3   Ibid, 30.
4   Flenley 1911, 141 (modern spelling by the author).
5   Maurer 2003, 117; Wolffe 1981, 285; Johnson 1988, 152.
6   Flenley 1911, 141; Hardy 1873, 686.
7   Wolffe 1981, 285; Storey 1999, 160.
8   *Calendar of Close Rolls, Henry VI, Vol V* 69–75 (hereafter *CCR HV VI*).
9   Storey 1999, 160; Wolffe 1981, 285.
10  Johnson 1988, 154–5.
11  Pollard 2007a, 29.
12  Hicks 1998, 114.
13  *Calendar of Patent Rolls, Henry VI, 1452–1461 Vol V*, 553 (hereafter *CPR HVI VI*); Pollard 1990, 248, 272; Pollard 1976. Pollard describes Pickering as 'one of those organising and leading Nevill gangs against Percy retainers' in 1453. He later fought alongside Salisbury and his sons at the battle of Blore Heath.

14   Harris 1907, 282–3.
15   Ibid.
16   Ibid.
17   Myers 1967, 276.
18   Johnson 1988, 156.
19   Given-Wilson 2005a.
20   Ibid.
21   Armstrong 1960, 18–9. Armstrong's 'Politics and the Battle of St Albans, 1455' is still by far the most comprehensive account of the battle and, in particular, the days and hours leading up to it. Boardman 2000 goes into more detail about the battle itself.
22   Given-Wilson 2005a.
23   Armstrong 1960, 22, 28.
24   Ibid, 30.
25   Ibid, 38.
26   Gairdner 1904b, 25–9 (modern spelling by the author).
27   Ibid.
28   Armstrong 1960, 39.
29   Gairdner 1904b, 25–9.
30   Ibid.
31   Davies 1841, 72; Gairdner 1904b, 25–9.
32   Armstrong 1960, 42–3, 46; Flenley 1911, 155.
33   Davies 1841, 72; Gairdner 1876, 198; Gairdner 1904a, 32–3.
34   Armstrong 1960, 44.
35   Gairdner 1904b, 25–9.
36   Armstrong 1960, 48; Gairdner 1904b, 25–9.
37   Gairdner 1904b, 25–9.
38   Flenley 1911, 142.
39   Armstrong 1960, 55–6.
40   Ibid, 57.
41   Hicks 2000a, 186.
42   Given-Wilson 2005b
43   Gairdner 1904b, 43–5 (modern spelling by the author).
44   Ibid.
45   Ibid.


## 14. Lady Willoughby's Troubles

1    Griffiths nd, 381.
2    Rawcliffe 1993.
3    Ibid.
4    Ibid.
5    Rawcliffe 1992; Friedrichs 2000, footnote 214.
6    Ibid.
7    Ibid.
8    Seaton 1961.
9    Jones 2005, 208; Seaton 1961.
10   Seaton 1961.
11   Lysons 1811, 498.

12  Hicks 2004d; Friedrichs 2006, 215–6.

13  Friedrichs 2006, 79.

14  Hicks 2004c.

15  Friedrichs 2006, 80 (modern spelling by the author).

16  Clark 1914, 62.

17  Ibid, 63.

18  Clark 2004a.

19  *CCR HVI V*; *CPR HV VI*, 64.

20  Seaton 1961, 495. The full text of this poem is available at https://en.wikibooks. org/wiki/The_Devonshire_Manuscript/Ye_know_my_herte_my_ladye_ dere. It is often attributed to Thomas Wyatt, but Seaton's attribution to Roos is generally accepted.

21  We do get one tantalising glimpse, through a copy of the *Canterbury Tales* bearing both Thomas and Maud's signatures. It may have been a wedding gift (perhaps from the dowager duchess of Suffolk) or an early joint purchase. The two signatures do suggest they saw this book as joint property. See Seaton 1964, 395.

22  Payling 2014, 5.

23  Friedrich 2006, 79, footnote.

24  Ibid.

25  Ibid; Payling 2014, 10.

26  Friedrich 2006, 107–8.

27  Ibid, 108–9.

28  Payling 2014, 11.

29  Friedrich 2006, 109.

30  Ibid, 111.

31  Ibid, 112.

32  Ibid, 110–1; Friedrichs 2006, 220–1. One of the complaints made by Maud and Jane in the 1470s was that the combined income of the properties did not equal the amount promised. John Leynton, a long-term servant of Cromwell's who knew his estate well, responded: 'And where my Master Radcliffe [Jane's second husband] says his livelihood is not worth four hundred marcs by year, it was when it was delivered to my lady his wife and her husband little worse than six hundred by year. And though they have let it go in decay we are not to blame, therefore we are not bound to be their bailiffs as their husbands…'. Quoted in Friedrichs 2006, 219 (modern spelling by the author).

33  *CPR HVI VI*, 275.

34  Ibid. The properties left to Maud and Jane were those that could not be sold but must be passed on to members of Cromwell's family.

35  Gairdner 1904a, 73–4.

36  Ibid.

37  Ibid, 50.

38  *Formulare Anglicarum*, 102 (modern spelling by the author).

39  Ibid, 103.

40  Ibid.

41  McCarthy, et al. 1990, 160.

42  Ibid, 158–9.

43  Ibid, 157, 159.

## 15. A Murder in the West Country

1    Storey 1999, 169.
2    Ibid, 165–75.
3    Some sources have William and Katherine married in 1455, others in 1458.
4    Storey 1999, 169.
5    Ibid.
6    Ibid.
7    Ibid; quoted in Radford 1912, 258. Radford refers to the document simply as the 'Indictment' against Devon.
8    Radford 1912, 258.
9    Ibid, 170–1; Kekewich et al. 1995, 262–3.
10   Kekewich et al. 1995, 262–3 (modern spelling by the author).
11   Ibid, 263.
12   Radford 1912, 260.
13   Ibid, 261; Lander 1960, 52–6.
14   Given-Wilson 2005a (modern spelling by the author).
15   Ibid.
16   Storey 1999, 173–4.
17   Johnson 1988, 173; Gairdner 1904b, 74–6. An act of resumption involved recalling all grants made by the crown after a specific date. There were always petitions for exemption, which were, more often than not, granted.
18   Johnson 1988, 173.
19   Gairdner 1904b, 74–6.
20   Johnson 1988, 173, and footnote.
21   Given-Wilson 2005d.
22   Johnson 1988, 173, 174.

## 16. Calais and Love Day

1    Hicks 1998, 144; Gairdner 1843, 70–1.
2    Nichols 1852, 20.
3    Curry 2004c ; Gairdner 1843, 70–1; Richmond 2008, 177–8.
4    *Calendar of Patent Rolls, Henry VI*, 1452–1461, 403.
5    Hicks 1998, 144.
6    Ibid.
7    *CPR HVI VI*, 413.
8    Nicholas 1831b, 294.
9    *CPR HVI VI*, 439.
10   Anderson 1919, 584–5; Richmond 2007, 7.
11   Pollard 2007a, 31; Harriss 1960, 40; Given-Wilson 2005b.
12   Harriss 1960, 42–3.
13   Nicholas 1835b, 276–9
14   Ibid.
15   *CPR HVI VI*, 154.
16   Given-Wilson 2005a.
17   Harriss 1960, 46.
18   Hicks 1998, 130–1.
19   Ibid; Given-Wilson 2005d; Woodger 2004.

20  Gairdner 1904b, 116–8; Richmond 2008, 180.
21  Curry 2004c; Grummit 2008, 78.
22  Hicks 2004d; Higginbotham 2013, 17–8.
23  Grummit, forthcoming.
24  Maurer 2003, 127–8.
25  Flenley 1911, 144 (modern spelling by the author).
26  Ibid, 159.
27  Kingsford 1905, 167; Brie 1906, 523 (modern spelling by the author).
28  Gairdner 1904b, 107–9.
29  Ibid.
30  Nicholas 1835b, 293, 294–5.
31  Hicks 1998, 125; Davies 1861, 77 (modern spelling by the author).
32  Ibid.
33  Flenley 1911, 159.
34  Ibid.
35  Kingsford 1905, 168; Hicks 1998, 132.
36  Ibid.
37  Gairdner 1904b, 127; Kingsford 1905, 168.
38  Hicks 1998, 132–4.
39  Flenley 1911, 160.
40  Robbins 1959, 194–6. 'Love Days' were common practice in the 15th century,
    where disputes were settled and debts often forgiven. Henry VI's Love Day
    was on a larger, grander scale and dealt with matters of national, rather than
    local, importance.

## 17. Breaking the King's Peace

1   Gairdner 1904b, 129–30.
2   Ibid, 130.
3   Ibid, 130; Anderson 1919, 585.
4   Gairdner 1904b, 129–30.
5   Druery 1826, 172.
6   Hicks 1998, 139.
7   Ibid, 141.
8   Ibid, 150–1.
9   Richmond 2007, 3–8; Scammell 1962, 108–10, 119–20.
10  Hicks 1998, 150.
11  Ibid; *CPR HVI VI*, 438.
12  Pollard 2007a, 131; Kingsford 1905, 169 (modern spelling by the author).
13  Hicks 1998, 146–7.
14  Flenley 1811, 147.
15  Ibid.
16  Ibid; Hicks 1998, 147; Maurer nd. (Maurer's article 'The Great Westminster
    Pie-Fight: A Cautionary Tale' was, as at 12 February 2012, available through www.
    r3.org. The author has been unable to retrieve it subsequently and can find no other
    source for this paper.)
17  Stephenson 1861, 368–9.
18  *CPR HVI VI*, 443.
19  Pollard 2007a, 131; Davies 1856, 79; Griffiths 1981, 808.

20  Hicks 1998, 150–2; Ellis 1877, 125–6.

21  Brie 1906, 526 (modern spelling by the author).

22  Fabyan 1811, 634 (modern spelling by the author); Maurer nd.

23  Fabyan 1811, 654; Kingsford 1905; 169; Flenley 1911, 146.

24  Hicks 1998, 152–3; Ellis 1877, 368–9 (reported in a newsletter from the court of Burgundy to the king of France).

## 18. The Gathering Storm

1  Pollard 1976, 52; Griffiths 1981, 813.

2  Whitaker 1823 (Vol 2), 261.

3  Flemming 1921, 128–9; the date of this letter is disputed. Maurer (2003, 216–21) dates it to 1455; Flemming (1921) to 1454; Hicks (1998, 155–6) puts it much later, in 1459. Pollard (2007, 205) argues that it is more likely to have been written sometime between 1455 and 1459, and the context of the letter seems to support this. Given the events in the years immediately following the first battle of St Albans, 1457 sounds about right.

4  Pollard 1976, 59–60; Pollard 1990, footnote 59.

5  Ibid; Rawcliffe & Flower 1986, 158, 170–1.

6  Pollard 1976, 59–62, 64–5.

7  Ragg 1909, 283–4 (modern spelling by the author).

8  Pollard 1976, 61–2; Pollard 1990, 213.

9  Reeves 2004b.

10  Given-Wilson 2005c.

11  Ibid.

12  Nicholas 1831b, 303.

13  Pollard 2007a, 88–9; Wolffe 1981, 313–4.

14  Gairdner 1843, 71 (modern spelling by the author); Wolffe 1981, 315.

15  Gairdner 1904b, 138–9.

16  Griffiths 1981, 773–7, 798.

17  Davies 1856, 79 (modern spelling by the author).

18  Ibid, 79–80.

19  Hicks 1998, 156–7; Nicholas 1831b, 303.

20  Given-Wilson 2005b.

21  Maurer 2007, 165–6; Davies 1856, 79–80.

22  Griffiths 1981, 817–8.

23  Brie 1906, 526–7.

24  Griffiths 1981, 817.

25  Given-Wilson 2005c.

26  Ibid.

27  Fabyan 1811, 634.

28  Given-Wilson 2005c.

29  Haigh 1995, 16–18

30  Ibid, 19–20.

31  Given-Wilson 2005c.

32  Fabyan 1811, 634; Gairdner 1876, 204.

33  Gairdner 1876, 204.

34  Goodman 1981, 27.

35  Gairdner 1876, 204.

## 19. Ludford

1   Pollard 2007a, 40.
2   Ibid; Johnson 1988, 186–7.
3   Hicks 1998, 164.
4   Kekewich et al. 1995, 208–10.
5   Ibid.
6   Ibid.
7   Stow 1600, 671 (modern spelling by the author).
8   Pollard 2007a, 41; Johnson 1988, 187.
9   Hicks 1998, 187.
10  Davies 1856, 80–3.
11  Ibid.
12  Ibid.
13  Ibid.
14  Ibid.
15  Hicks 1998, 187.
16  Pollard 2007a, 41.
17  Gairdner 1876, 205; Pollard 2007a, 41.
18  Johnson 1988, 188–9.
19  Fabyan 1811, 634–5.
20  Johnson 1988, 199; Hicks 1998, 164.
21  Stevenson 1864, 512 (modern spelling by the author). Thomas Nevill was stripped of his post as Chamberlain of the Exchequer and replaced by Henry VI's Chamberlain Sir Richard Tunstall. See Pollard 1990, 573.
22  Fabyan 1811, 635.
23  Gairdner 1876, 207.


## 20. *Somnium Vigilantis* and the Parliament of Devils

1   Nicholas 1835b, 168.
2   Keir 1970, 82–90.
3   *CPR HVI VI*, 281.
4   Keir 1970, 91–2.
5   Gibson 1911, 512; Lander 1961, 120; Kekewich 2007. 30.
6   Lander 1961, 119–20.
7   Dunn 2003, 9–10.
8   Ibid.
9   Broertjes 2015, 14; Kekewich. 2007.
10  Gibson 1911, 521–2 (modern spelling by the author); Broertjes 2015.
11  Gibson 1911, 518–20.
12  Ibid.
13  Ibid.
14  Ibid.
15  Ibid, 520–1.
16  Ibid.
17  Ibid, 521–2.
18  Ibid.
19  Ibid.

20 Ibid.
21 Given-Wilson 2005c.
22 Ibid.
23 Ibid.
24 Ibid.
25 Ibid.
26 Ibid.
27 Ibid.
28 Ibid.
29 Ibid.
30 Ibid.
31 Ibid.
32 Ibid.
33 Ibid.
34 Ibid.
35 Gairdner 1876, 206; Given-Wilson 2005c, November 1459.
36 Given-Wilson 2005c.

## 21. Wives and Sisters Left Behind

1 Gairdner 1876, 206; *CPR HVI VI*, 542.
2 Gairdner 1876, 207.
3 *CPR HVI VI*, 561.
4 Ibid, 561, 572. In an entry in the Close Rolls of Henry VI dated 9 May 1459, Thomas Nevill is styled 'of Eresby'. See www.british-history.ac.uk/cal-close-rolls/hen6/vol6/pp300-317.
5 *CPR HVI VI*, 572.
6 Baldwin 2009, 26, 58. As discussed in Chapter 7, Alice Fitzhugh may have been the one exception to the family policy. Without a confirmed year of birth, it is impossible to state with any certainty just how old she was when her first child was born.
7 *CPR HVI VI*, 556, 563, 575, 624.
8 Given-Wilson 2005c
9 Bennett 2004c.
10 Ibid.
11 Ibid; Bennett 2004a.
12 Given-Wilson 2005c.
13 *CPR HVI VI*, 565.
14 Ibid. 565, 605, 607.
15 Pollard 1990, 276.
16 *CPR HVI VI*, 536.
17 Pollard 1990, 275.
18 Ibid, 274.
19 Johnson 1988, 193; Pollard 1990, 277–8.
20 Pollard 2007a, 41.

## 22. Lord of the Channel

1   Kingsford 1922, 545; Rous 1980, 56.
2   Waurin 1891, 278 [translation by the author and Sharon Bennett Connolly].
3   Ibid.
4   Hicks 1998, 169; Waurin 1891, 277.
5   Waurin 1891, 277. For a discussion of Waurin's confusion and two possible solutions, see Johnson 1988, 195; Hicks 1998, 169. Waurin has John Dynham purchasing the ship for Warwick but, as Hicks quite sensibly points out, Warwick, as lord of Glamorgan or Morgannock, would hardly have needed to borrow money to purchase, or hire, a ship in South Wales. The author suggests a third possibility, that Warwick attempted to sail to Ireland from the Bristol Channel before, as per both Johnson and Hicks, fetching up on the coast of north Devon, meeting John Dynham there and moving south, where the ship that eventually took them to the Channel Islands and Calais was bought and crewed by Dynham and his mother. See also Kleineke 2000, 71–7. For a discussion on Waurin's source for the 'Warwick Apology', see Visser-Fuchs, 2002.
6   Waurin 1891, 277.
7   Kleineke 2000, 71.
8   Ibid, 74, 75–7. A noble was a gold coin first issued in 1344; initially valued at a third of a pound (6s 8d), by 1465 it was revalued at 10s. See Cunningham, 2002.
9   Waurin 1891, 277, 278.
10  Ibid, 278.
11  Ibid.
12  Ibid, 278–9.
13  Ibid, 279.
14  Ibid.
15  Ibid, 281; Kingsford 1905, 170.
16  Waurin 1891, 281.
17  Richmond 2008, 183; *CPR HVI VI*, 555–6.
18  Brie 1906, 529; *CPR HVI VI*, 556.
19  Brie 1906, 528; Harriss 1960, 31.
20  Waurin 1891, 281.
21  Brie 1906, 528.
22  Ibid.
23  Waurin 1891, 282.
24  Ibid; Gairdner 1876, 206; Kingsford 1905, 170; Fabyan 1811, 635; Davies 1861, 85; Gairdner 1843, 72; *CPR HVI VI*, 554–5; Hicks 1988, 170.
25  Gairdner 1904, 204. Waurin mentions 'some words which had been said by the earl of March who had them brought before the earl [of Warwick] and others' but in an otherwise highly detailed account gives us no more. See Waurin 1891, 284.
26  Higginbotham 2013, 13; Waurin 1891, 284; Santiuste 2010, 26–7. At some point soon after this, Audley (whose father had been killed at Blore Heath) changed sides and joined the Yorkist cause.
27  Waurin 1891, 285. Waurin gives by far the most detailed account of Warwick's voyage to Ireland, his meetings with York and his return to Calais. Though there are errors – for example, Waurin is under the misapprehension that the duchess of York was in Ireland – it is probable that his account came first-hand from Warwick or one of his men.
28  Ibid, 286.

29  *CPR HVI VI*, 554–5, 566, 567, 577; Davies 1861, 9.
30  Stevenson 1864, 512–3 (modern spelling by the author).
31  Richmond 2008, 185; *CPR HVI VI*, 591.
32  Waurin 1891, 286.
33  Ibid, 286, 287.
34  Ibid, 287.
35  Santiuste 2010, 26–7.
36  Davies 1861, 85.
37  Waurin 1891, 288–9.
38  Richmond (2008, 187) poses the question: Why did this encounter not end in a full-scale sea battle? 'If Exeter, the Admiral, in the best ship to be had, failed to attack a rebel fleet when offered the opportunity … then something was badly amiss. Here was one of those critical moments when action was essential but was not forthcoming.' While the chroniclers suggest this was because Exeter's sailors owed more loyalty and favour to Warwick (Brie 1906, 529) or questioned Exeter's courage (Davies 1861, 85), Richmond suggests a more practical reason. Not only were Warwick's ships 'bigger and better' than Exeter's, he had more of them. Not only that, his navy was better organised. Exeter's crew was 'impressed' and 'heterogeneous', whereas Warwick commanded a 'homogeneous personal fleet' that behaved like a navy. His confidence that he could best Exeter at sea was not misplaced and Exeter's retreat to the safety of Dartmouth was a sign of prudence rather than a lack of courage.
39  Waurin 1891, 289, 290.
40  Ibid.
41  Davies 1861, 91; Brie 1906, 529.
42  Curry 2002, 71–2; Brie 1906, 529.
43  Brie 1906, 529; Hicks 1998, 177. Just when John Dynham received his leg injury is unclear. Some sources (including Brie) date it to the second raid on Sandwich, others to the first.

## 23. Invasion and Triumph

1   Gairdner 1876, 198; Davies 1861, 90.
2   Davies 1861, 90.
3   Ibid.
4   Richmond 2008, 185.
5   Hicks 1998, 177; Davies 1861, 94.
6   Davies 1861, 91–4; Robbins 1959, 209–11 (modern spelling by the author).
7   Davies 1861, 86–7, 86–9; Hicks 1998, 177.
8   Davies 1861, 88.
9   Ibid, 87–8.
10  Ibid.
11  Gilson 1911, 520.
12  Davies 1861, 89.
13  Ibid.
14  Flenley 1811, 149.
15  Ibid; Davies 1861, 94.
16  Ibid, 95; Flenley 1911, 150.
17  Davies 1861, 95.

18   Ibid.
19   Gairdner 1843, 74; Griffiths 1981, 861.
20   Griffiths 1981, 860, 862; Hicks 1998, 178. Perhaps ironically, the Bishop of Ely had thrown in his lot with the Yorkists in London.
21   Jack 1960, 34; Jack 2004; Wagner 2001, 101.
22   Davies 1861, 96.
23   Ibid 96–7. In this context, 'naked' means without armour.
24   Waurin 1981, 300, quoted in Jack 1960, 23.
25   Jack 1960, 24; Davies 1861, 97.
26   *Whetehamstede's Register*, 374, quoted in Jack 1960, 23.
27   Gairdner 1876, 207; Gairdner 1843, 74; Fabyan 1811, 636; Davies 1861, 97.
28   Davies 1861, 98.
29   Ibid.
30   Ibid.
31   Davies 1861, 98–9; Maurer 2003, 187; Gairdner 1876, 208–9.
32   Maurer 2003, 187.
33   Davies 1861, 98.
34   Ibid
35   Griffiths 1981, 863.
36   Ibid; Hicks 1998, 180.
37   Griffiths 1981, 863; Gairdner 1843, 75; Hicks 1998, 180.
38   Castor 2004.
39   Hicks 1998, 180; Gairdner 1843, 75.
40   Hicks 1998, 180, 181–2, 183, 184; Keir 1970, 95–7.
41   Hicks 1998, 184; *CPR HVI VI*, 589.
42   Hicks 1998, 180, 181–2, 183, 184; Hinds 1912a.
43   Hicks 1998, 180, 184.
44   Ibid, 184; Pollard 2007a, 43.

## 24. Sir Thomas Nevill and the Duke of York

1   Johnson 1988, 212, 215; Gairdner 1976, 208; Kingsford 1905, 171; Davies 1861, 99; Fabyan 1811, 637. In the Introduction to the Parliamentary Rolls for October 1460, the editors suggest that York's preparations were not for his coronation but to 'mark his royal status by going crowned to Westminster Abbey ... to celebrate the feast of St Edward the Confessor'. A letter to John Tiptoft, earl of Worcester (quoted in full in Johnson 1988, 213) reports that crowds gathered on 13 October to see 'who should have gone on procession crowned', which seems less of a reference to a coronation itself. The author of this letter is unidentified. See Given-Wilson et al. 2005.
2   Johnson 1988, 211–2; Carpenter 1997, 147; Gairdner 1876, 208; Hicks 1998, 185.
3   Gairdner 1876, 208; Johnson 1988, 214.
4   Gairdner 1904b, 233.
5   Given-Wilson 2005d
6   Ibid.
7   Kingsford 1905, 171; Davies 1861, 99.
8   Johnson 1988, 214–5.
9   Ibid, 215.
10   Davies 1861, 100–5; Given-Wilson 2005d.

11  Gairdner 1876, 208.
12  As early as July it was being reported that 'It is also thought that they will make a son of the duke of York king, and that they will pass over the king's son as they are beginning already to say that he is not the king's son. Similarly the queen also runs great danger.' See Hinds 1912a; *CPR HVI VI*, 567.
13  Gairdner 1976, 209; Maurer 2003, 189.
14  Gairdner 1976, 209.
15  Johnson 1998, 219, 222.
16  Ibid, 221; Gairdner 1876, 210; Kingsford 1905, 172.
17  Flenley 1911, 151–2; Johnson 1988, 220; Haigh 1996, 18–19. The Kentishman Lovelace is a figure of some mystery. Reported to have been killed at Wakefield, his name nevertheless crops up later in connection with the second battle of St Albans (see Chapter 25).
18  Haigh 1996, 19.
19  Ibid.
20  Ibid, 36–74.
21  Ibid.
22  Ibid, 76–81; *CWR*, lxxxiii.
23  Davies 1861, 107; *CWR*, lxxxiii.


## 25. Three Battles that Made a King

1   Haigh 1995, 46.
2   Dockray 2004; Pollard 2007a, 275.
3   Although Edward succeeded to the title Duke of York on his father's death, I have followed convention and continue to refer to him as 'March', as events were soon to propel him to a higher rank than duke. See Bentley 1831, 8–9.
4   Kingsford 1905, 174; Calendar of State Papers Relating to English Affairs in the Archives of Venice, Volume 1, 1202–1509 (hereafter *Venice Papers*). These were not just letters of reassurance but requests for the promotion of Francesco Coppini, Bishop of Terni and papal legate. Coppini had been sent to England to persuade Henry VI to join a crusade and to broker peace between the king and the Duke of York. Snubbed by an impatient Queen Margaret, Coppini turned to Warwick, who welcomed him into the circle of exiles in Calais. He remained attached to Warwick and the Yorkists until February 1461 when, panicked by the advance of the queen's army on London, he left England. Ambitious for a cardinal's hat, Coppini tried the patience of the pope, who eventually demoted him and confined him to an abbey. In April, he still had the confidence of George Nevill, Bishop of Exeter and Chancellor, though his long absence from England was noted. See Wagner 1001, 62–3; Hinds 1912b. For a concise examination of Coppini's rise and fall, and his relationship with the Yorkist cause, see Keir 1970, 184–92.
5   *Venice Papers*.
6   Haigh 1995, 41.
7   Davies 1861, 110.
8   Haigh 1995, 41–4.
9   Gairdner 1876, 211.
10  Ibid, 44.
11  Gairdner 1876, 212; Haigh 1995, 46.

12  Haigh 1995, 47.

13  Ibid, 46, 47-8; Pollard 2007a, 89, 121; Hicks 1998, 213; Jones 2004.

14  Burley et al. 2007, 85–6.

15  Haigh 1995, 48; Burley et al. 2007, 58.

16  Gairdner 1876, 213.

17  Gairdner 1876, 213. At over a metre, an arrow measuring an ell in length was too big and too heavy to be fired from a handgun. It is more likely this fearsome new arrow was fired from a cannon. See Burley et al. 2007, 58–9.

18  Ibid. After the battle, Andrew Trollope said he had killed fewer men than may have been expected of him because he had stood on a caltrap, thus injuring his foot. See Gairdner 1876, 213.

19  Burley et al. 2007, 61; Haigh 1995, 48–9. Poyning's first name is unclear. He was either 'Sir Edward' (Haigh 1995, 48–9) or 'Sir Robert' (Burley et al., 59–60). Gregory tells a different version of the story. 'But the day before the battle there was a journey at Dunstable; but the king's men lacked good guiding, for some were but ne men of war, for the chiefest captain was a butcher of the same town; and there were the king's men overthrown only by the northern men. And soon after the butcher, for shame of his simple guiding and loss of the men, the number of 700, for very sorrow as it is said, hanged himself; and some men said that it was for the loss of his goods, but dead he is – God knows the thought.' See Gairdner 1976, 212). It's unlikely that Poynings was mistaken for a local butcher. Perhaps the latter was the leader of a small local contingent who joined Poynings and his men. Poynings would seem to have somewhat fewer men than the 700 Gregory cites, and the unfortunate butcher's volunteers are likely to have numbered in the tens rather than the hundreds.

20  Burley et al. 2007, 64–7; Haigh 1995, 49–50.

21  Burley et al. 2007, 69–71; Haigh 1995, 50.

22  Burley et al. 2007, 71–3.

23  Haigh 1995, 50–3.

24  Davies 1861, 107.

25  Haigh 1995, 52–3; Burley et al. 2007, 74–5. In a letter to Francesco Coppini dated 7 April 1461, George Nevill writes: 'On the 13th kalends of March [17 February] we fought unsuccessfully near St Albans, the details of which action would be too long to narrate, but I think it right to give a summary of the battle. Lord Berners, brother of the Archbishop of Canterbury, with my brother lord Montagu and Sir Thomas Charleton, knight, were captured and taken as far as York. Lord Bonneville and Sir Thomas Kiryel were taken and beheaded, and many of inferior station on our side were destroyed.' See *Venice Papers*.

26  Haigh 1995, 52–3; Burley et al. 2007, 76–7.

27  Burley et al. 2007, 78.

28  Ibid, 78–9. Burley et al. dispute at least part of this story, as 'they were experienced military commanders and it seems unlikely their role in the battle would have been limited to looking after king Henry. It would seem more likely they were captured with Montagu during the fighting' (79). It should be remembered, though, that Bonville had already lost a son and grandson at Wakefield and this more passive, but important, role may have been assigned him in order to keep him safe. Whatever the truth of it, this mass execution of prisoners marks a turning point in the wars, an escalation that could not be easily wound back.

29  Ibid. For an in-depth analysis of the second battle of St Albans, see Burley et al. 2007, 81–6.

30   Ibid; Hicks 1998, 217–8.

31   Davies 1861, 109–10.

32   Kingsford 1905, 174. The writer of *Davies Chronicle* says that this delegation was headed by the duchess of Buckingham 'with many witty men with her'. See Davies 1861, 109.

33   Ibid; Gairdner 1876, 214.

34   Kingsford 1905, 174; Ross 1974, 32–3.

35   Armstrong 1948; Hicks 1998, 217.

36   Hicks 1998, 53.

37   Kingsford 1905, 173; Flenley 1911, 161.

38   Flenley 1911.

39   Hicks 1998, 217.

40   Ibid.

41   Flenley 1911, 161–2; Armstrong 1948, 59.

42   Flenley 1911, 162.

43   Fabyan 1811, 639.

44   Hinds 1912b.

45   *Calendar of Close Rolls, Edward IV, Vol. I, 1461–1468*, 55 (hereafter *CCR EIV !*).

46   Haigh 1995, 57–8.

47   Ibid, 58; Boardman 2000, 68; Haigh 1995, 58.

48   Boardman 2000, 59; Haigh 1995, 58. While the traditional view is that the battle of Towton took place the day after Ferrybridge and Dintingdale, Sutherland (2007) makes a strong case for all three happening on the same day. I have followed Sutherland's timing here.

49   *Venice Papers.*

50   Hall 1809, 254 (modern spelling by the author).

51   Ibid. I can find no other mention of an illegitimate son of the earl of Salisbury. Hall was writing some seventy years after the event and is known to have added embellishments of his own to the story; it is difficult, for example, to see how Hall knew Fitzwalter's thoughts and assumptions, or what weapon he had to hand, without corroboration from other sources. An acknowledged son, as the name 'Bastard of Salisbury' would suggest, would have been a vital member of Salisbury's affinity and would surely have shown up in the record before this, had he existed. Fitzwalter, though mortally wounded during the dawn raid, survived a week before succumbing to his injuries. See Haigh 1995, 58.

52   Ibid.

53   *Venice Papers.*

54   Haigh 2002, 71–2; Sutherland 2007, 19; Gairdner 1976, 216.

55   Hall 1809, 254.

56   Boardman 2000, 66–7.

57   Haigh 1995, 60.

58   Ibid. For an in-depth description of the battlefield and the deployment of both armies, see Boardman 2000, chapters 5 and 6.

59   Hall 1809, 254–5.

60   Boardman 2000, 107.

61   Ibid, 111–2; Haigh 1995, 61–2.

62   Boardman 2000, 113–7; Haigh 1995, 62; Hinds 1912b.

63   Boardman 2000, 118; Haigh 1995, 62–3. Norfolk died later that year and was succeeded by his son John, who was just 16 years old.

64  Haigh 1995, 63; Boardman 2000, 124–7.
65  Hinds 1912b.
66  Hinds 1912b; Boardman 2000, 126.
67  Boardman 2000, 126–7; Haigh 1995, 64.


## 26. Resistance and Conspiracy

1   Ross 1974, 51–2.
2   Ibid.
3   Haigh 1995, 74–5; *CWR*, 104.
4   *CWR*, 104; Haigh 1995, 74.
5   Jones 2004a.
6   Ibid; Gairdner 1904b, 52.
7   Hicks 1991, 293; Lander 2011, 167.
8   Ross 1974, 45; Pollard 2007a, 51.
9   Ross 1974, 46; Pollard 2007a, 51.
10  Haig 1995, 70–1; Pollard 2007a, 51.
11  Macdougall 2004; Haigh 1995, 70.
12  Haigh 1995, 70–1; Gairdner 1904a, 276.
13  Haigh 1995, 71; Ross 1974, 48–9.
14  Haigh 1995, 70.
15  Fauconberg had by this time been elevated to the earldom of Kent.
16  Horrox 2004f; Baldwin 2009, 97.
17  Given-Wilson 2005e.
18  Ibid.
19  Ibid.
20  Ibid.
21  Ibid.
22  Ibid.
23  Ibid.
24  Ibid; *CCR EVI I*, 7, 25.
25  Given-Wilson 2005e.
26  Hinds 1912c; Ross 2011, 38.
27  Hinds 1912c.
28  Ibid.
29  Gairdner 1904, 32–3.
30  Hinds 1912c.
31  *CWR*, 11. For a deeper analysis of the Oxford plot, see Ross 2011, 38–46.
32  Ross 2011, 50–1.
33  Haigh 1995, 71.
34  Ibid, 72; Pollard 2007a, 52.
35  *CWR*, 12–3.
36  Haigh 1995, 72.
37  Given-Wilson 2005e.

## 27. John Nevill's War

1  Haigh 1995, 72.
2  Ibid.
3  Kingsford 1905, 177–8; *CWR*, 13; Gairdner 1876, 218–9.
4  Kingsford 1905, 177–8; *CWR*, 13.
5  Kekewich et al. 1995, 171–2.
6  Ibid.
7  Ibid; Kingsford 1905, 178; Haigh 1995, 73. In time to come, lord Strange's daughter would marry George Stanley, oldest surviving son of Thomas, lord Stanley and Alianor Nevill.
8  Gairdner 1904b, 60.
9  *CCR EVI I*, 215.
10  Storey 1999, 194.
11  Haigh 1995, 74; Gairdner 1876, 219.
12  Ibid.
13  Ibid.
14  Ross 1974, 53; Pollard 2004b; Pollard 2007a, 53. Fauconberg, like his brother Salisbury, was 60 years old at the time of his death and still active as a soldier and commander. They were by no means the only two men around their age still active in the field. The received wisdom that 60 was considered 'ancient' in the fifteenth century must be contextualised. Though many more people died before reaching that age than do now, what carried them off was disease, infection and injuries in battle – all of which are either treatable or avoidable in the twenty-first century.
15  Pollard 2004b.
16  Ibid.
17  Ibid.
18  Ross 1974, 53; Haigh 1995, 75.
19  Gairdner 1876, 220.
20  Ross 1974, 53; Haigh 1995, 75.
21  Hicks 1998; Pollard 2007a, 53.
22  Pollard 2007a, 54.
23  Ibid, 53; Haigh 1997, 77.
24  Gairdner 1876, 220–1.
25  Pollard 2007a, 53; Haigh 1995, 77.
26  Pollard 2007a, 53; Haigh 1995, 76; Gairdner 1876, 221.
27  Pollard 2007a, 53–4.
28  Gairdner 1876, 219; Jones 2004.
29  Jones 2004; Gairdner 1876, 219.
30  Gairdner 1876, 219.
31  Jones 2004; Haigh 1995, 78.
32  Gairdner 1876, 223.
33  Haigh 1995, 79.
34  Ibid.
35  Ross 1974, 59; Gairdner 1876, 223.
36  Haigh 1995, 80; Gairdner 1876, 223–4. Humphrey was the son of lord John Nevill, who had betrayed the Yorkists at Wakefield and lost his life at the battle of Towton.
37  Haigh 1995, 80.
38  Ibid, 80–1.

39　Ibid; Hammond, 2004.

40　Haigh 1995, 83.

41　Ibid, 85. Robert, lord Willoughby had been pardoned after the battle of Towton. He subsequently attached himself to the Nevills, an association that was to last the rest of his life. See Hicks 2004d.

42　Haigh 1995, 85.

43　Ibid, 85–6.

44　Kingsford 1905, 178, 318.

45　Gairdner 1876, 225.

46　Jones 2004b. Gregory's chronicle, gives a curious codicil to the battle of Hexham: 'And beside Newcastle, in the same month, there was taken [Sir William] Tailboys in a coalpit, and he had much money with him, both gold and silver, that should have gone to king Harry; and if it had come to Harry, late king of England, it would have caused much sorry sorrow, for he had ordained harness and ordinance enough, but the men would not go on foot with him till they had money. And they waited daily and hourly for money that this Tailboys should have sent to them or brought it; the sum was 3,000 marks. And the lord's men of Montagu were sore hurt and sick, and many of his men were slain in the great journeys, but this money was departed among them, and was a very wholesome salve for them. And in the day following Tailboys lost his head at Newcastle.' See Gairdner 1876, 226.

47　Hicks 1998, 246. Though John Nevill was now earl of Northumberland, in the interests of avoiding adding yet another layer of complexity to the already confusing roster of names, titles and honours, he will continue to be referred to as 'Montagu' throughout.

48　Ibid.

49　Haigh 1995, 83.

50　*CCR EV I*.

51　Hicks 1998, 246–7.

52　*CWR*, lxxxvii; Halliwell 1839, 38–9.

53　Halliwell 1839, 38.

54　Ibid, 39.

55　*CWR*, lxxxix; Halliwell 1839, 39.

56　Hicks 1998, 247; Pollard 2007a, 55.


## 28. More Troubles for Lady Willoughby

1　Grose & Astle 1897, 315; Fox-Davies 1909, 388.

2　Grose & Astle 1897, 315.

3　Ibid, 315.

4　Ibid, 315–6.

5　Ibid, 316 (modern spelling by the author). The Bishop of St Asaph at the time was Thomas Bird, sometimes known as Thomas Knight. Some time in 1463, he went into voluntarily exile in France, becoming Margaret of Anjou's confessor. Just how a bishop who was, at the very least, questioning his loyalties came to play a prominent role in the earl of Salisbury's funeral is not clear. His parish centred around Gwynedd in Wales, which was associated strongly with Warwick but not his father. See Griffiths, 2000, 87.

6　Pollard 2007a, 83.

7   Hicks 2002, 61–2.
8   Grose & Astle 1897, 315.
9   Ibid, 315–6.
10  Ibid, 316.
11  Ibid.
12  Ibid.
13  Ibid, 316–7.
14  Ibid.
15  Ibid.
16  Grummit, forthcoming.
17  *CCR EVI I*, 277. James Strangeways's son was married to Joan Fauconberg's daughter Elizabeth.
18  Ibid, 283; Pollard 2004b ; Raine & Clay 1865, 336. It should be noted that this licence was issued by the archdiocese of York, not by the king.
19  Ross 1974, 26, 121, 325.
20  Friedrichs 2006, 80.
21  Friedrichs 2000, 222; C1/66/96-96, Magdelene Misc. (My thanks to David Grummit for providing me with a copy of this document.)
22  C1/66/96-96.
23  Grummit, forthcoming; Friedrichs 2006, 80.
24  *CCR EVI I*, 330.
22  Wydeville, who was executed in 1483 during the brief reign of Edward V and the protectorate of Richard, Duke of Gloucester, went some way to making amends to Maud in his will: 'Also I will that my lady Willoughby, late the wyfe of Syr Gerveis Clifton', be comond w' all by myne executours, towching such stuffes as Syr Ewan pson' of Wolverton' and other my servantes had awey from hyr place; and she to be delt wt therin and answerid acording to goode right and conscience.' My thanks to Susan Higginbotham for providing me with a copy of this document.
26  Friedrichs 2000, 222, 226.
27  Ibid.

## 29. Secrets and Celebrations

1   Ross 1974, 90.
2   Ibid, 84–5. Isabella, later Queen of Castile in her own right, still bore a grudge against Edward more than twenty years later: 'the queen of Castile had turned in her heart from England in time past for the unkindness the which she took against the king last deceased, whom God pardon, for his refusing of her and taking to his wife a widow of England.' See Gairdner 1861, 32.
3   Ross 1974, 85.
4   For a discussion of the wedding between Edward and Elizabeth, how it came about, who was in attendance and possible dates, see Higginbotham 2013, 26–32.
5   Ross 1974, 87.
6   Lander 1976, 109. On the marriage of the duke and duchess of Bedford, the early career of Sir Richard Wydeville and the secret marriage to the widowed duchess, see Higginbotham 2013, 9–25.
7   Pollard 2007a, 56; Hinds 1912d.
8   Ross 1974, 91–9; Pollard 2007a, 56.

9    Fahy 1961, 663–5.
10   Hall 1809, 254.
11   Ibid; Gairdner 1876, 226; *CWR*, 15.
12   Fabyan 1811, 854.
13   Ross 1474, 90.
14   Pollard 2007a, 55.
15   Ross 1974, 91–2; Pollard 2007a, 56; Lander 1976, 107–8.
16   Hinds 1912d.
17   Ibid.
18   Ibid.
19   Pollard 2007a, 56; Ross 1974, 91.
20   Lander 1976, 114.
21   Keir 1970, 116.
22   Ibid. A pallium is a collar of fur or wool worn about the shoulders.
23   Ibid 116, 118–20. William Percy had died in 1462 and succeeded as Bishop of
     Carlisle by Richard Scrope, whose family had been retainers and associates of the
     Nevills for generations.
24   Ibid.
25   Leland 1752, 2–4 (modern spelling by the author).
26   Leland 1752, 2; White 1998, 403.
27   Ibid, 2–3. The menu included items not on the introductory list, such as larks,
     tench, salmon, crabs, eels, shrimps, quinces, dates, herrings and turbot.
28   Ibid.
29   Ibid, 4; Nichols 1790, 94. Though there were undoubtedly uncomfortable
     moments, it would have been a gross breach of protocol to fail to invite the earl of
     Westmorland and, on his part, to have excused himself without good reason.
30   Leland 1752, 2.
31   White 1998, 406–7.
32   Leland 1752, 5, 7.
33   Ibid, 9.
34   Ibid, 7.
35   Ibid. The carver at this feast was Robert, lord Willoughby, son of Joan Willoughby
     and Richard Welles.
36   Ibid, 3–5. Alianor, lady Stanley is not listed as attending the feast, though her
     husband is. She may have been unwell, preparing for or recovering from the birth
     of a child.
37   White 1998, 406.
38   Ibid, 44–5; Pollard 2007a, 57.


## 30. Rumblings of Discontent

1    Ross 1974, 110; Pollard 2007a, 60–1; Hicks 1998, 253–4.
2    Ross 1974, 110.
3    Keir 1970, 122–3.
4    Ibid, 138.
5    Emery 2000, 278; Halliwell 1839, 25.
6    Weiss 1957, 108; Halloran 2011, 20–1.
7    Hicks 1998, 234.

8    Halliwell 1839, 5. The account of the chronicler, John Warkworth, is geographically confused. Bungerley Hippingstone is near Hexham in Northumberland, not Lancashire.

9    Rous 1980, 7. Anne Nevill and Gloucester clearly knew each other as children. The myth that they were 'childhood sweethearts' should be addressed, however, as Gloucester was some five years older than Anne. When their paths crossed again as young adults, this age difference meant little but at 14 and 9 respectively, it would have counted for a good deal.

10    Hicks 1998, 249.

11    Ibid. Ross 1974, 93. Anne, duchess of Exeter's story is fascinating, but outside the scope of the current work. In 1464, she was granted her exiled husband's lands and titles. Some time in the 1460s she took a lover, Thomas St Leger, and finally married him after she was granted a divorce in 1472. See Hicks 2004b.

12    Hicks 1998, 262; Ross 1974, 104–25.

13    Ibid.

14    Pollard 2007a, 59; Ross 1974, 104–25.

15    Ibid.

16    Ibid; Scobie 1877, 126.

17    Scobie 1877, 125. Charles was not Duke of Burgundy until the death of his father Philip in June 1467.

18    Riley 1908, 1457.

19    Kekewich 2004.

20    Ibid.

21    Pollard 2007a, 60; Hicks 1998, 262; Ross 1974, 109.

22    Pollard 2007a, 60; Ross 1974, 104–25.

23    Pollard 2007a, 60–1; Ross 1974, 104–25.

24    Pollard 2007a, 61; Ross 1974, 104–25.

25    Hinds 1912f.

26    Pollard 2007a, 61; Ross 1974, 104–25.

27    Ibid. These secret plans put Edward IV in a difficult position. Hicks writes: 'If he thought higher for his brother, it was an insult to Warwick; if he wanted Clarence as a diplomatic pawn, it was offensive to the duke; if he feared to strengthen the earl, his action served to make him into the threat that he wished to dispel' (1998, 264).

28    Hinds 1912f.

29    Hicks 1998, 264; Pollard 2007a, 60; Ross 1974, 104–25.

30    Vergil, 2005.

31    Ibid.

32    Ibid.

33    Hicks 1998, 265; Ross 1974, 104–25.

34    Pollard 2007a, 60; Ross 1974, 104–25; Hicks 1998, 266.

35    Pollard 2007a, 62; Ross 1974, 104–25.

36    Hicks 1998, 268; Ross 1974, 104–25.

37    Pollard 2007a, 62; Hinds 1912f.

38    Hinds 1912f.

39    Pollard 2007a, 63; Ross 1974, 104–25. For full first-hand accounts of the wedding, see Bentley 1831, 223–39; Gairdner 1904b, 297–9.

40    Gairdner 1904b, 299.

41    Pollard 2007a, 63; Hicks 1998, 262, 264; Ross 1974, 104–25.

42    Hicks 1998, 267–8; Ross 1974, 10 Ross 1974, 104–25.

43    Pollard 2007a, 64; Ross 2011, 58–9.

44  Pollard 2007a, 64; Gairdner 1904b, 304.
45  Higginbotham 2013, 53.
46  Ibid, 65.
47  Connor 2010, 125.
48  Ibid, 126–7.
49  Nichols 1790, 98.
50  *CWR* 1845, 219.

## 31. Robin of Redesdale and the Capture of the King

1   *CWR* 1845, 219.
2   Ibid; John Fogge was related to earl Rivers and his name was likely included to appeal to a largely Kentish audience. See Hicks 1980, 35; Griffiths 2004a; Lewis 2011, 100.
3   Lewis 2011, 100.
4   Griffiths 2004c.
5   Ibid, 222; *CWR* 1845, 219–20.
6   Ross 1974, 130; Haigh 1995, 100.
7   Haigh 1995, 99.
8   Summerson 2004.
9   Haigh 1995, 99.
10  Lewis 2011.
11  Ross 1974, 127–2; Gairdner 1904c, 35.
12  Harris 1907, 341–2.
13  Ibid, 343.
14  Ibid, 345.
15  *CWR* 1845, 24; Haigh 1995, 100.
16  Haigh 1995, 100–1.
17  Ibid, 102.
18  Lewis 2011, 103.
19  *CWR* 1845, 23–4.
20  Ross 1974, 132.
21  Haigh 1995, 102–3.
22  *Croyland Chronicle*, in Riley 1908.
23  Ibid, 103.
24  Hinds 1912g. There are other chroniclers who held the queen and her kin responsible for Warwick and Clarence's disaffection. The *Croyland Chronicle* records that 'the king, being too greatly influenced by the urgent suggestions of the queen, admitted to his especial favour all the relations of the said queen, as well as those who were in any way connected with her by blood, enriching them with boundless presents and always promoting them to the most dignified offices about his person; while, at the same time, he banished from his presence his own brothers, and his kinsmen sprung from the royal blood, together with the earl of Warwick himself, and the other nobles of the realm who had always proved faithful to him.' This probably overstates the influence of the queen, and the rewards to her kin, as well as the degree to which Warwick and Clarence were excluded.
25  Ibid.
26  Ibid.

27  Ross 1974, 134; Pollard 2007a, 66.
28  Ross 1974, 134–5.
29  Riley 1908.
30  Ross 1974, 134–5; *CWR*, 112.
31  Ross 1974, 135.

## 32. The Lincolnshire Rebellion

1   Gairdner 1904c, 62.
2   Ibid, 63.
3   Ibid.
4   Higginbotham 2013, 60.
5   Riley 1908.
6   Hinds 1912h; Ross 1974, 37.
7   Hicks 1980, 48–9.
8   Ibid, 51.
9   Ibid, 51–2.
10  The difficulty with the Lincolnshire Rebellion, and identifying when exactly
    Warwick and Clarence became involved, is that the most coherent and
    comprehensive account is Edward IV's official record, the *Chronicle of the Rebellion
    in Lincolnshire*, which 'is of importance, only because it relates circumstances not
    elsewhere recorded, but also because it evidently proceeded from one who had
    consequently the best means of information; appealing, indeed, to documents
    throughout his narrative'. See Nichols 1847, 4. While it no doubt fits loosely under
    the heading 'propaganda', being the official record of the reigning king, dismissing
    the chronicle solely on this basis is unwise. Ross (1974, 441–2) and Hicks (1980,
    52–4) discuss this in some detail.
11  Hicks 1980, 55.
12  Nichols 1847, 21 (modern spelling by the author).
13  Hicks 1980, 55–6; Mackman 1999, 148.
14  Nichols 1847, 6, 22.
15  Haigh 1995, 106; Hicks 1980, 56; Nichols 1847, 6.
16  Nichols 1847, 6.
17  Ibid, 6, 7.
18  Ibid.
19  Ibid.
20  Ibid, 10.
21  Haigh 1995, 107.
22  Ibid. 107–8; Nichols 1847, 10; Hicks 1980, 57.
23  Ibid, 10–1; Haigh 1995, 109.
24  Nichols 1847, 13.
25  Ibid, 15.
26  Ibid, 12, 15.
27  Haigh 1995, 110.
28  Ibid; Hicks 1990, 286; Pollard 2007a, 68; Goodman 1981, 73; *CWR*, 114.

## 33. Strange Bedfellows

1   *CWR*, 226–9.
2   Hicks 1990, 287; *CWR*, 114–5.
3   Scoble 1877, 184.
4   Ibid, 184–5.
5   Ibid, 185.
6   Ibid, 184, 186; Rous 1980, 56.
7   Hicks 1990, 287–8.
8   Ibid, 287, 289.
9   Ibid, 288–9.
10   Hicks 1980, 63–5.
11   Hicks 1990, 288.
12   Hicks 1980, 65.
13   Hinds 1912h.
14   Kekewich et al. 1995, 268–9.
15   Ibid.
16   Ross 2011, 60.
17   Ibid.
18   Ibid.
19   Scoble 1877, 188–9.
20   Kekewich et al. 1995, 215–8.
21   Hinds 1912h.
22   Kekewich et al. 1995, 216.
23   Ibid, 216, 217.
24   Ibid, 217–8.
25   Ibid, 218.
26   Hicks 1989, 69–70.
27   Hinds 1912e. My thanks to Susan Higginbotham for her insights into the character of Edward, Prince of Wales.
28   Scoble 1877, 189.
29   Ibid, 190.
30   Kekewich et al. 1995, 220–1.
31   Ibid.
32   *CWR*, 116.

## 34. Endgame

1   Gairdner 1904c, 80.
2   Pollard 2007b, 69–70.
3   Scoble 1877, 116; Ross 1974, 152.
4   Ross 1974, 152; Pollard 2007a, 71.
5   Scoble 1877, 117.
6   Kleineke 2006, 2.
7   Pollard 2007a, 71–2.
8   Ibid.
9   Scoble 1877, 119–20; Ross 2011, 63.
10   Stapleton 1839, 19; Ross 2011, 59–62.
11   Ross 2011, 63; Gairdner 1904c, 63.

12 Hicks 1980, 87; Ross 1974, 157.
13 Pollard 2007a, 112.
14 Myers 2007, 114–5; Hicks 1980, 91.
15 Pollard 2007a, 72; Hull 1966, 65; Ross 1974, 83; Myers 2007, 114–5.
16 Myers 2007, 114.
17 Scoble 1877, 196–7.
18 Scoble 1877, 195; CWR, 119; Ross 1975, 156.
19 For a detailed examination of the readeption, see Hicks 1980, 73–91.
20 Hicks 1980, 88.
21 Visser-Fuchs 1995, 92–100.
22 Ibid, 92, 100.
23 Ross 1974, 160; Bruce 1838, 2 (modern spelling by the author).
24 Bruce 1838, 2; Pollard 2007a, 112; Ross 2011, 63; Gairdner 1904c, 95; Bruce 1838, 2.
25 Gairdner 1904c, 95.
26 Bruce 1838, 3.
27 Pollard 2007a, 72–3; Bruce 1838, 3.
28 Bruce 1838, 6.
29 Pollard 2007a, 72–3; Bruce 1838, 6.
30 Pollard 2007a, 72–3; Bruce 1838, 7–8; Haigh 1995, 117.
31 Bruce 1838, 9.
32 Ibid.
33 Ibid, 10–1.
34 Ibid.
35 Ibid, 12.
36 Ibid.
37 Ibid, 16–7.
38 Ibid, 17; Clark 2007, 38.
39 Clark 2007, 41–2, 43.
40 Ibid 44; Bruce 1838, 18.
41 Haigh 1995, 121.
42 Bruce 1838, 19; Haigh 1995, 121.
43 CWR, 124–5; Ross 2011, 66.
44 Haigh 1995, 121–2.
45 Ibid; CWR, 124–5. Warkworth's well-known account of the confusion of Edward IV's sun in splendour and Oxford's 'streaming star' is examined and called into question in Ross 2011, 66–7.
46 Haigh 1995, 122; Bruce 1838, 20; CWR, 125. Warkworth, and only Warkworth, tells the story of Montagu's betrayal. He had 'agreed and appointed with king Edward, and put upon him king Edward's livery; and a man of the earl of Warwick's saw that and fell upon him, and killed him'. See CWR, 125. There are two problems with this story. The first is that Warkworth had earlier stated that Montagu had come to hate Edward IV, and the second is the story is not found in The Arrivall, where much would have been made of it were it true. It is likely to be inspired by the confusion between Montagu's men and Oxford's when the latter returned from rallying his troops.

## 35. Embers of Resistance

1 Haigh 1995, 125; Bruce 1938, 22; Hinds 1912i.
2 Haigh 1995, 125; Bruce 1938, 22.
3 Bruce 1838, 22.
4 Haigh 1995, 125–7.
5 Ibid, 129.
6 Ibid, 131–3.
7 Ibid, 133–4; Bruce 1838, 30.
8 Haigh 1995, 134–5.
9 Ibid, 389.
10 Sharpe 1895, 387; 388.
11 Ibid, 389.
12 Ibid.
13 Ibid, 389–90.
14 Ibid, 391.
15 Richmond 1970, 676–8.
16 Sharpe 1895, 391–2.
17 Richmond 1970, 678–81.
18 Bruce 1895, 39.
19 Richmond 1970, 678–82; Gairdner 1905c, 109, 113. Little, if anything, is known about Fauconberg's brother.
20 Hicks 2004a.
21 Gairdner 1904c, 131; Hicks 2004c.
22 Hicks 2004c.


## 36. The Earl and the Archbishop

1 Gairdner 1904c, 101.
2 Ibid.
3 Ibid, 102.
4 Ibid, 137.
5 Ross 2011, 69.
6 *CWR*, 136–7; Gairdner 1904c, 137.
7 Meyer 2001, 65; Keir 1970, 177–8.
8 Hinds 1912j; Gairdner 1904c, 184; Ross 2011, 70.
9 Gairdner 1904c, 186, 188–9.
10 Milan 1473.
11 Ibid.
12 Ibid. For a discussion of the identity of the duke, see Ross 2011, 72.
13 Ross 2011, 72; *CWR*, 137–9
14 *CWR*, 139.
15 Fabyan 1811, 663; Ross 2011, 78, 80.
16 Keir 1970, 147, 225, 227.
17 Ibid, 149–50, 152–3.
18 Gairdner 1904d, 1–2.
19 Fabyan 1811, 663; Ross 2011, 81–2.
20 Ross 2011, 82, 85, 97.

## 37. Bitter Harvest

1   Riley 1908, 469–70; Hicks 1991, 327.
2   Hinds 1912k.
3   Riley 1908, 470.
4   Green 1846, 101–4.
5   Hicks 1991, 294, 296.
6   Ibid, 296.
7   *Calendar of Close Roles, Edward IV, 1468–1476*; Hicks 1991, 292.
8   Richmond 1992, 122.
9   Friedrichs 2000, 223–4.
10  Higginbotham 2013, 183 (modern spelling by the author).
11  Friedrichs 2000, 227 footnote.
12  Rolls of Parliament Edward IV 1472.
13  See Hicks 2006. Various historical novelists have also subscribed erroneously to this interpretation of the act.
14  Given-Wilson 2005f.
15  Ibid.
16  Rous 1990, 58. For a full account of Clarence's trial, see Hicks 1980, Chapter 4.
17  Rous 1990, 62.
18  Baldwin 2009, 108.
19  See Haigh 1995, 164–81.
20  Gairdner 1904d, 91–2.
21  Ibid, 92–9.
22  See Haigh 1995, 154–65.
23  Ross 2011, 82, 85, 97.

# PICTURE CREDITS

1   DeFacto, Wikimedia Commons.
2   Draco2008, www.flickr.com.
3a  JThomas, www.geograph.org.uk.
3b  CJW, Wikimedia Commons.
4   Chemical engineer, Wikimedia Commons.
5   Nigel Cox, cropped by Jappalang, Wikimedia Commons.
6   Greenshed, Wikimedia Commons.
7   Tim Felce, Wikimedia Commons.
8   Richard Whitaker, www.flickr.com.
9a  JThomas, www.geograph.org.uk.
9b  J.W. Robinson, Wikimedia Commons.
10  Rs-nourse, Wikimedia Commons.
11  G. Wheeler.

# BIBLIOGRAPHY

## Primary Sources

Anon, 1845, *The Chronicles of the White Rose of York*, James Bohn, London.

Bentley, Samuel (ed.), 1831, *Excerpta Historica*, Samuel Bentley, London.

Bloom, J.H., 1919, 'A Letter from the "Kingmaker"', *Notes and Queries*, 12s-V (88) (May), 120.

Brie, Friedrich W.D., 1905, *The Brut*, Early English Text Society, London.

Bruce, John (ed.), 1838, *Historie of the Arrivall of Edward IV and the Finall Recouerye of his Kingdomes from Henry VI, AD MCCCCLXXI*, Camden Society, London.

*Calendar of Close Rolls, Edward IV, Vol. I, 1461–1468*, 1949, ed. W.H.B. Bird and K.H. Ledward, HMSO, London.

*Calendar of Close Rolls, Edward IV, 1468–1476*, 1953, HMSO, London, www.british-history. ac.uk/cal-close-rolls/edw4/vol2/pp327-342.

*Calendar of Close Rolls, Henry VI, 1447–1454, Vol. V*, Kraus Reprint, 1971.

*Calendar of Patent Rolls, Henry VI, 1441–1446 Vol. IV*, Kraus Reprint, 1971.

*Calendar of Patent Rolls, Henry VI, 1446–1453 Vol. V*, Kraus Reprint, 1971.

*Calendar of Patent Rolls, Henry VI, 1452–1461, Vol. VI*, Kraus Reprint, 1971.

*Calendar of State Papers Relating to English Affairs in the Archives of Venice, Volume 1, 1202–1509*. Originally published by HMSO, London, 1864, www.british-history.ac.uk/cal-state-papers/venice/vol1/pp92-126.

Chambers, R.W. (ed.), 1911, *A Fifteenth-Century Courtesy Book*, Early English Text Society, Oxford.

Connor, Meriel (ed./trans.), 2010, *John Stone's Chronicle, Christ Church Priory, Canterbury, 1417–1472*, Medieval Institute Publications, Kalamazoo.

Davis, John Silvester, 1856, *An English Chronicle*, Camden Society, London.

Dupont (ed.), 1843, *Anchiennes Croniques d'Engleterre par Jehan de Wavrin, Vol. 3*, La Société de l'Histoire de France, Paris.

Ellis, Henry (ed.), 1825, *Original Letters Illustrative of English History Vol. I*, Harding, Triphook and Lepard, London.

——, 1827, *Original Letters Illustrative of English History, Second Series Vol. I*, Harding and Lepard, London.

Fabyan, Robert, 1811, *New Chronicles of England and France*, F.C. & J. & Rivington etc., London.

Flenley, Ralph, 1911, *Six Town Chronicles of England*, Clarendon Press, Oxford.

*Formulare Anglicorum*, 1702, 102–03.

du Fresne de Beaucourt, G. (ed.), 1893, *Chronique de Mathieu d'Escouchy 1452–1461*, Chez Jules Renouard, Paris.

Gairdner, James (ed.), 1843, *Three Fifteenth-Century Chronicles*, Camden Society, London.

——, 1864a, *The Paston Letters, AD 1422–1509, Vol. II*, Chatto & Windus, London.

——, 1876, *The Historical Collections of a Citizen of London in the Fifteenth Century, [Gregory's Chronicle]*, Camden Society, London.

——, 19094a, *The Paston Letters, AD 1422–1509, Vol. 2*, Chatto & Windus, London.

——, 1904b, *The Paston Letters, AD 1422–1509, Vol. 4*, Chatto & Windus, London.

——, 1904c, *The Paston Letters, AD 1422–1509, Vol. 5*, Chatto & Windus, London.

——, 1904d, *The Paston Letters, AD 1422–1509, Vol. 6*, Chatto & Windus, London.

Given-Wilson, C. (gen. ed.), Paul Brand, Seymour Phillips, Mark Ormond, Geoffrey Martin, Anne Curry, Rosemary Horrox (eds), 2005a, 'Henry VI: March 1453', Parliament Rolls of Medieval England, www.british-history.ac.uk/no-series/parliament-rolls-medieval/march-1453.

——, 2005b, 'Henry VI: 1455', Parliament Rolls of Medieval England.

——, 2005c, 'Henry VI: November 1459', Parliament Rolls of Medieval England, www.british-history.ac.uk/no-series/parliament-rolls-medieval/november-1459.

——, 2005d 'Henry VI: October 1460', Parliament Rolls of Medieval England, www.british-history.ac.uk/no-series/parliament-rolls-medieval/october-1460.

——, 2005e, 'Edward IV: November 1461', Parliament Rolls of Medieval England, www.british-history.ac.uk/no-series/parliament-rolls-medieval/november-1461.

——, 2005f, 'Edward IV: October 1472', Parliament Rolls of Medieval England, www.british-history.ac.uk/no-series/parliament-rolls-medieval/october-1472.

Green, Mary Anne Everett Wood (ed.), 1846, *Letters of Royal and Illustrious Ladies of Great Britain, Vol. I*, Henry Colburn, London.

Grose, Francis & Thomas Astle (eds), 1807, *The Antiquarian Repertory Vol. 1*, Edward Jeffrey, London.

Hall, Edmund, 1809, *Hall's Chronicle*, J. Johnson et al., London.

Halliwell, James Orchard (ed.), 1839, *A Chronicle of the First Thirteen Years of the Reign of King Edward the Fourth by John Warkworth, DD, [Warkworth's Chronicle]*, Camden Society, London.

Hardy, Thomas, 1973, *Rymer's Foedera Syllabus Vol. II*

Harris, Mary Dormer (ed.), 1967, *The Coventry Leet Book*, Early English Text Society, London.

Henbey, Ralph, 1911, *Six Town Chronicles of England*, Clarendon Press, Oxford.

Hinds, Allen B. (ed.), 1912a, *Milan: 1460 in Calendar of State Papers and Manuscripts in the Archives and Collections of Milan 1385–1618*, HMSO, London, www.british-history.ac.uk/cal-state-papers/milan/1385-1618.

——, 1912b, *Milan: 1461 in Calendar of State Papers and Manuscripts in the Archives and Collections of Milan 1385–1618*, HMSO, London.

——, 1912c, *Milan: 1462 in Calendar of State Papers and Manuscripts in the Archives and Collections of Milan 1385–1618*, HMSO, London.

——, 1912d, *Milan: 1464 in Calendar of State Papers and Manuscripts in the Archives and Collections of Milan 1385–1618*, HMSO, London.

——, 1912e, *Milan: 1467 in Calendar of State Papers and Manuscripts in the Archives and Collections of Milan 1385–1618*, HMSO, London.

——, 1912f, *Milan: 1468 in Calendar of State Papers and Manuscripts in the Archives and Collections of Milan 1385–1618*, HMSO, London.

——, 1912g, *Milan: 1469 in Calendar of State Papers and Manuscripts in the Archives and Collections of Milan 1385–1618*, HMSO, London.

——, 1912h, *Milan: 1470 in Calendar of State Papers and Manuscripts in the Archives and Collections of Milan 1385–1618*, HMSO, London.

——, 1912i, *Milan: 1471 in Calendar of State Papers and Manuscripts in the Archives and Collections of Milan 1385–1618*, HMSO, London.

——, 1912j, *Milan: 1473 in Calendar of State Papers and Manuscripts in the Archives and Collections of Milan 1385–1618*, HMSO, London.

——, 1912k, *Milan: 1474 in Calendar of State Papers and Manuscripts in the Archives and Collections of Milan 1385–1618*, HMSO, London.

Hull, Felix (ed.), 1966, *A Calendar of the Black and White Books of the Cinque Ports, 1432–1955*, HMSO, London.

Kingsford, C.L. (ed.), 1905, *Chronicles of London*, Clarendon Press, Oxford.

——, 1913, *English Historical Literature in the Fifteenth Century*, Burt Franklin, New York/ Clarendon Press, Oxford.

Leland, John, 1752, *Antiquarii de Rebus Britannicis Collectanea Vol. VI*, Richardson, London.

Lower, Mark Antony, 1851, *The Chronicle of Battle Abbey*, John Russell Smith, London.

Magdalen College Misc MSS 363.

Munro, Cecil (ed.), 1863, *Letters of Queen Margaret of Anjou, Bishop Beckington and Others Written in the Reigns of Henry V and Henry VI*, Camden Society, London.

Nicholas, Harry, 1831a, *Proceedings and Ordinances of Privy Council, Vol. V*, Record Commission.

——, 1831b, *Proceedings and Ordinances of Privy Council, Henry VI, Vol. VI*, Record Commission.

Nichols, John (ed.), 1790, *A Collection of Ordinances and Regulations for the Government of the Royal Household*, Society of Antiquaries, London.

Nichols, John Gough (ed.), 1847, *Chronicle of the Rebellion in Lincolnshire, 1470*, Camden Society, London.

——, 1852, *Chronicle of the Grey Friars of London*, Camden Society, London.

Nicolas, Harris (ed.), 1827, *A Chronicle of London*, Longman, Rees, Orme, Brown and Green; and Henry Butterworth, London.

Pearsall, Dereck (ed.), 1990, *The Floure and Leafe, The Assemblie of Ladies and the Isle of Ladies*, Medieval Institute Publications, Kalamazoo.

Raine, James & John William Clay (eds), 1865, *Testamenta Eboracensia: A Selection of Wills from the Registry at York, Vol. 3*, Surtees Society, London.

Riley, Henry (trans.), 1908, *Ingulph's Chronicle of the Abbey of Croyland, [Croyland Chronicle]*, George Bell & Sons, London.

Rous, John, *Rous Roll*, Alan Sutton, Stroud, 1980.

*Rymer's Foedera, Vol. XI*, Apud Joannem Nuelme, London, 1739.

Scoble, Andrew (ed.), 1877, *The Memoirs of Philippe de Commines, Vol. I*, George Bell & Sons, London.

Sharpe, Reginald R., 1985, *London and the Kingdom Vol. III*, Longmans, Green & Co., London.

Sinclair, Alexandra (ed.), 2003, *The Beauchamp Pageant*, Paul Watkins, Donnington.

Society of Antiquaries of London, 1812, *Archaeologica Vol. XVI*, T. Bensley, London.

Staley, Lynn (ed.), 1996, *The Book of Margery Kempe*, Medieval Institute Publications, Kalamazoo.

Stapleton, Thomas (ed.), 1839, *Plumpton Correspondence*, Camden Society, London.

Stevenson, Joseph (ed.), 1861, *Letters and Papers Illustrative of the Wars of the English in France, Vol. 1*, Longman, Green, Longman and Roberts, London.

——, 1864, *Letters and Papers Illustrative of the Wars of the English in France, Vol. 2 Part 2*, Longman, Green, Longman, Roberts and Green, London.

Stow, John, 1600, *Annales of England*.

Sutton, Dana F, 2005, Virgil, Polydore, *Angelica Historica* (1555 Version), University of California, Irvine, www.philological.bham.ac.uk/polverg/

Swallow, Henry J, 1885, *De Nova Villa: Or the House of Nevill, In Sunshine and Shade*, Andrew Reid, Newcastle-on-Tyne.

Waurin, Jehan de (ed. William Hardy and Edward C.P. Hardy), 1891, *Recueil de Croniques et Anchiennes Istories de la Grant Bretaigne*, HMSO, London.

## Secondary Sources

Anderson, Marjorie, 1945, 'Alice Chaucer and Her Husbands', *PMLA*, Vol. 60, No. 1 (March), 211–47.

Anderson, R.C., 1919, 'The Grace of Dieu of 1446–86', *English Historical Review*, Vol. 134, No. 136 (October), 584–86.

Archer, Rowena E., 2004a, 'Neville, Katherine, Dowager Duchess of Norfolk, (c1400–1483)', *ODNB*, Oxford University Press (OUP), Oxford, online ed.

——, 2004b, 'John Mowbray (V), Second Duke of Norfolk (1392–1432)', *ODNB*, OUP, Oxford.

Armstrong, C.A.J., 1948, 'The Inauguration Ceremonies of the Yorkist Kings and their Title to the Throne', *Transactions of the Royal Historical Society*, 4th Series, Vol. 30, 51–73.

——, 1960. 'Politics and the Battle of St Albans, 1455', *Bulletin of the Institute of Historical Research*, No. 87 (May), 1–72.

Baldwin, David, 2009, *Kingmaker's Sisters*, The History Press, Stroud.

Barratt, John, 2010, *War for the Throne: The Battle of Shrewsbury* (Campaign Chronicles), Pen & Sword Military, Barnsley.

Bennett, Michael J., 2004a, 'Stanley, Thomas, First Earl of Derby (c1433–1504)', *ODNB*, OUP, online ed.

—— 2004b, 'Stanley, Sir William (c1435–1495)', *ODNB*, OUP, online ed.

——, 2004c, 'Stanley, Thomas, first Baron Stanley (1406–1459)', *ODNB*, OUP, online ed.

Boardman, A.W., 2000, *The Battle of Towton*, Sutton Publishing, Stroud.

Boardman, Andrew, 2006, *The First Battle of St Albans*, Tempus, Stroud.

Booth, Peter, 1997, *Landed Society in Cumberland and Westmorland c1440–1488: The Politics of the Wars of the Roses*, PhD thesis, University of Leicester.

—— 2003, 'Men Behaving Badly: The West March towards Scotland and the Percy/Neville Feud', in Linda Clark (ed.), *The Fifteenth Century: Authority and Subversion*, Boydell Press, Woodbridge.

Brears, Peter, 2012, *Cooking and Dining in Medieval England*, Prospect Books, Totnes.

Brindley, David, 2001, *Richard Beauchamp: Medieval England's Greatest Knight*, Tempus, Stroud.

Broertjes, Andrew, 2015, 'The Lancastrian Retreat from Populist Discourse? Propaganda Conflicts in the Wars of the Roses', *Limina*, Vol. 20, No. 3, 1–20.

Brown, A.L. & Bruce Webster, 1966, 'The Movements of the Earl of Warwick in the Summer of 1464 – A Correction', *English Historical Review*, Vol. 81, No. 318, 80–82.

Burley, Peter, Michael Elliot & Harvey Waston, 2007, *The Battles of St Albans*, Pen & Sword Military, Barnsley.

Butler, Archibald & Rouge Croix, 1917, 'The Rous Roll', *The Burlington Magazine for*

*Connoisseurs*, Vol. 30, No. 116 (January), 23–31.

Campbell, John, 1851, *The Lives of the Lords Chancellor, Vol. 1, (3)*, Blanchard and Lea, Philadelphia.

Carpenter, Christine, 1980, 'The Beauchamp Affinity: A Study of Bastard Feudalism at Work', *English Historical Review*, Vol. 95, No. 376 (July), 514–32.

—— 1997, *The Wars of the Roses: Politics and the Constitution in England, c1437–1509*, Cambridge University Press, Cambridge.

——, 2004a, 'Beauchamp, Henry, Duke of Warwick, (1425–1446)', *ODNB*, OUP, online ed.

——, 2004b, 'Beauchamp, Richard, Thirteenth Earl of Warwick (1382–1438)', *ODNB*, OUP, online ed.

Castor, Helen, 2004, 'Scales, Thomas, Seventh Baron Scales (1399?–1460)', *ODNB*, OUP.

Cherry, Martin, 2004a, 'Bonville, William, First Baron Bonville (1392–1461)', *ODNB*, OUP, online ed.

——, 2004c, 'Courtney, Thomas, Thirteenth Earl of Devon (1414–1461)', *ODNB*, OUP, online ed.

Clark, David, 2007, *Barnet 1471, Death of a Kingmaker*, Pen & Sword Military, Barnsley.

Clark, Linda, 2004a, 'Bourchier, Thomas (c1411–1486)', *ODNB*, OUP.

——, 2004b, 'Bourchier, Henry First Earl of Essex (c1408-1483)', *ODNB*, OUP, online ed.

Cokayne, G.E. (ed.), 1887, *Complete Peerage Vol. I*, George Bell & Sons, London.

—— (ed.), 1887a, *Complete Peerage Vol. IV*, George Bell & Sons, London.

—— (ed.), 1887b, *Complete Peerage Vol. IX*, George Bell & Sons, London.

—— (ed.), 1887c, *Complete Peerage Vol. I*, George Bell & Sons, London.

—— (ed.), 1887d, *Complete Peerage Vol. IX Part 2*, George Bell & Sons, London.

—— (ed.), 1887e, *Complete Peerage Vol. VIII*, George Bell & Sons, London.

—— (ed.), 1940a, *Complete Peerage Vol. XIII*, St Catherine Press, London.

Crawford, Anne, 2001, 'The Queens Council in the Middle Ages', *English Historical Review*, Vol. 116, No. 469 (November), 1193–211.

Cunningham, Hugo S., 2002, 'Medieval Coinage – the Gold "Noble"', www.cyberussr. com/hcunn/gold-bri-noble.html.

Curry, Anne, 2002, *Osprey Guide to the Hundred Years' War, 1337–1453*, Osprey Publishing, Oxford.

——, 2004a, 'Montagu, Thomas, Fourth Earl of Salisbury (1388–1428)', *ODNB*, OUP, online ed.

——, 2004c, 'Kyriell, Sir Thomas (1391–1461)', *ODNB*, OUP, online ed.

Dobson, R.B., 2004, 'Neville, Alexander (1332–1392)', *ODNB*, OUP, online ed.

Dockray, Keith, 1983, 'The Yorkshire Rebellions of 1469', *The Ricardian*, Vol. 6, No. 82 (December), 246–57.

——, 2004, 'Greystoke Family (per 1321–1487)', *ODNB*, OUP.

Dockray, Keith & Richard Knowles, 1992, 'The Battle of Wakefield', *The Ricardian*, Vol. 9, No. 117, 238–56.

Druery, John Henry, 1826, *Historical and Topographical Notices of Great Yarmouth*, Nichols & Son, London.

Dunn, Alistair, 2003, 'Henry IV and the Politics of Resistance in Early Lancastrian England, 1399–1413', in Clark, Linda (ed.), *The Fifteenth Century III: Authority and Subversion*, Boydell Press, Oxford.

Dunn, Diana E.S., 2004, 'Margaret, (1430–1482)', *ODNB*, OUP.

Embleton, Gerry & John Howe, 1994, *The Medieval Soldier, 15th Century Campaign Life*,

Crowood Press, Ramsbury.

Emery, Anthony, 2000, *Great Medieval Houses of England and Wales, Vol. 2*, Cambridge University Press, Cambridge.

Fahy, Connor, 1961, 'The Marriage of Edward IV and Elizabeth Woodville: A New Italian Source', *English Historical Review*, Vol. 76, No. 301 (October), 660–72.

Fisher, Eric, 1954, *Some Yorkshire Estates of the Percies, 1450–1650*, PhD thesis, University of Leeds.

Ford, L.L., 2004, 'Vaux Nicholas, First Baron Vaux (c1460–1523)', *ODNB*, OUP, online ed.

Fox-Davies, Arthur Charles, 1909, *A Complete Guide to Heraldry*, Bonanza Books, New York.

Fraser, C.M., 2004, 'Ogle, Robert (VI), First Baron Ogle (1406–1469)', *ODNB*, OUP, online ed.

Fredrichs, Rhoda Lange, 1974, *The Career and Influence of Ralph, Lord Cromwell 1393–1456*, PhD thesis, Columbia University.

Fredrichs, Rhoda L., 1998, 'Ralph, Lord Cromwell and the Politics of Fifteenth-Century England', *Nottingham Medieval Studies*, XXXII, 207–27.

——, 2000, 'Rich Old Ladies Made Poor: The Vulnerability of Women's Property in Medieval England', *Medieval Prosopography*, XXI, 223–29.

——, 2006, 'The Remarriage of Elite Widows in the Later Middle Ages', *Florilegium*, Vol. 231, No. 1, 69–83.

Gibson, J.P., 1911, 'A Defence of the Proscription of the Yorkists in 1459', *English Historical Review*, Vol. 26, No. 103 (July), 512–25.

Gillespie, James L., Thomas Mortimer & Thomas Molineux, 1975, 'Radcot Bridge and the Appeal of 1397', *Albion*, Vol. 17, No. 2 (Summer), 161–73.

——, 1985, 'Ladies of the Fraternity of St George and of the Society of the Garter', *Albion*, Vol. 117, No. 3 (Autumn), 259–78.

——, 2004, 'Holland, Thomas, Sixth Earl of Kent and Duke of Surrey', *ODNB*, OUP, online ed.

Given-Wilson, C., 1993, *Chronicles of the Revolution 1397–1400*, Manchester University Press, Manchester.

——, 2004, 'Fitzalan, Richard (III), Fourth Earl of Arundel and Ninth Earl of Surry (1346–1397)', *ODNB*, OUP, online ed.

Goodman, Anthony, 2004, 'Montagu, John, Third Earl of Salisbury (c1350–1400)', *ODNB*, OUP.

Goodwin, George, 2011, *Fatal Colours*, Phoenix, London.

Gray, Douglas, 2004, 'Chaucer', *ODNB*, OUP, online ed.

Green, Richard Firth, 1981, 'The Short Version of the Arrival of Edward IV', *Specuum*, Vol. 56, No. 2 (April), 324–36.

Griffiths, R.A., 1975, 'Duke Richard of York's Intentions in 1450 and the Origins of the Wars of the Roses', *Journal of Medieval History*, I, 187–209.

——, 2004b, 'Percy, Thomas, First Baron Egremont (1422–1460)', *ODNB*, OUP, online ed.

——, 2004c, 'Herbert, William, First Earl of Pembroke (c1423–1469)', *ODNB*, OUP, online ed.

Griffiths, Ralph A., 1965, 'Local Rivalries and National Politics: The Percies, the Nevilles and the Duke of Exeter, 1452–1455', *Speculum*, Vol. 43, No. 4 (October), 589–632.

——, 1981, *The Reign of King Henry VI*, University of California Press, Berkeley.

——, 1984, 'The King's Council and the First Protectorate of the Duke of York, 1453–1454', *English Historical Review*, Vol. 99, No. 390 (January), 67–82.

Griffiths, Ralph, 2000, 'The English Crown, Provinces and Dominions in the Fifteenth Century', in Anne Curry & Elizabeth Matthews (eds), *Concepts and Patterns of Service in the Late Middle Ages*, Boydell Press, Woodbridge.

Grummit, David, 2007, 'The Defence of Calais and the Development of Gunpowder Weaponry in the Late Fifteenth Century', *War in History*, No. 3, 253–72.

——, 2004a, 'Henry Percy, second Earl of Northumberland, (1394–1455)', *ODNB*, OUP, online ed.

——, (1968), 'The Trial of Eleanor Cobham: An Episode in the Fall of Humphrey Duke of Gloucester', *Bulletin of the John Rylands Library Manchester*, No. 51, 381–99.

—— 2008, *The Calais Garrison: War and Military Service in England 1436–1588*, Boydell Press, Woodbury.

——, (forthcoming), *Clifton, Gervase, History of Parliament* [private communication].

Haigh, Philip A., 1995, *The Military Campaigns of the Wars of the Roses*, Alan Sutton, Stroud.

—— 1996, *The Battle of Wakefield, 30 December 1460*, Sutton Publishing, Stroud.

——, 2002, *From Wakefield to Towton*, Leo Cooper, Barnsley.

Hall, S.C. & Llewellyn Jewitt, 1876, 'The Stately Homes of England (Occasionally Open to the Public) – Raby Castle, Durham', *The Art Journal* (1875–87), New Series, Vol. 2, 233–35.

Halloran, Erin Michelle, 2011, *The Influence of Humanism on English Social Structures through the Actions of Thomas Linacre and John Colet*, MA dissertation, Louisiana State University.

Hammond, P.W., 2004, 'Percy, Sir Ralph (1425–1464)', *ODNB*, OUP.

Hanham, Alison, 2008, 'The Curious Letters of Friar Brackley', *Historical Research*, Vol. 81, No. 211 (February), 28–51.

Harper-Bill, Christopher, 2004, 'Cecily, Duchess of York (1415–1495)', *ODNB*, OUP, online ed.

Harriss, G.L., 1960, 'The Struggle for Calais', *English Historical Review*, Vol. 75, No. 294, 30–53.

——, 2004a, 'Richard Earl of Cambridge (1385–1415)', *ODNB*, OUP, online ed.

——, 2004b, 'Eleanor, Duchess of Gloucester (c1406–1482)', *ODNB*, OUP, online ed. 2008.

——, 2004c, 'Willoughby, Robert (III), Sixth Baron Willoughby (1385–1452)', *ODNB*, OUP, online ed.

——, 2004d, 'Beaufort, Henry (1375?–1447)', *ODNB*, OUP, online ed.

——, 2004e, 'Beaufort, Henry, Duke of Somerset (1404–1444)', *ODNB*, OUP, online ed.

Hicks, M.A., 1994, 'Edward IV, the Duke of Somerset and Lancastrian Loyalism in the North', *Northern History*, Vol. 20, No. 1 (January), 23–37.

Hicks, Michael, 1991, *Richard III and his Rivals: Magnates and their Motives in the Wars of the Roses*, Hambledon Press, London.

——, 1998, *Warwick the Kingmaker*, Blackwell, Oxford.

——, 1999, 'Between Majorities: The "Beauchamp Interregnum" 1439–1449', *Historical Research*, Vol. 72, No. 127 (February), 27–43.

——, 2000a, 'Propaganda and the First Battle of St Albans', *Nottingham Medieval Studies*, XLIV, 167–83.

——, 2000b, 'Bastard Feudalism, Overmighty Subjects and Idols of the Multitude during the Wars of the Roses', *History*, Vol. 85, No. 279 (July), 386–403.

——, 2002, *English Political Culture in the Fifteenth Century*, Routledge, New York.

——, 2004a, 'Neville, George (1432–1476)', *ODNB*, OUP, online ed.

——, 2004b, 'Holland, Henry, Second Duke of Exeter (1430–1475)', *ODNB*, OUP.

——, 2004c, 'Richard Welles, Seventh Baron Willoughby and Seventh Baron Welles (c1428–1470)', *ODNB*, OUP.

——, 2004d, 'Neville, Thomas (d 1471)', *ODNB*, OUP, online ed.

——, 2004e, 'Woodville, Richard, First Earl Rivers (d1469)', *ODNB*, OUP, online ed.

——, 2004e, 'Dynham, John, Baron Dynham (c1433–1501)', *ODNB*, OUP, online ed.

——, 2006, *Anne Neville, Queen to Richard III*, Tempus, Stroud.

Higginbotham, Susan, 2013, *The Woodvilles*, The History Press, Stroud.

Holland, P., 1988, 'The Lincolnshire Rebellion of March 1470', *English Historical Review*, No. 103 (October), 849–69.

Horrox, Rosemary, 2004a, 'Egremont, Sir John (b1459?, d in or after 1505)', *ODNB*, OUP, online ed.

—— 2004b, 'Conyers Family (per c1375–1525)', *ODNB*, OUP, online ed.

——, 2004c, 'Harrington Family (per c1300–1512)', *ODNB*, OUP.

——, 2004d, 'Parr Family (per c1320–1517)', *ODNB*, OUP, online ed.

——, 2004e, 'Neville, John, Marquess Montagu (c1431–1471)', *ODNB*, OUP, online ed.

——, 2004f, 'Hastings, William, First Baron of Hastings (c1430–1483)', *ODNB*, OUP.

Ingram, Mike, 2015, *The Battle of Northampton 1460*, Northampton Battlefield Society, Northampton.

Ives, E.W., 2004, 'Fortescue, Sir John', *ODNB*, OUP, online ed.

Jack, R.I., 1960, 'A Quincentenary: The Battle of Northampton, 10th July 1460', *Northamptonshire Past and Present*, No. 3, 21–25.

Jack, R. Ian, 2004, 'Gray Family (per 1325–1523)', *ODNB*, OUP, online ed.

Jambeck, Karen K., 1996, 'Patterns of Women's Literary Patronage, 1200–ca1475', in June Hall McCash (ed.), *The Cultural Patronage of Medieval Women*, University of Georgia Press, Athens.

Johnson, P.A., 1988, *Duke Richard of York 1411–1460*, Clarendon Press, Oxford.

Jones, Michael K., 1989, 'Somerset, York and the Wars of the Roses', *English Historical Review*, No. 409 (April), 285–307.

——, 1997, 'Edward IV, the Earl of Warwick and the Yorkist Claim to the Throne', *Historical Research*, Vol. 70, No. 173 (October), 342–52.

——, 2004a, 'Beaufort, Henry, Second Duke of Somerset (1436–1464)', *ODNB*, OUP, online ed.

——, 2004b, 'Beaufort, Edmund, Styled Third Duke of Somerset (c1438–1471)', *ODNB*, OUP, online ed.

Jones, Nigel R., 2005, *Architecture of England, Scotland and Wales*, Greenwood Publishing, Westport.

Keir, Gillian, 1970, *The Ecclesiastical Career of George Neville, 1432–1476*, BLitt thesis, University of Oxford.

Kekewich, Margaret Lucille, 2004, 'Wenlock, John, First Baron Wenlock (d 1471)', *ODNB*, OUP, online ed.

Kekewich, Margaret Lucille, Colin Richmond, Anne E Sutton, Livia Visser-Fuchs & John Watts (ed.), 1995, *The Politics of 15ᵗʰ Century England: John Vales Book*, Alan Sutton, Stroud.

Kelly, Catherine, 1986, 'The Noble Steward and Late-Feudal Lordship', *Huntington Library Quarterly*, Vol. 49, No. 2 (Spring), 133–48.

Kingsford, C.L., 1921, 'On Some London Houses of the Early Tudor Period', *Archaeologia*, second series, Vol. 17 (January), 17–54.

——, 1922, 'The Earl of Warwick at Calais in 1460', *English Historical Review*, Vol. 37, No. 148 (October), 544–46.

Kleineke, Hannes, 2000, 'Lady Jane Dinham – A Fifteenth-Century West Country

Matriarch', in Tom Thornton (ed.), *The Fifteenth Century: Social Attitudes and Political Structures*, Sutton Publishing, Stroud.

——, 2006, 'Gerhard von Wesel's Newsletter from England, 17 April 1471', *The Ricardian*, Vol. 16, 1–10.

Kohl, Benjamin G., 2004, 'Tiptoft, John, First Earl of Worcester (1427–1470)', *ODNB*, OUP, online ed.

Lander, J.R., 1960, 'Henry VI and the Duke of York's Second Protectorate, 1455 to 1456', *Bulletin of the John Rylands Library*, Vol. 43, No. 1, 49–69.

——, 1961, 'Attainder and Forfeiture, 1453–1509', *The Historical Journal*, Vol 14, No. 2, 119–51.

——, 1963, 'Marriage and Politics in the Fifteenth Century: The Nevilles and the Wydvilles', *Bulletin of the Institute of Historic Research*, Vol. 36, No. 94, 119–52.

Laynesmith, J.L., 2004, *The Last Medieval Queens*, OUP, Oxford.

Laynesmith, Joanna L., 2000, 'Fertility Rite or Authority Ritual? The Queen's Coronation in England, 1445–87', in Tom Thornton (ed.), *The Fifteenth Century: Social Attitudes and Political Structures*, Sutton Publishing, Stroud.

Lewis, Barry, 2011, 'The Battle of Edgecote or Banbury (1469) through the Eyes of Contemporary Welsh Poets', *Journal of Medieval Military History*, No. 9, 97–117.

Lyson, Daniel, 1811, *The Environs of London, Vol. I, Part II*, Cadell & Davies, London.

MacCracken, Henry Noble, 1911, 'An English Friend of Charles of Orleans', *PMLA*, Vol. 26, No. 1, 142–80.

Macdougall, Norman, 2004, 'Mary (d 1463)', *ODNB*, OUP.

Mackman, Jonathan S., 1999, *The Lincolnshire Gentry and the Wars of the Roses*, DPhil thesis, University of York.

Mate, Mavis, 1992, 'The Economic and Social Roots of Medieval Popular Rebellion, 1450–1451', *Economic History Review*, Vol. 45, No. 4 (November), 661–76.

Maurer, Helen, 2003, *Margaret of Anjou*, Boydell Press, Woodbridge.

—— nd, 'Reporting the Wars: The Great Westminster Pie Fight, a Cautionary Tale', www.rs.org/wood/papers/maurer.html (no longer available).

McCarthy, M.R., H.R.T. Summerson & R.G. Annis, 1990, *Carlisle Castle: A Survey and Documentary History*, Historic Buildings & Monuments Commission for England.

McCulloch, D. & E.D. Jones, 1980, 'Lancastrian Politics, the French War and the Rise of the Popular Element', *Speculum*, Vol. 58, No. 1 (January), 95–138.

McDonald, Nicola F., 2001, 'Chaucer's Legend of Good women, Ladies at Court and the Female Reader', *The Chaucer Review*, Vol. 35, No. 1, 22–42.

Morgan, D.A.L., 1973, 'The King's Affinity in the Polity of Yorkist England', *Transactions of the Royal Historical Society*, Vol. 23, 1–25.

Moyer, Ann E., 2001, *The Philosophers' Game: Rithmomachia in Medieval and Renaissance Europe*, University of Michigan Press, Ann Arbor.

Myers, A.R., 1967, 'The Household of Margaret of Anjou, 1466–7: I', *John Rylands Library*, Vol. 50, No. 1, 207–35.

——, 2007, 'The Outbreak of War between England and Burgundy in February 1471', *Historical Review*, Vol. 33, No. 87 (October), 114–15.

Myers, J.N.L., 1927, 'The Campaign of Radcot Bridge in December 1367', *English Historical Review*, Vol. 42, No. 165 (January), 20–33.

Payling, S.J., 1989, 'The Ampthill Dispute: A Study of Aristocratic Lawlessness and the Breakdown of Lancastrian Government', *English Historical Review*, Vol. 104, No. 413 (October), 881–907.

——, 2014, 'The "Grete Laboure and the Ling and Troublous Tyme"? The Execution of the Will of Ralph, Lord Cromwell, and the Foundation of Tattershall College', in Linda Clark (ed.), *The Fifteenth Century XIII, Exploring Evidence Commemoration, Administration and the Economy*, Boydell Press, Chapel Hill, 1–29.

Philips, Kim, 2005, 'The Invisible Man: Body and Ritual in a Fifteenth Century Noble House', *Journal of Medieval History*, No. 31, 143–62.

Pollard, A.J., 1976, 'The Northern Retainers of Richard Neville, Earl of Salisbury', *Northern History*, XI, 52–69.

——, 1990, *Northeastern England during the Wars of the Roses*, OUP, Oxford.

——, 2004a, 'Neville, Robert (1404–1457)', *ODNB*, OUP, online ed.

——, 2004b, 'Neville, William, Earl of Kent (1401?–1463)', *ODNB*, OUP, online ed.

——, 2004c, 'Neville, Ralph, Second Earl of Westmorland (b in or before 1407, d 1484)', *ODNB*, OUP, online ed.

——, 2004d, 'Neville, Richard, Sixteenth Earl of Warwick and Sixth Earl of Salisbury [Called the Kingmaker] (1428–1471)', *ODNB*, OUP, online ed.

——, 2004e, 'Neville, Richard, Fifth Earl of Salisbury (1400–1460)', *ODNB*, OUP, online ed.

——, 2007a, *Warwick the Kingmaker*, Hambledon Continuum, London

——, 2007b 'Lord Fitzhugh's Rising in 1470', *Historical Research*, Vol. 52, No. 126 (November), 170–75.

Pollard, Anthony, 2004f, 'Neville, Sir Humphrey (1439–1469)', *ODNB*, OUP, online ed.

Powell, Raymond A., 2005, 'Marjery Kempe! An Exemplar of Late Medieval English Piety', *The Catholic Historical Review*, Vol. 99, No. 1 (January), 1–23.

Power, Eileen, 1941, *The Wool Trade in English Medieval History*, OUP, Oxford.

Pugh, T.B., 1988, *Henry V and the Southampton Plot of 1415*, Alan Sutton.

——, 2004, 'Neville, Edward, First Baron Bergavenny (d 1476)', *ODNB*, OUP, online ed.

——, 2007, 'Richard Duke of York and the Rebellion of Henry Holland Duke of Exeter in May 1454', *Historical Research*, Vol. 63, No. 152, 248–62.

Radford, G.H., 1912, 'The Fight at Clyst in 1455', *Report and Transactions of the Devonshire Association*, Vol. 1 No. XLIV.

Ragg, Frederick W., 1909, 'Indenture in English of 1431 between Richard Earl of Salisbury and Sir Henry Threlkeld (of Yarmouth)', *Transactions of the Cumberland and Westmorland Antiquarian and Archaeological Society*, new series, Vol. IX, 282–86.

Rawcliffe, Carole, 1987, 'Richard Duke of York, the King's "Obeisant liegeman": A New Source for the Protectorate of 1454 & 1455', *Historical Research*, Vol. 60, No. 42 (June), 232–39.

——, 1993, 'Stanhope, Sir Richard (c1374–1436) of Rampton, Notts', *History of Parliament, Member Biographies*, www.historyofparliamentonline.org/volume/1386-1421/member/stanhope-sir-richard-1374-1436.

——, 2004, 'Stafford Humphrey, First Duke of Buckingham (1402–1460)', *ODNB*, OUP, online ed.

Reeves, A.C., 2004, 'Cromwell, Ralph, Third Baron Cromwell, (1393?–1456)', *ODNB*, OUP, online ed.

Richmond, C.F., 1970, 'Fauconberg's Kentish Rising of May 1471', *English Historical Review*, Vol. 85, No. 237 (October), 673–92.

——, 2007, 'English Naval Power in the Fifteenth Century', *History*, Vol. 52, No. 174, 1–15.

Richmond, Colin, 1992, 'A Letter of 19 April 1483 from John Gigur to William Wainfleet', *Historical Research*, Vol. 65, No. 156, 112–16.

——, 2004a, 'Mowbray, John (VI), Third Duke of Norfolk (1415–1461)', *ODNB*, OUP online ed.

——, 2004b, 'Mowbray, John (VII), Fourth Duke of Norfolk (1444–1470)', *ODNB*, OUP online ed.

——, 2008, 'The Earl of Warwick's Domination of the Channel and the Naval Dimensions of the Wars of the Roses 1456–1460', in Susan Rose (ed.), *Medieval Ships and Warfare*, Ashgate Publishing, Aldershot.

Robbins, Russell Hope (ed.), 1959, *Historical Poems of XIVth and XVth Centuries*, Columbia University Press, New York.

Rose, Susan, 2008, *Calais: An English Town in France, 1347–1588*, Boydell Press, Woodbridge.

Roskell, J.S., 1953, 'The Office and Dignity of the Protector of England, with Special Reference to its Origins', *English Historical Review*, Vol. 68, No. 267 (April), 193–33.

Roskell, J.S., & Linda Clark (ed.), 1993, 'The Composition of the Merciless Parliament [Feb 1388]', *The History of Parliament: The House of Commons, 1386–1421*, http://www.historyofparliamentonline.org/volume/1386-1421/survey/appendix-c1-composition-merciless-parliament-(feb-1388).

Roskell, J.S. & L.S. Woodger, nd, 'Bonville, Sir William (1392–1461) of Chewton Mendip. Somerset, and Shute, Devon', *History of Parliament, Member Biographies*, www.historyofparliamentonline.org/volume/1386-1421/member/bonville-sir-william-ii-1392-1461.

Ross, Charles, 1974, *Edward IV*, University of California Press, Berkeley & Los Angeles.

Ross, James, 2011, *John de Vere, Thirteenth Earl of Oxford (1442–1513): 'The Foremost Man in the Kingdom'*, Boydell Press, Woodbridge.

Rowley, Ian, 1984, 'The Hastings Affinity in Staffordshire and the Honour of Tutbury', *Historical Research*, Vol. 57, No. 135 (May), 35–45.

Sadler, John, 2011, *Towton: The Battle of Palm Sunday Field, 1461*, Pen & Sword Military, Barnsley.

Sadler, John & Alex Spiers, 2007, *The Battle of Hexham in its Place*, Ergo Press, Hexham.

Santiuste, David, 2010, *Edward IV & the Wars of the Roses*, Pen & Sword Military, Barnsley.

Scammell, G.V., 1962, 'Shipowning in England, 1450–1550', *Transactions of the Royal Historical Society*, Vol. 12, 105–22.

Scofield, Cora L., 1914, 'An Engagement of Service to Warwick the Kingmaker, 1462', *English Historical Review*, Vol. 29, No. 116 (October), 719–20.

——, 1921, 'Five Indentures between Edward IV and Warwick the Kingmaker', *English Historical Review*, Vol. 36, No. 141 (January), 67–70.

——, 1922, 'The Capture of Lord Rivers & Sir Anthony Woodville, 19 January 1460', *English Historical Review*, Vol. 37, No. 146 (April), 253–55.

Seaton, Ethel, 1961, *Sir Richard Roos c1410–1482: Lancastrian Poet*, R. Hart-Davis, London.

Stansfield, M.M.N., 2004, 'Holland, John, First Earl of Huntingdon and Duke of Exeter (c1352–1400)', *ODNB*, OUP, online ed.

Stapleton, Thomas (ed.), 1839, *Plumpton Correspondence*, Camden Society, London.

Storey, R.L., 1957, 'The Wardens of the Marches towards Scotland, 1377–1489', *English Historical Review*, No. 285, 593–615.

——, 1970, 'Lincolnshire and the Wars of the Roses', *Nottingham Medieval Studies*, Vol. 14, 64–83.

——, 1999, *The End of the House of Lancaster*, Sutton Publishing, Stroud.

Summerson, Henry, 2004, 'Robin of Redesdale (fl 1469)', *ODNB*, OUP.

Sutherland, Tim, 2009, 'Killing Time: Challenging the Common Perception of Three Medieval Conflicts – Ferrybridge, Dintingdale and Towton – "The Largest Battle on British Soil"', *Journal of Conflict Archaeology*, Vol. 5, No. 1, 1–25.

Thomson, J.A.F., 1971, '"The Arrival of Edward IV", the Development of the Text', *Speculum*, Vol. 46, No. 1 (January), 84–93.

Tuck, Anthony, 2004a, 'Beaufort, Joan, Countess of Westmorland (1379?–1440)', *ODNB*, OUP, online ed.

——, 2004b, 'Richard II (1367–1400)', *ODNB*, OUP, online ed.

——, 2004c, 'John, fifth Baron Neville (c1330–1388)', *ODNB*, OUP, online ed.

——, 2004d, 'Neville, Ralph, First Earl of Westmorland (c1364–1425)', *ODNB*, OUP, online ed.

——, 2004e, 'Neville, Ralph, Fourth Lord Neville (c1291–1367)', *ODNB*, OUP, online ed.

Vale, M.G.A, 1969, 'The Last Years of English Gascony, 1451–1453', *Transactions of the Royal Historical Society*, Vol. 19, 119–38.

Virgoe, Roger, 1965, 'The Death of William de la Pole, Duke of Suffolk', *John Reynolds Library*, Vol. 47, No. 2, 489–502.

——, 1973, 'William Tailboys and Lord Cromwell: Crime and Politics in Lancastrian England', *John Rylands Library*, No. 55, 459–82.

Visser-Fuchs, Livia, 1995, 'Il n'a plus lion ne lieppart, qui voeulle tenir de sa part': Edward IV in Exile, October 1470 to March 1471', in Jean-Marie Cauchies (ed.), *L'Angleterre et les pays bourguigons*, Centre European d'études bourguignonnes, Neuchatel.

——, 2004, 'Waurin, Jean de (b 1399/1400, d in or after 1473/4)', *ODNB*, OUP.

Visser-Fuchs, Carolina Theodora Livia, 2002, *Warwick and Wavrin: Two Case Studies on the Literary Background and Propaganda of Anglo-Burgundian Relations in the Yorkist Period*, PhD Thesis, University College London.

Wagner, John A., 2001, *Encyclopaedia of the War of the Roses*, ABC/CLIO, Santa Barbara.

Walker, Simon, 2004a, Katherine, Duchess of Lancaster, (1350?–1403), *ODNB*, OUP, online edn Jan 2008.

——, 2004b, 'John, Duke of Aquitaine and Duke of Lancaster, Styled King of Castile and Leon (1340–1399)', *ODNB*, OUP, online ed.

Ward, Jennifer C., 1992, *English Noblewomen in the Late Middle Ages*, Longman, London and New York.

Watts, John L., 1995, 'Polemic and Politics in the 1450s', in Margaret Kekewich et al. (eds), *The Politics of the Fifteenth Century England: John Vate's Book*, Alan Sutton, Stroud.

Watts, John, 2004a, 'Beaumont, John, First Viscount', *ODNB*, OUP.

——, 2004b, 'Pole, William de la, First Duke of Suffolk (1396–1450)', *ODNB*, OUP.

Weiss, Michael, 1976, 'A Power in the North? The Percies in the Fifteenth Century', *Historical Journal*, Vol. 19, No. 2, 501–09.

Weiss, R., 1957, 'Learning and Education in Western Europe from 1470–1520', in G.R. Potter (ed.), *The New Cambridge Modern History*, Cambridge University Press, Cambridge, 95–126.

Whitaker, Thomas Dunham, 1823, *An History of Richmondshire in the North Riding of Yorkshire, Vols 1 & 2*, Longman, Hurst, Rees, Orme & Brown, London.

White, Eileen, 1998, 'The Great Feast', *Leeds Studies in English*, No. 29, 401–10.

Wolffe, Betram, 1981, *Henry VI*, Eyre Methuen, London.

Wood, Anthony, 1876, *The History of Antiquities of the Colleges and Halls in the University of Oxford* (ed. J Gutch), Clarendon Press, Oxford.

Woodgers, L.S., nd, 'Ingoldisthorpe, Sir John [1361–1420] of Ingoldisthorpe and Raynham, Norf', *History of Parliament, Member Biographies*, www.historyofparliamentonline.org/volume/1386-1421/member/ingoldisthorpe-sir-john-1361-1420.

Wright, C.E., 1956, 'The Rous Roll: The English Version', *British Museum Quarterly*, Vol. 210, No. 4 (June), 77–81.

Young, Charles, 1974, 'The Forest Eyre in England During the Thirteenth Century', *American Journal of Legal History*, Vol. 18, No. 4 (October), 321–31.

——, 1996, *The Making of the Neville Family 1166–1400*, Boydell Press, Woodbridge.

# INDEX